# The Grand Strategy
# of the Russian Empire, 1650–1831

# The Grand Strategy
# of the Russian Empire, 1650–1831

John P. LeDonne

OXFORD
UNIVERSITY PRESS
2004

# OXFORD
## UNIVERSITY PRESS

Oxford   New York

Auckland   Bangkok   Buenos Aires   Cape Town   Chennai
Dar es Salaam   Dehli   Hong Kong   Istanbul   Karachi   Kolkata
Kuala Lumpur   Madrid   Melbourne   Mexico City   Mumbai
Nairobi   São Paulo   Shanghai   Taipei   Tokyo   Toronto

Published by Oxford University Press, Inc.
198 Madison Avenue, New York, New York, 10016

www.oup.com

Oxford is a registered trademark of Oxford University Press

Library of Congress Cataloging-in-Publication Data
LeDonne, John P., 1935–
The grand strategy of the Russian Empire : 1650–1831 / John P. LeDonne.
p. cm.
Includes bibliographical references and index.
ISBN 0-19-516100-9
1. Russia—Territorial expansion.  2. Russia—History—1613–1917.
3. Imperialism. I. Title.
DK43.L4 2003
947—dc21        2002044695

2 4 6 8 9 7 5 3 1

Printed in the United States of America
on acid-free paper

For Priscilla
with gratitude

# Preface

I must begin with a caution and a plea. Some readers will argue that writing a first book on Russian grand strategy without the benefit of monographs concentrating on specific problems—decision making, for example—is running the risk of writing about the "virtual past."[1] They will argue that what is presented here is nothing but "virtual strategy," in which the author attributes to the Russian political elite a vision they never had. I answer that if we must wait until enough monographs have been published—especially on eighteenth-century history, which has been so neglected—we condemn ourselves to purely descriptive history for a long time to come. But there is a more serious argument. One can think of history writing as the patient accumulation of facts which eventually yields an insight—or none at all. That is the work of the caterpillar, in Ihor Ševčenko's felicitous contrast between two types of historic writing.[2] But if the inductive work of patient accumulation adds to our knowledge of a historical period or subject matter, it often contributes nothing to an understanding of it. One can write an entire book on diplomatic negotiations or military operations without an understanding of their context, of their continuity with previous activities, and without seeking to elucidate why they took place. The inductive historian who gains an insight—not all do—after many years of research and contemplation may enlarge it into a vision that informs the period or subject matter. It is then for the scholar to select among the mass of facts those which support his vision and contribute to the building of an integrated and intelligible whole. That is the work of the butterfly, who sees a field of flowers where the caterpillar sees grains of sand and tiny leaves.

Facts by themselves are dead matter. They acquire life by becoming connected with other facts by the power of the imagination; the connections are virtual because they are fundamentally subjective. The historian's vision will help him create a historical interpretation reflecting both his personality and his own times. That is why, as William Walsh puts it, "each generation finds it necessary to write its histories afresh."[3] That we need to create such connections is especially urgent in Russian military history. Much information is available in collections of various materials, be they "protocols" of Anna Ivanovna's Cabinet and Catherine II's Council or the papers of various army commanders, but they often contain very little that may be useful in constructing a paradigm of grand strategy as the term is understood here: an integrated military, geopolitical, economic, and cultural vision. What is striking in these documents is the abundance of details, as if the strategic purpose of a war had been taken for granted all along. The focus is on the modalities of execution: recruiting, troop transfers, logistics, appointments, and promotions. The papers of individual commanders tell us for the most part next to nothing about the goals of the war. The archives may tell us more, but one should not expect too much, and they will certainly tell us nothing about a grand strategy.

That the strategic goals of wars seem to be so seldom discussed is easily explained. Continental states usually did not have the choices available to sea powers. Making war on Sweden in 1700 meant for the Russians to dislodge it from its Baltic provinces and, after 1721, there was no alternative to the occupation of Finland and the Åland Islands as a prelude to a landing on the Swedish coast and a move on to Stockholm. Making war on the Turks did present a choice: either focusing on the conquest of the Crimean Khanate before moving toward the Danube or marching toward the Danube directly while keeping the Crimean Tatars at bay. After 1771, there was no alternative to a strategic offensive against the Turks alone for the purpose of establishing a permanent presence on the Danube. And any move against Persia meant launching an expedition from Astrakhan and, after 1804, from Tiflis as well. We know almost nothing about decision making in Petersburg; we have various projects, but what was done with them remains an enigma. In the absence of monographs throwing light on these matters, virtual history must remain undistinguishable from "real" history. This is certainly true when we discuss Russia's grand strategy. In a country where no public existed, where correspondence between members of the elite was routinely opened by the political police, where public policy was carefully fragmented so that each sector was the responsibility of individuals who jealously protected their turf against curious outsiders and sought to keep an open channel to the ruler alone, one could hardly expect to hear the debate so necessary to the articulation of a grand strategy combining military strategy with economic policy and geopolitical activities in the peripheral regions. Therefore, critics will say there could be no grand strategy.

But would it be true? The historian is perfectly justified in claiming there was one by establishing connections between what was repeatedly done in the diplomatic, military, and economic fields, by using a mass of disparate facts as so many building blocks for an integrating synthesis that infuses life where there was none. At least we know that the Russians had a sense of history and continuity in the eighteenth century—memories transmitted from one generation to another in elite families—and that Peter the Great's work was a constant reference. If anything, that work expressed the integrating vision of a great man: one cannot separate his military strategy from his commercial ambitions, his economic policy and his diplomacy. While he probably never said he had a grand strategy, are we justified in saying he did not have one? It would be very much like saying that he did not know what he was doing.

Even if we refuse to accept that we cannot know the past in all its complexity, that the historical past remains beyond our reach while the virtual past is ours for the making,[4] an integrated vision of the past offers a model with which one can agree or disagree. Disagreement is the engine of progress. But it must be a disagreement at the same conceptual level. Those who disagree with the model of a grand strategy in this book will have to come up with a different model, and a clash of models will sharpen our understanding of Russia's perceptions of the outside world. It has been said that a theory cannot be proved, that it can only be disproved. If this debate can encourage scholars to raise their sights and doctoral students to study in detail the various ingredients that went into the formation of a grand strategy, this book will have served its purpose.

# Acknowledgments

I wrote a first complete version of this book at the Institute for Advanced Study (Princeton), where I spent a most pleasant year and learned a great deal from Ambassador Jack F. Matlock, Jr., whose Tuesday lunches offered a challenging opportunity to hear about late Soviet politics and policy making. I rewrote it at the Davis Center, Harvard University, and I thank Timothy Colton for giving me the peace and hospitality so necessary to sustained scholarship.

I have benefited from the advice of several people who read the manuscript and suggested changes: Eric Lohr, who read the original version, and whose comments helped me eliminate much factual information that only cluttered the text; Sally Paine, who asked very pertinent questions and whose close reading remains a source of wonderment; Marc Raeff, of course, who raised larger issues and continued to stimulate my thinking as he has for so many years; Richard Wortman, for an opportunity to present my views to a seminar at the Harriman Institute, Columbia University; Edward Keenan, who, despite his move to Dumbarton Oaks, keeps inspiring me with his skeptical detachment and inquisitive mind; Donald Ostrowski, for bearing with me when I seemed to lose my way and for many challenging conversations; and Jarmo Kotilaine, for encouraging my study of Russian economic history, a field in which he already possesses much knowledge and wisdom.

In other matters, I thank Donna Griesenbeck for a splendid idea that led to the writing of this book; Lisbeth Tarlow, for financial assistance in preparing the manuscript and her unfailing courtesy; Melissa Griggs, for transferring the typed manuscript to the word processor; and especially, Heidi Penix, for painstakingly putting the second version of the manuscript into final shape. I do not forget Ruth Mathewson for her meticulous editing, and thank Susan Ferber of Oxford University Press for believing in the manuscript from the beginning. Last, but not least, thanks are due to Patrick M. Florance and Alison L. Connor for the cartographic design.

# Contents

Maps     xv

Introduction     3


I. *The Formation of Russia's Grand Strategy, 1650–1743*

1. The Geopolitical Background     15
   The Western Theater     15
   The Southern Theater     23
   The Eastern Theater     29
2. Mobile Armies     38
   Strategic Penetration     38
   Concentrated Deployment     44
   The Economic Foundation     52
3. Client States and Societies     61
   Client States: The Western Theater     61
   Client Societies: The Western and Southern Theaters     67
   Client Societies: The Eastern Theater     74


II. *Hegemonic Expansionism, 1743–1796*

4. Deep Strikes     85
   Sweden, France, and Prussia     85
   The Russo-Turkish Wars     93
   Marking Time     100
5. Peripheral Deployment     108
   After the Seven Years' War: 1763     108
   The Emerging Force Structure: 1765–1796     116
   The Fragmentation of the Strategic Force: 1796–1801     123
6. Economy, Culture, Client Societies     132
   The Economy     132

The Ideology of Russia's Grand Strategy   139
Client States and Societies   145

III.  *The Territorialization of the Empire, 1797–1831*

7.  Strategic Penetration   155
Italy, Holland, Sweden, and Turkey, 1799–1812   155
The War with France, 1812–1815   162
Persia, Turkey, and Poland, 1815–1831   168
8.  Dispersion of the Strategic Force   177
Growth of the Army and Deployment, 1801–1812   177
War and Peace, 1812–1831   184
Peripheral Deployment   192
9.  Fortress Empire   198
The Economy   198
Client States and Societies, Old and New   205
Army, Police, Ideology   212

Conclusion   219

Notes   235

Bibliography   251

Index   259

# Maps

The Western and Southern Theaters    16
The Eastern Theater (Kazakh Steppe)    30
Deployment of 1725    45
Rivers and Canals    56
The Polish Sector    88
The Danubian Sector    95
Deployment of 1763    109
Deployment of 1796    124
The Caucasian Sector    169
Deployment of 1819    190

# The Grand Strategy
# of the Russian Empire, 1650–1831

# Introduction

This book is part of an ongoing project devoted to the formation of the Russian Empire from the 1650s to the Polish Revolt of 1830–31, which brought to an end the first and crucial phase of the empire's expansion. The seven generations separating the Thirteen Years' War from the crushing of the Polish Revolt witnessed the transformation of Muscovite Russia into a hegemonic empire in the basins of the eastern Baltic, the Black Sea, and the Caspian, the culmination of an offensive that had taken the Russians far beyond their original goals and had given the empire mastery of the continental Heartland, defined as the huge land mass stretching from the Norwegian Alps to the Sea of Okhotsk and bounded by the continuous chain of mountains from the Dinaric Alps of the former Yugoslavia to the Stanovoi Mountains of northern Manchuria. This period deserves to be studied as the most dynamic in modern Russian history, and the concept of grand strategy provides an excellent tool to help us understand its uniqueness.

The Thirteen Years' War (1654–67) marked the beginning of an offensive strategy directed against the Polish Empire, Moscow's main rival and enemy. Its ultimate goal was to gain hegemony in the eastern marches of that empire—between the Niemen and the Dvina, between the Bug and the Dniepr—the old lands of Kievan Rus'. The peace gave Russia Smolensk and Kiev—one the gate to Lithuania, the other to the Right-Bank Ukraine. The Polish Revolt took place fifteen years after the Vienna settlement, which gave the Russian Empire the larger part of the Polish core and made the Russian emperor tsar of Poland, two hundred years after the son of a Polish king had been elected tsar of Russia. The crushing of the revolt settled the fate of Poland within the Russian Empire until the fall of the Romanov dynasty. The Thirteen Years' War was also directed against Sweden and aimed at gaining access to the Gulf of Finland. One hundred and fifty years later, the Russians were established on the Gulf of Bothnia. The Treaty of Turkmanchai with Persia (1828) advanced the periphery of the empire to the Araks, and the Treaty of Adrianople with the Ottomans (1829) consolidated Russian rule in Georgia and Bessarabia. The empire had reached its greatest territorial extent in the western and southern theaters,[1] and only minor changes would later be brought about by the Treaty of Paris (1856) and the Congress of Berlin (1878).

This period in Russian history was unique in several ways. It is almost an axiom of Western historiography, and one also cultivated by the Russians themselves, that Russia was always on the defensive, surrounded and threatened by enemies, real and imaginary, and that the creation of a vast empire covering eleven time zones resulted from the need to secure protection against the encroachments of malevolent neighbors. It is certainly true that the invasions by Mongols, Crimean Tatars, and Teutonic Knights, followed by the creation of the Polish-Lithuanian empire, created in centrally located Moscow a psychosis of encirclement, heightened by the Time of Troubles, which followed Ivan IV's determination to break that encirclement in his campaigns against Livonia, Kazan, and Astrakhan. It is also true that the rise of Germany and Japan in the late nineteenth century, which took place in the larger context of a century-long cold war with Britain, renewed old fears of encirclement, upon which Stalin would build in the 1930s to whip up enthusiasm among his countrymen for the five-year plans. But it is also just as true that Moscow's central location was ideally suited to launch powerful deep thrusts seeking to destroy the regional hegemonies of Sweden, Poland, and Ottoman Turkey and replace them with Russia's own hegemony in the Heartland. Alastair Johnston, in his study of Chinese "strategic culture," has argued that scholarship has been too willing to accept at face value the traditional Confucian-Mencian central assumption that a benevolent China always emphasized accommodation and peacemaking in accordance with an all-encompassing vision that placed China at the center of the universe while overlooking the violent and offensive strategies that often dominated imperial thinking.

The period under consideration in this book also requires a new vision. It witnessed the rise of a self-confident Russia that developed a long-range offensive strategy—not in response to an immediate threat, because none of the powers that had threatened the Russian core in the past were in a position to threaten it in the eighteenth century, but rather guided by its own expansionist urge in the basins of the Baltic, the Black Sea, and the Caspian. It was not Charles XII who declared war on Russia but Peter I who declared war on the king. Only Napoleonic France can be portrayed as a clear enemy, even though the conflict of 1812 can best be seen as the clash of two offensive strategies for the control of Central Europe. No Russophobia is involved here. Russian overland expansion paralleled that of the European powers across the seas with the same determination and ruthlessness. The Russians, like their European brethren, were on the ascendant in the eighteenth century and were no more threatened than the Europeans by the objects of their ambitions.

This period was unique in other ways. It witnessed the emergence of a ruling elite and a ruling class that crystallized during Peter's reign under the leadership of the Romanov house, bound together by serfdom, with which they rose and fell together. It was marked by a steady economic upsurge, which placed Russia among the great economic powers of the day and created the appearance of a convergence with the economies of the Coastland, while concealing from contemporaries deep structural flaws that would not appear until after 1831. It also witnessed the consolidation on a truly continental scale of an original foreign policy inspired by the politics of the steppe, in which Moscow-Petersburg looked upon states and frontier societies in the Heartland from the Gulf of Bothnia to the Irtysh as so many clients to which the imperial government extended its patronage in return for their willingness to serve the empire's interests. Finally, this period witnessed the building of a powerful army capable of winning victories no matter where it fought, against Tatars, Turks, and Persians, Swedes, Poles, and Prussians. Its only defeats after 1700 were on the Prut in 1711 and in 1805–7. These were, in fact, more humiliations than shattering defeats. As a result, the empire projected a perception of invincibility enhanced by a cult of raw military power centered on Petersburg, built in the midst of a swamp by the indomitable will of a tsar and commander in chief, for whom brutality in the choice of means served the larger vision of an empire whose will must be irresistible among clients everywhere. Such a situation Russia had never enjoyed before Peter's reign and would not enjoy again during the imperial period after the reign of Nicholas I.

The structure of this work was inspired by Edward Luttwak's *The Grand Strategy of the Roman Empire*, a broad and stimulating study of Roman troop deployment and the client system along the imperial periphery from the reign of Augustus to that of Diocletian more than two hundred years later. Luttwak traces the evolution of that grand strategy in three phases. There was at first no demarcated imperial frontier and no system of fixed frontier defense. The legions were deployed astride major routes and served as mobile striking forces. Beyond the core area of the empire, there were client states creating an invisible frontier, still facing no empire-wide threat, and kept in subjection by their perceptions of Roman power. The second phase was marked by the appearance of such a threat and resulted in the creation of defended perimeters, networks of roads linking the frontier garrisons with one another, and the transfer of legions from the inner zones to the periphery. This in turn brought about the development of a policy of centralization and annexation that eventually destroyed the client system. A consequence was the administrative-territorial fragmentation of the empire and the creation of optimal regional perimeters from which a forward defense strategy sought to intercept and destroy enemy troop movements beyond the imperial periphery. The third phase witnessed the concerted offensive of the Teutonic peoples along the entire perimeter from the north to the Black Sea; it forced the Romans to fall back on a defense-in-depth strategy, in which the former surge capability of the legions had disappeared and the Romans were left with the defense of the rear until they were finally overwhelmed. Phases one and two provide extremely valuable lessons for a study of Russian grand strategy from the 1650s to the 1830s.[2] The Russian case is an excellent one to study the operation of the client system, and it had much in common with that of ancient Rome. In both cases, the imperial client system represented an extension of sociopolitical networks within the core to relationships with the elites beyond the core area. Much work remains to be done to clarify this process in the Russian Empire, but a beginning has been made, paving the way for more detailed studies of individual networks and subnetworks.[3]

The book attempts to do for the Russian Empire what Luttwak did for that of Rome: to formulate on the basis of much disparate information a number of principles that, taken together, contributed to elaborate an imperial grand strategy at various stages of the empire's evolution. They will also provide a conceptual framework for a debate on the strategic factors underpinning the formation of the empire.

What, then, is grand strategy? It is not just strategy on a grand scale, as is often suggested in the literature. It is not even a purely military concept. Strategy is the art of deploying troops on the map, then on the ground, in order to reach a specific objective, which is the defeat of the enemy in a given theater of war.[4] It relies on strong logistical support, for an army cannot fight without food and ammunition; in eighteenth-century campaigns, more men died of malnutrition and resulting diseases than from enemy fire.[5] A successful strategy depended on the mobilization of economic resources; this was the responsibility of the political leadership. Grand strategy required the mobilization of the political and military establishment, of the economy, and of the country's leading cultural and ecclesiastical figures, in order to realize a global vision, which in Russia's case was the establishment of its hegemony within the Heartland.[6] The Mongols once had a similar vision when they planned a simultaneous invasion of Poland and Korea. Russia's global theater of operation was the Heartland,[7] and only seldom would the empire cross its periphery, usually with unfavorable results. Such a vision determined the means, including the creation of a client system requiring constant management, the shaping of an economic policy encouraging the formation of a military-industrial complex, and the reaching of an agreement on the nature of Russia's economic relations with the outside world. Russia was a warrior state, its nobility defined as a service class whose identity was inseparable from action on the battlefield in defense of the ruling house and the Orthodox faith. As a result, the ruling elite would not recognize a sharp distinction between the politicians and the high command until the late nineteenth century. Until then, general and lower-grade officers were found everywhere in the agencies of the government. It was a combined civil and military elite,[8] in which military objectives played a disproportionate role in decision making, though subject to the countervailing influence of the ruler as the supreme "politician" expected to impose a truly political solution—if he or she had the will and the ability to do so. Russia's military history supplies enough evidence to show how the more forceful rulers shaped strategy at a given time to fit the requirements of a grand strategy as they understood it, tilting the balance within the ruling elite in favor of political solutions. This work takes all these factors into account and traces the evolution of Russia's grand strategy in three major phases. One stretched from the 1650s to the 1730s, when such a grand strategy began to crystallize. During the second phase, from the 1740s to the end of the eighteenth century, Russia gradually won a position of hegemony within the Heartland. During the third, from the beginning of the nineteenth century to the Polish Revolt of 1830–31, it consolidated its hegemony for another generation.

Did such a vision exist? If the answer is sought in the existence of a single document, an official "position paper" analyzing Russia's options and capabilities on a continental scale, it must be negative. Such documents, drawn during various stages of the empire's expansion, probably never existed, if only because they would have been seen as usurpation of the power of the ruler who, in the ideology of the autocratic state, must always be allowed to initiate policy and retain his freedom of action. Outsiders, however, were quite conscious of a Russian grand design, and those who forged the Testament of Peter the Great saw things insiders must have taken for granted. Adam Czartoryski, a Pole who was foreign minister of the empire from 1804 to 1806, wrote that no other state had pursued such vast designs with "indefatigable perseverance," seeking "the submission of the greater part of Europe and Asia, plus the arbitration of the destinies of its rivals."[9] At any rate, Peter's actions speak for themselves. In 1689, Russia had but a small—and short—access to the ocean at Arkhangelsk. In 1700, it had gained access to the Sea of Azov, which turned into a dead end once the Turks built forces at Kerch and Enikale barring entrance into the Black Sea. In 1711, Peter fought the Turks on the Prut after failing to reach the Danube ahead of them. In 1714, his troops occupied Finland, and in 1716, after Poland had been devastated by Russians and Swedes for nearly a decade, they were in Denmark, poised to cross the Sound for an invasion of Sweden. That same year, the Russians were on the Irtysh seeking a way to the mysterious city of Erkent, rumored to abound in gold, while others crossed the Caspian on their way to Khiva at the gates of Central Asia. And six years later, Russian troops marched to the coastal road from Astrakhan to Rasht to win from a disintegrating Persia the entire southern coast of the Caspian. Whether these moves succeeded or failed is irrelevant; what is certain is that they embodied a determination to demonstrate Russian power in the Heartland from the Baltic to the Caspian. While launching these deep strikes within the Heartland's periphery, the tsar set out with grim determination to build almost from scratch a powerful industrial base geared to produce the weapons of war and a new navy to wrest naval hegemony in the Baltic from the Swedes. He continued to dream, as had his predecessors, that Russia could become the intermediary between the commerce of the East and that of the West, a vast transit space occupied by the valley of the Volga and that of the Volkhov, which he connected by a canal, creating a single waterway between the Caspian and the Baltic. Last but not least, he encouraged a cult of power, a cult of Russia's "awesomeness,"[10] which churchmen and writers happily developed as the ideological support of Russia's striving toward hegemony. From this outline of a continental vision of Russia's role within the Heartland, there clearly emerges a grand design.

But what of his successors? Anna Ivanovna was steeped in old Muscovy, and the Crimean campaigns of 1736–38 were more a throwback to Vasilii Golitsyn's campaigns of the 1680s than to the Prut campaign of 1711, but the expansion of the industrial base continued. Most of her advisers had begun their careers under Peter, notably those most likely to take part in the formulation of a grand strategy, like Heinrich Ostermann, Burhard von Münnich, James Bruce, and Feofan Prokopovich, all of non-Russian origin. The role of Germans, Scots, and Ukrainians, not to mention Moldavians, like Cantemir, and later in the century, Greeks and Poles, in the formulation of a program of empire building and expansion has been neglected but deserves to be studied. Their knowledge of the outside world, where the empire would have to be built, their own interest in inviting Russian expansion, matched the imperial urge of the elite to create a powerful current drawing the high command into the three great sea basins of the Heartland. Anna's 1733 intervention in the Polish succession crisis and the dispatch of Russian troops to the Rhine two years later, together with her tariff policy, evidenced no deviation from the guidelines set by Peter. Elizabeth, Peter's daughter, made it clear she would rule in accordance with her father's precepts; her flamboyant reign witnessed a surge of Russian national self-consciousness and Orthodox proselytizing. While downgrading Russian activities in the southern theater, she continued to resort to a forward strategy in the valley of the Ural and Irtysh, and landed troops in Stockholm before fighting a bloody war with a Prussian client whose recalcitrance threatened to destabilize the client system along the western periphery of the Heartland. Russia's power had become truly awesome by 1762 and was about to become even more so in the last three decades of the century. Catherine II was a German usurper who needed to be more Russian than the Russians themselves. Her road to success lay in being faithful to the Petrine legacy, as she herself recognized in the inscription on Peter's statue in Senate Square. In her wars with the Ottomans and Persians she acknowledged following in Peter's footsteps. By 1796 she had established Russia's position as arbiter in the tense relationship between Austria and Prussia, confirming Russia's hegemony in the Heartland. Despite warning signs, the Russian economy continued to do well, and Petersburg became one of the great capitals on the periphery of Europe. Are we to claim that this extraordinary progression of Russian power and influence took place in a fit of absentmindedness, without the ruling elite's possessing a continent-wide vision of its ambitions and a sustained determination to realize them?

Alexander may have been less concerned with the Petrine legacy,[11] partly because he had nothing to prove (unlike Elizabeth, who was born out of wedlock, and Catherine II, who was a foreigner), and also because his reign resembled Peter's in some ways, bringing to a close a long eighteenth century that had begun in 1696, if not 1689. Like Peter, Alexander spent most of his reign at war with the greatest military commander of the day and left his country financially exhausted. Both carried out important domestic reforms inspired by the necessity to cope with the demands of war; both built powerful armies far exceeding in size those of their predecessors; and both reigns ended with the imposition of a prohibitive tariff wall. But Peter's reign signaled the acceleration of Russian expansion begun by his father, while Alexander's carried out the work of his grandmother to its logical completion. Czartoryski, who wrote his memoirs in the 1840s, noted under the year 1804 that "the spirit of Peter still hovered over his empire," and General Filippo Paulucci, a former commander of the imperial forces in the Caucasus, wrote in a memorandum of 1816 that the establishment of new boundaries with the Ottoman and Persian empires would bring the projects of Peter the Great to their completion.[12] Peter surely would have felt proud satisfaction in the annexation of Finland, in Russian troops stationed in Paris to weaken a France that had been Russia's major rival throughout the century, in the establishment of a quasi-protectorate over the Danubian Principalities, and in the defeat of the Ottomans and Persians in Transcaucasia from a new base of operations in Georgia. Contemporaries who had read up in ancient history could not fail to hear in the monster parades that marked the latter half of the reign after 1815 an echo of the tramping of the Roman legions returning from victory in Gaul and Egypt. Never had Russia appeared so awesome as it did then. It cannot of course be claimed that such achievements had been planned all along, but Russia's victories in the 1810s and 1820s were nevertheless the logical realization of the Petrine vision of Russia as the hegemon in the Heartland, protected by high tariff walls, with a strong economy capable of supporting an invincible military establishment and with a cult of power to impose submission on client states and enemies alike. That vision, no doubt, owed something to the older Mongol vision of hegemony in the immense world of the steppe and to that of Ivan IV, who was ahead of his times, but it was Peter who laid the durable foundations for the transformation of that vision into realistic policy and Nicholas I who completed it.

This study of Russia's grand strategy will also suggest the need for a fresh look at the old and perhaps insoluble question of Russia's relationship with "Europe." It is a well established assumption in Western historiography that with Peter's reign Russia entered the European state system and became Europeanized, as its ruling class adopted European manners and enjoyed and copied European art and literature. The depth of Russia's Europeanization very much remains to be assessed. Its manifestations may well be seen as forms of grandstanding and playacting before the rulers who became less and less Russian and genetically more and more German as the Romanov dynasty grew older. Indeed, a historian of eighteenth-century Russia, Iurii Got'e, would ask in the summer of 1917, soon after the collapse of the old regime, whether the Petersburg civilization, which had been equated for so long with Russian civilization, had not in fact been but a "thin veneer"[13] that had fooled the unsuspecting observer. Surely the fact that so many Russians, and not just the Slavophiles, before 1917—and the Bolsheviks for seventy-five years thereafter— insisted that Russia was not part of Europe or the "West" and showed open contempt for it should give pause to those who insist uncritically that it was (and remains) part of a Europe stretching from the Atlantic to the Urals, Siberia's place in "Russia" being conveniently ignored. A persistent Eurocentric attitude has presented Russia as an isolated eastern margin of Europe that must sooner or later be brought into the fold. The Moscow-centered Russians could with better justice and with a greater appreciation of their history and geography claim that the European Coastland was the margin, more dynamic indeed, but also alien to a way of life based on the mastery of great spaces, the exercise of arbitrary power by the very few over a largely passive population, and an Eastern Orthodoxy declared incompatible with Latin Christianity since 1054. It is suggested here that Russia was not part of Europe. It certainly was not so for the eighteenth-century contemporaries of its expansion, like Louis XV of France and Frederick II of Prussia, who said so openly. In 1770, in Neustadt in Moravia, the Prussian king and Joseph II, the Holy Roman emperor, agreed that Russia was a menace to European civilization.[14] In our own day, Walther Mediger entitled his major monograph on eighteenth-century Russian foreign policy *Moscow's Advance toward Europe* and Christopher Duffy called his book on Russia's strategy *Russia's Military Way to the West*, obviously implying that Russia was not part of either Europe or the "West." It was instead a sui generis Eurasian state seeking hegemony in the Heartland stretching from the Elbe to eastern Siberia and manipulating not only the European state system to achieve its goals but also the system of states and societies in the immense steppe from the Danube to Lake Baikal.

Ensconced in the forests of the Volga-Oka Mesopotamia and with its back to the wastes of the White Sea and Arctic Ocean, the Muscovite state had a mission defined by the church as the standard bearer of Eastern Orthodoxy against Latin Christianity and Islam and which behaved as the proponent of political, economic, and cultural autarky. It steadily consolidated its power in the forest and wooded steppe zones until it came up against the outer peripheries of those two civilizations—in the Baltic frontier, in the eastern marches of the Polish Empire, in the successor states of the Golden Horde. From their position of strength, the Russians took advantage of the weakening hold of the Swedes, Poles, and Ottomans on their frontier zones in order to manipulate client relationships within those empires, transforming frontier societies and even core areas like Prussia into clients of their growing empire. But they manipulated those relationships from the outside, not from within. It would greatly help our understanding of Russian history, strategy, and foreign policy if we chose to see the Russians not always as part of something else, but as the bearers of an autonomous civilization engaged in an age-long competition within the Heartland with the other two great civilizations of Latin Christianity and Islam with which they had (and still have) so little in common.

The emergence of the Russian Empire was a long process. The principality of Moscow developed in the heart of a vast hydrographic network linking it with the Baltic, the Black Sea, and the Caspian. It was subjugated by the Mongols in 1237. For the next three centuries the nomad ruled supreme not only in the steppe but even in the forest zone, where the principality became a pliable yet recalcitrant client. The Moscow princes rose to power by taking full advantage of that favorable geographical location and by obtaining from the khan of the Golden Horde, headquartered north of Astrakhan, the political charter that eventually established their legitimacy over the entire Russian land and confirmed their position as chief vassal of the steppe khan.[15] Meanwhile, the Teutonic Knights had consolidated their hold on Livonia and established a Germanic empire along the eastern Baltic coast. It would have become a territorially contiguous empire had it not been for the rise of Lithuania around 1300. The new state rapidly expanded to include by the end of the fourteenth century almost the entire valley of the Dniepr to the Black Sea, encroaching into the southern steppe, the domain of the nomad. The stage was thus set for Moscow's relations with three political configurations: the Germans, the Lithuanians, and the Turco-Mongols, in two theaters, the Baltic and the Black Sea, from which trails and rivers led to Moscow and from Moscow to the sea. In 1386, the grand prince of Lithuania married the heiress to the Polish throne to create a powerful empire soon dominated by Poland, and Poland would become Russia's rival for the lands of the Lithuanian principality that had once been part of Kievan Rus', to which the Muscovite church claimed to be the heir after the incorporation of Novgorod in 1478. After the conquest of Constantinople in 1453 and the final destruction of the Byzantine Empire by the Ottoman Turks, Ivan III married a Romanized Byzantine princess in 1472. The grand princes who had derived their legitimacy for so long from the Mongol khans now saw themselves as the heirs to the Byzantine Empire, a claim that would eventually set the stage for the long and bitter Russo-Ottoman conflict over hegemony in the Black Sea basin.

If empires are "relationships of political control imposed by some political societies over the effective sovereignty of other political societies,"[16] they also contain a strong ethnic component. They are political systems in which an ethnic group or a "super-ethnicity"—like the "French," the "British," the "Russians"—imposed their will on other ethnic societies. The Athenian empire of the Delian League and the Holy Roman Empire of the German Nation may have been the only exceptions, and the latter with substantial reservations. In such a case, the formation of the Russian Empire began with Ivan IV, who was crowned tsar in 1547 and launched an expedition against Kazan in 1552 and another against Astrakhan in 1556, resulting in the annexation of the entire valley of the Volga below Sviiazhsk to the Caspian, leaving only the Crimea beyond Russian control. Two years later, in 1558, in the wake of the secularization of the lands of the Teutonic Knights, who embraced Protestantism and committed political suicide, Ivan sent his troops into Livonia in order to enlarge the narrow frontage Russia possessed on the Gulf of Finland. The war went well at first, but Russia found itself face to face with Poland and Sweden, which also claimed the legacy of the Knights. Their combined opposition rolled back the Russian advance, and when peace was made in 1581–82, Ivan had lost all his former gains. The appearance of Sweden was a momentous event. This new power, created in 1526 when Gustav Vasa broke with Denmark, was embarking on a course of expansion that would soon establish its hegemony in the Baltic and make it Russia's main enemy in the region. Russia would face the oppositions of two powers in the western theater.

Its expansionist surge was in evidence in the east as well. Peace had hardly been made with the Swedes and the Poles when an expedition was sent across the Urals against the Siberian Khanate, followed by the annexation of "Siberia" and the construction of Tobolsk in 1587, which would remain the capital of the new territory for 180 years. The Time of Troubles (1598–1613) put Moscow on the defensive. When the new Romanov dynasty ascended the throne, the Swedes were established in Livonia and the Poles beyond Smolensk and Kiev: the two powers, although rivals, exercised a joint hegemony in the western theater and barred Russia's access to the Baltic. The Ottoman Empire, with the help of its client societies in Moldavia-Wallachia and the Tatars in the Crimea and on the mainland to the Kuban, blocked Russia's access to the Black Sea. It had become the undisputed hegemon in the southern theater. Beyond the Volga and the Urals, an indeterminate eastern theater was taking shape while a powerful Manchu dynasty was about to seize control of China. By 1650, however, Russia was ready to resume its expansionist surge. The consolidation of the dynasty, the emergence of a ruling class whose raison d'être was the management of the country's resources, and the tremendous energy released by the civil war that had brought the dynasty to power combined to transform a defensive into an offensive posture.[17] The geopolitical environment had created three theaters, two of them, the western and the southern, dominated by hegemonic powers. The means of a grand strategy operating within a remarkable constant geopolitical environment were the modernization the army, the foundation of an industrial base, and the maximum extraction of resources from an increasingly dependent population; the goal was to challenge Swedish, Polish, and

Ottoman hegemony, eventually destroy it, and replace it with Russia's own hegemony within the larger territorial framework of the Heartland. The offensive began during the reign of Alexei Mikhailovich (1645–76), paving the way for his son Peter I (1689–1725) to openly challenge the hegemonic powers and work out a number of principles underlying a Russian grand strategy. We must now turn to an examination of the three theaters and the expansionist surge in each before turning to the elaboration of a grand strategy during Peter's reign.

# PART I

# THE FORMATION OF RUSSIA'S GRAND STRATEGY, 1650–1743

# The Geopolitical Background

A knowledge of the geopolitical context in which Russia's grand strategy developed is a fundamental necessity. Not only did that context shape a global vision, it helps us understand the relative strengths and weaknesses of the rival powers engaged in a struggle for hegemony in the three theaters making up the Heartland, and it determined what was possible at a given time as well as the stakes involved in committing military power to the transformation of that vision into a blueprint for troop movements and diplomatic negotiations.

## The Western Theater

The western theater included the entire basin of the Baltic Sea and the broad corridor between the Dniepr and the Prut along the eastern curve of the Carpathian Mountains. The Baltic Basin was the aggregate of the basins of all the rivers flowing into the Gulf of Bothnia, the Gulf of Finland, and the Baltic proper, from Lübeck to Reval. The Norwegian Alps and the Elbe River descending from the Sudeten Mountains formed the outer periphery of the western theater and of the Heartland as well, beyond which began the European Coastland facing outward toward the Atlantic Ocean.[1] This periphery was an arc of a circle on which the distances from Moscow to Hamburg and to Magdeburg on the Elbe via Warsaw and Berlin were within a 2,000-kilometer radius. The geography of the western theater created a natural system of radial roads emanating from Moscow toward the northwest, the west, and the southwest, intersecting a succession of "vertical" roads following the course of rivers—the Volkhov, the Dvina, the Niemen, the Vistula, the Oder, and the Elbe—and in the south, the Dniepr, the Dniestr, and the Prut. This network of intersecting roads provided axes of penetration and retreat, interior lines for communication, reinforcements, troop circulation, and supply.

The theater of effective Russian operations within this broadly conceived western theater was smaller and can be divided into three sectors. Lake Il'men, with Novgorod at its northern end, drained the waters of the Valdai Hills and gave its

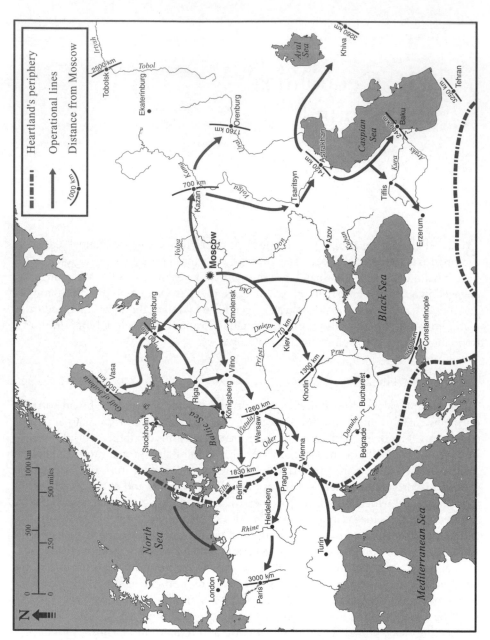

The Western and Southern Theaters

basin a western orientation similar to that which Ladoga and the Neva would later give to Petersburg, while the rivers descending from the Norwegian Alps gave Sweden an eastern orientation toward Livonia and Lake Ladoga. The Dvina, flowing into the Baltic below Riga, drained the waters of its vast hinterland stretching all the way to the Moscow-Smolensk morainic ridge; the Niemen descending from the Bielorussian watershed between the basins of the Baltic and the Black Sea turned Lithuania outward toward the Baltic. Riga was 950 kilometers from Moscow; Vasa, on the Gulf of Bothnia, 1,500 kilometers. Riga and Novgorod had once belonged to the Hanseatic League; they exported the products of the Muscovite center and the former Novgorod fur empire that had reached as far as the White Sea. By their very success and wealth, however, they had also transformed the entire basin of the eastern Baltic into an area of contention and invited Muscovite expansion. The focus of the contention was the extremity of the Gulf of Finland: whoever controlled it would derive the greatest profit from all the export trade in the basin of Lake Ladoga.[2] The site of the future Petersburg at the end of the Gulf of Finland was about halfway between Stockholm and Moscow, but Riga was much closer to Stockholm and accessed more easily by sea than overland from Moscow.

The second sector was the basin of the Vistula and the Oder. Both rivers took their source in the same region, one descending from the Czech upland between Olmütz and Ostrava, the other from the Beskids forming the boundary between Poland and Slovakia, another watershed between the basin of the Baltic and that of the Black Sea. The two rivers, with the Elbe to the west and the Niemen to the east, formed another succession of vertical roads intersecting the Moscow-Warsaw-Berlin highway. The Vistula carried the rich grain trade of the Polish towns to Danzig, from which the grain was then exported to other Baltic towns or to the Coastland, while the Oder carried the textiles of Silesia to Stettin. All these rivers drained fresh water to the Baltic, forming a layer over the salt water brought in from the Atlantic. This layer flowed steadily toward the ocean, creating a sustained westward movement of economic life, transporting the products not only of the entire Baltic basin but also of northern Russia toward the Scandinavian Sound.[3] Distances from Moscow were comparable: 1,260 kilometers to Warsaw and 1,700 to Frankfurt on the Oder.

The two sectors belonged to the forest zone of chiefly coniferous trees, from the "desert" of Finland,[4] "the land of the thousand lakes" (even though there were many more) but easily crossed in winter, to the nearly impenetrable forests of Lithuania and the Pripet marshes beyond which deciduous trees announced the Ukrainian steppe. Much of the region was a climatic frontier "where arable soils dwindle and the climate defeats the farmer,"[5] but there were also islands of good soil and excellent pastures where the soil was rich with moisture. The Gulf of Bothnia, the Gulf of Finland, and the rivers froze over in winter, and so Finland was cut off from Sweden. Springtime was known for the mud that turned much of the countryside into a nightmare for men and horses. Poland began at the Oder; it was one of the great corridors of the Eurasian landmass, "with its immense horizons opening out toward Asia."[6] Altogether, the two sectors were a frontier where Slav and Teuton, Russians and Swedes in the eastern Baltic, then Poles and Russians south of the Baltic confronted one another for centuries until Russia would achieve hegemony toward the end of the period under consideration.

The third sector belonged not to the Baltic basin but to that of the Black Sea. It must be included in the western theater, however, because it was part of the Polish Empire, one of its eastern marches separated from the other in Lithuania and Bielorussia by the Pripet swamps. It did not include the entire corridor between the Dniepr and the Dniestr but stopped along the Siniukha, the Vys, and the lower Tiasmin which formed the border with the Ottoman Empire or, more precisely, with the nomadic Tatars who roamed the steppe between the Danube and the Kuban. Its northern part was still in the forest zone that ended along a line running from Pulawa on the Vistula through Lutsk and Zhitomir to Kiev, but the remainder stood squarely in the wooded steppe zone stretching just beyond the border where the Tatar steppe began.[7] This sector was very much an interlocking frontier — Russo-Polish certainly, but also Turco-Polish and Turco-Russian. Politically and economically, it gravitated toward Poland: its grain trade linked the region with the Baltic via the Western Bug and the Vistula. But that orientation was an artificial one: geographically, the entire sector faced the Black Sea, drained as it was by the tributaries of the Southern Bug flowing toward the coast of that sea. It was rich country with good soils as soon as the ground rose above the drainage basin of the Pripet, coveted by the Russians as an excellent base of operations against Poland and the Ottoman provinces. It was still a long way from Moscow, however. Kiev was 800 kilometers away, from Kiev to the future Odessa another 500 kilometers, and to Khotin, the great Ottoman fortress facing the no less imposing Polish fortress of Kamenets-Podolsk, was also 500 kilometers. Nevertheless, Vasa, Warsaw, and Khotin were at about the same distance from Moscow, within a radius of 1,500 kilometers. Reaching those three key places would give the Russians hegemony in the western theater, leaving Brandenburg along the Heartland's periphery exposed to continuous Russian pressure. The occupation of the third sector would also bring the Russians to the edge of the Ottoman Empire and threaten the Tatars' age-long hegemony in the steppe.

This vast theater witnessed a long epic struggle between Poles, Swedes, and Russians for access to its resources, the allegiance of its populations, and control of its trade routes. The Russo-Swedish rivalry in Finland went back to the thirteenth century. Long wars that followed with the Novgorodians barred their access to the Gulf of Finland, and the Swedes built forward positions in Vyborg, Kexholm, and Oreshek (Noteburg). The first Swedish king, Gustav Vasa, who died in 1560, made his younger son Johan duke of Finland, but the difficulties of administering the territory, cut off from Sweden in winter, were already apparent. It would become a grand duchy in 1581, a status it would retain until 1917. In the eastern Baltic, Sweden's policy would concentrate on controlling the mouth of the Neva and the Narova and the narrow coastal corridor along the Gulf of Finland.[8] The Russians took advantage of Sweden's internal difficulties to break its hold on the eastern Baltic shoreline, in Karelia and Ingria, prompting a crackdown in Stockholm against the Finnish nobility and its separatist ambitions. Boris Godunov's death in 1605 ushered in a period of civil war in Russia during which Swedish aid was purchased by the cession of the Kexholm district.[9] The Swedes took Novgorod in 1611, the year Gustav II Adolf came to the Swedish throne. The Stolbovo Peace (1617) retroceded Novgorod but rolled back the Russians "to prehistoric times" in Finland,[10] expelling them from Karelia and Ingria and cutting them off completely from the Gulf of Finland. The Swedish defensive perimeter would run from Lake Peipus to Lake Ladoga, and Gustav Adolf and his daughter Christina (1632–54) went on to integrate Finland more closely into the new Swedish Empire.

In Livonia, the Reformation destroyed the Teutonic Order.[11] The area between the Vistula and the Niemen became known as the Duchy of Prussia, which was inherited by the Electors of Brandenburg in 1618 — a momentous event that gave Brandenburg-Prussia a stake in Russo-Polish relations for two hundred years. There too, the Russians sought to take advantage of the political confusion; Ivan IV (1533–84) invaded Livonia and captured some twenty strongholds in 1558, but he found himself at war with Poland and Sweden, which coveted the lands of the Order. In 1561, when the Order finally broke up, the northern part of Livonia (Estland) gave its allegiance to Sweden; the central part (Livland), with Riga as its main city, placed itself under Sigismund II; so did the southern part (Kurland), which was granted special status within the Polish Empire. The fortunes of war turned against the Russians, leaving ruin and desolation after nearly thirty years (1558–82). Once the Swedes had made peace with the Russians in 1617, they went to war against the Poles to gain Livland, the most valuable prize, and expelled them in 1621. Thus, of all the former lands of the Order, the Poles retained only Kurland and a small corner of Livonia. Gustav Adolf's foreign policy was guided by both strategic and commercial considerations. Sweden's determination to keep Russia without access to the Baltic was all the more necessary after the founding of the new Romanov dynasty in 1613 on the crest of a national reaction against foreign interventions. The king also saw the establishment of Swedish control over the Baltic shoreline as a profitable way of milking the custom revenue collected in the Baltic ports to sustain his military machine.[12]

Russia's other great rival in the western theater was Poland. Its early capital was Kraków, and the great event of its early history was the marriage of Jadwiga, the Polish queen, with Jagiello, the grand duke of Lithuania, in 1386. The Lithuanian state had grown around the Vilno-Grodno area; by 1300 it had reached the shores of the Black Sea between present-day Odessa and the mouth of the Dniepr. A century later, it would reach beyond Smolensk to include the headwaters of the Western Dvina and the Dniepr. The marriage laid the foundations of the Polish Empire with its eastern marches in Lithuania and on the Right-Bank Ukraine, where great Polish lords built enormous estates. The capital was moved to Warsaw in 1526, and the empire was considerably strengthened by the Union of Lublin (1569), when Poland incorporated the Right-Bank Ukraine — the third sector of the western theater — to form a unitary state and proclaimed an indivisible union with Lithuania.[13] The conflict with Russia began in earnest under Sigismund II (1548–72), who challenged Ivan the Terrible for the inheritance of the Teutonic Order, and continued under Stephen Batory (1575–86), who rolled back the Russians from eastern Bielorussia as far as Pskov. It was under Sigismund III (1587–1632), the half-Vasa king, that the Polish Empire reached its largest territorial extent. The reign coincided with the disintegration of the Muscovite kingdom and the founding of the Romanov dynasty. The intervention of the Poles on the side of the pretenders to the Russian throne led to the invasion of Russia in 1609 and the occupation of the Kremlin a year later. It appeared for a short while that the Russian and Polish crowns might be united when Sigismund's son was elected tsar. But the king's rejection of the offer and the national reaction forced the Poles out of the Kremlin in 1612, initiating a long process of rolling back Polish power. A truce was signed at Deulino in 1618, the Poles keeping the major fortresses of Smolensk and Novgorod-Seversk. In 1632, the Russians tried to take Smolensk but failed.[14] The stage was set, however, for a Russian counteroffensive that would end in 1815 when the Russian tsar became king of Poland.

The reign of the first Romanov tsar, Mikhail (1613–45), was a time of recovery and consolidation; the tremendous energy generated by the civil war also sought new channels of activity. A reinvigorated ruling class laid down the foundations of its power in a socioeconomic order based on serfdom, sanctioned in the Law Code of 1649, during the reign of Mikhail's son, Alexei (1645–76). It was then, during the latter half of the seventeenth century, that the great expansion begun during the preceding century turned into a systematic forward strategy in both the western and southern theaters. In the former, the Russian advance seeking both to restore access to the Baltic and to force Poland into accepting a union of both crowns under the Russian tsar brought about a long war with Poland and Sweden.

The Russians stepped into a geopolitical situation, which channeled their new energy westward along paths well trodden by past conquerors. The rivalries between Poles and Swedes had been struggles for hegemony in the basin of the eastern Baltic. Religion had been a factor in those struggles, but not more so than trade converging from deep inland toward the coast and then westward toward the open sea. Geography, religion, and trade had carved out a geopolitical universe in which ambitious rulers sought hegemony for their house. By about 1650, the Romanov house and the ruling elite were ready to stake a claim for participation in the governing of that universe, but that claim could be satisfied only by war against Sweden and Poland, either separately or simultaneously. Such a war could not be fought for limited objectives—except in the short run—because it was bound to become a war for hegemony, with its ultimate objective the destruction of Sweden's and Poland's political and military capabilities. The limited size and well-defined physiognomy of the Baltic sector admitted no other outcome. On the other hand, any offensive against the Polish Empire would have to proceed beyond the Baltic sector into the Black Sea or southern theater, where Poland remained the hegemonic power in the valley of the upper and middle Dniepr. Thus, the expansionist impulse, which gathered momentum after 1650, was inseparable from a geopolitical vision determined by the configuration of the Swedish and Polish Empires and had to aim at the eventual establishment of Russian power and influence on the Gulf of Bothnia, the Oder, and the Dniestr. In order to realize that vision, it was necessary to work out an offensive political and military strategy based on the development of Russia's economic potential, deep strategic strikes with which the Russians had been familiar since the days of the Mongol invasion, and a client system that had been for centuries the foundation of "international" relations in the steppe.

The impetus to expansion came from a series of Cossack uprisings in the Left-Bank Ukraine against Polish rule. In 1648, the Cossacks found a leader in Bohdan

Khmelnytsky, who took the oath of allegiance to the tsar in 1654. In alliance with the Cossacks the Russians returned to war against the Polish Empire, and the so-called Thirteen Years' War began in 1655. The Russians occupied Lithuania, including Vilno, but their intervention brought Sweden into the war. The ambition of Charles X (1654–60) was to force the Polish king, Jan Casimir (1648–68), to give up his claims to the Swedish crown and accept instead a reunion of both crowns under the Swedish scepter. It was also to incorporate Lithuania into the Swedish Empire in order to strengthen the anti-Russian bulwark in the eastern Baltic.[15] The Swedes, allied with Brandenburg, advanced quickly. They landed at Riga and Danzig. From these two bases of operation they contained the Russians in Lithuania and captured the main cities on the Vistula — Thorn, Warsaw, and Kraków — in 1656, advancing as far as the Carpathians, Przemyshl on the San, and Brest-Litovsk on the Western Bug. But all was not well on the Swedish front. Stalled in Lithuania, the Russians attacked Riga, Oreshek, and Kexholm, where they could count on the support of the Orthodox population. The Swedes faced the danger of losing their control of the Gulf of Finland. Worse still, the Danes, who had not become reconciled to the defection of Gustav Vasa a century earlier, declared war in 1657, forcing Charles X to withdraw from Poland and concentrate his forces against Denmark, landing on Seeland a few miles from Copenhagen the following year. The defeated Danes had to surrender their last holdings in southern Sweden and the bishopric of Trondheim. By then, the Swedes had overextended themselves, Poland had been devastated, and the Russians had made no decisive headway against Swedish resistance. It was time for a general peace. At Oliva near Danzig in 1660, Jan Casimir renounced his claims to the Swedish crown and recognized Sweden's hold on Livonia except for Kurland. At Kardis, south of Reval, in 1661, the Russians had to abandon their gains and accept the border agreed upon at Stolbovo. Poland and Russia remained at war, however, but Poland's brighter prospects were dimmed by a rebellion in its eastern marches in 1664, and it had to accept Moscow's terms three years later. By the Truce of Andrusovo (1667) the Russians returned Polotsk, Vitebsk, and Polish Livonia on the Western Dvina but gained Smolensk and the entire left bank of the Dniepr to the mouth of the Samara. Kiev, on the right bank, was to remain in Russian hands for two years, but it was never returned.[16] The war had embroiled all three powers — Sweden, Poland, and Brandenburg — in Russia's western theater. It ended in what was essentially a first partition of the Polish Empire, from which Russia gained two key positions in Smolensk and Kiev. They would become bases of operations in any invasion of Lithuania and the Right Bank Ukraine, placing the Polish core area at Russia's mercy.

Despite the fact that Russia and Sweden had been at war with each other, the conflict with Poland had actually been a combined Russo-Swedish operation directed against the Polish Empire. The geopolitical underpinning of Polish foreign policy had long been a determination to control the Baltic–Black Sea isthmus; in order to succeed, it had to stem the tide of Russian-Orthodox and Turkish-Muslim westward expansion.[17] In addition, despite the dynastic alliances, Polish and Swedish ambitions in the eastern Baltic were incompatible, partly because of the bitterness of the Catholic-Lutheran antagonism, partly for geopolitical reasons such as the rivalry over Lithuania and Latvia, with Riga the major port in the region. The

Polish Empire had passed its high point, reached during the reign of Sigismund III. The king had been forced to recognize the so-called Henrician Articles of 1573 severely restricting the royal power and requiring the convocation of a diet every two years. Every subsequent monarch had to swear allegiance to them, thereby leading Poland down the path to political anarchy, while his neighbors in Sweden and Russia (and Prussia) were consolidating their own absolute monarchies.[18] The weakening of royal power resulted from and increased the growing political weight of the great lords in the eastern marches of the empire and encouraged separatist tendencies, until by the seventeenth century the empire had come to resemble a loose federation of fifty to sixty sovereign states.[19] The empire was under siege by the Swedes, the Russians, and the Tatars who ravaged Podolia and Volhynia in the 1670s. The Thirteen Years' War devastated the empire's economy, ruining its towns and its trade, worsening the enserfment of the peasant population, and arousing religious intolerance against Protestants, Jews, and Orthodox, where there had been an exceptional level of tolerance. In the election of 1697, there were no fewer than eighteen candidates, and Peter I's government took a strong stand against the French (and Ottoman) choice, deploying troops along the Lithuanian border to help the election of the Saxon candidate, who became king as Augustus II (1697–1733).[20] The stage was set for the transformation of Poland into a client state of Russia, leaving France as Russia's main enemy in Europe.

The Swedish Empire had also passed its prime by the mid–seventeenth century, even though it remained the great Baltic power. Much of its foreign policy was focused on Denmark, from which it had seized the southern provinces in 1660, breaking the Danish hold on the Sound while holding a defensive position toward the Russians in the eastern Baltic. Despite the strength of its monarchy and of its economy, based on iron, copper, and naval stores, and occasional French subsidies, long wars had exhausted the treasury. The solution for Charles XI (1660–97) was to tighten control and carry out the so-called *Reduktion*, a policy of reclaiming landed properties the Crown claimed had been unlawfully acquired from its own domains. Between 1652 and 1700 the nobility's holdings were reduced by half in Sweden proper, by 90 percent in Finland and Livonia.[21] The consequence was, paradoxically, the same as in the Polish Empire: the "reclamation" stimulated separatist tendencies both in Finland, where they went back at least to the beginning of the seventeenth century,[22] and in the Baltic provinces, where the Germanic nobility strongly resented Stockholm's policy of centralization and such social engineering projects as the emancipation of the peasantry. Members of a protesting delegation led by Johann von Patkul found themselves accused of high treason and sentenced to death in 1692. Patkul managed to flee to Dresden, Saxony's capital, where he concocted with Augustus II a plan to partition the Swedish Empire.[23] But it could not be carried out without Russian participation. As a result, discontent in Livonia led to a Russian alliance with Poland-Saxony, into which the Danes were naturally drawn, creating an irresistible opportunity for a dynamic new tsar, Peter I, to challenge Sweden's defensive stance — but in the process arousing the no less dynamic energy of a new Swedish king, Charles XII (1697–1718), to strike at Denmark, Poland, and Russia in a last bid to maintain his country's hegemony in the Baltic.

## The Southern Theater

The southern theater included the northern basin of the Black Sea from the Danube to the Kuban as well as the western basin of the Caspian from Astrakhan to the mountains of northern Persia. It was naturally divided into an Ottoman and a Persian sector. North of the Danube, the sea was fed by four major rivers descending from the Podolian Highland and the Central Upland, with the Dniepr watering the broad plain between them. The Dniepr began as far north as the latitude of Moscow, only a short distance from the source of the Volga; the Don began outside Tula, ignored the Oka flowing north toward the Volga, then seemed to repent and quietly flowed toward the lower Volga before turning sharply westward and losing itself into the Sea of Azov. The Dniestr and the Southern Bug gave the southeast marches of the Polish Empire their Black Sea orientation; directly across the Crimean peninsula, the Kuban gathered the waters of the western Caucasus. The geographic center of the Ottoman sector was the peninsula around which the entire sector formed an amphitheater of steppe country—the grazing grounds of various Tatar hordes.

These rivers gave that sector a structure different from that of the western theater. Radial roads from Moscow toward the Danube via Kiev intersected vertical roads formed by the Dniepr, the Southern Bug, and the Dniestr. Beyond the Dniestr the steppe continued into Moldavia and Wallachia, until it abutted against the Carpathian crescent, and the Balkan and Rhodope Mountains, the Heartland's southern periphery in Europe. East of the Dniepr, however, the Moscow-Tula-Orel road continued toward Kursk and Belgorod, crossing the steppe all the way to the Crimea without encountering any linear obstacle until it reached the Black Sea coast. The region was thus opened to invasion from the south, and much of its history was marked by Tatar raids into Ukrainian and Russian settlements and, on several occasions, even as far as Moscow. To the east of this corridor of Tatar—and later Russian—incursions we find the familiar pattern once again: the Don and its right-bank tributaries flowing across another corridor of invasion, from Riazan to the Tsaritsyn watershed between the Don and the Volga; the Manych, its left-bank tributary; and, across the steppe, the Kuban, barring the way to the approaches to the western Caucasus. Beyond the chain, the Ottoman sector thus formed a huge triangle. Its base, a straight line from Galati on the Danube to Poti on the Rion, was nearly 1,200 kilometers long; one side, from Galati to Moscow, 1,400 kilometers; the other, from Moscow to Poti, over 1,500 kilometers.

This immense sector consisted of four ecological zones, which critically determined the type of settlement and the importance of migration in Russia's expansion. The northern part was in the forest zone: its southern border ran beyond Kiev via Briansk to Kaluga, then along the Oka to Riazan and Nizhnii Novgorod. It was a zone of poor soils degraded by ancient forests. South of it was the wooded steppe with its oaks in the west and birches in the east, a zone of good soils and deep ravines. Its southern limit ran from Beltsy in Bessarabia to Ananev on the very edge of the Podolian Highland, to Kremenchug, Poltava, Valuiki (past Kharkov), Borisoglebsk, and Saratov on the Volga. The third zone was the steppe itself, a vast continental ocean, treeless save for the forested island of the Donets heights, rising toward the Stavropol upland and ending along the foothills of the western Caucasus. Its rich black soil was among the best in the world, but until the nineteenth century it produced only grass to feed the flocks of nomadic Tatar horsemen.[24] The forest zone was the land of the settler, the steppe that of the nomad, and the wooded steppe the frontier between them. Russia's advance toward the Black Sea was thus the advance of the settler into nomadic territory until the nomad was either destroyed or integrated into the world of the settler. Beyond the steppe lay the broad Caucasus and the swampy Rion Valley, a zone of eternal snows in the mountains and tropical rains and heat south of them, on the approaches to the Taurus Mountains of Anatolia, the Heartland's periphery.

The Black Sea gave these disparate regions and countries of the Ottoman sector a common destiny, very much as the Baltic gave most of the western theater its internal unity. The Black Sea was less "closed" than the Baltic, because the Turkish Straits were deeper and a strong current of fresh water flowed out into the Aegean Sea. They were closed, however, in a political sense, because the Ottomans controlled both banks, very much as Denmark had closed the Sound until 1660.[25] The Muscovite and Anatolian core areas faced each other in crablike fashion across the Black Sea, each extending its claw around one half of its coastline, transforming Moldavia-Wallachia and the Caucasus into the most strategically sensitive zones in their rivalry.

The Persian sector was smaller and its ecology very different. It began along the almost imperceptible watershed of the Ergeni Hills between the basin of the Black Sea and that of the Caspian. Its boundary then followed the valley of the Kuma to its source in the high mountains of the Caucasus separating the basin of the Kuban from that of the Terek. In Transcaucasia, it followed the Adzhar-Imeretian and Suram Ranges separating the valley of the Rion from that of the Kura, which received toward the end of its course the Araks descending from deep in the Taurus, the watershed between the Black Sea and the Persian Gulf. In the north, the sector's boundary was the lower Volga with Astrakhan, the only town of importance north of the Caucasus, on its large delta, a region of sandy soils and treeless saline marshes and lakes. The broad Dagestan Mountains were arid, unlike the western Caucasus, but they could be bypassed by the only two major roads linking both flanks of the Caucasus: one across the Darial Gorge to Tiflis, the other, the coastal road to Baku. The broad zone between the Araks and Dagestan was filled by the Armenian Highlands and the Murgan Depression. Two peaks overlooked the whole of Transcaucasia: Mount Elbrus, the highest at 5,633 meters, and Mount Ararat at 5,156 meters.[26] This sector also formed a triangle: the overland distance from Astrakhan to Astara was 1,300 kilometers, from Astrakhan to the Borjom Defile via Grozny and Tiflis, 900, and from Borzhom to Astara about 1,000 kilometers.

The alignment of the entire sector was northwest-southeast and favored the extension of Persian influence along the Kura and the Araks and into the mountains along the coastal road. But it also invited Russia's advance from Astrakhan, by sea and overland. Thus, in both sectors the course of rivers dictated a pattern of expansion toward the seas until the Russians reached the Danube and the Araks. These two rivers, with the Gulf of Bothnia, formed three moats of crucial strategic importance; they formed lines of optimum conquest, blocking invasion routes into the empire and giving Russia a commanding position on the imperial periphery. Beyond them, however, farther expansion would be counterproductive because it would penetrate core-area territory in which the Russians could not possibly gain staying power, as in Poland and Persia, an alien and impenetrable political and cultural world.

The Ottoman Empire became Russia's greatest and most lasting opponent.[27] The axis of Ottoman expansion had been an east-west one, from the Dinaric Alps to the Black Sea–Caspian watershed. It was largely determined by the alignment of the Balkan Mountains and the parallel chains of the Taurus. But there was also a northern orientation. For the Ottomans, the Black Sea was a moat that, like a mountain chain, required the expanding power to control its approaches from the other side. Without this elementary precaution, the moat would become the stepping board of expansion for any power established on that other side.[28] The Ottomans needed client states and societies on the northern shore of the Black Sea in order to concentrate their energies on the Balkans and the Caucasus. Moldavia and Wallachia were ideally suited to become such client societies; so was western Georgia. The client state was the Crimean Khanate. The allies, or rather the clients, of the Crimeans were the Nogai Tatars who roamed the entire steppe zone between the Dniestr and the Kuban. All these nomads lived on booty and kept the steppe and wooded steppe zones in a state of permanent insecurity.[29]

The turbulence of the frontier created the Cossacks, a social phenomenon characteristic of the southern and eastern theaters. The word means "freebooters": they were men who lived on the edge of the frontier, attracted by its freedoms and dangers. They sought to avoid the constraints of Polish power but were useful to it in fighting off nomadic raids, hence the ambiguity that always distinguished Cossack relations with the Poles and later with the Russians. The Poles favored the development of a Cossack force but also wanted to control it. In 1516, the Cossacks were divided into twenty territorial regiments of 2,000 men, each named after a town. Half of them were always on call; the others remained in the town's garrison. Their privileges, however, attracted townsmen and peasants. As their numbers grew, so did the instability and the dangers. In 1625, the Poles sought to dampen the turbulence by reducing the Cossack force to 6,000 registered members. The policy was bound to fail. Cossacks were moving south along the Dniepr like the nomads looking for booty. Life in the frontier brought about a social convergence between friends and foes, both seeking to maximize the opportunities the frontier had to offer. These Cossacks eventually settled beyond the Dniepr rapids and were called Zaporozhians. They developed their own raiding tactics against the Crimean Tatars and the Ottomans: in 1605 they devastated Varna, and Ochakov ten years later. In 1613, they took Sinop, in 1616 Trebizond, on the Anatolian coast. Other Cossacks would later move east, into the frontier of the Muscovite core along the edge of the Central Upland, east of the Sula River. They settled just ahead of the line the Russians were building to stop Tatar raids, and they became exposed to the full force of these sometimes devastating raids. These Cossacks were called Slobodians because they settled in large communities called *slobody*. Farther east were the Don Cossacks, settled in 1650 in some thirty *gorodki* along the Don and its three major tributaries, the Donets, the Khopër, and the Medveditsa. They were of mixed origin, some from the southern lands of Muscovy, others from among the Dniepr Cossacks who wandered eastward. These three Cossack groups formed a militia spread between the Dniepr and the Volga; they were client societies, sometimes paid by the Poles and the Russians to check nomadic raids into the Polish Empire and the Muscovite lands.[30]

The creation of these Cossack communities, a largely organic phenomenon, fitted in very well with Russian strategy in the southern theater. The great threat came from the Crimean Tatars who sent periodic raids along well-defined trails, of which the most famous was the *Muravskii shliakh*, a succession of watersheds between the Orel and the Donets, the Vorskla, and the Donets past Valuiki and Belgorod. These trails met at Livny, ran past Tula, and crossed the Oka at Serpukhov. To block these raids, the Russians built lines (*cherty*, later *linii*), artificial perimeters of fortified outposts across the steppe running from west to east. An early one was built along the Oka. Kursk and Voronezh were founded in 1586, Belgorod perhaps in 1593, Tambov in 1636, and Simbirsk in 1648. A line had already been built at the beginning of the seventeenth century between the Vorskla and the Don; Belgorod became Russia's chief military headquarters in the region. To the south, territorial regiments of Slobodian Cossacks were created in the 1650s in Sumy, Akhtyrka, and Kharkov.[31]

There was less disturbance in the Russo-Persian sector. A new Safavid dynasty had come into being with Ismail I (1502–24), whose adoption of the Shia branch of Islam brought about a long series of wars with the Ottoman Sunnis. In 1587, the Ottomans reached the Caspian, but they were rolled back in the 1600s until the two Muslim powers divided Transcaucasia among themselves in 1639. The Russians were little affected by these east-west conflicts, but they were determined to establish their influence in the mountains following the annexation of Astrakhan in 1556. One of the wives of Ivan the Terrible was a Kabardian princess. Astrakhan, much more than Cherkassk on the Don, the headquarters of the Don Cossacks, led to the Caucasus. There were two Cossack formations in the region. One was the "Greben" Cossacks, who may have split off from the Don Cossacks, moved to the Terek River in 1582, and later settled beyond it, as far as the Sunzha River. They and the Kabardians and Chechens would later become both friends and foes. Closely related to them were the Terek Cossacks who settled at the same time on the lower course of the river.[32] Across the mountains, the Turco-Persian wars caused enormous losses in Georgia, and several embassies were sent to Moscow seeking its support against the Muslim powers.

If the Ukrainian Cossack Uprising was a major factor in inducing the Russians to pursue an offensive strategy against the Polish Empire in the western theater, it also destabilized the southern theater. The Cossacks were Orthodox, the Poles Catholic. The Cossacks were free men who came from the peasantry and the urban poor. The Polish magnates on their huge properties in the eastern marches of their empire sought to bind the peasantry to the soil and to themselves. The Poles wanted strong measures against the Crimean Tatars; the Cossacks often found a modus vivendi with the Tatars, whom they resembled in their way of life. In 1649, Bohdan Khmelnytsky was recognized as hetman of the entire Cossack community. He made Chigirin on the right bank of the Dniepr his capital and entered into direct relations with foreign powers, including the Ottoman Empire. But the Poles refused to recognize the new Cossack state, and Khmelnytsky's separatist ambitions brought about a war in 1651 in which the Poles defeated the Cossacks. Moscow re- fused to help. Three years later, however, steady Polish pressures forced Khmelnyt- sky to turn to Moscow once again, and at Pereiaslav, east of Kiev, he gave his alle- giance to the tsar. The Muscovite tsar, as was his custom, assumed no obligations and invested the hetman with the symbols of authority.[33] The development was typ- ical of the fate of frontier societies. Determined to assert their independence from one core area, the Cossacks remained exposed to counterpressures they could not resist. Unable to build the foundations of a strong state, they were inevitably com- pelled to turn to other core areas for protection and end up as clients of one of them.[34] After the truce of Andrusovo (1667) the hetmanate became a client society of Muscovy. The Cossack community broke up: those on the right bank of the Dniepr were either wiped out or moved en masse across the river to become the Slobodian Cossacks and were placed under the Belgorod governor (*voevoda*); those on the left bank became known as the Little Russian Cossacks; those below the rapids retained the name Zaporozhian and, despite their autonomy, they too be- came a client society of Moscow. To the east, the growth of serfdom in the core area accelerated the flight of peasants to the Don Cossacks, who were forced in 1671 to give the oath of allegiance to Moscow and repeat it every year.

Behind this zone of Cossack client societies the perimeter of Russian outposts was advancing into the steppe. The Belgorod Line, built in the 1650s, began at Akhtyrka and continued via Belgorod, Voronezh, and Tambov to Simbirsk. A south- ern extension was later built via Penza to Syzran on the Volga. Another line, begin- ning in Poltava, bounded the Slobodian Cossack settlements in the south: this Izium Line followed the Merl, then swerved past Valki, followed the Mzha to the Donets, this river past Izium, then turned northward along the Oskol to Userd where it merged with the Belgorod Line.[35] The consequence was to place a Cos- sack client society for the first time behind the defensive perimeter of the empire and to inaugurate a process of disintegration.

The advance of the line into the steppe was part of a broad offensive strategy di- rected against the Crimean Khanate. The Truce of Andrusovo gave the Russians a free hand in the southern theater. Twenty years later, Vasilii Golitsyn assembled an army of over 100,000 men along the Izium Line between Poltava and Valki: it would cross the steppe to Perekop, which guarded the entrance to the peninsula, and move on to the khan's capital, while the Zaporozhian Cossacks cleared the lower Dniepr and the Don Cossacks directed their efforts against Azov. This coordi- nated offensive announced Russia's future strategy in the southern theater: a broad pincer movement directed against the enemy's capital. The Russians reached the Konka (Konskie Vody) River, the de facto boundary of the khanate, only to discover that the Tatars had set the steppe afire, creating enormous health and logistical haz- ards. To avoid a major disaster, Golitsyn returned to base camp, losing a third of his army to hunger and thirst. He tried again in 1689, starting early to avoid the sum- mer heat. The Russians reached Perekop in May, but found that the Tatars had dug a fosse across the entire isthmus, barring the way to the Russian cavalry and artillery and forcing another retreat.[36] While both campaigns were failures, they were also rehearsals of enormous strategic importance. For the first time since the nomad had imposed his rule on the steppe, an army recruited in settler territory was challenging his dominion in his own territory. Although it would take another century to annex the khanate, the Tatars had lost the initiative to the Russians.

Peter I's expedition against Azov was an offshoot of Golitsyn's campaigns. Almost sixty years earlier, in 1637, the Don Cossacks had taken this key strategic fortress on the Ottoman's defensive perimeter, held it against an amphibious counterattack, and offered it to the tsar in vain. But in 1695, Russia was on the offensive. An army of 30,000 troops trained by western mercenary officers sailed down the Volga and marched across the Volga-Don watershed; Azov, however, turned out to be another dead end: it could not be invested from the sea side without a navy, and two assaults failed with heavy losses. Peter then built a navy of river vessels and barges at Voronezh which sailed down the Don in 1696, negotiating the maze of channels forming the river's delta and forcing the fortress to surrender. Because Azov was not well located for a naval headquarters, Peter built the rudiment of a seagoing navy at Taganrog across the bay.[37] Russia's establishment on the Sea of Azov cut the Crimea's overland communication with the Nogai Horde in the Kuban steppe and threatened the Ottoman fortress of Kerch, which controlled the exit into the Black Sea. The Azov expedition raised the level of confrontation in the southern theater: in the 1680s, the Russians challenged a client state of the sultan; in the 1690s, they challenged Ottoman power directly. This encounter was the first of a dozen wars the Russians would fight with the Ottomans up to 1917.

The Cossack Uprising of the 1650s and the subsequent civil wars that lasted for twenty years were the foremost factor in the destabilization of the entire southern theater and the encouragement of Russian expansion. This theater had not been, like the western theater, a vast geopolitical space where two powers competed for hegemony, but one where an unsteady balance had been maintained by a long-lasting stalemate between the settler and the nomad. But the settler was advancing out of the forest zone in the seventeenth century, attracted by good land where trees did not even have to be uprooted because there were so few of them, and the steppe, where there were none at all. The destabilization stirred up mass raids by the nomads who played a major role in the struggles between Cossacks against Poles and later the Russians, once they became the patron of the new Cossack hetmanate. Not the Ottoman Turks but the Crimean Khanate was still the major player in the southern steppe, where rivalries were fought out beyond the perimeter of immediate Muscovite interests. But the acceptance of the hetmanate as a client society created a strategic threat for the khanate and opened up a new period marked by a struggle for hegemony in the steppe. Such a struggle, which placed the khanate on the defensive, could not be won by piecemeal additions of territory—every boundary line across the steppe had to be temporary—but only by the destruction of the khanate and the occupation of its capital deep in the peninsula. As a result, the destabilization of the southern theater called for the preparation of deep strikes into nomad lands and an eventual massive onslaught against Bakhchisarai, 1,400 kilometers from Moscow. However, such strikes were difficult to carry out, what with the great distances, the emptiness of the land, the heat, and the lack of wood and water. Nevertheless, the emerging geopolitical situation shaped, as it did in the western theater, a strategy of deep penetrations into enemy territory, supplemented by a policy of strengthening clientage relationships between Moscow and various communities.

There was more. The Crimean Khanate was not an independent player, but a vassal of the Ottoman sultan. If the Tatar raids against Cossack territories were henceforth certain to be seen as direct threats to Russia's vital interests, any sustained move by Moscow against the khanate was transformed into a threat to the integrity of the Ottoman Empire. This in turn created a certain ambivalence in Russian strategic planning by the end of the century: should the major effort be directed against the khanate itself, or toward the Danube in order to break the Ottomans' hold on the khanate? An anti-Ottoman strategy would in turn necessitate the extension of the client system to as many communities as possible in the Ottoman frontier, from the Balkans to Transcaucasia, notably in Moldavia and Wallachia, in Armenia and Georgia. It would also require the formulation of a long-term strategy calling for deep strikes not only toward the Danube but toward the Kuban as well, supported by Cossack auxiliary forces and the militias of local client communities ready to overthrow Ottoman domination and throw in their lot with the Russians. Thus, a deep strike strategy was inseparable from a well-developed client system capable of facilitating the operations of the strategic force and giving the Russians staying power along the shores of the Black Sea. In both the western and southern theaters, Moscow's expansionist urge beginning in the 1650s resulted in the articulation, still in the most general terms, of a similar political and military strategy designed eventually to establish Russia's hegemony in the vast geopolitical space between the Baltic, Black, and Caspian Seas, well within the Heartland's periphery.

## The Eastern Theater

This third theater stretched from the Volga to Nerchinsk. Its axis was a network of trails and rivers connecting Kazan with Tiumen (1,420 kilometers), with a northern branch to Tobolsk (250 kilometers), Tiumen with Omsk (630 kilometers), and Omsk with Irkutsk (2,590 kilometers). From Irkutsk the trail rounded Lake Baikal and ended at Nerchinsk, 1,250 kilometers away. Tobolsk, the capital of Siberia during the eighteenth century, was 2,500 kilometers away from Moscow; Irkutsk, 5,470 kilometers.

It consisted of three sectors. One, the Orenburg sector, was bounded by the Volga, the Kama, the middle and southern Urals and the Mygodzhary hills forming the watershed between the Caspian and the Ob basin, and the Ustiurt upland between the Aral and the Caspian seas. Its major feature was the so-called *Obshchii Syrt*, a broad plateau of spurs from the southern Urals, the watershed between the Volga and the Ural River; it was the northern end of the Aralo-Caspian Depression. It was also the land of the Bashkirs, a Turco-Mongol people who fell prey after the breakup of the Golden Horde to the Kazan and Siberian Khanates and the Nogai Horde roaming farther south. There, the Caspian Depression marked the end of the broad zone of desiccated land edging the great deserts of Central Asia and the Heartland's periphery, and sharply different from the wet steppe of the southern theater. Distances were already considerable in the smaller sector: from Kazan to

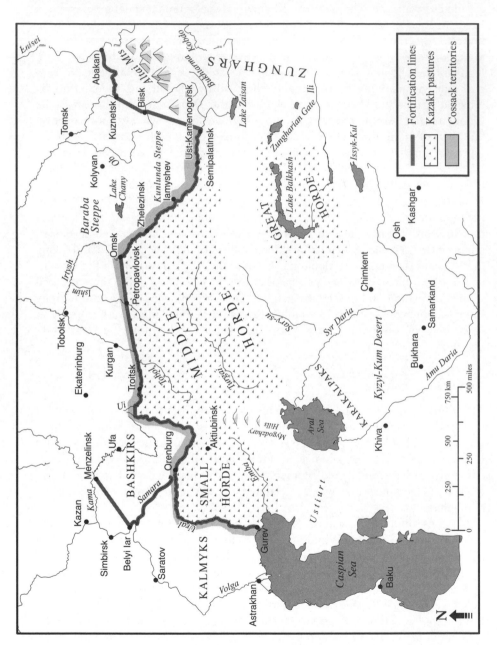

The Eastern Theater (Kazakh Steppe)

Fortification lines
Kazakh pastures
Cossack territories

Orenburg via Ufa 930 kilometers, from Orenburg to the Aral Sea about 1,250 kilometers, and between Saratov and Aktiubinsk 990 kilometers. Khiva, the first great oasis announcing Central Asia, was about 3,260 kilometers from Moscow.[38]

The second was the Tobolsk, later Omsk, sector comprising the basin of the middle and upper Ob. The river began at the confluence of the Katun and the Biia, both descending from the watershed between the Altai ("Gold Mountains") and the Kobdo Depression. On the Ob's long way to the Kara Sea it picked up the Irtysh, its source in the Mongolian Altai, the watershed between Zungaria and the Kobdo Depression, and flowed through an elongated trough called Lake Zaisan. Its course separated the Ishim steppe to the west, the most fertile part of Siberia, from the Baraba and Kunlanda steppes, all three known for an abundance of freshwater and saltwater lakes, an irresistible attraction for both the Kazakh nomad and the Russian Cossack. After entering the "Great Lowland,"[39] the Irtysh picked up the Ishim descending from the Kazakh upland and winding its way across the steppe bearing its name. Farther down, it received the Tobol with its many tributaries issuing from the Ural Mountains. This was the land of the Siberian Khanate, the fourth successor khanate after the breakup of the Golden Horde. This second sector also included the land of the Kazakhs stretching in a vast crescent from the Caspian and the Emba River to the Zungar Alatau and Tarbagatai Range, where the Zungar pastures began. It was a land of barren and sandy steppe but also of rich pastures and good soil. The climate was at times forbidding: dangerous snowstorms (*burany*) drove entire flocks of cattle and horses to their death and terrible frosts killed young shoots and caused mass hunger.[40] This sector was a zone of constant tensions over access to pastures among Kazahs, Kalmyks, Bashkirs, and Zunghars (Western Mongols). It formed a huge triangle. Distances as the crow flies were 1,200 kilometers from Tobolsk to Semipalatinsk, 1,400 from Semipalatinsk to the Emba River, and another 1,400 from that river to Tobolsk.

These two sectors also formed a succession of ecological zones from north to south. The forest zone ended along the Tura River and a line tracing Ishim–Kolyvan on the approaches to the Altai, the wooded steppe, along a line from Troitsk to Omsk, Lake Chany, and Barnaul on the Ob. The steppe formed another narrow zone bounded in the south by a Saratov-Uralsk-Temir-Turgai perimeter reaching the Irtysh below Semipalatinsk. Then came a semidesert zone including the entire northern shore of the Caspian from the Sulak River in the northern Caucasus to the Ustiurt upland and, beyond the Aral Sea, to the northern shore of Lake Balkhash and the Zungharian Gate, which led into Eastern Turkestan.[41]

The third was the Irkutsk sector. Like Orenburg and Tobolsk, the city was at the center of a vast hydrographic network. In Siberia, with its enormous distances, rivers were the chief avenues of exploration and transportation. Although the three most important rivers, the Ob, the Enisei, and the Lena, flowed in the northward direction, many of their tributaries created an almost continuous waterway between them; it was possible to cross Siberia from the Urals to Irkutsk by using only one portage, between the Ket and the Enisei. But this territory was of little importance in the shaping of a Russian strategy, because it was separated from China not by a populated frontier but by the almost impassable Saian Mountains. However, the Irkutsk hydrographic network also included Lake Baikal, which received the

Selenga that began in the Hangayn Mountains, forming the watershed between the lake's basin and the Kobdo Depression. Among the Selenga's many tributaries, the Khilok issued from the Iablonoi Range, the Heartland's boundary and the watershed between eastern Siberia and the Pacific. A portage between the Khilok and the Ingoda led to the Amur, which flowed across territory inhabited by the Tungus, a collection of peoples of which the Manchus would become the most prominent. Thus from Irkutsk, the Selenga led into Mongolia, the Khilok-Ingoda into Manchuria, and the Amur to the Pacific.[42] The configuration of the two Siberian sectors of the eastern theater established an indirect contact between Russia and China in three places: in the area of Lake Zaisan, in Mongolia, and in Manchuria. This third sector also formed a huge triangle: from Irkutsk to Peking as the crow flies, it was 1,700 kilometers, from Irkutsk to Nerchinsk 850, and from Nerchinsk to Peking 1,400 kilometers, but real distances were of course much longer.

The eastern theater was thus a patchwork of swampy forest land, vast and well irrigated plains, and semideserts separated by watersheds creating few obstacles to the movement of men, horses, and cattle. Like so much of the southern theater, it was the domain of the nomad between the forests of the Russian core area and, here, the great plains of China. Its fate would eventually be settled by those two great powers, but Russian strategy during the period under consideration would assume a defensive posture against Manchu China. It would be based on lines of fortified outposts seeking to achieve what nature had refused to do—to place insuperable obstacles to the movement of the nomads, until nomad societies, deprived of their life-giving freedom of movement, would begin to disintegrate from within and would invite the Russian advance.

Russia's expansion across Siberia had little in common with its advance into the other two theaters. Distances were enormous, resistance was insignificant, local societies were loosely organized, and there was no danger of meeting the armed opposition of a powerful state. It took place from west to east across an essentially open frontier, fueled by the fur trade that would eventually take the Russians to Alaska. Geopolitically, the so-called conquest of Siberia was the logical continuation of the process of collecting the inheritance of the Golden Horde. There was a Siberian Khanate beyond the Urals, which stirred opposition to the Russians on the western slopes of the mountains. Ermak's expedition of 1582 eliminated the khanate and Tobolsk was founded in 1587. From Tobolsk, the advance continued eastward along the Ob and its tributary, the Ket, then over to the Enisei Valley, where the Russians founded Eniseisk in 1619. From there, Cossacks and fur traders moved upstream and planted Krasnoiarsk two years later on the foothills of the Saian Massif. The advance continued into the land of the Buriat Mongols toward Lake Baikal, near which Irkutsk was founded in 1651. Nearly twenty years earlier, however, the Russians had sailed down the Lena and built Iakutsk in 1632, then crossed the nearly impassable mountain range forming the Heartland's boundary and founded Okhotsk in 1648, having tramped the entire length of Siberia in sixty-six years. In this open frontier they collected a tax in furs (*iasak*) from the natives, who had previously paid it to their past overlords. It was paid in various fortified outposts and shipped to Moscow, where a central agency, the Siberian Chancery, was made responsible for the entire administration of Siberia.[43]

This immense territory would have never become a geopolitical frontier if the advance had not branched off southward following the course of the rivers. Immediately after the conquest of Kazan, the Russians crossed the Volga and entered the land of the Baskhirs between the Kama and the Samara; the territory became a dependency of the Kazan headquarters. Samara on the Volga and Ufa on the Belaia in the heart of Bashkir country were both founded in 1586. This region would become a highly turbulent one because the intrusion of a sedentary civilization, with its officials, garrisons, and peasants, aroused opposition among the nomads, and attempts to extend serfdom and restrict the nomads' freedom of movement struck at the foundation of the Bashkir's way of life. The appearance of the Cossacks was an additional factor. The oldest Cossacks in the region were the Ural Cossacks (the Ural River was known as the Iaik until 1775). Their origin went back to the late sixteenth century, when a group of Cossacks raiding merchants on the Volga crossed the river after antagonizing Moscow and established their own settlement at Uralsk. From there, they founded outposts along the river all the way to its mouth on the Caspian coast. Even though they were placed in 1629 under the Chancery of Foreign Affairs, they behaved as they pleased, raiding Kazakh and Kalmyk pastures and robbing Russian traders on the Volga. Finally, it was also a turbulent frontier because Bashkiria was at the western end of the great steppe expanse of nomadic life, where Bashkirs, Nogais, Kalmyks, and Kazakhs maintained often hostile relationships. And beyond that steppe expanse there was China, which would play such an important role in the region in the eighteenth century.[44]

The Russians came into contact with the Sino-Mongol world in the Altai Mountains. In 1567, a chieftain named Sholoi founded the so-called Altyn Khanate. Its core was the Kobdo Depression, but by the time of his death in 1627, it had expanded to include the entire territory between the Mongolian Altai and Lake Khusugul, known as western Mongolia, beyond which lay the basin of the Selenga or the land of the eastern Mongols or Khalkas. The Altyn khan became the rival of the Siberian khans for the fiscal allegiance of various tribes in the valley of the Ob and the Irtysh. The elimination of the Siberian Khanate brought the Russians into contact with these tribes and into rivalry with the Altyn Khanate. Contacts began in 1616, and in 1632 an emissary from the khan arrived in Tomsk (founded in 1604) offering tribute and military aid. It was later agreed that Tomsk would become the center of Sino-Mongol-Russian trade: the khan had heard of the rise of the Manchus and the allegiance they had already extracted from the eastern Mongols. He offered to become the Russians' intermediary with Mongolia and China.[45]

The western Mongols consisted of four main tribes. One, the Torguts, who later became known as the Kalmyks, began a full-scale emigration across the Kazakh country in 1627 and settled in the area between the Emba and Volga in the 1630s. The other three formed in 1640 the so-called Zunghar Confederation under the leadership of Batur (1634–53) and sought to recreate a Mongol state that would also include the Khalkas. They invaded Tibet in 1638, placed the Dalai Lama on his throne, and adopted Tibetan (yellow) Buddhism. They were already at war with the Kazakhs and posed a formidable threat to the Manchus, who were about to begin their invasion of China.[46] The Russians were interested observers. Since their advance proceeded from west to east, they had every interest in protecting their southern flank against the Kazakhs and in settling their differences with the Zunghars in the Altai Mountains, where rumors of gold finds attracted them. But the Russians also faced a dilemma: supporting the Kazakhs meant antagonizing the Zunghars, while supporting the Zunghars was certain to increase Kazakh pressure on Russian settlements and raised the possibility of a conflict with China.

The Kazakhs were a people of Uzbek-Turkic stock who broke away from the Uzbek Khanate in the middle of the fifteenth century and crossed the Syr-Daria to settle in the Muiunkum Desert between the Talas and the Chu Rivers. There, they formed a separate khanate that expanded westward all the way to the Emba River, beyond which began the pastures of the Volga Kalmyks. By the 1640s, they roamed across what we now know as the Kazakh steppe and into the Ishim and Kunlunda steppe across the Irtysh. The lack of boundaries in such open country was a source of constant conflicts over grazing lands, and the ambitions of an occasionally powerful chieftain only made the situation worse. Although they still recognized the authority of a single khan, the Kazakhs were already divided into three hordes, the Small, the Middle, and the Great, running from west to east, each moving along its own corridor from south to north and back between summer and winter.[47] Their transhumance across a vast frontier would give the Zunghars and the Russians many opportunities to intervene to weaken the Kazakhs.

The Russians also came into contact with the Sino-Mongol world east of Lake Baikal. The fur trade led them eastward into the valley of the Lena, since Mongolia was of little interest because of the poor quality of the fur, but there were rumors of silver deposits in the region. Important political developments were also taking place there that would soon revolutionize the geopolitical situation in Eurasia and create a Russo-Chinese frontier. Tribes living on both sides of the Amur River, known as Tungus, divided into a large number of clans. The chief of one of them, Nurgaci, assumed the title of khan and claimed supremacy over all the others by founding a new dynasty only three years after the beginning of the Romanov dynasty in 1613. By the time of Nurgaci's death in 1626, his dynasty was at war with the Ming dynasty of China, and his successors were determined to overthrow it. In 1635, they adopted the term Manchu as a name for their people and in 1636 called their ruling dynasty the Ch'ing (Qing) dynasty, the name by which it would be known until its overthrow in 1911. That same year, they won the allegiance of the Khalkas. The Manchus entered Peking in 1644. In the meantime, they had reached the Sea of Okhotsk, which they called the North Sea, in 1636, and between 1639 and 1643 consolidated their control of the Amur and Shilka river basin including Nerchinsk and its silver deposits. By 1650 the "border" of the new empire followed the Iablonoi and Stanovoi Mountains, the Heartland's periphery in the Far East.[48]

To say that Russia switched to an offensive strategy in the eastern theater in the 1650s, as it was doing in the other two theaters, may seem inappropriate in view of the steady advance across Siberia for the three previous generations. Yet it was then that the Russians shifted their interests toward Transbaikalia across the Iablonoi-Stanovoi periphery, toward the valley of the Amur. The change was motivated by a realization that they had reached a dead end on the coast of the Sea of Okhotsk and by rumors that the valley of the Amur was rich in sables, had good land for agriculture, and contained deposits of gold and silver. But in so doing, they invaded territory the Manchus considered their own, and only there would they meet the armed opposition of a powerful state. Albazin and Achansk, both on the Amur, were founded in 1651, Irkutsk, the future capital of eastern Siberia and military and (inland) naval headquarters of Russia's presence in the Far East, in 1652, Nerchinsk in 1654. Fifteen years earlier, in 1639, the Russians had built a fort at the mouth of the Uda, which would become the collecting point for the best sable in Siberia. The Russians were thus claiming the valley of the Zeia and the Bureia, the two major left-bank tributaries of the Amur, filling the space between the Stanovoi and the Amur, and Achansk was the base for the exploration of the Sungari, the Amur's right-bank tributary, which watered the Manchurian plain. The Manchu emperors could hardly ignore this Russian invasion of their ancestral lands.

They considered the Cossacks and fur traders another variety of nomads, counterattacked early, and by 1650 had destroyed Albazin and Achansk. Albazin was rebuilt in 1665 and would become for the next twenty years a thorn in the flesh of the Manchus who were preoccupied at the time with putting down a rebellion in southern China and could not give undivided attention to their northern theater. The Russians sent embassies to Peking in 1654, 1657, 1670, and 1675, seeking a settlement of border disputes and permission to trade with the empire they saw as a source of precious metals and precious cloth, another India like the one they were trying to reach via Bukhara and the Silk Road. But the embassies all failed when the Russians refused to perform the kowtow. By 1682, the Kang-hsi emperor (1662–1722), the first of the two great emperors of the Manchu dynasty, was ready to deal with the threats from the north. In 1685, Albazin was burned and occupied the following year when the Russians returned, at the very time another Russian embassy headed by Fedor Golovin was on its way to seek a border settlement.[49]

Golovin arrived in Selenginsk in November 1686, after a two-year journey from Moscow, but the extremely tense situation between the Manchus and the Mongols forced both sides to move the site of their conference to Nerchinsk, where a treaty was signed in September 1689. The Manchus enjoyed military superiority over the Russians but were politically on the defensive. Concerned over the possibility of a Russian alliance with the Mongols who were then making substantial progress, they decided to compromise. Originally, they wanted the Russo-Chinese border to run along Lake Baikal and the Stanovoi chain, forcing the Russians to abandon Nerchinsk and the entire valley of the Amur as well as any claims on the Selenga. The treaty, however, barred the Russians only from access to the Amur, leaving the fort on the Uda and Nerchinsk on the Russian side. It also provided for the return of fugitives, an extremely sore point with the Manchus. The treaty was seen in Moscow as a victory for the Russians in view of their military weakness in the region. It would keep the peace between the two empires for over 150 years.[50]

The treaty must also be placed in the context of the geopolitical situation of the time. The greatest threat to Manchu rule was not so much Russian penetration as the ambitions of Galdan Boshugtu, the Zunghar chieftain (1671–97), to unify all the Mongols under his leadership. The Altyn Khanate had already been brought into the confederation in 1667, and the Zunghars had become Russia's rivals over the right to collect the tribute from the forest tribes in Altai. Galdan began his offensive in 1678, seizing Turfan and Hami in 1679 and Kashgar in 1680, thereby gaining control over the Silk Road from the Great Wall to the Pamirs. After seeking in vain an alliance with the Russians against China, he invaded the basin of the Selenga in 1688, going as far as the Kerulen, sending tens of thousands of Khalka refugees into China before moving into Transbaikalia and besieging Golovin in Selenginsk. Golovin was able to free himself and moved on to Nerchinsk. However, the Zunghar attack had the effect of creating a common interest between the Russians and the Manchus against the nomads, a fundamental fact in the history of Russia's strategy in the eastern theater. Seventy years later, an unwritten Russo-Chinese alliance would seal the fate of the nomadic frontier, without the Russians ever having to use force. After 1689, they assumed a defensive posture, secure in the knowledge that the alliance was the best guarantor of their security. Peace with the Russians allowed the Kang-hsi emperor to counterattack. Galdan was on his way to Peking but was stopped three hundred kilometers from the capital at the battle of Ulan Butong (near present-day Ulan Bator) in 1690. In 1691, the Khalka lands were annexed to the Manchu Empire.[51]

The great nomadic frontier extending from the Volga to Manchuria was an organic frontier of successive zones merging imperceptibly into one another, so that events in one zone had repercussions in the others. The expansion of the Zunghars took them into the Kazakh upland via the Irtysh Valley and the "Gate of Nations" (also called the Zungharian Gate), which led to Lake Balkhash. There was constant strife between Kazakhs and Mongols, the former abducting Mongol women and acquiring with the passage of time, more than any other Turkic people, a sturdy Mongol appearance. Zunghar attacks had begun in 1643, and by the 1680s Galdan, in an attempt to control the two trade routes from Tobolsk and Ufa to Tashkent and Bukhara, had taken possession of almost the entire southern part of the upland beyond Lake Balkash, swallowing up most of the Great Horde. The last Kazakh khan, Tauke (1680–1718), who kept his headquarters near Turkestan City, sent several embassies to Moscow in the 1680s asking for help. The Russians could not afford any help, but the Mongol-Kazakh conflict created a second fundamental fact: while the expansion of the Zunghars cemented the Russo-Manchu flanking alliance, it also laid the foundation of a Russo-Kazakh alliance, paving the way for a Russian forward strategy in the Kazakh steppe that would end two hundred years later with the conquest of Central Asia. Farther west, the Kalmyks of Khan Ayuki (1669–1724) were slowly becoming a client society of the Russians. Despite their constant fighting on both sides of the Caspian, they were doing the Russians' work, and when Peter I left for Europe in 1697, he entrusted to them the defense of the steppe frontier. The Russians were also advancing deeper into Bashkiria. A new Trans-Kama Line was built in the 1650s linking Belyi Iar on the Volga with Menzelinsk. The progress of the settler and the corruption of officials brought about a first Bashkir Uprising in 1662–64 and a second in 1675–83, put down with the help of the Kalmyks.[52]

In the three theaters during this latter half of the seventeenth century, one can detect in Russia's expansion the appearance of three principles that would later combine to form a grand strategy with its own internal logic. One was the determination to project military power over great distances in order to weaken the power of Poland and the Crimean Khanate, if not yet the Ottoman Empire, while even longer distances and the reliance on Cossacks forced Moscow to recognize the un-challengeable superiority of Manchu power. The second was the creation along-side the old militia of a regular army, modeled after the European armies of the day and stationed for obvious reasons in the Moscow area. The third was the develop-ment of a system of "international" clientage, to a large extent a broadening of the domestic one, in order to extend the range of Muscovite power. But only the trau-matic experience of the Northern War and the emergence of a powerful ruler at the head of the Romanov house could compel these three elements to coalesce into a grand strategy.

Much progress had already been made, however. Peter the Great's father, Alexei Mikhailovich, had secured in Afanasii Ordin-Nashchokin (who died in 1680) the services of a first-rate statesman capable of articulating a geopolitical vision en-compassing almost the entire Heartland. The government, he claimed, must de-velop the productive forces of the country, especially metallurgy and manufactures, in order to support the modernization of the army along Western models. This army must be concentrated on the periphery, chiefly in the Novgorod-Pskov area, in order to impress the Poles and the Swedes and be ready to move in the direction of the Baltic and Bielorussia. It must also be deployed south of the Oka facing the Ukrainian frontier and the Crimean Khanate. For what purpose? In order to weaken the Polish Empire by taking from it the Ukrainian lands on both banks of the Dniepr; then, once Poland had ceased to be a dangerous rival, to harness its en-ergies to strike a decisive blow at Sweden's hegemony in the eastern Baltic by taking Riga and at least the southern shore of the Gulf of Finland. The Polish alliance would also help Russia against the Crimean Khanate and facilitate the develop-ment of commercial and cultural relations with Moldavia. In this southern theater, kept insecure by Crimean raids, Ordin-Nashchokin envisaged an offensive against the Ottoman Empire in which the major objective would be Azov; its capture would force the Ottomans to restrain the Crimean Tatars and establish a durable peace in the region.

This military and diplomatic strategy was part of a much grander vision of Rus-sia's role in the Heartland. With the help of the Armenians in Persia, Russia must deflect existing commercial patterns and reroute the trade of the east through Moscow toward the Baltic and Europe, once Sweden's grip on the eastern Baltic had been broken. Moscow was already beginning to draw traders from Khiva, Bukhara, and India, and the trade with China was growing, using Mongol interme-diaries. The development of Russian manufactures was necessary not only to sup-port growing military power but also to make friends—shall we say "clients"?— among the peoples of the Caucasus and Persia and by implication in Mongolia as well, at a time when Ordin-Nashchokin could not yet realize the implications of the Manchu seizure of power in China. Such a comprehensive vision of Russia's role—which bore some resemblance to that of Ivan IV a century earlier, when Rus-sia was much weaker—was inseparable from the surge of self-confidence that marked the reign of Peter's father. It also bequeathed the great tsar a concrete pro gram of action.[53]

# 2

# Mobile Armies

## Strategic Penetration

One of the first principles of Russia's grand strategy was the determination to maintain highly mobile armies in order to carry out deep strategic penetrations across the frontier and into the enemy core areas. Here, the Russians were well ahead of their times: they pursued a Napoleonic strategy long before Napoleon was born. His strategy would be "to beat the enemy—to shatter him—to gain the capital—to drive the government into the last corner of the empire—and then, while the confusion was fresh, to dictate the peace."[1] The Northern War was an excellent example of such a strategy. It began in 1700 as a joint offensive operation, in alliance with Poland and Denmark, designed to take advantage of the youth of Charles XII in order to break Swedish hegemony in the Baltic.

There were two phases in that war. Peter I committed about 34,000 men to move into Ingria and Estonia but was met by Charles XII at Narva in November and thoroughly trounced. However, the Swedish king had fallen into a trap. If he pursued the Russians, he would expose his rear to Polish-Saxon troops besieging Riga; if he turned against these, he would expose his rear to Russian raids. The Swedes still looked upon the Poles as the main enemy and fought the war as they had fought it in 1656–60. The king relieved Riga, left a token presence in the Baltic provinces, and began a long pursuit of Augustus II which led him first to Warsaw, where he imposed his candidate, Stanislas Leszczynski, on the Polish throne in August 1704, and then all the way to Altränstadt outside Leipzig, where he forced the former Polish king to make peace in September 1706. Meanwhile, the Russians were forming a new army and mobilizing their enormous economic potential. They took Oreshek in October 1703, renamed it Shlisselburg, and reached the end of the Gulf of Finland in May 1703, where Peter laid the foundation of Petersburg. The conquest of Ingria followed, and the second battle of Narva in August 1704 was a Russian victory. The Russians then took the war into the Polish Empire, gaining supporters in Lithuania, which did not recognize Stanislas, while beating back Swedish attempts from Finland to regain control of the Neva. By the end of 1705, they had reached Grodno on the Niemen, but were stalled by a Swedish counter-attack, which failed largely because the Swedes ran out of provisions. The Russian advance resumed, and a Swedish force was defeated at Kalisz in western Poland in October 1706, the first substantial victory over the Swedes. By then, Charles XII had made peace with Augustus and secured his rear before turning against the Russians, inaugurating the second phase of the war. Rather than meeting the Swedes in general battle, Peter I chose the indirect approach, letting the Swedes penetrate deeper into Russian territory until their provisions were exhausted, then dealing a massive blow that would knock them out of the war. In September 1707, Charles was back in Grodno with about 30,000 men. A year later, he was marching toward Smolensk and eventually Moscow, when the capture of a train of supplies coming from Riga forced him to move south into the Left-Bank Ukraine. He wintered there, and at Poltava in June 1709, 24,000 Swedes faced 42,000 Russians expecting some 30,000 Kalmyks. Their defeat was catastrophic, and the king fled to Bendery (Tighina) in Ottoman territory.

But the blow did not compel them to capitulate. The Russians had a choice. They could assume a defensive posture, conducting essentially mopping operations in the Baltic provinces, safe in the knowledge that this granary of Sweden was now in their hands. This they did, taking Reval, Riga, and Vyborg in 1710, and also Kexholm on Lake Ladoga, which they had been forced to surrender in 1617. But the war had developed its own momentum, and the Russians continued to pursue an offensive strategy, now aiming at deep strategic penetrations into the Swedish Empire. In 1711, they besieged Stralsund in Swedish Pomerania and in 1712 began the invasion of Finland with 35,000 men, while a new fleet of galleys was being built to transport both men and provisions along the dangerous Finnish coast. Stralsund, Stettin, and Åbo were taken in 1713. In 1714, they reached Vasa, and a detachment even sailed across the Kvarken to Umeå on the Swedish side of the Gulf of Bothnia, while ships of the line and the galley fleet inflicted a major defeat on the Swedish navy at the battle of Hangö, the naval equivalent of Poltava. After Charles XII returned to Sweden and refused to negotiate, it was decided to carry out a landing in southern Sweden across the Sound. By the summer of 1716, 27,000 Russians were encamped around Copenhagen, over 2,500 kilometers away from Moscow. But the operation was cancelled at the last minute, largely for logistical reasons. That same year Peter arranged the marriage of his niece to the duke of Mecklenburg, opening the possibility that Wismar might in due time become a Russian naval base. Even the death of Charles XII in December 1718 did not compel the Swedes to capitulate, but systematic naval attacks along the Swedish coast designed to destroy the country's industrial capabilities and pave the way for an amphibious landing finally succeeded in bringing them to the negotiating table. Peace was signed at Nystadt (Uusikaupunki) in 1721.

One major lesson was drawn from that war. The Russians were determined and able to project a very significant amount of force at considerable distances from Moscow in order to force the enemy to accept a peace favorable to them. An expedition across Germany required the cooperation of allies who were neither disinterested nor always forthcoming, but the Russians always had the other option of striking at Sweden across the Gulf of Bothnia. However, the gulf, about 75 kilometers at the narrowest point across the Kvarken and 240 kilometers along the Åland archipelago, was a treacherous body of water which cut off Finland from Sweden in winter and required an invading force to maintain considerable and always vulnerable logistical support in order to gain staying power on the Swedish side. And a major capital was always certain to be heavily defended. Thus, as early as the 1720s, the Gulf of Bothnia emerged as a moat forming for the Russians a line of optimum conquest, a defensive perimeter serving the dual purpose of protecting the security of the new capital and launching devastating raids against the Swedish coast. Finland had to be abandoned in 1721, but a strategic lesson had been learned.[2]

Another conflict would soon test Russia's determination to carry out deep strategic penetrations. International relations during the first half of the eighteenth century were dominated by the Franco-Austrian rivalry for hegemony in continental Europe. Austria and Russia were natural allies because of their common hostility against Islam and Ottoman ambitions; Austria's enemies were also Russia's. By the 1720s, it had become clear that France's system of alliance with the Swedes, the Poles, and the Ottomans was directed against Austria and by implication against Russia as well. When Austria found itself at war with France over the election of the same Stanislas Leszczynski as king of Poland in 1733 and suffered reverses, it called on Russia to send an expeditionary force of 20,000 men to link up with its forces in Heidelberg prior to beginning joint operations against the French. After overthrowing the Polish king, the Russians left Warsaw, already 1,260 kilometers from Moscow, in April 1735, reached Częstochowa in May, crossed the Moravian Gate, and reached Plzeň via Prague in July. They were in Nüremberg in July, and met the Austrians in Heidelberg, about 25 kilometers from the Rhine and 2,500 from Moscow, in August. They had marched 1,240 kilometers at a leisurely pace in about 120 days.[3]

By then, Austria and France had made peace, and the expedition lost its purpose, but it had shown Russia's ability to send a substantial force across the Heartland's periphery for the first time and its determination to fight a Coastland power if need be. This determination would remain a major article of Russian strategy until 1814.

The Copenhagen expedition of 1716 was in fact not the first long-range penetration within the Heartland. Five years earlier, while his troops were besieging Stralsund, Peter had gone to war against the Ottomans. From Bendery on the Dniestr, Charles XII had been inciting the sultan to enter the conflict by opening a second front for the Russians at a considerable distance from the Baltic coast. The War of 1711 was thus an extension of the Northern War with Sweden. After the Turkish declaration of war, both sides rushed to the Danube, the 44,000 Russians hoping to block an Ottoman crossing of the river at Isakcha (Isaccea). They failed, and the encounter took place instead on the Prut River, about 75 kilometers south of Jassy.[4] It was a disaster, the Russians barely escaping annihilation, but it contained a lesson for the student of Russian strategy. The battlefield was 1,400 kilometers from Moscow, and Russian detachments reached the Danube at Galats (Galati), another 250 kilometers away. For the first time, the Russians had directed their main force in the southern theater not against the Crimean Khanate but against the Ottoman army in Moldavia. The Danube was emerging as a second moat in Russia's perceptions: it would defend a Russian presence in Moldavia and Wallachia, two Christian territories, and become a base of operations into Christian Bulgaria, on the way to Constantinople. The major thrust was accompanied by a secondary one from Kazan with less than 3,500 men. This small force sailed down the Volga, gathered 20,000 Kalmyks at Tsaritsyn, marched on to Azov, and crossed the steppe to ravage "Cherkess" settlements along the Kuban, then returned to Kazan.[5] The city was already 800 kilometers from Moscow; the distance from Kazan to Tsaritsyn was 1,100 kilometers, from Tsaritsyn to the Kuban via Azov another 800. The expedition thus marched 2,000 kilometers to punish Ottoman allies. Taken together, these two thrusts formed a huge pincer movement directed from Moscow, one prong aiming at the Danube, the other at the Kuban. This pincer movement would in later campaigns aim across the Caucasus at eastern Anatolia and across the Balkans at Constantinople. It would remain a key element in Russia's strategic planning against the Ottomans until World War I.

The war with Sweden was barely over when Peter forced a showdown in the Persian sector. The weakness of the Safavid dynasty created chaotic conditions in eastern Transcaucasia, and Russian merchants had already suffered substantial losses in Shemakha, the region's great commercial entrepôt, in 1712 and 1720. An Afghan leader based in Kandahar was advancing on Isfahan, the shah's capital, and took it in October 1722. Historians have obscured the reasons for Russia's intervention. It was assumed that the Afghan advance was certain to bring about an Ottoman invasion of the Azeri Khanates to the Caspian shores, even of the Persian core area itself, as in the days of Suleiman the Magnificent, and that a Russian Empire on the rise could not accept the potential unification of the entire southern theater under Ottoman overlordship.[6] These fears were not unfounded. In fact, however, the Russians had a strong interest themselves in taking advantage of the weakness of Persia, which offered possibilities of gaining trade concessions from a shah with a weak hand, including the right to cross the country on the way to India and gaining a monopoly of the caviar and silk trade. Russia's commercial interests in the region had an old history, and Peter's move was part of an offensive strategy designed to take full advantage of favorable circumstances.

During the winter of 1721–22, troops returning from the western theater gathered around Moscow and along the Volga and the Oka prior to boarding ship for Astrakhan. Stores of provisions were set up along the Volga. The expeditionary force consisted of about 56,000 men, including 10,000 Kalmyks and Cossacks from the Don and Left-Bank Ukraine. The tsar left Moscow in May 1722. At Astrakhan, the infantry went on by ship while the cavalry took the overland route to Derbent, which controlled the narrow defile leading into Transcaucasia. The town surrendered in August, but the expedition stopped there: a storm destroyed the transport ships carrying the provisions, forage, and fresh water. The troops returned to Astrakhan, but the Caspian flotilla carried out an amphibious operation in Enzeli Bay that took Resht (Rasht) in December. Russian objectives remained the capture of Baku and the occupation of the entire southern shore of the Caspian, the source of the caviar and silk trade. In Tiflis (Tbilisi), Tsar Wakhtang IV deserted the shah, his nominal suzerain, and went over to the Russians. Peter I returned in 1723, taking Derbent again and Baku in July, and signed in September a treaty of alliance with the shah, who ceded the two towns and the three provinces on the southern shore.[7] It was only then that the defection of eastern Georgia prompted Ottoman troops to invade the country: they occupied Tiflis in July, at the very same time the Russians were taking Baku. Other Ottoman troops invaded Persia proper, raising the danger of a direct confrontation with the Russians. This was avoided when the two sides agreed in 1724 to partition eastern Transcaucasia, the Russians retaining their conquests along the Caspian coast, the Ottomans annexing the rest.

This Persian campaign, which took the Russians to Baku, over 3,000 kilometers from Moscow and another 500 to Rasht, can be seen in retrospect as an essential part of a broad strategic offensive against the Ottoman Empire, in which eastern Georgia played a crucial role. The Russians could not gain staying power on the Caspian shore: the climate was unbearable, and the Caspian flotilla too small to provide steady logistical support. When a reaction began in Persia, led by Nadir Shah, who launched a counteroffensive in 1730 to dislodge the Ottomans from eastern Transcaucasia, the Russians wisely cut their losses and retreated to Astrakhan. They also used the opportunity of the Ottomans being on the defensive to make war on their client in the Crimea in 1735.

The operational plan was extremely ambitious. It envisaged a four-year campaign: to win control of the steppe in 1736, conquer the khanate and the Sea of Azov in 1737, take Moldavia and Wallachia in 1738, cross the Danube and capture Constantinople in 1739. Faithful to their strategy of launching sweeping operations in the form of pincer movements, the high command assigned an army of 85,000 to invade the Crimea via the Perekop Isthmus, and another of 45,000 to attack it from the Azov side. This initial concentration on the Crimea reminds us of Golitsyn's campaigns and had the same baneful results. The zone of operation, here the steppe, was empty and hostile territory because of harassment by elusive nomads. There were no peasant settlements or towns to supply provisions, which had to be dragged along in countless slow-moving ox-drawn wagons. There was no timber to repair them and sometimes no firewood to bake bread, resulting in severe intestinal problems, which killed tens of thousands of men. There was often no fresh water, and when there was, the enemy had poisoned the wells, as they did after the Russians reached Bakhchisarai, the khan's capital, in 1736. Worst of all, there was the oppressive heat, which exhausted both men and horses.[8] Only a definitely offensive strategy underestimating the difficulties of the terrain and the resourcefulness of the enemy while neglecting the crucial importance of logistical support could explain such ambitious and unrealistic projections of military force in the southern theater.[9]

A measure of other such ambitious and unrealistic projections was the expedition of Lt. Col. Ivan Bukhgolts to the Irtysh and that of Guard Captain Alexander (Bekovich) Cherkasskii to Khiva. Reports were received in the early 1710s from Governor Matvei Gagarin in Tobolsk and from Turkmen traders in Astrakhan that there was gold dust (*pesochnoe zoloto*) in the bed of the upper Amu Daria, gold, silver, and copper ore in the region of the upper Irtysh. Gold dust was also found in some mysterious town called Erkent in "Little Bukhara" (eastern Turkestan). These reports stimulated the tsar's interest for two reasons: Russia did not have indigenous sources of precious metals—save for the Nerchinsk silver, which began to be mined in 1704[10]—and its participation in international trade was still too small to generate a substantial amount of hard currency; with the invasion of Finland in 1713, the government sorely needed additional revenue and trade would supply it. Despite their limited knowledge of the geography of this immense region between the Caspian Sea and the Irtysh, the Russians decided to launch two expeditions at the same time, actually two detachments of a single expedition designed to place the Kazakh upland and the khanates in a vise—another pincer movement to establish fortified outposts at strategic locations and control trade routes. Such an enterprise also underestimated the baneful effects of the heat to which the Russians were not accustomed, the difficulties of the terrain, the exhausting distances, and the resistance of the Khivans and Zunghars who had everything to lose if it succeeded.

In June 1714, Bukhgolts was instructed to proceed to Tobolsk and take command of a military force put together by Gagarin, to sail the Irtysh upstream to Lake Iamyshev, a salt lake of great attraction to nomads, to build a fort and winter there, and move on to Erkent (Iarkend) the following spring. In 1715, his mission was expanded to include the exploration of the Lake Zaisan and upper Irtysh region in search of gold, silver, and copper deposits. He left Tobolsk in July with 3,000 men and 1,500 horses and built the fort at Lake Iamyshev, but in the spring of 1716 found himself surrounded by 10,000 Zunghars determined to starve him away. He withdrew in April 1717, but built a fort downstream at the confluence of the Om, a location so successful that Omsk would later become the military capital of western Siberia. He then reported that there was no overland or river route to Erkent and that it would take over three months to reach it. Bukhgolts's mission thus had only partially failed: he never had a chance to discover Erkent and the mineral wealth of the Altai, but he had established a Russian military presence 3,300 kilometers from Moscow. The Russians were still too weak to challenge Zunghar power directly, but they had plans for settlements on Lake Zaisan and in the Altai that would continue to stimulate their advance into the Russo-Chinese frontier. Two years later, in 1719, another expedition was sent to the upper Irtysh to discover the mysterious city but also failed, although its commander, Guard Major Ivan Likharev, founded Ust-Kamenogorsk, 1,000 kilometers upstream from Omsk at the very gate of the Altai Mountains. In 1721, the Zunghars had a change of heart following their defeat by the Manchus in eastern Turkestan and offered the Russians free transit for their gold prospectors in exchange for an anti-Manchu alliance. Nothing came of it, however, as the Manchus withdrew their forces after the death of the Kang-hsi emperor in 1722.[11]

Cherkasskii's expedition was even less successful. In Central Asia, Khiva was in turmoil. In 1700 an envoy had proposed to the tsar that the khanate become a client state in return for military support. Peter agreed and confirmed the khanate's new status in the charter of 1703 sent to the new khan, but it was largely a formal gesture because the Russians could offer no military assistance. By 1714, however, Peter switched to an offensive strategy against both Zunghars and Khivans. The purpose of the expedition was to establish a string of forts on the eastern shore of the Caspian and determine how far Erkent was from that sea. The Russians were still so ignorant of the topography of Central Asia that they did not appreciate the distance between Khiva and the Irtysh, and Likharev would be asked in 1719 to determine if any rivers in the area of Lake Zaisan flowed into the Aral Sea.[12]

Cherkasskii was ordered in May 1714 to go to Khiva to congratulate another new khan on his accession and to discuss trade matters. There was much more to it, however, than this modest goal. He was given 1,500 men by the Kazan governor and sailed on to Astrakhan from which he reached Gurev, near the mouth of the Ural River, in October, but he returned to Astrakhan when his flotilla was threatened by ice. In 1715, he rounded out the northern end of the Caspian and landed on the Tiub-Karagan promontory of the Mangyshlak peninsula, directly across the sea from Astrakhan. There began the main caravan route to Khiva, and Turkmen traders told Cherkasskii that the lower course of the Amu Daria could be diverted to reenter its old channel to Krasnye Vody on the Caspian. This was of major interest to the tsar, who hoped to use the river (which takes its source in the Pamirs) to establish trade relations with Mogul India. Cherkasskii was instructed in 1716 to follow the old bed to Khiva, to confirm the khan's status as a client, to send from there embassies to Bukhara and India, and to march on to the Syr Daria in search of Erkent. He built three forts on the eastern shore of the Caspian, including Alexandrovsk on the promontory and Krasnovodsk, and sent presents to the khan announcing he was coming as an envoy of peace, but the khan was not fooled.

The march on Khiva took place in 1717, at the same time Bukhgolts was returning to Tobolsk after founding Omsk. Rather than following the old bed to the Amu Daria, Cherkasskii gathered his force of about 4,000, including Ural (Iaik) and "Greben" Cossacks, with six guns in Gurev and left in June, almost the worst time of the year, when the oppressive heat began. From Gurev, the expedition reached the Emba River, marched on to the Ustiurt, crossed this desolate region nearly 800 kilometers long, and reached the Amu Daria in August, after covering 1,350 kilometers in 66 days. It was then 150 kilometers from Khiva. Cherkasskii was betrayed by his Kalmyk detachment, which disappeared in the night to warn the khan that the envoy's intentions were not so peaceful. The khan decided to give battle, but could not force a decision and resorted to a ruse. He agreed to sign a peace treaty and invited the Russians to come to Khiva, claiming however that the city was too small to accommodate the expedition; it should instead be broken up into smaller units. Cherkasskii made the error of agreeing, and almost the entire force was massacred. Cherkasskii, who was a Kabardian prince, had styled himself the "conqueror" (*pokoritel' vladenii*); he paid with his life, and his head was sent to the Bukhara khan. Although he failed and even the Caspian forts were abandoned, he nevertheless had brought Russian power to Khiva, 3,300 kilometers from Moscow, the same distance as Omsk.[13]

Thus, by the end of the 1730s, the new Russia, steeled by the traumatic experience of the Northern War, had built a powerful standing army and strategic force and worked out a grand strategy of which a first principle was the determination to project military force across enormous distances in all three theaters in order to strike at enemy capitals, Stockholm, Warsaw, Constantinople, the northern cities of Persia, and Khiva. We must now turn to the deployment of that force in peacetime.

## Concentrated Deployment

One of Peter's major achievements was to transform a seventeenth-century army consisting of occasional mounted levies, obsolete infantry detachments, and "new

Deployment of 1725

formation troops" built on the western model into a standing and disciplined force of infantry and cavalry regiments. By the 1720s, the field army consisted of forty-two infantry regiments (a paper strength of 60,144 men) and thirty-three cavalry regiments (all dragoons, for 41,349 men), a total force of about 100,000 men. There was, in addition, the so-called Southern Corps (*Nizovyi korpus*), stationed in the conquered Persian provinces and consisting of about 25,000 men. I shall call this standing army the strategic force.[14]

With the return of peace, a second principle of Russia's emerging grand strategy became clear: the strategic force must be withdrawn from the border regions and concentrated in the Muscovite core. There, it would form a single army, not committed to territorial or perimeter defense, but ready to move into the western and southern theaters with the strength appropriate to the importance of the objective, in order to achieve specific foreign policy goals, either political or commercial. Only the Southern Corps, stationed as it was at considerable distances from Moscow, was assigned the task of fixed perimeter defense, facing the Persians and the Ottomans across a largely undefined border. This second principle, closely related to the first—deep strategic penetrations—subordinated the use of force to the attainment of political objectives against rival core areas and the maintenance of the client system.

Moscow was the natural hub of this concentrated deployment. Seven roads, rudimentary but already well traveled, radiated from it: toward Tver, Novgorod, and Petersburg, the new capital, and toward Smolensk on the approaches to the western theater; toward Kaluga, Orel, Kursk, and the Dniepr; toward Tula, Elets, Voronezh, and the Donets, both rivers and the space between them forming the frontier with the steppe nomads; toward Riazan and Tambov, the lower Don and the lower Volga, the gateway to the northern Caucasus. A sixth road led to Vologda and Arkhangelsk, Russia's old window on Western Europe, now partly supplanted by Petersburg. The seventh led to Vladimir, Nizhnii Novgorod, Kazan and beyond, into Bashkiria in the eastern theater. These vertical roads had become Russia's corridors of expansion. The Volga and Oka, flowing from west to east and merging at Nizhnii Novgorod, formed horizontal roads intersecting the vertical roads to Tver, Iaroslavl, Kaluga, and Riazan, facilitating lateral transfers from one sector of the hub to another. Concentrated deployment was thus designed to maximize the strategic force's surge capability in any direction whenever the high command chose to undertake offensive operations against a perceived enemy.

Sixteen of the seventy-three regiments[15] were stationed at the very center of the hub, eight in Moscow and its province, the other eight in the triangle formed by the Moscow-Tver and Moscow-Iaroslavl roads, intersected by the upper Volga, which picked up the Sheksna and Mologa at Rybinsk, a region of intense commercial activity along the great river. The two guard regiments were stationed in Petersburg and its environs. There were six regiments in Novgorod and Pskov, with one battalion posted at Velikie Luki, in the great space between Novgorod and Smolensk. Two dragoon regiments patrolled the Moscow-Smolensk road, a third the Smolensk-Briansk horizontal road, which ran to Orel and merged with the Moscow-Kursk road. South of Moscow, sixteen regiments were echeloned along two belts, eight along the Kaluga-Tula-Riazan belt, on the edge of the wooded steppe, along the old fortified line that had once faced the steppe nomads launching raids against Moscow, the other eight, all dragoons, along a line from Elets to Tambov to Shatsk, between the Don and the Tsna, forming a horizontal line intersecting the Moscow-Voronezh road. The Oka separated two clusters of regiments. West of it, nine regiments, all infantry, were concentrated in the triangle formed on two sides by the Moscow-Iaroslavl and Moscow-Vladimir roads; east of it, twelve dragoon regiments were deployed in Nizhnii Novgorod, Arzamas, Alatyr, Sviiazhsk, and Penza, filling the space between the middle Volga and the Simbirsk Line and even ahead of it, on the fringe of Nogai Tatar country between the line and the Don. Completing the circle around Moscow were four infantry regiments in Viatka and Solikamsk, and one of dragoons patrolled the area between the Kama and Galich, where two infantry regiments were stationed. One regiment of dragoons was in Bashkiria, one of infantry in Siberia proper. No regular troops were left in the Baltic provinces or in the Left-Bank Ukraine or, for that matter, south of a line running from Briansk to Tambov via Orel and Elets. In those territories, regular troops were replaced by garrisons with a dual mission: to maintain Russia's presence and to operate as forward bases, with provisions, guns, and ammunition, to support a forward thrust by the strategic force into the western and southern theaters, as well as into Bashkiria, where the situation remained tense.

Such a concentrated deployment served a number of purposes. Regular troops maintained order in and around Moscow, the old capital—still far more important than the new one in Petersburg—along the Volga waterway, and in sparsely populated territory south of the Oka, where the settler was beginning to encroach into the world of the nomad, creating tensions and challenging the nomad to carry out occasional desperate sorties against peasant settlements. Forward defense was provided by client societies forming a broad frontier of agricultural or semi-agricultural settlements separating the Muscovite center from the enemy core areas. It also resulted from policy considerations of a fiscal and economic nature. To facilitate their supply, regiments were settled in provinces and districts with a specific number of taxable males enrolled in the census of 1719. The proceeds of the tax, the capitation, were assigned exclusively to meet the needs of the army.[16] An army in the field resembled a moving town: it was a large consuming unit depending on a surrounding agricultural base. Like a town, regiments were expected to stimulate the activities of the market towns along the rivers, where grain, meat, salt, and spirits were always available. There is some evidence that Peter even contemplated a resettlement of the population from the fringes back into the area of concentrated deployment, in order to improve tax collection and increase the productive capabilities of the population.[17] The army would thus become an agent of economic transformation in the basin of the upper and middle Volga. Such a policy would create a garrison state, a "Fortress Russia," where the labor of a rigidly controlled population would be channeled to increase the striking power of the strategic force.

Finally, concentrated deployment around the Muscovite center with an outer ring of garrisoned strongholds would create an infrastructure of roads, depots, and stores offering an impregnable defense. But the strategic posture was not defensive, it was offensive. The strategic force was a mobile army that could transform itself temporarily into a number of armies capable of striking in any direction or even in all directions at once, toward Finland, Poland, the Danube, and the Crimea, even the Caucasus and Persia. Gathered up in one central location, it could take full advantage of Russia's interior lines, and the high command could switch forces from one sector or theater to another, as Peter's campaigns had clearly shown. Concentration also magnified the "awesomeness"[18] of Russian power toward enemies and client states alike, thereby creating an economy of force on an empire-wide basis. In the near absence of territorial commitments, the strategic force's surge capability was maximized.

Major steps were taken after Peter's death to consolidate the infrastructure of fortified outposts, patrols, and military settlements in the steppe, as peasant colonization kept advancing toward the Dniepr and the middle Volga, countering Peter's expectations that it might be contained within the Muscovite core. However, the elemental process of colonization toward the richer lands of the south undermined the principle of concentrated deployment of the strategic force in the old forest zone in two ways. Regiments had to follow the peasants if they were to remain close to their source of provisions and thereby minimize their logistical difficulties. But the southern lands were also the most exposed to nomadic roads. No settled life could survive within the raiding range of steppe nomads unless provided with a reliable defense in depth capable of intimidating the nomad with the prospect of severe losses in case of attack and the threat of retaliatory strikes into his territory. Priority was given to the southern theater for both defensive and offensive purposes; it would culminate in the ill-fated war against the Crimean Khanate, when the nomad was able for the last time to stem the settler's advance into the steppe and toward the Black Sea.

The 1730s witnessed the accelerated construction of fortified lines that rendered obsolete their predecessors built in the 1640s and 1650s. A new "Ukrainian Line" was designed to block access to the Ukraine of Settlements west of Kharkov and to the Donets.[19] It began on the Orel, close to the border between the Russian Empire and the Crimean Khanate, followed the Berestovaia, crossed the steppe to the Bereka, and followed it to the Donets above Izium. It was about 250 kilometers long, and its headquarters was at Fort Belev, near present-day Krasnograd. Beyond the Donets, the Don Cossacks stood guard all the way to the Don. Beyond the Don, the so-called Tsaritsyn Line linked the elbows of the Don and Volga, and sought to pin the Nogais in the triangle between the Khopër and the Volga, separating them from their brethren in the Kuban steppe. It also kept the Kalmyks beyond the Volga. Farther south, the Terek Line barred the mountain peoples from the North Caucasus steppe.[20] These lines divided the nomadic world by corralling individual tribes within a definite space. Within each such separate space, forts became so many anchor points for settlers to stake a claim to the land and to challenge the nomad's hegemony until the Russians could establish their own and expel or domesticate him. These forts backed by garrisons in their rear, with garrisons backed by units of the strategic force, formed the outer perimeter of an in-depth infrastructure that not only defended the Muscovite center but also sustained an offensive posture toward the steppe horsemen. As they advanced into the steppe, the lines remained the vanguard of the strategic force, which they imperceptibly drew into the new areas of settlement. This had become obvious by the 1740s.

The lines extended beyond the Volga. While the Bashkir Uprising of 1735–37 was in progress, the Russians built a series of forts along the entire course of the Samara between the Volga and the Ural River, both to facilitate expeditions into Bashkiria and to separate the Bashkirs from the Kalmyks, who roamed between the Samara, the Volga, the Ural, and the Caspian.[21] This Trans-Kama Line, after reaching the Ural, became the Orenburg Line almost all the way to the river's headwaters, then followed the Ui River to its confluence with the Tobol. It served to demarcate the western boundaries of the Kazakh world and to separate the Kazakhs from the Bashkirs, with whom they were in constant warfare. Bashkiria became completely surrounded between the Volga, the Kama, and the Ural prior to its full incorporation into the empire and the systematic colonization of its lands. In 1735, Orenburg was founded at the confluence of the Or with the Ural and moved to its present location in 1742. It would soon become Russia's major military headquarters in the region, the last, after Riga, Kiev, and Astrakhan, of the four great regional military headquarters along the periphery of the Russian Empire of the day, forming a huge semicircle around the Muscovite core. The same policy of breaking up immense spaces into manageable territories and confining nomads within them was in evidence beyond the Tobol as well. By the 1730s, there were three major fortresses on the Irtysh, in Omsk, Iamyshev, Semipalatinsk, and a smaller one at Ust-Kamenogorsk: they formed the backbone of the Irtysh Line.[22] It separated the Ishim steppe from the Baraba and Kunlunda steppes and demarcated Kazakh territory in the east, blocking the nomads' transhumance into designated areas of Russian settlement on the foothills of the Altai Mountains. Beyond the Saian Mountains, the rudiments of another line were being sketched, linking Irkutsk with Selenginsk and Nerchinsk and guarding the approaches to Lake Baikal.

To provide support for the operation and maintenance of the lines, Moscow had created in the seventeenth century military colonies of single-family homesteaders (*odnodvortsy*), who were given a plot of land adequate for one man and his family.[23] Peter mobilized this loose frontier society to create a separate military formation. In 1713, in anticipation of another war with the Ottomans, five regiments of "land militia" were created, each of 1,400 officers and men. These regiments were settled just beyond the limit of deployment of the strategic force. In 1711, the force was enlarged to consist of twenty regiments, sixteen of them mounted, and in 1736, all twenty regiments (22,730 men) were reorganized into mounted troops and called the Ukrainian ("border") Land Militia Corps, under its own commander, a lieutenant general, stationed at Fort Belev. To support this force of irregulars, peasants in Belgorod and Voronezh provinces in the vicinity of places of settlement were required to pay forty kopecks per soul in addition to the standard seventy kopecks that went, as elsewhere in Russia proper, to support the regular army.[24] The pattern of deployment shows that the territory assigned to the land militia filled the great space between the Desna and the Khopër, a forward perimeter about 670 kilometers wide that barred all the Tatar invasion routes. Some of the regiments were stationed on the Ukrainian Line, others remained in their place of settlement. This land militia of military colonists was another instrument of strategic control. Together with the Cossacks of Little Russia, the Ukraine of Settlements, and the Don, its mission was to provide in-depth defense against Tatar invasions without having to bring the strategic force into action. There was also a Trans-Kama land militia created in the 1730s, consisting of three mounted regiments stationed in Bashkiria and a regiment of infantry deployed along the Samara River, forming a force of about 4,500 men.[25] It consisted of the same kind of people, *odnodvortsy*, and also descendants of *streltsy*, gunners, and various *raznochintsy*, drafted into an auxiliary force of military colonists. The total strength of the land militia was thus about 27,000 men. There may also have been a Siberian land militia, but its location is uncertain. The Trans-Kama land militia became largely obsolete after the founding of Orenburg, but it remained in existence until the 1760s.

The deployment of the strategic force was tested on three occasions after Peter's death. In 1733, when the Polish succession crisis began, three separate corps were created with regiments detached from the force, one concentrated around Riga, another around Smolensk, the third around Starodub.[26] However, the invasion of Poland was carried out by the Riga corps alone, consisting of eleven regiments of infantry and three of dragoons, which marched through Kovno, Grodno, Tikocin, and Nur, took Warsaw, and imposed the Russian candidate on the Polish throne. Two years later, two armies were sent against the Crimea, one along the Dniepr, the other from Azov. The war lasted four years, until 1739. The entire strategic force was committed to this war, which caused the Russians enormous casualties. Finally, Russia found itself at war with Sweden once again in 1741, when Sweden declared war.[27] The security of the imperial capital was at stake, and over 75,000 troops, or about 60 percent of the strategic force, were shifted to the Baltic sector between Riga and Vyborg. Only 26,000 actively took part in the operations; the remainder were committed to a defense-in-depth strategy of interception in Vyborg province, within the imperial territory, in the event the offensive into Finland should fail. When the war came to an end in 1743, a new deployment of the army was carried out, showing some differences from that of 1725 and the evolution of Russian strategic thinking.

The table of October 1743 showed eighty-one regiments, including three of cuirassiers, forty-six of infantry (of which nine were stationed in Stockholm to carry out the peace settlement), twenty-nine of dragoons, and three of hussars.[28] Seven of the nine regiments detailed to Stockholm came from Moscow Province, which at the time extended southward beyond Kaluga, Tula, and Riazan, and eastward to Nizhnii Novgorod. Another five were shifted to the Petersburg area, four to the Baltic provinces, and one to Alatyr in the east. Of the twenty-four regiments that had been deployed in Moscow Province, there remained only eight, including one of dragoons. As a result, there had taken place a substantial redeployment of the strategic force away from concentration in the Muscovite core toward the Petersburg region. There were now ten infantry regiments in that province, in addition to one of Guard cuirassiers (created in 1731) and three Guard infantry regiments (the third was created in 1730), not included in the table. To maintain security between Moscow and Petersburg along the waterway linking the Volga with Lake Ladoga, two dragoon regiments were shifted from Kazan and Arzamas and one of infantry was transferred from Moscow to Ladoga. In Smolensk Province, there remained only one regiment of dragoons. South and east of Moscow, few changes had taken place, with eight regiments still stationed in Elets, Tambov, and Shatsk and nine dragoon regiments in Nizhnii Novgorod Province, in Sviiazhsk, Penza, and Kazan. If we exclude from the eighty-one regiments the nine stationed in Stockholm but add the three Guard infantry regiments, we have a total of 75 regiments, of which only 48 or 64 percent remained in Russia proper. A new area of concentrated deployment had developed around the new capital, while the regiments remaining around Moscow were being transformed into a strategic reserve held uncommitted in the deep rear.

Another novelty was the deployment of relatively large forces in the Baltic provinces, in the Ukraine, and the southeast. In Vyborg province, where there had been only one infantry regiment, there were now three; in Estland, where there had also been only one, there were now five; and in Livland, two infantry regiments were shifted from Kostroma and Smolensk to join the existing three and a cuirassier regiment. In the Baltic provinces, there were now fourteen regiments instead of five. The Baltic sector, including the environs of Petersburg—with twenty-eight regiments—had become a second core. It owed its new importance to two factors. Swedish hostility, not expected in 1725 after Russia had signed with Sweden a treaty of alliance the previous year, exposed the vulnerability of Petersburg, which by 1743 was developing as a great capital, the rival of Stockholm in the eastern Baltic. The peace treaty of 1743 transferred to the Russians a number of fortified places along the edge of Lake Saimaa, destroying Sweden's ability to launch offensive operations overland.[29] The new deployment did not serve only a defensive purpose, however; it was also offensive: the Baltic sector was becoming a base of operations against Sweden in Finland. The provisioning department of the army was located in the northern capital to facilitate logistical support. Troops could rapidly move along the northern shore of the Gulf of Finland toward Åbo, supported by the two Baltic squadrons anchored in Kronstadt and Reval and the galley fleet. Moreover, the Baltic provinces, with their good land and pastures, were also a much better base of operations against Poland than the Smolensk region. All the invasions of the Polish Empire via Lithuania would begin in Riga, and a strong military presence in Livonia was an explicit threat to Königsberg and East Prussia. The old concentrated deployment was gradually giving way to a regional one as the high command became increasingly committed to a permanent deployment in the peripheral regions.

Regular troops were also deployed in the southern borderlands. There were two infantry regiments in Kiev, six of dragoons in Little Russia, another two in the Ukraine of Settlements, together with three hussar regiments. Finally, five infantry regiments were stationed in St. Anna (Rostov), Tsaritsyn, and Astrakhan. This forward deployment into territories where the Russians had until then maintained only garrisons was a direct consequence of the treaty of Belgrade (1739) and the changing situation in Transcaucasia. The treaty called for the razing of Azov and left the site a neutral zone between the Ottomans and the Russians, but it also allowed the Russians to build another fort (St. Anna) on the Don.[30] Also in 1739, near the end of the war, Swedes and Ottomans had signed a treaty of alliance, in the (vain) hope of creating a second front for the Russians in the south. In the new strategic perspective following the Russo-Swedish war, the Swedish and Ottoman-Crimean questions became linked once again, as they had been in 1711. Russia's posture in the southern theater was also offensive. The failure of the operations against the Crimea had taught the high command that the main enemy would have to be not the khanate but the Ottoman Empire, and every war with it would have to begin with a race to the Danube to block an early Ottoman strike into Wallachia and Moldavia. In such circumstances, the pressure was irresistible to abandon concentrated deployment and transform the peripheral territories into bases of operation. The imperial government was thus creating territorial commitments with serious consequences for the operation of the client system, as we shall see presently. In the southeast, the forward deployment of regular troops was an insurance against a possible destabilization of the situation in the mountains and in Transcaucasia, at a time when Nadir Shah was rumored to be planning an attack on Kizliar and was reincorporating eastern Georgia into the Persian Empire.[31] Concentrated deployment in the Muscovite core was being replaced by a bipolar deployment in the Baltic and Black Sea sectors, with an uncommitted reserve around the old capital to take advantage of Russia's interior lines between Moscow and Petersburg and between Moscow and Kiev. Yet the strategic force remained unfragmented, because its two poles or wings were not committed to perimeter defense — there were no fixed, "scientific" borders in the early 1740s, only lines drawn across the land for tactical or topographical convenience. The two wings remained part of a single force capable of reconcentration for a massive show of offensive power in either the western or southern theater, as the Seven Years' War of the 1750s and the Russo-Turkish War of 1768–74 would clearly show.

## The Economic Foundation

Grand strategy is more than strategy, more than the deployment of troops in peacetime and their concentration in the field in order to engage the enemy in wartime and compel him to seek peace. It must also deal with the economic foundations of military power and forge an industrial policy most conducive to providing the wherewithal of war. Economic policy, no less than the great strategic choices about the purpose of war — to enhance security or seek hegemony — also results from political decisions based on an ongoing consensus among the ruling elite.

The commitment made during the reign of Alexei Mikhailovich, Peter's father, to build new formations modeled after Western armies was inseparable from the determination to develop a native Russian metallurgy. There was poor quality iron ore in the Tula region that enabled the government to build mills, foundries, and gun works, and the Moscow-Kaluga-Tula triangle became the first center of a metal industry dedicated to weapon production. A second center developed on the western shore of Lake Onega, at Olonets, where iron of similarly poor quality was also found. There were shipyards in Kazan on the Volga and Briansk on the Desna, which flowed into the Dniepr just above Kiev. And there were salt works in Solikamsk on the western approaches to the Urals. Because that industry remained inadequate to equip the new formations, the Russians had to depend on a high level of imports from Europe via Dutch and English intermediaries. By the end of the seventeenth century, Russia's production of iron — approximately 250,000 *pudi* or 4,500 tons — was a mere tenth of the Swedish output.[32]

The first battle of Narva in November 1700, when the Russians lost all their artillery to the Swedes, was a great date in the history of Russian industry, because it compelled the tsar and a critical mass of the ruling elite to face up to the urgency of tapping Russia's potential, one much greater than that of Sweden, to build a powerful industry geared to the production of war material for the army and navy. The new industry made its appearance on the Gulf of Finland soon after the founding of Petersburg in 1703. It was built on those three preexisting geographical foundations—Tula, Olonets, and Solikamsk—but with an emphasis on the development of the resources of the Urals, where the iron and copper ore was of excellent quality. Private capital and free labor being scarce, especially there, the ruling elite had to gather up the fiscal resources of the government and mobilize serf labor to build shipyards in Petersburg and Voronezh, harbors in Rogervik (Baltiiskii Port) and Taganrog, smelters and foundries in the Urals. By the end of Peter's reign, a new tax (the poll tax or capitation) had been set aside for the needs of the army and navy; it was collected and accounted for separately, to pay the troops and purchase provisions. An essential component of Russia's new grand strategy was the determination to build a garrison state based on serf labor and to stretch the serf economy in order to extract a maximum of resources from it. Therefore, this grand strategy did not really include a commitment to the development of an industrial economy with equally strong civilian and military sectors but rested on the development of a traditional economy based on subsistence agriculture and a metal industry based on serf labor. It would take a century to stretch it to its penultimate limits. The consequences of that commitment would become painfully clear after 1825.

In the meantime, the production of iron rose rapidly to 14,818 tons in 1725, and 27,273 tons in 1740, nearly 75 percent coming from the Urals.[33] But it was necessary to translate this production into guns, muskets, bayonets, saber blades, anchors, and cannonballs, among many other requirements. The 1711 table of organization of the army required 122,600 muskets for the infantry and 49,800 for the dragoons; that of 1733, 7,200 carbines for the (projected) ten regiments of cuirassiers, 21,120 muskets for the twelve of dragoons, 50,274 for the thirty-eight regiments of infantry, with an additional 60,551 for the garrisons and a reserve of 17,848 muskets and 1,800 carbines. A musket was expected to last five years. In other words, the same amount of muskets had to be produced, at least in theory, every five years, giving an average of about 35,000 a year after 1711 and 26,400 after 1733.[34]

There were no specialized armament factories at the beginning of the eighteenth century; rather muskets and bayonets were manufactured with other metal goods in the new industrial plants. However, domestic production was inadequate to meet the needs of the army. During the first ten years of the century, between 10,000 and 20,000 muskets alone had to be imported every year, chiefly from England and Holland, Russia's main trade partners. After 1712, Tula began to specialize in the manufacture of muskets, bayonets, and pistols, and seems to have been able to cover current needs, but there were lean years when the works did not produce enough due to technical difficulties. As operations moved increasingly to the northwest after Poltava, the ironworks of Olonets joined in the production of muskets, but their major contribution was to produce guns and anchors for the new Baltic fleet, built at first at nearby Lodeinoe Pole, then in the Petersburg shipyards, one of the largest enterprises of the empire. The Lipetsk ironworks, upstream from

Voronezh, also produced muskets and small arms for the army, the garrisons, and the Azov fleet, abandoned after 1712. They were of much lesser importance and their production, together with that of the Olonets works, declined sharply after Peter's reign. The production of muskets at Olonets was moved in 1724 to Sestroretsk, twenty-eight kilometers north of Petersburg. Heavy guns and anchors for the Baltic fleet were increasingly being built in the Urals, especially at the Neniansk, Alapaevsk, Utkinsk, and Isetsk ironworks, from which they were shipped to Kazan via the Kama River, and from there to Petersburg. Iron was also shipped to the Tula works to be turned into musket barrels. Gunpowder was produced in Moscow and Kazan and at the Okhta plants in Petersburg, but the raw material (saltpeter) came mostly from the Left-Bank Ukraine and the Volga provinces below Kazan. Domestic production was more than enough to meet all the needs of the army and navy.[35]

However, Russia was highly deficient in the production of cloth for army uniforms, in part because Russia's climate was not favorable to the raising of sheep, in part because the pre-1700 army did not wear standardized uniforms and there were no specialized craftsmen to process the wool. The production of army cloth began in Moscow in the area of Voronezh, and on the Left-Bank Ukraine, from the wool of locally raised sheep. Most of this textile industry, unlike the heavy metallurgy of the Urals, was privately owned. By 1725, fourteen factories were producing 213,300 meters of cloth. Production seems to have stabilized at 426,600 meters in the 1730s. Nevertheless, domestic production remained inadequate. Cloth had to be imported from England and Holland, and also Prussia, Poland, Silesia, and as far away as Spain and Turkey. As late as 1732, despite the remarkable growth of the industry, Russia still imported 166,260 meters, which meant that it produced only about two-thirds of its needs. Moreover, Russian cloth acquired a reputation for poor quality, just good enough for common soldiers. Russia also had to develop a leather industry, and it managed to produce enough to cover its needs for boots, belts, and cartridge bags. The industry was concentrated on Moscow, Vladimir, and Voronezh.[36] A tremendous effort, stimulated by the exceptional energy of a powerful tsar, succeeded in creating a military-industrial complex, in which army generals who formed the core of the elite, together with their allies among the ruling families, dominated industrial production and made social policy. Their goal was to transform Russia into a hegemonic power in the Heartland by maintaining a military establishment capable, when need be, of projecting great power across enormous distances while keeping the population in a condition of servitude.

The successful operation of the military-industrial complex very much depended on the existence of a well-developed road and river network. Soil and climate—and the undeveloped state of commerce—combined to leave roads in a deplorable state, but there were postal and carriage roads—getting narrower as one moved across Europe from the Coastland into the Heartland and beyond Poland into Russia[37]—linking Moscow with Riga, Smolensk, Kiev, Astrakhan, and Kazan. In the open steppe, it mattered little if there were any roads at all. A tolerably efficient road linking Moscow with Petersburg was not built until the 1740s. Until then, Petersburg remained virtually cut off overland from the old capital.

But Russia, northern Russia at least, was blessed with a remarkable hydrographic network that mightily contributed to the creation of an industrial base around Moscow and made it one of the natural transit points between Ekaterinburg, the mining capital of the Urals, and Petersburg on the Baltic.[38] The low gradient of the Russian plain slowed the flow of water so that rivers were used as channels of communication in both directions, interrupted, however, by occasional rapids, sandbars, and changes in the water level that often rendered them inoperable in the summer. On the other hand, many of those rivers froze over for more than half of the year, making them into excellent roads for the rapid transportation of people and lightweight goods. The Volga, over 3,300 kilometers long, drained the entire interior of European Russia and the Urals toward the Caspian, but also drew the entire trade of Astrakhan with the east, the fur trade of Siberia, and the iron and copper shipments of the Urals toward Moscow. Its two major tributaries were the Oka and the Kama. The former meandered over 1,500 kilometers from the Central Upland to Nizhnii Novgorod, picking up the Moskva on the way and giving Moscow a water link with the Volga. The Kama, 1,800 kilometers long, wound its way along the approaches to the Urals and received the Chusovaia, which crossed the central Urals past Ekaterinburg on the eastern slope facing Siberia. The Kama also received the Belaia, descending from the southern Urals across Bashkir country, but also drawing Russian settlers into nomad territory. A third tributary was the Sura, 840 kilometers long, which drained the Penza upland northward. In the first three decades of the eighteenth century, this territory was still a fringe of settlement facing the Nogais, and most of the dragoon regiments were stationed there.

These rivers were the channels of trade that gave the Moscow region its economic compactness and made it an ideal logistical base for the strategic force. Long lines of river boats forming "caravans"—the word belonged to the terminology of the steppe, boats replacing camels—brought salt from the brine fields of Solikamsk on the upper Kama, iron and copper with guns, cannonballs, and anchors from the plants of the central and southern Urals, and coins from the Ekaterinburg mint. The Volga drew the grain trade of the wooded steppe, "grain caravans" sailing down the Sura and the Oka past Orel and Kaluga, and then upstream from Nizhnii Novgorod continuing westward toward Rybinsk and Tver. The Tula gun works were linked with the Urals by the Oka and the Upa, dammed to provide water power to the mills. The Oka's major tributary was the Moksha, which began just west of Penza and had its own tributary, the Tsna, which flowed past Tambov; they drew this vast region, still sparsely settled, northward toward the great semicircle around Moscow formed by the Oka and the Volga.

From Nizhnii Novgorod, grain shipments also went east to Kazan, the great market of eastern Russia. The city was located a short distance north of the confluence of the Kama and the Volga, and the caravans of boats loaded with iron, copper, and salt sailed past this capital of the former khanate, where people and architecture reminded contemporaries that it was the gate to the eastern theater. The Siberian trail passed through it, and the city was linked with the heart of Bashkiria via the Belaia. Its oak forests were already well known, and a naval station had existed there since the seventeenth century. Kazan was the entrepôt for grain shipments destined for the Urals and the fortified lines in Baskhiria and Siberia. The Commissary and the Provision Chancery maintained a branch there, from which

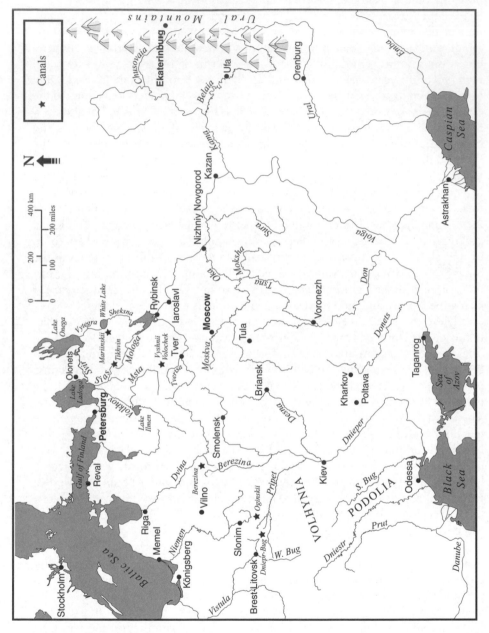

Rivers and Canals

the troops and garrisons beyond the Volga were paid and provisioned. Kazan was also the gate to central Russia for caravans of boats loaded with salt and fish coming up from Astrakhan, accompanied by Armenian, Persian, and Indian traders on their way to the great fair in Nizhnii Novgorod. Finally, Kazan was the military head-quarters for operations down the Volga toward the Caucasus and Central Asia, like those of Petr Apraksin in 1711 and Bukhgolts and Cherkasskii in 1714. The Volga below Kazan led to the Sea of Azov. A landing was built at Dubrovka in 1734 from which goods, especially timber in which the steppe was deficient, were trans-shipped on oxcarts to Kachalinsk on the Don, fifty-eight kilometers away, and for-warded to the river's delta; the Russians, who had gained Azov in 1696 and lost it in 1712, regained the delta in 1739 and built Fort St. Dmitrii, which replaced St. Anna before becoming Rostov on the Don.

The weakest link in this great hydrographic axis between the Baltic and the Urals was the watershed between the Volga basin and the sea. Without the ability to bridge it, the new capital would be unable to develop a profitable hinterland, and its growth would be stunted by its inability to receive not only the raw materials for its industries but also the basic necessities of life for its population. Some of these came from the Baltic provinces, with Riga their main port, thereby contributing to the formation of an economic region that could well support a substantial number of troops. But more was needed. The solution was found in cutting a canal linking the Tvertsa, a tributary of the Volga—Tver is on the confluence of the two rivers—with the Msta, which flows into Lake Il'men, from which issues the Volkhov, which flows into Lake Ladoga. This was the Vyshnii Volochek canal, begun in 1703, when the northern capital was founded; navigation was opened in 1709, the year of Poltava. It remained dangerous, however. The Tvertsa was shallow, reservoirs had to be built to regulate its flow in the summer, its current was unusually swift, and boats heading for Petersburg had to sail against it. The canal was 2.9 kilometers long and needed sluices for passage from one river to the other. The most dangerous place on the Msta was the Borovichi Rapids, the scene of many shipwrecks. Lake Il'men was known for its sudden storms. So was Lake Ladoga. Therefore, a second canal had to be cut along its shore, between the Neva and the mouth of the Volkhov. Begun in 1719, and completed in 1731, much of it was built by 15,000 Cossacks and 12,000 dragoons under the command of a Guard captain and later no less than Münnich himself, the future commander in chief of the strategic force. Both canals were considered part of the so-called Vyshnii Volochek system. Between the Volga and Petersburg, it stretched over nearly 1,000 kilometers, equivalent to the entire length of France from Belgium to the Spanish border.

Thus, by the late 1730s, the Ural industry was in full bloom, the Court, after some hesitation, had committed itself to remain in Petersburg, and the northern capital had become linked with Moscow and the Urals by an uninterrupted water-way. This extensive economic region had become the foundation of Russia's indus-trial power, the economic backbone of its strategic force. The result was an unri-valled concentration of power in the Heartland, within which the new empire could hope, in alliance with its client states and societies along its western and southern peripheries, "to win victory by awesomeness" over any potential rival.

But all was not well in this economic policy that propped up the grand strategic

vision. Except for a few cities along the Volga and the new Petersburg, which engaged in foreign commerce both over land and across the sea, Russian towns were
merely trading towns tied to their rural environment. Peter was seeking to create
"another Russia"[39] of commercial nodes that would become a source of wealth for
their societies and for the emerging ruling class of the empire. But that was fated to
fail down to our own day, because overland river-based trade was already a very poor
cousin to seaborne commerce in the eighteenth century. As a result, the commercial cities never developed the necessary autonomy from the administrative state
rooted in a subsistence agriculture and the servitude of its population. Perceptions
of Russia as a great commercial power (inspired by Peter's visit to England and Holland) soon shrank to become a more restrained autarkic outlook on commercial exchanges. Russia would remain the intermediary between the overland trade of the
East and that of the West, a trade bypassing the network of the trading towns, but
taxable as it had been by the Mongols, and still was by the Central Asian khanates,
the Zunghars, and the Persians. The consequence of that mutual isolation between
trade and commerce would be the continued backwardness of the trading towns of
the interior, the lack of incentives to build roads where no rivers were available, and
the inability to develop a native industry in order to encourage the export trade, as
well as lagging urbanization. At the same time, this autarkic outlook became a necessary prerequisite to the formulation of a grand strategy seeking hegemony in the
Heartland alone, because hegemony based on economic weakness required pre-
venting penetration by outside powers that might create an economic dependence
and undermine a hegemony based on raw military power and obedient clients.
Autarky, hegemony, and the primacy of military power were closely related.[40]

In the seventeenth century, trade relations with Europe had been centered in
Arkhangelsk, linked with Moscow via the Northern Dvina and, past Vologda, by the
road that crossed the Volga at Iaroslavl. One of the reasons, arguably the major one,
for making war on Sweden in 1700 was to seize the resources Sweden had gained
from its custom house in Nienshants, at the site of the future Okhta gun works in
Petersburg, which since the 1650s had been increasingly drawing the overland trade
of northern Russia, from Lake Onega to Lake Ilmen in the basin of the Baltic, separated from the White Sea and the Volga-Caspian basin by the Valdai Hills. It was
hoped that the founding of Petersburg would redirect the flow of silk, precious
stones, caviar, and furs shipped to Amsterdam and London or dropped off in
Wismar, a Swedish enclave in Mecklenburg, and from there transported into the
German lands.[41] The acquisition of Wismar or at least its inclusion into Mecklenburg would, in addition, strengthen the latter's position as a client state of the empire. Victory in war gave Russia Sweden's ports in Estland and Livland, especially
Riga, which had conducted a brisk trade with Sweden and was Petersburg's natural
rival. In order to concentrate Russia's foreign trade in the new capital, the 1724 tariff
raised duties in Arkhangelsk by 25 percent above those collected in Petersburg and
retained in the Baltic provinces the lower tariffs that went back to the days of
Queen Christina (1632–54), while forbidding goods imported there to be reexported
elsewhere in the empire.

The foreign trade pattern that emerged during the first forty years of the century would become characteristic. Russia would export raw materials such as timber

and iron and semimanufactured products like tar and potash, even sailcloth, which combined to form the so-called naval stores on which the British navy would depend until the Napoleonic wars. In exchange, it would import colonial goods such as coffee and sugar, rum and also wines, as well as the manufactured products, chiefly textiles, from more advanced economies. These exports and imports would be carried in British and Dutch bottoms, Russia remaining without a native merchant marine, its population unable to overcome a strong aversion to the sea, and its merchants, with their chronic shortage of capital and lack of insurance, unable to risk the capital necessary for overseas ventures. A merchant marine was the traditional nursery of sailors, and one of the main purposes of a navy was to protect the merchant marine. As a result, the Russian navy would be the creation of feverish efforts without follow-up, manned by recruits drawn from inland villages, and likely to rot away as soon as the effort was exhausted. When it did operate beyond the home waters, it would be on the sufferance of the Coastland powers, chiefly Britain.

The tariff of 1724 was the logical expression of this autarkic retrenchment.[42] It was certainly protectionist and was even called prohibitive; the Prussian ambassador reported to his king that it was "a knife at the throat of the entire trade."[43] It imposed duties ranging from 25 to 75 percent, but in fact retained only one prohibition from the long list of goods, which had been previously forbidden in the seventeenth century. The heaviest duty was imposed on goods that the government considered were produced in adequate quantities in Russia, thus precluding competition that would raise quality. They included textiles, iron goods, needles, and hides. There were also duties on the export of goods, although much lower. Peter's policy was not truly mercantilist, because it did not encourage the development of domestic industries working for export, as Peter must have known that their production would not be competitive anyway. For him, Eurasian trade and trade beyond the Heartland served a fiscal rather than an economic purpose. What emerges out of this economic and trade policy, if we see it as part of a grand strategy, is a vision of a Fortress Russia largely concentrated in the forest zone, revolving around the Petersburg-Moscow-Ekaterinburg axis of a continuous waterway linking major centers of industrial and military production to form a vast network of interdependent elements. It would be protected against competition from the outside world, but also needed to export the raw materials Russia possessed in abundance in order to obtain the badly needed precious metals in which it would remain deficient until the exploitation of the Altai mines. Fortress Russia was the geographical, economic, fiscal, and logistical foundation for a strategic force concentrated in the Moscow region and ready to strike in any direction.

The tariff of 1724 generated much opposition, among both Russian and foreign traders, and a reduction of duties began as early as 1726 until a new tariff was promulgated in 1731.[44] In 1724, it had been assumed that high duties would prohibit the importation of certain goods and thereby encourage domestic production, a non sequitur since the opposite was more likely to happen because the civilian sector remained in a natural state close to self-sufficiency. In addition, the practice of taxing goods ad valorem had led to widespread cheating as merchants undervalued their goods and the collection of revenue suffered accordingly. The new tariff imposed lower duties, but they were assessed according to weight and size. Domestic producers were subsidized by allowing them to export some of their goods and import certain raw materials duty-free, and nonnoble producers retained the right to buy serfs for their factories in order to reduce costs (but also the quality of their products). Arkhangelsk was no longer a rival of Petersburg, and the 25 percent surcharge was abandoned. Despite these changes, the tariff remained protectionist, in a largely vain attempt to prevent Russia from becoming dependent on outside economies. In the 1730s, the geographical foundation of the strategic force expanded northward and southward—expanded quantitatively but not qualitatively, in a continuing attempt to stretch the servile economy to its limits. But the lack of consumer demand and shortage of capital kept casting a persistent shadow on the Petrine vision.

# 3

# Client States and Societies

## Client States: The Western Theater

Russian grand strategy was an essentially political concept, recognizing no discontinuity between peace and wartime. The decisions that shaped it proceeded from a consensus worked out among the ruling elite not only on military and economic policy but also on diplomatic relations with neighboring territories. Most of those territories were found within the Heartland. Some were core areas, others were frontiers between them and Russia. Russia's diplomatic vision was largely confined to the Heartland. Muscovy and the empire—even if the term *empire* did not come into official use until Peter's reign—had grown since the mid–sixteenth century by co-opting local elites and becoming a multi-clan and multi-ethnic political configuration, in which the tsar was the grand patron of a complex system of clientage. Much of Russian diplomacy in the seventeenth and eighteenth centuries sought to expand this system of patronage, from which the Romanov house derived great prestige. Relations with peripheral states and societies were rooted in the traditional pattern of patron-client relationships at the Muscovite court. This brings us to the third principle underlying Russia's emerging grand strategy: if one was the determination to carry out deep strategic penetrations within the Heartland and only occasionally beyond its periphery, and the second the deployment of the strategic force originally in the old Muscovite core, the third was the creation of a glacis of client states and societies beyond which there sometimes stretched an "invisible frontier" of client relationships with other peoples along the Heartland's periphery or even beyond it.

The definition of a patron-client relationship does not come easily, because patrons do not always demand the same type of services from different clients and, as a result, clients play a variety of roles. Different roles in turn establish a hierarchy of clients. A buffer state is not a client, because it can afford a neutral stance between two rival great powers. A "friendly kingdom"[1] is another great power; it assumes a friendly stance and benefits from the imperial power's friendship, because common interests require that they cooperate on a number of issues, no matter how much tension and resentment may surface from time to time. A client state, however, is a smaller territorial and weaker political entity, with an army and foreign policy, but with a political leadership willing (or compelled) to enter into a relation of client-age with the ruling elite of the empire. Client societies are looser associations of families, clans, and tribes seeking protection against hostile neighbors or against one another. Generally, a client state/society is one where the native political leadership is willing to translate imperial desires into reality, often because to do so is in its own interest. The crucial fact is that there must be a great disparity of size and resources between the imperial power and its client.

Relationships were, as a rule, intensely personal. Leading families would send their sons to the imperial capital for the purpose of an "education," which meant above all absorbing some elements of the imperial culture, identifying with its achievements, establishing personal connections with members of the ruling elite, and marrying into it. Those who went back would receive valuable gifts and a "salary." The sons might also be used to undermine their fathers' position, should the latter become recalcitrant clients. In the world of the steppe, but not only there, it was customary to send "hostages" who also came from leading families, even from that of the local ruler. They were kept for a number of years before being replaced by others, serving as security for the good behavior of their relatives and their continued compliance with the wishes of the imperial power, while also learning to appreciate the imperial power's reputation for invincibility, its awesomeness. This had been the case in Rome; this was the case in China and Russia as well.

Clients played positive and negative roles. They provided auxiliary troops, interposed forces between rival imperial powers, absorbed threats, and created enough geographic depth to enable the patron power to keep its forces in reserve at a substantial distance from an eventual battlefield. Their contribution was not only additive but also complementary: their light cavalry and "militias" complemented the heavy infantry of the imperial power and had the great advantage of being adapted to the terrain and the tactics of the enemy. They supplied provisions and carts when the imperial army went to war across their territory at great distances from its bases of operation. They also contributed local administrators devoted to the cause of the imperial power who knew the languages and customs of their own peoples. In both military and civilian affairs, clients enabled their patrons to practice an economy of force and resources while facilitating the spread of their influence. Although the relationship between patron and clients was not one between equals, it often worked both ways. Clients had their own interests. The same families that sent their sons for an "education" or as "hostages" sought to use the imperial power for their own ends, whether to consolidate their rule or restore their land to its past glory. Their support contributed to the "honor" of the patron, but also reinforced their own; the more awesome the imperial power was, the greater their prestige among their own people. As a result, their own ambivalence, the product of distrust, envy, and interest, often invited the imperial power's advance, weakening their powers of resistance until they became fully integrated into the formal territorial and administrative structure of the empire. Only then did they have to make a full commitment to join its ruling elite, even at the cost of losing their power base in their old country, but gaining full access to prestigious positions in the army and civilian establishments.

Clients also played a negative, destabilizing role. Client states and societies, by the very fact that they were frontier communities caught between the ambitions of rival imperial powers, were often wracked by internal dissensions, either between weak rulers and powerful clans, or between families drawn, some to one imperial power, others to its rival. They became fifth columns, motivated by religion, cupidity, or narrow personal interests. Their actions had the divisive effect of creating a power vacuum, which also invited an imperial power's advance, until they too became incorporated into its political system and harshly brought to heel when their subversive activities ceased to be acceptable. The political environment of client states and societies was thus highly unstable and required constant management by the imperial power. Clients had to be made to feel the consequences of disobedience if they deviated from the course expected of them, but the system had to be kept in equilibrium without recourse to direct imperial intervention. One of its cardinal rules was that clients could not aggrandize themselves without the explicit sanction of the imperial power, but for this to happen, the clients' perception of the imperial power's awesomeness had to remain unchallenged. The successful management of the system thus depended on a combination of implicit threat with a steady mediation between competing clients, which created and maintained for the imperial power a position of indispensable arbiter within the system. Its occasional breakdown brought about the rapid intervention of the strategic force, followed by the temporary or final annexation of the frontier territories and the termination of the client relationship.

It is quite clear that in the wake of its victory over Sweden Russia was determined to transform both Sweden and Poland into client states. The task was easier in Poland. Russia's natural enemy had been France since the 1650s, because France and Sweden were the guarantors of the new international order created by the Peace of Westphalia (1648), and France had formed alliances with Sweden, Poland, and the Ottomans, openly directed against the Austrian Habsburgs but implicitly also against Russia, since these three empires were Russia's rivals for hegemony in the western and southern theaters. During the Northern War, Poland suffered terrible destruction by Swedish and Russian troops and the country was in great turmoil. The Russians had grown used to treating it as occupied territory; the tsar saw himself as the protector of the Polish Empire, with the right to veto any change in its constitution and any foreign policy move considered hostile to Russian interests. A prostrate Poland fit only to contribute some cavalry units and to supply a Russian army on the move ceased to be the age-old threat to the Russian core area, instead providing geographical depth against a potential enemy, as well as a safe invasion route toward the Vistula and the Oder, beyond which Russia could reasonably expect to build its hegemony in the Heartland. The major Russian objective was thus to keep the Polish Empire both weak and in fear of Russia's awesomeness.

The Polish elective monarchy was a major cause of Poland's weakness. The election of a Saxon prince in 1697 had been a victory for Russia because he was considered preferable to the French candidate. Augustus II, ambitious and devious, sought to make the crown hereditary in his house and found himself in constant conflict with the Polish nobility that insisted on its rights and privileges as the ruling class of the empire. A settlement was imposed by the Russians in 1717, which reduced the Polish army to 24,000 men, a size far too small to enable Poland to defend itself. The Russian envoy, Grigorii Dolgorukov, was the first of a long line of proconsuls who would lay down the law in Warsaw until the final partition of the Polish Empire in 1795. When Augustus II died in 1733 and Poland elected the French candidate, the same Stanislas Leszczynski with whom the Swedes had briefly replaced Augustus in 1704 and who, by then, had become the father-in-law of the king of France, the Russians—without, however, accepting the principle that the monarchy had become hereditary—intervened militarily to impose the son of the dead king, who would rule as Augustus III until 1763. Petersburg could not accept any foreign interference in the management of its client system.

A second weakness was the rivalries among powerful magnate families, based mainly in the eastern marches of the empire, which naturally opposed a strong monarchy in Warsaw but were also unable to reach a consensus on a viable form of government. Political warfare was dominated by the Czartoryskis and the Potockis, the former seeking to reform the Polish government in alliance with the Russians, the latter opposed to reforms and leaning toward France. The Czartoryskis and some of their allies were related to families in the imperial ruling elite who descended from the fourteenth-century grand prince of Lithuania and belonged to the Naryshkin-Trubetskoi network in Russia, while the Potockis were distantly related to the Saltykovs, who led the other network.[2] The politics of the Polish client state mirrored to some extent the rivalry between the two Russian networks.

A third weakness contributing to making Poland into an obedient tool of the Russians was the persecution of the Protestants and the Orthodox that began after 1717. Since the Peace of Andrusovo (1667) the tsar had been the protector of Orthodoxy in the Polish Empire and thereby gained a means to influence Polish internal affairs. Most of the Orthodox lived in the eastern marches, where the religious question merged with the obstructionist politics of the great magnates.

There were similarities and differences in Russia's treatment of Sweden. The similarities were obvious to contemporaries. From London in 1720, it appeared that Russia was seeking hegemony in the Baltic and determined to lay down the law in both Poland and Sweden. In 1721, a French envoy concluded the tsar would use factionalism to bring Sweden under his dominion; in 1722, the Russian envoy called Sweden "a real Poland"; and in 1735, a Swedish commission compared the Russian empress to Providence, which overthrows kings and places new ones on the throne, as she had just done in Poland and might want to do in Sweden.[3] The Swedish economy too had been severely damaged by the war, especially by the loss of the Baltic provinces. The Treaty of Nystadt pledged Russia to continue the grain trade between Riga and Stockholm—vital to the maintenance of domestic peace in Sweden—unless Petersburg decided to suspend it for "important" reasons. In addition, Russia promised not to interfere in Swedish domestic affairs but also to oppose any attempt to subvert the constitution of 1720, which cut down the powers of the monarchy and strengthened parliament. This assembly would become the scene of bitter partisan warfare between two parties: the Hats, consisting of nobles, officers, civil servants, and great merchants, wanted a war of revenge to regain the Baltic provinces in alliance with France and Britain, while the Caps, consisting of clergy, petits bourgeois, and peasants, wanted peace and were pro-Russian. The Russians spent enormous sums to keep their supporters in line and to win over members of the Hats in the central government and during local elections, but were less successful than in Poland because the prestige of the monarchy had not been so irretrievably damaged and because their power to intimidate the Swedes by awesomeness was much mitigated by their inability to apply force directly in Sweden itself. The deployment of Russian troops in the Baltic provinces prior to the invasion of Poland enhanced Russia's awesomeness, but its performance in the war against the Crimea in 1735–38 damaged its prestige and paved the way for the Swedish-Ottoman alliance of 1739 and the Swedish offensive against Russia two years later. The revolt of the client state, abetted by France, was put down in 1742, a few months after Russia's awesome threat to destroy Finland by fire and sword. The settlement of 1743 sought to bring the Swedish crown under Russian control. Charles XII, who had died in 1718, was succeeded by his younger sister, who was elected by the estates before the kingship passed to her husband, Frederick I, a German prince. But her elder sister, who had greater rights to the throne, had a son, Charles Frederick, duke of Holstein, who married the tsar's daughter in 1724 and kept claiming his rights to the Swedish throne. The Russians cultivated his supporters in Sweden, but the duke died in 1739. Nevertheless, the Russians withdrew from Finland in 1743 in return for the election of their candidate, a first cousin of the duke, heir to the Swedish crown.[4] Nine regiments were sent to Stockholm to enforce the settlement, which, in addition, stripped Sweden of its fortresses along the new border with the Russian Empire and made it defenseless in Finland.

The weakness of the monarchy and the venality of Swedish politics undermined Sweden's hold on its eastern march, Finland. There, as had already happened in the eastern marches of the Polish Empire, nobles were developing a separate identity and were beginning to consider whether their interests would not be better safeguarded by seeking an agreement with the Russians and abandoning the Stockholm government, which seemed incapable of protecting them; even the peasantry, which deeply distrusted the Russians, felt that way during the war. The manifesto of 1742 raised for the first time the option of a partition of Sweden, a new Finland providing geographical depth against another Swedish revolt and guaranteeing the security of Petersburg.[5]

Russia's client system in the western theater needed to be buttressed by the collaboration of another two powers, Austria and Prussia. Austria was the "friendly kingdom." The Austrian Habsburgs and the French Bourbons were bitter enemies, and Austria was Russia's natural ally. It was also the most powerful state in the Holy Roman Empire; it stood, in theory at least, above all the other monarchs of Europe. But the empire was a crazy quilt of large and small territories divided along religious lines, the northern German states being Protestant, the rest Catholic. For the Russians, the Holy Roman Empire provided fertile ground for creating client states: they would become footholds in a vast region where Austrian influence was predominant and where Austria was certain to remain the anchor in the international relations of the German states. The friendly kingdom found itself becoming willy-nilly an accomplice to Russia's penetration into the Germanic regions of the European Coastland. The 1735 expedition to the Rhineland was only the most dramatic illustration of Austria's dependence on a natural ally against France's century-old bid for hegemony in the region; the occasional strains between Austria and other members of the empire established Russia as the natural arbiter of Germanic destinies.

Russia's interests during Peter's reign were focused on the northern German states as a major sector of operations during the Northern War, Sweden being still in possession of western Pomerania with Stettin and the bishoprics of Bremen and Verden, which were also part of the Holy Roman Empire. The Russians already had a client state in Saxony, where Augustus II, who resided mostly in Dresden, was also king of Poland. In 1711, Peter's heir, Alexei, was married to a princess of Wolfen-büttel, but the marriage gave Russia few political dividends. Five years later, in 1716, the tsar arranged the marriage of his niece Ekaterina to the duke of Mecklenburg. The stationing of Russian troops in the duchy threatened Swedish Pomerania and offered the possibility of establishing a naval base and supply depots on the coast, from which they would seek to dominate the western Baltic. However, Vienna's support of the Mecklenburg nobility against the duke damaged relations with the Russians, who eventually had to withdraw. In 1724, however, one of the tsar's daughters was married to the duke of Holstein, a key location facing both the Baltic and the North Sea. This search for client states in northern Germany was part of a strategic design to establish Russia as the commercial intermediary between Asia and Europe and the dominant naval power. From such a position of strength, Russia would be able to enforce a client status on Sweden and overpower the commercial cities of Danzig, Lübeck, and Hamburg. Russia's success in northern Germany depended on Austrian support. The treaty of 1724 promised Russian assistance in the event of war and the opening to Russian ships of ports on the North Sea coast and those of Spain in the Atlantic and Mediterranean. Austria was doing its best to translate Russia's imperial but unrealistic desires into reality.[6]

Russia and Austria also had common interests against the Ottoman Empire. The last great Ottoman offensive in the Balkans had been stopped in 1683 at the gates of Vienna by the Austrians and the Poles. Peter's reign witnessed the Austrian counteroffensive into Hungary and Serbia, while the Russians took Azov and made their first attempts toward the Danube. Orthodoxy and Catholicism cooperated for once in the crusade against the infidel, who happened to have the strong support of France. As in Germany, the Austro-Russian alliance was directed against their common natural enemy. Their alliance, which enabled the Russians to maintain their client system in equilibrium without direct intervention, was sealed by the emergence of Prussia following the accession of Frederick II in 1740.

Brandenburg was the largest state of the Holy Roman Empire, but it was a poor country at the beginning of the eighteenth century. A wooded land of sandy soils and marshy valleys east of the Elbe, the Heartland's periphery, it had been ravaged by the Thirty Years' War, and an epidemic of plague added to the devastation half a century later. Its rulers were ambitious, however, and one of them won in 1701 the Holy Roman emperor's permission to style himself king—although not in Brandenburg but outside the empire in Prussia, acquired in 1618.[7] The Prussian kings' determination to round out the possessions of Brandenburg-Prussia—to be called henceforth simply Prussia—on the one hand, and the great disparity between its relative poverty and the rising might of Russia on the other, clearly marked the new kingdom as a potential client. Frederick I, aware of his country's vulnerability to Swedish attacks, hesitated to commit himself in the Russo-Swedish conflict until 1709, when the Poltava victory left no doubt that Russia was winning the war. But Prussia's gains required Russia's assent because Prussia was not yet a power factor in the region: when the king died in 1713, his son and successor Frederick William I (1713–40) had to sell his collection of paintings to find some additional revenue.[8] To bind Prussia as a client state, the Russians, who took Stettin in 1713, offered it to the king, and the peace treaty of 1720 confirmed the transfer. Stettin was a major acquisition, because it controlled the trade of the Oder Valley and the exports of Silesia, Austria's richest province; in fact, it was Austria's only outlet on the Baltic coast. The potential conflict with the friendly kingdom paved the way for Russia's becoming the arbiter between the two Germanic powers. The price was that Berlin would have to follow Russian policy unconditionally;[9] Russian activities in Mecklenburg and Holstein left it no choice anyway, placing Prussia in a vise as they did. A loan of tall grenadiers of whom the king was very fond was the "salary" that confirmed the king's new status as a client of the empire. But he too, like most clients, understood there were two sides to the relationship. The client who contributed to the power and glory of his patron could also use him in the pursuit of his own interests. Frederick William said in 1719 that he wanted the tsar to be powerful "because as result, I will be given consideration when I hold on to him like a leech."[10] This would be Berlin's policy until 1740.

Prussia also sought to use its relationship with Russia to establish its influence in Kurland, which had been part of the dominion of the Teutonic Knights. But in 1710, Peter's niece Anna, the future empress Anna Ivanovna, was married to the duke of Kurland, who died soon afterward. The marriage was intended to transform Kurland into another client state. When Berlin sought to arrange another marriage with a Prussian prince, the Russians warned the Kurland nobles they would be deported to Siberia if they chose a candidate not acceptable to them. The Russian candidate was Anna's lover, Biron.[11] On the other hand, to keep Prussia as a client state, the Russians were led, unaware of the fateful road they were embarking upon, to accept its help in keeping the Polish client subservient to Russian interests: a major component of Berlin's foreign policy had been for some time to acquire Polish territory in order to link Brandenburg with the old duchy of Prussia and gain what they had won with Stettin on the Oder vis-à-vis Austria: the control of Danzig and the Polish grain trade on the Vistula. Thus, by the late 1730s, Petersburg, the capital of an emerging Eurasian empire that was not part of the European state system, had managed to create in that system a network of clients on the approaches to the Heartland's periphery. It was anchored in Austria as the friendly kingdom, which shared a common interest in keeping it in equilibrium. No client in this network could afford to upset the system without inviting Russia's awesome retaliation. Frederick II would learn that hard lesson in the 1750s.

## Client Societies: The Western and Southern Theaters

The most prominent of the client societies in the western theater during the first decades of the eighteenth century was that of the Baltic Germans. It is true that after 1710, and certainly by 1721, they had been brought within the imperial periphery, but the considerable autonomy they received at the peace settlement, much greater than the autonomy they had enjoyed under Swedish rule, gave them a unique status. They too translated imperial ambitions into reality, contributing, if not foot soldiers, at least large numbers of officers to the imperial army and administering the Baltic provinces on behalf of the imperial government. They formed an intermediate zone between Russia proper and the "invisible frontier" beyond the imperial periphery. There, large numbers of Germans from the Holy Roman Empire discovered the pull of Russia's awesomeness and moved to Petersburg to help lay the foundations of a new imperial Russian civilization resting on military power and a client system of peripheral states and societies.

While still under Swedish rule, the Baltic Germans, many of them descendants of the Teutonic Knights, had secured a body of "rights and privileges," one of them the right to enserf the local population at the beginning of the seventeenth century, when Sweden included Livonia into its empire. Sweden's relations with its Baltic German frontier were not always friendly. Long before the Russians at the end of the nineteenth century, the Swedish monarchy had pursued a policy of integration and administrative unification in the Church, the Courts, and the schools, looking askance at serfdom, which was unknown in Sweden and Finland. Its need for money brought about the so-called reversion (*Reduktion*), according to which landed properties held by the nobility without sufficient evidence of lawful title reverted to the crown, causing much resentment.[12] At the same time, the nobility gained the right to elect its own leader (*Landmarshal*) and councillors (*Landräte*). In its determination to create a caste within a client society, the old nobility eventually clashed with the royal power, and in 1694, the posts of councillor and *Landmarshal* were abolished. Stockholm's policies created a secessionist movement in which Johann von Patkul was a leading figure, and it was he who brokered the Russo-Danish-Polish alliance of 1699 against Sweden; there would be no active opposition against the Russians in the 1700s.[13]

Peter I, once the war had devastated the provinces, chose to pursue a policy of conciliation that amounted to a rejection of Swedish policies. The nobility recognized its transfer to the Russian orbit, accepted the tsar's "high protection" (*pokrovitel'stvo*), and pledged loyalty to him as their "supreme leader" (*verkhovnyi pravitel'*). In return, the imperial government pledged to restore "the rights, privileges, and customs" granted since the days of the Teutonic Knights, including those in the charter of Sigismund II of 1561, when Livonia was part of the Polish Empire. No one seems to have known the nature of its provisions, however: When summoned by Charles XI of Sweden to submit the charter, the Livonians had claimed they could not find the original, and they were already known for the "manifold wondrous legal conceits, of which this land is replete in every scattered corner."[14] The twelve councillors and the *Landmarshal* were restored to their posts; the first assembly (*Landtag*) met as early as December 1710. Some of the most prominent families threw in their lot with the Russians. Patkul, who was executed by the Swedes in 1706, had not been known for his Russian sympathies, but the Löwenwoldes took the lead in brokering the transformation of Baltic German society into a client society of the Russian Empire. Among others were the von Tiesenhausens, von Platers, von Buddenbrocks, and especially the von Mengdens, who had worked hard since the mid-seventeenth century to establish the nobility as the true ruling class of Livonia. No wonder that at the end of Peter's reign "the nobility felt that its struggle with Sweden had not been in vain."[15]

The integration of the Baltic Germans into the imperial elite accelerated after Peter's death and especially during the reign of Anna Ivanovna (1730–40), when Biron—a Kurland nobleman whose real name was Ernst von Bühren—became one of the leading dispensers of patronage. But he had to share power with Heinrich Ostermann from Westphalia, the de facto foreign minister, and Burchard von Münnich, the "war minister." Some of the Baltic Germans who settled in Petersburg or, like Rudolph von Bismarck in the Ukraine, were given major military commands lost their ties to their homeland and felt little affinity with its interests; others used their wide-ranging connections to strengthen their rule over Livonia. Of no small interest for the operation of the client system was the fact that two of the four envoys to Warsaw in the 1730s were Baltic Germans: Karl von Löwenwölde, the son of Gerhard, sentenced to death with Patkul in 1695, who played a key role in 1710, and Herman von Keyserlingk. These Germans, now members of a client society of the Russian Empire, became new brokers in an age-old struggle between Poland and the Germanic world whom the Russians were determined to use in their own interests—or so they thought. Clients were set off against clients in accordance with the well-tested policy of divide and rule. Moreover, these Germans became the backbone of the imperial foreign service in Russia's relations with its "invisible frontier" in the Holy Roman Empire and beyond.

In Livonia itself, they continued to administer the two provinces on behalf of Petersburg, which was only slowly emerging as the new imperial capital and knew little about local conditions. The governors were occasionally Russian but for the most part belonged to local families: the Lacys (of Irish origin) in Livland, the Löwens and Douglases in Estland. Baltic nobles entered the imperial service with the same rights as Russians, acquiring estates and serfs. But important developments were taking place within the nobility. At the accession of every new ruler, it was expected to petition for the confirmation of its rights and privileges, and it used the opportunity to ask for more of them. Thus, the Livland nobility in 1725 and the Estland nobility in 1728 gained the right to bequeath real property, in the absence of male heirs, in the female line to the fifth generation, while Swedish law had allowed transfers only in the male line.[16] Article 11 of the Nystadt Treaty confirmed the cancellation by Sweden of the reversion in 1700 but, as a result, deprived the peasantry of the small degree of protection afforded by the crown, especially after Baron Otto von Rosen declared in 1739 that the nobility's title to its dominion over the peasantry went back to the conquest of the land by the Teutonic Knights. The charter of 1742, however, struck a new note, calling the Baltic Germans "vassals of the empress" (*vsepoddaneishie vassaly*)[17] and reminding them, as if to echo Rosen's views, that their land had been conquered by force of arms, so that Petersburg exercised over them the same dominion as the one they claimed over the local population.

But the major event of the 1730s was the decision to draw up the so-called matriculation rolls (*Matrikuly*), begun under Swedish rule but never completed. It was an attempt to preserve the Germanic character of the nobility by excluding non-Germans as well as Germans of nonnoble origin who had risen up in the army and, in accordance with the Table of Ranks, had become noble with their promotion to the first officer rank: this entitled them to buy landed property and serfs. All those claiming to be nobles were invited in 1733 and again in 1737 to submit proof to a commission that included two Patkuls.[18]

In the southern theater, the Cossacks were the most prominent client society. The Little Russian Cossacks on the left bank of the Dniepr, mostly in the wooded steppe between the swamps and forests of southern Bielorussia and the edge of the steppe, had recognized the Muscovite tsar as their patron in 1654. The election of a new hetman required the tsar's confirmation: he had to take an oath of perpetual and faithful submission (*vechnoe i vernoe poddanstvo*) to the ruler.[19] In exchange for military protection and the tsar's recognition of the Cossacks' rights and privileges—the right to elect their officers among others—the hetman had to accept his full inclusion into the orbit of Russian influence and pledge not to engage in correspondence with other powers. That was why Hetman Mazepa's siding with Charles XII in 1708 was considered in Moscow to be treason—for betraying a patron and offering his services to another. The tsar's reaction was harsh. The hetmanate was incorporated into Kiev Province and placed under its governor, Prince Dmitrii Golitsyn. Petersburg imposed a new hetman, Ivan Skoropadskii, to manage it with a Russian minister watching over him. Following Skoropadskii's death in 1722, the management of the territory was vested in a Little Russian College stationed in Kiev consisting of Russian and Cossack officers. A third hetman, Danil Apostol, whose daughter married Skoropadskii's son, was in office between 1727 and 1734, but he had no successor until 1750. During that time, the former hetmanate, now called Little Russia, was administered by a "governor" (*pravitel'*), a Russian general from among the great families of the empire. Until Peter's reign, the Cossacks had provided light cavalry troops in the southern theater, where they were better suited than the heavier Russian cavalry to fight the Tatar nomads, as well as excellent auxiliaries to carry out reconnaissance missions and forage in the steppe. They were now used unceremoniously along with units of the regular army in Peter's campaigns against the Swedes, the Ottomans of course, and the Persians. In 1734, there were 13,000 of them in Poland, where they served without pay. Worse still, they were deported in large numbers to build canals linking the Volga with the Gulf of Finland, in the forest zone, which was totally alien to them.

The client society was changing in other ways. The size of the Cossack force was not permanent, as peasants and townsmen joined it while some Cossacks left to engage in other occupations. Limits began to be placed on such transfers, seeking to keep non-Cossacks out while facilitating the transformation of Cossacks into peasants.[20] A new class of regimental colonels and officers, hetmanate officials, and landowners was emerging, forming the so-called *starshina*, eager to acquire landed property and serfs, and seeing themselves as the descendants of the Polish landowners against whom their ancestors had rebelled. Serfdom and Orthodoxy, together with steady pressure by the Russian patron, were shaping a new ruling class in the hetmanate more favorable to the imperial cause and ready to become a reliable client on what was still the empire's periphery along the Dniepr.

The transformation went farther in the Ukraine of Settlements, in the steppe zone stretching to the Oskol. In 1700, the strength of the five regiments of Slobodian Cossacks was fixed at 3,500, and many of them were used in the Persian campaign. Originally placed under the Belgorod *voevoda*, they passed in 1709 under the jurisdiction of the commander of the Ukrainian ("Border") Division; Cossacks, along with peasants, were drafted to build the Ukrainian Line in the 1730s. By then, these Cossacks, like their brethren in Little Russia, had become divided between the better-off Cossacks, who carried out their service obligations, and their "helpers" (*podpomoshchniki*), who supported them with their labor. In the Ukraine of Settlements, the trend toward the degradation of the latter to the status of serfs was already well advanced. There were also attempts to equate Cossack ranks with those in the regular army and to introduce Russian laws. One regiment was formed in Chuguev in the 1730s, consisting of Cossacks and baptized Kalmyks. It became part of the regular army. In 1734, the territory was placed under the authority of Lt. Gen. Alexei Shakhovskoi, the "governor" of Little Russia.[21]

The "disciplining" of the Zaporozhian Cossacks had not gone so far yet, because their territory was largely beyond the reach of the army in peacetime and remained a sensitive zone on the edge of the Crimean Khanate. Following Ivan Mazepa's "treason," their headquarters (*Sech*) on Khortitsa Island was destroyed and they fled to Aleshki, opposite present-day Kherson, where the khan allowed them to build a new one. Now a client society of the khanate, they launched raids against Polish landlords and their own countrymen. But the pull of Orthodoxy remained strong, and serving the infidel khan was a betrayal of all they had stood for since the beginning of their history. When the khan and the sultan ordered them to move into Poland to support Stanislas Leszczynski in 1733, they balked and went north instead, to reach an agreement with the Russians on the Podpilnaia (Kamenka) River, where they built their third headquarters and became once again a client society of the empire.[22] Their territory stretched on both sides of the Dniepr from the Southern Bug to the Kalmius and was bounded in the south by the Dniepr and the Konka River. It was divided into five territorial "regiments" called *palanki*, with a military administration elected every year by the Cossack assembly representing about 15,000 men. The Russians interfered little but kept a close watch on the Cossacks by means of fortified outposts built after 1735 along the Dniepr from the Ukrainian Line to the Great Meadow of the Dniepr on the khanate's border. They had become once again a frontline defense against Tatar raids and an auxiliary troop for the strategic force in the event of another war with the Crimeans and the Ottomans.

East of the Oskol began the territory of the Don Cossacks, who had grown to become the largest Cossack "host"—over 15,000 men—with the influx of fugitive peasants and Old Believers whom they were at first allowed to keep. This was a significant privilege, because landlords elsewhere were required to return fugitives to their lawful owners. But Peter's wars also destabilized this client society, which had done so much in the seventeenth century to advance imperial interests in the Black Sea. The Don Cossacks were forced to take part in the Azov campaign and in other wars. They were required to return the fugitives because the imperial government was always short of soldiers. When they refused, an armed expedition was sent to recover some 3,000 of them, provoking the Bulavin Rebellion (1707–8). The repression shook the Don Cossack society to its foundations, some Cossacks fleeing to the Taman Peninsula to become, like the Zaporozhians at Aleshki, clients of the Crimean khan who raided Russian settlements, others to the Danube delta to become clients of the Ottoman sultan. This induced the imperial government to build Fort St. Anna to watch over the Cossacks and to abolish the election of the "ataman," who was henceforth appointed by Petersburg. Thus, wars and deep penetrations by the strategic force into the frontier of client societies brought about similar results everywhere: an increased imperial presence in the form of fortresses and garrisons, and a restructuring of Cossack societies based on growing social differentiation. A reliable upper stratum of richer Cossacks was becoming an elite of landowners responsive to the dictates of the imperial government. A process of integrating the client societies into the military structure of the empire had begun.

The Don territory also became the mother house of other Cossack settlements in the region. In 1737, detachments settled in the environs of St. Anna were called Azov Cossacks. Five years earlier, in 1732, the Senate had called on volunteers from the Don to settle the Tsaritsyn Line linking the elbows of the Don and the Volga, blocking the Kalmyks from crossing the Volga and separating the North Caucasus Nogais from their brethren to the north. Half of the total colony of over 1,000 families came from the Don, the others from Little Russia. They were settled between Dubovka and the Balykleia River and eventually occupied the entire watershed between the Ilovlia and the Volga. To the south across the North Caucasus steppe, the Terek Cossacks were drafted to take part in the Persian War, but, following the abandonment of Baku and Derbent in 1735, they were withdrawn behind the Terek. The Greben Cossacks, very much weakened by their participation in the Khiva expedition, were settled farther west along the river. Both hosts were subordinated to the commandant of Kizliar, a fortress built on the Terek in 1735; he reported to the Astrakhan governor. They were replenished from time to time with families from the Don. These smaller hosts were creations of the imperial government and represented a cross between a client society and an auxiliary cavalry formation with a territorial base, but they nevertheless remained outside the force structure of the imperial army. They developed their own identity and a feeling of separateness, which gave them a certain autonomy from the dictates of the imperial government and a certain freedom of action vis-à-vis the peoples in the mountains whose raids into the plain it was their mission to check.

There were other client societies well beyond the imperial periphery, in the "invisible frontier": Georgians, Armenians, and Kabardians in the Caucasus, Moldavians, Wallachians, and Greeks in the Balkan sector. Georgians had lived in Moscow since the sixteenth century. An Imeretian prince, Tsarevich Alexander Imeretinskii (1673–1711), was Peter's first chief of the artillery; he was taken prisoner at Narva and died in Swedish captivity. Following the treaty of 1724 with the Ottomans who occupied eastern Georgia, Tsar Wakhtang VI (1675–1737), with his sons and a suite of 1,200, moved to Russia and set up a colony in Moscow, while other communities, well supplied with landed properties, sprang up in Astrakhan, Kizliar, and the Ukraine. One of Wakhtang's sons, Bakar, a full general in the imperial army, married a princess Dolgorukova, and their daughter married a prince

Golitsyn. Once he had joined the imperial elite and become in fact a hostage, Wakhtang was expected to translate imperial ambitions into reality. In 1726, he was sent to Persia to establish contacts with the shah and organize a Russo-Persian campaign against the Ottomans, but failed. He went again in 1734 and in Derbent met with Armenian delegates and their patriarch, who in 1722 had sent a mission to Peter in Astrakhan asking for protection against the infidel. Armenians had long been well disposed toward the Russians.[23] Religion played a powerful role— Georgians and Armenians were Christian, caught between the Sunni Ottomans and the Shiite Persians. But commercial interests, especially for the Armenians who controlled the Persian silk trade, and the instinct for survival kept religious strivings in check. After Peter's death, Russia's awesomeness was no longer so impressive: the Crimean War exposed the limits of imperial power, and Nadir Shah led the reconquest of eastern Georgia and Armenia. Despite the massacres and religious profanations that usually accompanied warfare in Transcaucasia, members of the Georgian elite answered Nadir Shah's call to lead a contingent of Georgian troops in his expeditions to Mogul India in 1737 and 1740. The Georgian elite served the shahs as faithfully as it would have served the Russians if they had established themselves in Tiflis. The loyalty of client societies was always fickle; its strength depended on the power of the patron. In the 1730s, the Ottomans and Persians were more awesome than the Russians.

Relations with Kabarda also had a long history. Maria Cherkasskaia (†1569) was the second wife of Ivan the Terrible. One of her converted cousins married a princess Prozorovskaia and their grandson married Princess Maria Golitsyna, granddaughter of Boris Golitsyn, Peter I's tutor, who administered for thirty years the former khanates of Kazan and Astrakhan. Alexander Bekovich (son of a *bek* or prince), who led the expedition against Khiva, was kidnapped from his parents in Little Kabarda and, as a hostage, found a ready-made political education in this circle. His biographer, who showed little interest in genealogy, wrote that a "rich Golitsyna" took pity on him and raised him in the family of Boris Golitsyn: he would in fact marry Marfa Golitsyna, Maria's sister, and become known as Cherkasskii. Thoroughly imbued with imperial civilization, he was sent in 1711 to Kabarda to bring the territory over to the Russian side in opposition to the Kuban Horde. He would later claim he had succeeded, although the claim was premature.[24] Nevertheless, the Treaty of Belgrade (1739) declared the Kabardas to be a barrier between the Russian and Ottoman Empires: such a declaration was already a Russian victory. The Cherkasskiis belonged to what I have called the Naryshkin-Trubetskoi network, which would build later in the century an extensive clientage system in the southern theater.[25] Members of the local elites who married into it became brokers between the imperial government and their homeland and eventually agents of the integration of the client society into the empire.

In the Balkan sector, the Prut campaign (1711) heralded the formation of a client society in Moldavia and Wallachia along the Danube, which the Russians would later consider the southern moat of their empire. Although the campaign was a disaster, it shook the foundations of the Ottomans' client society in the principalities and caused an exodus of people not unlike that of the Cossacks in the opposite direction after Poltava, two years earlier. Among the prominent families that followed the retreat of the Russian army and were settled, chiefly on the Left-Bank Ukraine where they received large estates, were the Cantemirs, descendants of a rich Tatar who had converted and settled in Moldavia in 1540. Dmitrii (1673–1723), appointed in 1710 *hospodar* (governor) of Moldavia, a largely autonomous province of the Ottoman Empire, was born in Constantinople and kept as a hostage there. He learned Turkish and Persian and later occupied high positions. But he went over to the Russians in 1711 with a thousand of his *boyars* (nobles), was made a prince, and was given a pension. A decade later, he would head the tsar's field chancery during the Persian campaign. His first wife was a princess Kantakuzen, the descendant of a Byzantine emperor and the daughter of a *hospodar* of Wallachia, but the second was a princess Trubetskaia, the daughter of Ivan, field marshal, governor general of Kiev, and founder of the Naryshkin-Trubetskoi network, whose brother was married to a princess Cherkasskaia. His son Antioch (1708–44) became a leading figure in the world of Russian letters and was ambassador to London and then Paris, where he died. He remained single, but one of his brothers and one of his sisters married into the Golitsyn family. Andrei Kheraskov from Wallachia belonged to those families that accompanied the Cantemirs; his grandson Mikhail (1733–1807), born in Poltava, would become an epic poet of Russian classicism; another family was that of Iurii Mechnikov, Moldavian boyar and judge (*mechnik*), who also received large estates.[26] What is striking about this emigration from Georgia and Moldavia-Wallachia is its size; 1,000 members from the elite of a small country represented a substantial share. As members of an elite in emigration, they retained close ties with those who stayed behind and became potential supporters of the Russians. And beyond the two principalities there was the "invisible frontier" of the Greek Orthodox world, its high clergy partly financed by the Russians, and the Balkan Slavs, especially the Serbs and the Montenegrins, who looked with hope to the rising might of the empire.

## Client Societies: The Eastern Theater

Client societies in the eastern theater were of more recent origin; in fact, most were created during the first forty years of the eighteenth century. The fundamental geopolitical fact during that period was the continuing struggle between the Manchu dynasty and the Western Mongols or Zunghars and the resulting turbulence in the Kazakh steppe. A first lull after Galdan's death in 1697 was followed by another Manchu offensive beginning in 1715, by a second lull after the death of the K'ang-hsi emperor in 1722, a renewed offensive during the reign of the Yungcheng emperor (1723–35), and a final and massive onslaught that destroyed the Zunghars in 1755–57.[27] On the Russian side, the progress of colonization in Bashkiria—so similar in many ways to the advance of the American settler into Indian territory[28]—caused growing unrest that eventually erupted in the War of 1705–11, followed by another uprising in 1735–38 and the pacification of the territory. Occupation always brings about collaboration. The Russians found among the Bashkirs and Tatars who had emigrated from the old Kazan Khanate enough clients willing to carry out diplomatic missions in the Kazakh steppe, among peoples with whom they shared a long, if not always friendly, history.

The permanent turbulence in a huge frontier stretching from the Volga to the Altai Mountains brought to the fore hard-line administrators, one of them Ivan Kirilov, the Senate's senior secretary. He submitted in 1734 one of the most remarkable sets of recommendations in the elaboration of a Russian grand strategy; his reward was an appointment to Bashkiria with a mission to establish a forward position from which Russia would dominate the entire frontier.[29] The project, like Peter's grand strategy in general, was motivated by commercial and military considerations. Russia must gain access to the riches of Mogul India, in much the same way that Portugal and Spain gained access to those of the Americas. There was gold, which flowed into Persia, and precious stones, especially lapis lazuli, used chiefly for ornamental purposes, from Badakhshan, in the northern province of modern-day Afghanistan. There was lead and silver in the mountains of present-day Kirgizia. But access to those riches was blocked by the Zunghars, who roamed between the Altai and the Syr Daria and, from their headquarters in Turkestan City, were at war with China and in a state of latent hostility toward the Kazakhs. Kirilov proposed that Russia ally with China to destroy the Zunghars in return for China supplying gold and giving the Russians access to the Amur River. However, Russia must not (and could not) use her own troops but must treat Kazakhs and Karakalpaks not so much as subjects (*poddanye*) but as "privileged peoples" (*privillegirovannye narody*)—in other words as clients—and turn them against the Zunghars. After all, had not Alexander the Great reached India more with the help of Asiatic peoples than with his own European troops? Russia's forward position would be on the Ural River, on the outer periphery of Bashkiria. From that military headquarters it would work to draw the Kazakh steppe into the orbit of Russian influence and the trade of Bukhara and Tashkent toward the Urals and the Volga. Kirilov already felt confident that the Bashkirs and Kalmyks (and Cossacks) who had been used against the Swedes, the Poles, the Turks, and the Crimeans could also be turned against the Zunghars and even the Kazakhs, should they refuse to accept their Russian patron.

But there were few forces at Kirilov's disposal, and the Cossacks would remain as a rule the most reliable client society in the eastern theater. They made it possible for the imperial government to practice an economy of force by keeping the regular army out of the region, save in exceptional circumstances. However, these Cossacks had a history different from that of their brethren in the southern theater. They were the Siberian Cossacks, not yet known under this collective name, descendants of Ermak's Cossacks who had "conquered" Siberia in 1582. They settled in various towns or fortified outposts, their ranks replenished from time to time by other Cossacks banished from the southern theater and local Tatars with whom they intermingled. The northward advance of the Zunghars into the Kunlunda steppe in the late seventeenth century and the threat they represented to Russian expansion from west to east across Siberia brought about a countermovement of Cossack outposts from Tobolsk upstream along the Irtysh and toward the upper Ob in the foothills of the Altai, toward Kuznetsk, Krasnoiarsk, and Minusinsk, to protect Russian colonists and Akinfii Demidov's mining operations in the mountains. Later, following the creation of fortified outposts defended by garrisons between Omsk and Ust-Kamenogorsk, they were used to maintain communications between them and were placed under the commander of the Siberian Line. But they remained a very small force of about 3,000 men, scattered over enormous distances, and without the traditions and esprit de corps of the Ukrainian and Don Cossacks.[30]

A similar situation prevailed in Bashkiria. Cossacks there also came from European Russia, caught in the great eastward movement of people seeking both adventure and freedom from the constraints imposed by the Muscovite government on its dependent population. They took the name of the place or river where they settled: there were Samara, Sakmara, Ufa, Iset, and Nagaibatsk Cossacks, recruited from among pagans, Muslims, and Christians in the area, even including Persians, Arabs, and Afghans. Like all Cossacks, they were the enemy of the nomads, whom they resembled in many ways, because they competed for booty (people and horses) and for land, which they carved out from the nomads' pastures and transformed into settlers' land where they raised their own cattle. They moved on toward the Ural River, where the first fortified outposts were founded by Kirilov in 1735–37, including Orenburg at its original location, at the confluence of the Or and Ural rivers, Russia's new forward position in the eastern theater. These various Cossack communities were gathered up in 1748 to form the Orenburg Cossack Host, with a total strength of 5,887 men.[31]

If one may question whether these Siberian and Orenburg Cossacks truly formed "client societies," there was no doubt that the Ural (Iaik) Cossacks did. Their origin went back to perhaps 1584, when a party of Don Cossacks established a settlement on the middle course of the river. They later received a charter allowing them to build settlements all the way to the Caspian Sea. In the seventeenth century, they raided merchantmen on that sea and even carried out a coup de main against Khiva. But they also became involved in the turbulence of the frontier, attacking Russian settlements and merchant caravans on the Volga, notably during the Razin Uprising (1670–71), although they had already entered into a client relationship with Moscow when they recognized the authority of the first Romanov tsar. In 1670, they were included in the jurisdiction of the Kazan Chancery headed by Boris Golitsyn, but passed in 1720 under that of the College of War; their immediate local commander was the Astrakhan governor until 1744. In 1723, they numbered 6,124 men, while the original land grant had been for only 600. These Cossacks fulfilled some of the basic functions of a client society, supplying auxiliary formations to the imperial army. They contributed 1,500 men to Cherkasskii's Khiva expedition, detachments to the Southern Corps stationed in northern Persia, where they suffered heavy losses, and to the north Caucasus. The purpose of their settlements along the Ural River was to demarcate the pastures of the Kalmyks from those of the Kazakhs. In return, the imperial government recognized their rights and privileges to elect their officers and ataman and to fish in the river, their main source of income. But these Cossacks were an unruly society, "democratic" to the point of anarchy. As elsewhere in other Cossack societies, an upper stratum of well-to-do "elders" was emerging, eager to secure landed properties on which to settle fugitive peasants and to seek Russian support against the mass of their own Cossacks. The resulting conflict pitted the elected ataman, Grigorii Markurev, against some of his men who denounced him to Petersburg. However, he was appointed ataman for life in 1723 and given the empress's portrait—a significant honor—a gold goblet and saber, and 100 rubles; his men already received an annual salary of 1,500 rubles. Repeated denunciations finally led to his dismissal in 1740, but Anna Ivanovna's death kept him in office.[32] By constantly inviting imperial intervention, the host was taking the path of self-destruction as a client society.

While steps were being taken to "discipline" the Siberian and Orenburg Cossacks, Kalmyk society was entering a period of decline. The imperial government depended on them to keep order in the steppe across the Volga at the end of the seventeenth century, using them against the Nogais, the Bashkirs, and the Kazakhs. As a client society in what was still the "invisible frontier," they were the foundation of Russian power between the Volga and the Emba, between the Samara and the Caspian. But they also depended on the Russians. Although they considered themselves independent, contacts with the Russians had forged ties of economic dependence. They needed access to the Russian market to barter their livestock (horses and sheep) for metal goods (kettles and buckets, needles and mirrors), vodka and tobacco, tunics and boots. And they were a large market for the Russians: there may have been 150,000 Kalmyks of both sexes in the 1720s, although they could never muster more than 20,000 men in the field. They were also an unruly lot, praising military values and highly dependent on booty in the absence of an agricultural base.[33]

Like the Cossacks, they were used to police the steppe and to form a pool of auxiliary troops for the strategic force operating in the western and southern theaters. During the Astrakhan Uprising of 1705–6, their contribution was crucial to the imperial government's victory: it also yielded substantial spoils. They sent 10,000 horsemen to crush the Bashkir Rebellion of 1705–11 and another 10,000 against Bulavin in 1707–1708, prompting the Kazan governor, Petr Apraksin, to concede it was difficult for the imperial government to function in the region without their assistance. They were used in the Northern War against the Swedes. In 1707, 3,000 Kalmyks were on their way to the Baltic front, but turned back before reaching Moscow, kidnapping one hundred families of Russian settlers on their return journey. Others, however, carried out the missions assigned to them as auxiliary troops—reconnaissance, capturing prisoners, burning villages, foraging. They left such a bad memory that when Reval capitulated in 1710, its representatives insisted that no Kalmyks be stationed in the vicinity of their city.[34] Their 3,300 horsemen arrived too late to take part in the battle of Poltava, but not before the rumor that 30,000 of them were on their way had caused panic among the Swedes. In the eyes of European troops, Kalmyks, Bashkirs, and Cossacks were "Asiatic" horsemen who brought back memories of Genghis Khan, no small contribution to the awesomeness of Russian power. In 1711, when Apraksin was sent from Kazan to destroy Nogai villages along the Kuban River, he stopped on his way to meet Khan Ayuki on the Volga below Tsaritsyn and obtained from him a commitment of 20,000 Kalmyks to join his 1,000 Ural Cossacks and his own 3,400 dragoons. They caused immense devastation and captured an enormous booty. In 1719, the French consul reported that the tsar planned an invasion of Sweden during the winter with 20,000 regulars and 40,000 Kalmyks. They also took part in the Persian expedition of 1722–23 and the Crimean War of 1735–38.[35]

The awareness of their power and usefulness under Khan Ayuki went to the Kalmyks' heads and blinded them to the true nature of their relationship with the empire. Ayuki treated the first governor of Astrakhan, Artemii Volynskii, as an inferior, while the imperial government demanded that he correspond with the governor on an equal footing, subjecting both to the same level of dependence on the tsar. On more than one occasion, the khan had faced domestic opposition, including that of his oldest son, and he had been restored to power by the Russians. Increasing raids by Kazakhs and Karakalpaks worsened the Kalmyks' dependence on the Russians. The imperial government, which had grown used to Ayuki and had counted on him as a client strong enough to mobilize his people in a frontier where it was still weak, began to change its policy for at least three reasons. The khan was getting old, there were no rules of succession, and a period of instability was inevitable. Ayuki had betrayed Cherkasskii in 1717 during the Khiva expedition for personal reasons, but such a betrayal was by then also treason to the empire. Russian power was growing in the frontier, rendering a disciplining of the Kalmyk client society indispensable. On his way to Derbent in 1722, the tsar had visited the Kalmyk steppe and had selected Ayuki's nephew, Dorji-Nazar, to succeed the khan. But there were other candidates: Dosang, the khan's oldest grandson (his father had died that year), the main candidate; Cheren-Donduk, the oldest of the khan's living sons; and Donduk-Ombo, Ayuki's adopted grandson and favorite, whose descendants would become imperial princes under Alexander I under the name of Dondukov-Korsakov. Their best-known members would be Mikhail (1794–1869), curator of Petersburg University (1832–52) and vice president of the Academy of Sciences (1835–52), and his son Alexander (1822–89), governor general of the Right-Bank Ukraine (1869–78) and commander of the Caucasian military district (1882–89).

When Ayuki died in 1724, Petersburg ordered Volynskii to proclaim Dorji-Nazar khan and take his son as hostage, but the governor found himself facing open revolt in the steppe, the Kalmyk elite siding with Cheren-Donduk and preparing for war against the Russians. Volynskii, with the help of the Cossacks, was able to prevent a showdown and reached a compromise by which Cheren-Donduk was proclaimed acting khan (*namestnik*). He was also the first khan required to take the oath of allegiance to the Romanov house. His incompetence suited the Russians only too well, determined as they now were to strengthen the role of the clan leaders and weaken the authority of the khan. But he also established relations with the Chinese, the Ottomans, and the Persians, unacceptable behavior for a client. The Russians finally lost patience with him in 1735, deported him to Petersburg, and chose Donduk-Ombo as his successor: he would rule until 1741. Before he died, Donduk chose his ten-year-old son to succeed him and sent an embassy to the Dalai Lama to secure his confirmation—the Kalmyks were Tibetan Buddhists (Lamaists) and the Dalai Lama had appointed their chief lama since the sixteenth century. But his widow knew where real power lay, and when the khan died, she sent a delegation to Petersburg to legitimize their son. However, the Russians had their own candidate, Donduk-Dashi, Dosang's brother, who had long been loyal to Russian interests, and he became acting khan in 1741. His twenty-year rule would witness the disintegration of the traditional Kalmyk client society. The Kazakh

Small Horde pasturing beyond the Emba was becoming the Russians' major client in the steppe, containing the Kalmyks from the east and barring their return to their Zunghar homeland. The khan was forbidden to conduct foreign relations, especially with China, in return for receiving the insignia of his office: a banner, a saber, a fur coat, and a fur hat. The client society had lost its freedom of action.

A rising imperial power is driven by its own momentum and by the geopolitical environment to create more client states and societies until it reaches a physical barrier beyond which farther expansion becomes counterproductive. For Russia in the eastern theater, that barrier was the Heartland's periphery along the Tienshan and Altai Mountains. The growing penetration of Kalmyk society by imperial officials and the renewed Manchu offensive against the Zunghars impelled the Russians to seek client societies among the Kazakhs, bringing about a far-reaching extension of imperial diplomatic control in the Kazakh steppe. Beginning in the 1730s the systematic construction of fortified outposts along the Ural, the Irtysh, and across the steppe would transform the territory of older client societies into forward bases of operations against the potential hostility of the Zunghars and even the Manchus.

The death of Khan Tauke in 1718—six years before that of Ayuki—marked the end of an era and the final division of the Kazakhs into three hordes. The Great Horde, with about 50,000 people, roamed between the upper Irtysh and the Ala Tau range around the eastern end of Lake Balkash. Its khan, Zholbarys, ruled until 1740, when he was assassinated on orders from Nadir Shah, who brought Persian rule to the Syr Daria. The Middle Horde wintered on the lower course of the river, west to the lake, and in summer migrated along the valley of the Sary-Su to the headwaters of the Tobol and the Ishim, tributaries of the Irtysh. It traded with the oasis towns of Central Asia and straddled the caravan routes from Siberia. Its khan, Semeke (Shah Muhammad), died in 1733 and was succeeded by his son Abul Muhammad (1733–71). The Small Horde's winter pastures were also on the Syr Daria, but it summered farther west, in the valley of the Irgiz and the Turgai and in the Mugodzhary Hills that formed the watershed with the basin of the Caspian, the land of the Kalmyks. Russian efforts naturally focused on this last horde. Its khan, Abul Khayr, Tauke's son, towered over his two brothers, Semeke and Zholbarys, and dominated steppe politics until his assassination in 1748. The khans were not autocratic leaders, however, but presided over fragmented societies in which their sons (sultans) and elders (*starshiny*), whose power rested on their leadership of the major clans, wielded effective power and often went their own way, in opposition to the khan's policies.

The Zunghars' westward expansion, prodded in part by the Manchu offensive, had a shattering effect on Kazakh society. Galdan had already claimed the pastures of the Great Horde, and his successor Tsewang Rabtan (1697–1727) went farther, crossed the Sary-Su into Middle Horde territory to the Syr Daria, and destroyed one of the chief settlements of the horde at Sairam near present-day Chimkent. The Great Horde migrated into disputed territory between Khiva and Bukhara in the Kyzylkum Desert; the Middle Horde settled in the Kazakh upland; and the Small Horde moved west toward Bashkiria and Kalmyk territory, raising tensions in the region over access to pastures. Abul Khayr's ambition was to reunite the Kazakhs under a single leadership, his own, and the disaster offered an opportunity. Every frontier society, caught in the turmoil of frontier warfare, needs a patron among the core area powers. Only one, Russia, was capable of protecting the Kazakhs against the Zunghars. By 1730, Abul Khayr had become convinced there was no alternative to becoming a client society of the empire by taking the oath of allegiance. He sent an embassy to Petersburg, which returned with rich gifts and accompanied by Alexander Tevkelev, a Tatar nobleman (originally called Mirza Kutlu Muhammad) who worked as a translator in the College of Foreign Affairs. He brought a saber, a sable coat, and a black fox hat, which, in the eyes of the Russians if not in those of the Kazakhs, represented the khan's regalia. But Tevkelev would have to stay more than a year with Abul Khayr before a critical mass of elders would agree to the transformation of the horde into a client society in 1731. They knew that the khan would seek to use Russian support to consolidate his power over them and realize his ambition to reunite the Kazakhs. Indeed, it was the khan who suggested to Kirilov the building of a fortress at the confluence of the Ural and the Or that might serve as a refuge for him, should his authority in the horde be successfully challenged. Thus it was that the leader of the new client society was instrumental in building the empire's forward military headquarters from which it would eventually spread its dominion over the entire steppe. In return for Russia's protection, Abul Khayr was required to send hostages. In addition, he would help the Russians crush the Bashkir Uprising of 1735–40 and would promise to bring the Khivans and "Aralians" (Araltsy or Karakalpaks) into the client system.

The Russians looked to their success as only a first step. In 1737, Abul Muhammad and Sultan Ablai, the most powerful man in the Middle Horde, stated their willingness to take the oath of allegiance, and they eventually did, in 1741. Growing Russian power was beginning to create competition for Russian support among powerful figures in Kazakh society, each intent on using that support for his own ends. Little progress was made in the Great Horde: it was too far away and too much under the sway of the Zunghars. Yet the outlook seemed promising in the delta of the Amu Daria. In 1741, after a three-year hiatus, Nur Ali, one of Abul Khayr's sons, wrote to Ivan Nepliuev, Kirilov's successor, that he had been invited to become khan of Khiva. However, Nepliuev, the new hard-line proconsul of the empire in the region, opposed accepting the invitation because it would strengthen Abul Khayr's authority among the Kazakhs, and the khan, a client of the empire, would become exposed to the countervailing influence of Persia. The management of the client system required that clients be forbidden to create their own subclients without imperial approval. Nepliuev's resentment could only grow at the news that 30,000 tents (*kibitki*), or about 150,000 Karakalpaks, had come to Abul Khayr in 1742 offering to become clients of the empire and that Nur Ali had nevertheless become their khan and that of Khiva. Relations rapidly cooled between the imperial proconsul and Abul Khayr, who began to realize that his relationship with the Russians was not one between equals. The oaths of allegiance left many questions unsettled. The construction of fortified outposts created a demarcation line that cut off some 80,000 square kilometers of Kazakh pastures by 1743, to be settled by Cossacks who launched from them raids against Kazakh *auly* (villages) to get the same booty the Kazakhs were seeking in imperial territory.[36]

Thus, from the Gulf of Finland to Mongolia, Russia's emerging grand strategy depended on a glacis of client states and societies between the area of deployment of the strategic force and the Heartland's periphery. Their purpose was to maximize imperial influence and diplomatic control while minimizing the use of force by the regular army. The client system was held together by personal relationships between the Romanov house and the empire's great families on the one hand and the client elites on the other, be they in Sweden, Poland, Moldavia, or Georgia, the Cossack hosts from the Dniepr to the Irtysh, or even the Kalmyks and the Kazakhs by the early 1740s. These personal relationships rested on the widespread perception of Russia's awesomeness, carefully cultivated by an ideology that glorified raw and invincible power and the majesty of the ruler. They found their rewards in rich presents, land grants, and positions in the imperial elite and were sustained by intermarriages creating a common interest between the imperial power and its clients in the Russo-Swedish, Russo-Polish, and Russo-Turkish frontiers.

# PART II

# HEGEMONIC EXPANSIONISM, 1743–1796

# 4

# Deep Strikes

## Sweden, France, and Prussia

We now turn to the evolution of Russia's grand strategy from the accession of Elizabeth to the death of Catherine II and to an analysis of its three major principles—strategic penetration, deployment, and the client system—at a time when Russia sought and achieved hegemony in the Heartland. Faced with the reluctance of the Swedish client to accept its place in the new international order created by the Treaty of Nystadt (1721) and ill-conceived attempts to regain some of its losses, the empire struck back with a determination to destroy Sweden's military capability and discipline it to accept Russia's overlordship. Russian troops were stationed in Stockholm for the first and only time. Determined likewise to teach the Prussian client that Russia alone was entitled to manage the client system anchored in the friendly kingdom, Russia fought the bloodiest engagements of the century against Frederick II, and its troops even briefly occupied Berlin. In the southern theater, imperial troops finally broke the Ottoman hold on the Black Sea and even crossed the Danube under the watchful apprehension of the Prussian client and Austria. Both were subsequently kept in line by an agreement to partition the Polish client. Farther east, a new client state was being created in Georgia. By the time of Catherine's death in 1796, Russian forces were poised for deep penetrations beyond the Heartland's periphery, in Holland and northern Italy. Russia's position as hegemon and arbiter of interclient disputes within the Heartland had become an incontrovertible fact.

The Russo-Swedish War of 1741–43 was a huge misunderstanding. Sweden's fearful realization that it was being treated like another Poland; the political dominance of the Hats; the perception of would-be weakness after the Crimean campaign of 1735–38; the summary execution by the Russians in 1739 of Major Malcolm Sinclair, a member of the Swedish parliament carrying dispatches to Constantinople; and French incitements convinced Stockholm to declare war in July 1741. Seldom was a war fought in such an incompetent manner. The Swedes' failure demonstrated conclusively that if they could declare war, it was the Russians who would impose the peace. By the time the war broke out, the Russians had moved 35,000 men to Vyborg, which was at the time only about five kilometers from the border, and another 33,000 to Estland and Ingria to block a Swedish landing and an attack on Petersburg. Included in the Russian army were Don Cossacks, whose commander "aroused wide comment by his determination to use the methods of the Turkish war to accomplish the physical destruction of the Swedish race in Finland,"[1] as well as Bashkirs and Kalmyks. The Swedes, who had declared war, had only 8,000 men in Willmanstand and Fredrikshamn (Hamina). The Russians were commanded by the same Marshal Lacy who had led them to Warsaw in 1733, Heidelberg in 1735, and the Crimea in 1738; the Swedes by Karl Lewenhaupt, whom Lacy had defeated at Tönningen in Denmark in 1714.[2]

Lacy moved on Willmanstrand and stormed it in September, causing the Swedes 4,600 casualties and the eventual execution of Lewenhaupt's second in command for dereliction of duty. But Lacy, claiming a shortage of provisions, did not exploit his success by moving on Fredrikshamn and bringing the war to a close. There was a weightier reason, however. Warfare in the eighteenth century, and in Russia perhaps more than anywhere else, was highly politicized. Military commanders saw themselves primarily as the executors of a political will, with strategic considerations taking second place. Lacy knew there had been great tension in the ruling elite since the death of Anna Ivanovna in 1740. It was not relieved until Elizabeth staged a coup in November 1741. By then, it was too late in the season to continue the war.

It could not resume until mid-May 1742, when the grass was tall enough to feed the horses. Although the Swedish army had grown to 23,700 men, the strength of the imperial forces had reached 70,000 regulars with 12,000 Cossacks, Kalmyks, and other irregulars, and a galley fleet was being built to ferry troops and provisions along the coast of the Gulf of Finland. The Russians moved on Fredrikshamn in June, only to discover the Swedes had abandoned it, one of those "strange and incomprehensible actions that posterity can hardly believe."[3] Nyslott and Tavastgus (Hämeenlinna) capitulated in August, followed by Helsingfors (Helsinki), after a Finnish peasant told the Russians that a trail once cut by Peter I's soldiers across the woods could quickly be restored to block the Swedes' retreat toward Åbo. For this disaster, Lewenhaupt was recalled and executed. Finland was now defenseless, and after a campaign of less than three months the Russians reached Åbo, Vasa, and Uleåborg, 1,140 kilometers from Petersburg and 1,830 from Moscow.

In accordance with a strategic doctrine calling for deep penetration in order to threaten the enemy's capital, the war could not end with the Swedish capitulation at Helsingfors, which provided that the ten Finnish regiments in the Swedish army were to lay down their arms and the Swedish regulars were to return to their homeland. Elizabeth, who "did not forget whose blood she had,"[4] was determined to force the Swedes to capitulate in Stockholm. Lacy was made commander in chief of all land and naval forces in May 1743, with Admiral Nikolai Golovin, who commanded the Baltic Fleet and had been envoy to Sweden (1724–31), subordinate to him. Their mission was to neutralize the Swedish fleet and ferry the troops across the Åland archipelago to the Swedish coast. Golovin was a cautious man, however, and refused to risk his seventeen ships of the line against Sweden's twelve, invoking

Peter's Naval Regulations that the Russians must not attack the Swedes unless the ratio was three Russian to two Swedish ships. The offensive never materialized because peace was signed in August. The Swedes surrendered Willmanstrand, Fredrikshamn, and Nyslott, key fortified strongholds that would henceforth serve as the basis for tactically offensive operations in Finland while denying that advantage to the Swedes against Russia. They had to accept the stationing of nine Russian regiments transported in galleys to Stockholm under General James Keith, Lacy's second in command.

The Russians also sought to reach the Rhine, once again at the invitation of the friendly kingdom. Following the accession of Maria Theresa in Vienna and Frederick II in Berlin in 1740, a new situation emerged: the king chose to take advantage of the perceived weakness of Austria to strike at its leadership in German affairs. The so-called War of the Austrian Succession was a challenge to the imperial patron, which could not accept a change in the client relationships carried out without its consent. At first, the Russians stood on the sidelines, until Austria made peace with Prussia, but then heeded Austria's request for an expeditionary corps of 30,000 to fight France, with which Austria was also at war. In 1748, 36,000 Russians (twenty-three infantry regiments, with some dragoons and Cossacks), under the command of Vasilii Repnin, set out for the Rhineland, as they had in 1735. Repnin left Riga in February, reached Grodno in March, crossed the Bug and the Vistula, and reached Kraków in May. From Kraków, he entered Moravia via Teschen, marched via Olmütz past Prague toward Nüremberg, reaching Ebensfeld, north of Bamberg, in July. The expedition was financed by British subsidies. Repnin's advance stopped with the beginning of peace negotiations completed at Aix-la-Chapelle (Aachen) in October.[5] Repnin had not reached the Rhine any more than Lacy had, but the expedition served notice that the empire, in alliance with the friendly kingdom, was determined to resist Franco-Prussian attempts to weaken Austria and challenge its position in the Heartland.

Frederick II's victories cemented the Austro-Russian alliance and focused Russia's attention on the ongoing transformation of the Prussian client into a potential enemy. Unless the king's ambitions were contained, the client system in Sweden and Poland would be in constant jeopardy and the Austrian anchor would become unstable. The king's youthful disregard of Russia's awesomeness needed to be challenged with a demonstration of overwhelming force in order to restore the system's equilibrium and assert Russian hegemony in the western theater. In 1742, Frederick II had dictated the peace to Austria, gaining Silesia, the rich agricultural valley of the Oder, with its well-known textile industry. Two years later, he was at war again, invading Bohemia and then Saxony, whose elector was the king of Poland. Peace was made in Dresden (1745), confirming the cession of Silesia and the county of Glatz (Klodzko), from which the Prussians, their back to the Oder, "the nourishing mother" of their supply bases,[6] could quickly march on Prague and Vienna via Brunn (Brno). The Russians made their displeasure clear, but to no avail. Military preparations by both sides only raised tensions until diplomatic relations were broken in 1750. Three years later, a joint meeting of senators and generals in Petersburg resolved that, in order "to reduce Prussia to its former modest state," 60,000 must be deployed in Livonia, with 4,000 Don Cossacks and 2,000 Kalmyks, and an addi-

The Polish Sector

tional 60,000 kept ready to move into Livonia when the war began.[7] An observation corps of 30,000 must also be stationed in Vyborg province for an invasion of Finland, should Frederick win Swedish support, one third of them to be transported in galleys to Finland and the Swedish coast for another attack on Stockholm. Russia was thus committing 150,000 regular troops to a war against Prussia that it already considered inevitable. War finally broke out in 1756 in the wake of the international realignment known as the Diplomatic Revolution, in which Prussia left its alliance with France for one with Britain, and Austria left its alliance with Britain for one with France, its old enemy. But this realignment changed nothing in the strategic alliance with the friendly kingdom. Russia found itself at war against Prussia with an Austria eager to regain Silesia and reduce Prussia to its previous modest state.

A so-called Conference was created in Petersburg in March 1756 consisting of the top leadership of the empire; it would seek to micromanage a war fought in the valley of the Oder, 1,750 kilometers from Moscow and 2,000 from Petersburg via Riga. This war, known as the Seven Years' War, began with a preemptive strike by Frederick into Saxony in August, and Russia joined it in December. The Conference decided to raise 130,000 men for an army commanded by Stepan Apraksin. He never got that many men, however, and by June 1757, two months after crossing the Dvina, he had only 65,000, with whom he marched on Königsberg, 375 kilometers from Riga. The city was the key to East Prussia, defended by 32,000 troops. Apraksin crossed the Niemen at Kovno and was advancing along the valley of the Pregel when he stumbled against the Prussians at Gross Jägersdorf at the end of August. It was a Russian victory, but one marred as usual by the excesses committed by Cossacks and Kalmyks, who "ravaged the country and terrorized the population with dire consequences for the supply and the intelligence of the army."[8] Apraksin was only 50 kilometers from Königsberg, but, invoking a shortage of fodder, he did not pursue his success and retreated to Memel, over 200 kilometers to the north. In fact, like Lacy in 1741, he was highly sensitive to political developments in Petersburg, where the empress suffered a stroke at the beginning of September. She recovered, however, and Apraksin was recalled and court-martialed. Königsberg was taken in January 1758.

Faithful to what had become a major principle of their grand strategy, and abetted by Elizabeth's well-known hatred of Frederick, the Russians prepared for an invasion of Brandenburg across the Oder, with the ultimate objective the capture of Berlin. Their political obsession with the king's refusal to accept his place in the client system and their devotion to a doctrine of strategic penetration over considerable distances at any cost blinded them to the fact they were playing into the hands of Austria, the friendly kingdom, for which the true purpose of the war was not an offensive on Berlin but the recovery of Silesia. To reduce Prussia to its previous modest state required the occupation of Pomerania with the fortress of Kolberg (Kołobrzeg) on the Baltic coast, which, following that of East Prussia and the recovery of Silesia, would have reduced Brandenburg to even less than its pre-1618 borders. The indirect approach promised much greater rewards than an all-out offensive against the Oder. However, such an offensive would have overlooked Frederick's strategic advantage. From Berlin to Frankfurt-on-the-Oder the distance was a mere 90 kilometers, to Prague via Dresden and from Breslau to Olmütz via Glatz about 320 kilometers. Frederick's reputation as the great commander of his day would rest largely on his ability to derive the maximum advantage from his "interior lines" within a radius of about 300 kilometers in densely settled and relatively well-off Saxony, Bohemia, and Silesia. These interior lines would enable him to move quickly against one enemy, beat him, and then turn against the other before the two could link up against him. In November 1757, while the Russians were retreating toward Memel, he won a major victory over the French at Rossbach, and in December over the Austrians at Leuthen, west of Breslau. In 1758, he was ready for the expected Russian offensive.

The imperial army was led by Wilhelm Fermor, a Baltic German with a good grasp of military realities and solicitude for his soldiers—unlike Apraksin, who had behaved like an "Oriental satrap" and neglected the well-being of his troops. From Königsberg, he moved with his 72,000 men to the Vistula, crossed it at Thorn and marched on Poznan, where the Russians established their main operational base, supplied by magazines set up along the lower course of the river. The main force advanced from Poznan, crossed the Wartha at Landsberg, and moved on Küstrin, at its confluence with the Oder, 30 kilometers north of Frankfurt, while a detachment was sent to Schwedt farther downstream to block an unexpected Prussian crossing of the Oder. But the king outwitted Fermor, crossed the river elsewhere, and moved to attack the Russian rear on the right bank. The two armies, Fermor's 42,500—depleted after leaving troops along the way to garrison towns and maintain communications—and Frederick's 33,000, met at Zorndorf in August to fight one of the bloodiest battles of the century. When it was over, Russians and Prussians had each lost 12,000 men, and neither side had truly won a decisive victory.[9] Fermor retreated to Landsberg and later withdrew behind the Vistula for the winter. In the meantime, an expedition had been sent under Petr Rumiantsev to Kolberg, the only port of any value on the bleak Pomeranian coast between Danzig and Stettin. But the operation was poorly conducted and the siege was lifted in November. And yet, Kolberg, the key to Pomerania, was eminently suited to become a temporary naval base for the unloading of provisions, munitions, and heavy guns from Petersburg and the Baltic provinces and for a combined land and naval offensive against Stettin. The Austrians did not disturb Frederick in 1758, in part because they were still reeling from their defeat the previous year, in part because of their ambivalence toward a Russian offensive that they both wanted and feared: Russia wielded sufficient power to upset the status quo in Central Europe, which it was in Austria's interest to maintain, at least once Silesia had been regained.

The Russians followed the same strategy in 1759, but among mounting concerns over the costs of the war and the reluctance, or inability, of the Austrians to coordinate their operations with theirs. With the approach of spring, magazines on the lower Vistula at Kulm (Chelmno), Graudentz (Grudzadz), Marienwerder (Kwidzyn), and Elbing (Elblag) were filled to capacity, tapping the profitable grain trade of the Vistula, the nourishing mother of the Russian war effort. Although the Russians who wintered in central Poland marched back and forth during the year between the Vistula and the Oder, creating many hardships among the population, traders were doing well selling them grain, salt, and meat, and neutralized the opposition of those who resented the passage of Russian troops across Polish territory. The French wondered why their Russian allies were not taxing the occupied parts of Brandenburg and Pomerania as ruthlessly as Frederick was taxing Saxony and Mecklenburg. The Russians answered that the population was too poor and that the king had removed all the currency from circulation. Another reason was most likely the hope that a Prussian defeat would result in the occupation of Pomerania, whose population had to be befriended beforehand. A Prussian defeat would create a Russian-controlled client society in Pomerania and return Silesia to Austria, relegating Prussia west of the Oder and reducing it to the status of a very modest client state.

Poznan remained the base of operations, 130 kilometers west of Warsaw and 180 east of Frankfurt. The command of the army was given to Petr Saltykov, of insignificant appearance, and little known outside court circles, where he was well connected. But he managed to earn the loyalty of his troops and win the greatest victory of the war. He set out from Poznan for the Oder with about 60,000 men, including the irregular cavalry, but the approach to the river was guarded by a Prussian force of 28,000. By a flanking movement, Saltykov cut them off from the river and defeated them at Palzig in July. The road to Frankfurt was open, and he expected the Austrians to join him in a massive offensive against the city beyond which it was only a week's march to Berlin. But the ever cautious Austrians were not inclined to commit their army to a decisive battle with Frederick and sent only 24,000 men under General Loudon, who lost his supply train on the way and disliked Saltykov. The king followed the same tactic as he had in 1758, crossing the Oder below Küstrin to outflank the Russian commander. The result was the Battle of Künersdorf, fought in August, at which Russians and Austrians inflicted on the king the greatest calamity he had ever experienced: he lost 20,000 men, or 48 percent of his army in the field. He retired in haste to Berlin for a final battle, which could have brought the war to an end.[10] But Saltykov found himself facing some very difficult decisions. The Austrians were short of supplies and began to retreat toward Dresden, destroying all hopes for a joint operation against Berlin. He had to feed Loudon's troops in addition to his own and experienced similar logistical problems, worsened by the fact that the country east of the middle Oder did not have the resources to support an immobile army much longer. It began to dawn on him that a strike against Berlin was fraught with great danger. Crossing a river like the Oder to carry the war into enemy territory against an agile commander like Frederick, whose interior lines would become shorter as he retreated toward Berlin, was a risky undertaking. The king, who still had 30,000 men against Saltykov's 60,000, could attack the Russians west of the Oder, cut off their rear from the main force and beat them in detail. Or he could cross the Oder as he had done on two previous occasions, destroy Saltykov's entrenchments on both sides of the river, and leave the Russians stranded in Brandenburg. The Russian commander, eager "to catch up with his bread" (*pour rejoindre son pain*)[11] — which should have been catching up with him instead — decided to withdraw to the Vistula for the winter. Such was the miserable end of a campaign marked by "the greatest Russian feat of arms of the eighteenth century considering the caliber of the enemy and the scale of combat."[12] There were some similarities between the Russians' position in Finland prior to an invasion of Sweden and their position in Poland before an invasion of Brandenburg. In both cases, a final strike against the enemy's capital carried with it the possibility of a major disaster: being cut off from their operational base by the moat of the Gulf of Bothnia in the event of a lucky strike by the Swedish navy or bad weather, or of a successful counterstrike on the Oder.

The campaign of 1760 was marred by confusion in Petersburg, where the Conference remained unable to work out a plan of operations to reconcile the unreconcilable—Russia's determination to reach Berlin with Austria's dependence on a war of attrition that would checkmate Frederick and force him to negotiate. It rejected Saltykov's project of a move on Kolberg to open up the Baltic coast in favor of a compromise plan according to which the Russians would move from Poznan into Silesia, link up with the Austrians to expel the Prussians from the province, and march on Berlin. The campaign did not begin well. Neither Saltykov nor Loudon could take Breslau; the Russians did not have the siege artillery to reduce Glogau; and the Austrians were mauled at Liegnitz. The battle for Silesia had been lost. Nevertheless, the Russians pushed on, crossing the Oder at Carolath and moving on to Guben, meeting little resistance from the Prussians, who were fully engaged in expelling the Austrians from Silesia. After the main force spread out in the valley of the middle Oder and Rumiantsev took Frankfurt in September, two Russian divisions, with some Austrians and Saxons, moved along the Spree toward Berlin, 1,830 kilometers from Moscow and 2,000 from Petersburg. The city capitulated in October, but it was a meaningless tactical victory.[13] Frederick was marching back from Silesia, threatening to cut off the Russians' retreat to the Oder. They withdrew at full speed behind the river, but not before their Cossack and Kalmyk irregulars left such devastation in Brandenburg that Frederick would never recover from the shock; he finally became convinced of Russia's awesomeness.

This monotonous succession of annual campaigns was drawing to an end, with all sides verging on exhaustion. Yet it was then, in 1761, that the Russians finally recognized that Frederick would not be forced to capitulate by a frontal assault on Berlin but by a successful offensive on his two flanks, in Pomerania and Silesia. In August, a separate corps of 20,000 under Zakhar Chernyshev linked up with Loudon's 70,000 men, moved into Silesia, and in October stormed the powerful fortress of Schweidnitz (Swidnica), with its enormous supplies. Its capture gave the allies the control of Silesia. Meanwhile, the Russians had laid siege to Kolberg, but had to face a Prussian invasion of Poland that destroyed their magazines in Poznan, ravaged the Kolberg hinterland, and vainly sought to relieve the fortress. Rumiantsev's 35,000 men kept up the siege with the effective support of the Revel squadron,[14] and the fortress capitulated in December. Frederick's two flanks had collapsed, and the king stated his readiness to begin negotiations in January 1762. The war soured relations between the Russians and the friendly kingdom: they suspected they had been used by the Austrians, even though Vienna did not recover Silesia. But the war also served Russian ends: another deep strategic penetration taught the recalcitrant state in Berlin that an independent policy in the Heartland that threatened to destabilize the client system would be met with a demonstration of overwhelming force. It was a lesson that Frederick would never forget.

## The Russo-Turkish Wars

Victories against the leading practitioner of the military art of the day gave the imperial army a degree of operational confidence it had not had since carrying out the sweeping operations that followed the battle of Poltava, between 1709 and 1721. The question is well worth raising whether, in spite of all appearances, Russian ambitions were not turning to the southern frontier from the beginning of Catherine's reign. Russia's hegemony in the western theater had become a fact, but it offered no further rewards to the crop of ambitious generals who got their first command responsibilities in the valley of the Oder. The new empress's yearning for fame—and her need of it to confirm the legitimacy of her rule—together with the restlessness of generals relegated to garrison duties, could find an outlet only in the southern theater. There the empire's grand strategy was indeed tested and reshaped to meet the needs of hegemonic expansion. The appointment in 1764 of Rumiantsev as governor general of Little Russia and commander of the Ukrainian Division—its troops deployed in the valley of the Dniepr to face both the southeastern march of the Polish Empire and the Crimean Khanate—hinted at a realignment of strategic priorities. That the Russians were taken by surprise by the Ottoman declaration of war in 1768 in no way undermines this hypothesis. The border incident in which Cossacks operating in Poland against confederates opposing the Russian-imposed settlement of the dissident question was only a precipitant. The cause of the war must be found in the new leadership's determination to carry out deep strategic penetrations into the Ottoman Empire in order to break its hold on the Black Sea littoral.

It was clear from the beginning that the objectives of the war were free navigation in the Black Sea and the "independence" of the Crimean Khanate, two objectives that so struck at the vital interests of the Ottoman Empire that only a crushing defeat could compel the Porte to capitulate. To achieve them, the imperial army must move to the Danube, occupying Moldavia and Wallachia, which, like the khanate, would become independent, while a naval expedition destroyed the Ottoman fleet, occupied the archipelago and blockaded Constantinople. Both the overland and naval expeditions involved strategic penetrations of considerable magnitude. Two armies were created. The First Army, under Alexander Golitsyn, gathered near Kiev in the spring of 1769, consisting largely of regiments drawn from central Russia and as far away as Petersburg. Its strength was fixed at 80,000 men. Its mission was to take Khotin and from Khotin to move on to Jassy: this had been Münnich's operational plan in 1739. The Second Army of 40,000 under Rumiantsev consisted of regiments stationed in the Left-Bank Ukraine. Its base of operations was Elizavetgrad, its mission to defend the left bank against Tatar raids and draw Ottoman forces away from Khotin. There was also an observation corps of 15,000 deployed in the Right-Bank Ukraine to block any attempts by Ottomans and Tatars to link up with the Polish confederates. The original plan thus envisaged an enveloping movement directed toward the Prut that would trap Ottoman and Tatar forces between that river and the Dniestr, annihilate them, and bring the imperial army to the lower Danube.[15]

Golitsyn crossed the Dniestr and reached Khotin in April. The fortress, with a large garrison of about 30,000, could withstand a long siege, and Golitsyn did not have siege artillery. He withdrew after discovering he could not take it by storm; he returned in August while Rumiantsev sent part of his force against Bendery, misleading the grand vizier moving along the Prut into believing that the Khotin operation was only a diversion. This gave Golitsyn the chance to take the fortress after all, but too late to prevent his recall for indecisiveness. Rumiantsev replaced him, after Petr Panin was given the command of the Second Army. Both operated under the guidance of the so-called Council (*Sovet*) consisting, like the old Conference, of key members of the ruling elite, and where Chernyshev, who had commanded the expedition against Berlin, was the major figure. The empress had quickly made her own the philosophy of the offensive that guided the high command: she wanted a forceful commander who could bring to her in Petersburg not only the grand vizier but also the sultan himself, and she found that Rumiantsev never moved fast enough.[16] Nevertheless, he took Jassy in September, and proclaimed in October the annexation to the empire of Moldavia and its "all-Russian Orthodox people." An advanced force entered Bucharest, Wallachia's capital, in November, and the principality was placed "under Her Majesty's scepter."[17] Strong Ottoman resistance blocked a farther advance to the Danube until the time came for the troops to take up their winter quarters. The empress was also hurrying Admiral Grigorii Spiridov to leave Kronstadt with a squadron of the Baltic fleet for a daring *naval* strategic penetration, unprecedented and unique in Russia's history until the 1905 expedition around the Cape of Good Hope to fight the Japanese navy in the Tsushima Strait. The squadron sailed through the Strait of Dover and past Gibraltar into the Mediterranean: its mission was to engage the Ottoman fleet and blockade Constantinople, which depended on grain shipments from the Greek archipelago. The high command thus committed nearly the entire imperial army and navy to a huge pincer movement directed against the Ottoman capital in order to force the sultan to capitulate on land and at sea. In addition, as if this strategic plan were not bold enough, a detachment of 3,000 troops gathered in Kizliar under Gottlob von Totleben, who had led the avant-garde against Berlin. They crossed into eastern Georgia in August and invested Sharopany, one of the Ottoman fortresses in western Georgia, in October.[18]

The year 1770 was the year of great victories but also of monumental logistical difficulties, which Rumiantsev kept complaining about in his reports to Petersburg. The distance from Khotin to Bendery was 400 kilometers and from Bendery to Galati on the lower Danube another 250. An army of 35,000 had to transport all its provisions across Moldavia, which did not have the resources to supply such a large force, not to mention Panin's Second Army of 45,000. From the beginning of the war, Rumiantsev envisaged a vast hinterland for the army reaching as far back as Mezhibozhe, Berdichev, and Polonnoe in Volhynia, nearly 900 kilometers from Galati. The agricultural resources of the Right-Bank Ukraine were mobilized to provide logistical depth, but the provisions had to be carted across the Podolian upland across the Dniestr to the Danube.[19] As in Poland during the Seven Years' War, these large purchases enriched the Polish landowners and created a vast market with outlets on the Danube. The consequence was a reorientation of the economy of the southeastern march of the Polish Empire toward the Black Sea, a factor

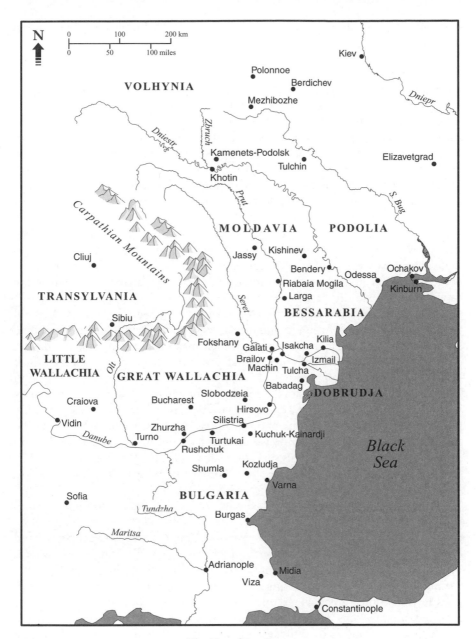

The Danubian Sector

that would eventually play a role in the annexation of the region to the empire in 1793.

Rumiantsev set out from Khotin in May, advancing along the Prut. In June, he defeated an Ottoman-Tatar force of 72,000 at Riabaia Mogila, and a few days later his 34,000 men defeated another 80,000 on the Larga, a tributary of the Prut. In July, a murderous battle against 150,000 Ottomans was fought at Kagul: the enemy suffered 20,000 casualties, the Russians 400. Never before had superior artillery wrought such carnage against an enemy cavalry. In September, Panin stormed Bendery, but with such losses that he was forced to retire. The Russians followed up their successive victories with the capture of two major fortresses on the lower Danube, Izmail and Kilia, but failed before Brailov. There was also a great victory at sea: in June, a force increased to four squadrons destroyed the Ottoman fleet in the battle of Chesme, off Chios Island. Totleben failed in Transcaucasia, however: there was a constant shortage of provisions and supplies coming from Mozdok across the mountains; the troops could not deal with the hot and humid climate of western Georgia and the insalubrious lowlands of the Rion Valley. Totleben could not take Poti, and his replacement in January 1771 signaled the end of the expedition.

These great victories on land and at sea did not yet open the road to Constantinople for two reasons. As in 1711 and unlike 1735, the Russians had focused on the Danubian sector, leaving the territory of the Crimean Khanate outside the theater of operations. But a farther advance to and across the Danube exposed the army's communications and supply lines to Tatar raids and the possibility of Ottoman landings on the peninsula and in the estuary of the Dniepr. The first task was to remove that threat. Once that was done, the advance still could not resume until Ottoman fortresses on the left bank of the Danube had been captured and until the river had been crossed. Rumiantsev would now have to cope with the same difficulties and dangers that Saltykov, his superior, had faced along the Oder in 1760. Only then could the Russians challenge the Ottomans in Bulgaria and move against Adrianople (Edirne), the sultan's summer capital.

Priority was thus given in 1771 to the occupation of the Crimea. The Second Army of 48,000 men, now led by Vasilii Dolgorukov, was deployed along the so-called Dniepr Line, built the previous year along the two steppe rivers, Konka and Berda, linking the Dniepr with the Sea of Azov to block all Tatar invasion routes into the Left-Bank Ukraine. Recalling Münnich's poor planning in 1735–38, the Council ordered the creation of large magazines along the line with adequate supplies for the entire campaign. Nearly half of the army's strength was assigned to cover communications between the advancing troops and the line to guarantee a steady flow of supplies. The campaign began in June, with operations on land supported by the Azov flotilla of galleys and landing crafts. Dolgorukov's main force crossed the Perekop isthmus and moved toward Kaffa, the major commercial port and slave trade center on the southern coast. Separate detachments took Kerch and Enikale and crossed the strait to capture Taman, opening the Black Sea to the flotilla that would become the core of the future Black Sea fleet. Other troops took Akhtiar, the site of the future Sevastopol, and the campaign ended with the occupation of Bakhchisarai, the khan's capital.[20] Münnich's Crimean campaign had taken three years, only to fail; Dolgorukov's took three weeks and brought the khanate to its knees. Russia's ability not only to carry out deep strategic penetrations into what had long been forbidden territory but also to gain staying power there had grown tremendously in thirty years; in another twelve, the Crimea would be annexed to the empire.

Rumiantsev did not remain inactive in the Danubian sector. His First Army of 45,000 men sought to consolidate Russia's hold on Wallachia. It was deployed along the Danube from Vidin to Kilia, but the Ottomans still retained two major fortresses on the left bank: Zhurzha (Giurgiu), on the shortest route between Bucharest and the Danube, and Turno (Turnu), near the confluence of the Olt, separating Great from Little Wallachia to the west. Military operations there had political implications, and the friendly kingdom began to look askance at Russia's project: Little Wallachia was the gate to Hungary and Serbia, and Belgrade led to Vienna. It was known that the Austrians were concentrating troops in Transylvania, from which it was easy to cross the Carpathians into Moldavia and Wallachia. A strategy of deep penetration into Ottoman territory, which would eventually trans-form the Danube into another moat along the imperial periphery, threatened to un-dermine the policy of relying on the friendly kingdom as the anchor of the client system in the western theater. A way had to be found to reconcile strategy with diplomacy: the partition of Poland would provide the solution. In the meantime, the Russians were testing their abilities to cross the river. Zhurzha was taken in Feb-ruary, retaken by the Ottomans, and taken back by the Russians, but Turno held out. Nevertheless, they ventured across the lower Danube into Dobrudja, taking Isakcha (Isaccea) in April and Tulcha (Tulcea) in October and reaching Babadag, where the grand vizier kept his headquarters at the time, while other detachments took Machin and Hirsovo (Harsova). All these fortresses were destroyed. These for-ays across the river eliminated the Ottomans' forward position, which, in the event of a crossing by Rumiantsev's main force between Turnu and Silistria, would threaten his rear in Moldavia. Still, he kept hesitating to commit himself to crossing the river and launching operations into Bulgaria because of a shortage of pontoons and fears that spring floods and ice would destroy the bridge and leave his forces stranded on the Ottoman side. He also complained of a shortage of trained recruits; his regiments were at half strength. Once on the other side, his troops advancing into Bulgaria would be threatened by strikes from three Ottoman fortresses on the right bank: Rushchuk (Ruse) facing Zhurzha, Turtukai (Tutrakan), and Silistria, forming the base of a triangle pointing to Shumla (Šumen), the Ottoman base of operation, from which reinforcements could move quickly to repel an invasion. Rumiantsev had every reason to believe that the Ottomans would check his every move in Bulgaria and might even cut off his retreat to the left bank.[21] An illegiti-mate son of Peter I, he must have remembered the Prut expedition and the tsar's humiliating defeat.

He was spared the necessity to reach a decision by the suspension of hostilities in 1772, while a congress was negotiating an end to the war. Important develop-ments in the western theater required the imperial government's attention: the par-tition of Poland; the coup d'état in Stockholm, which brought about the withdrawal of several regiments from the First Army to cope with expected disorders in Swe-

den; and Swedish troop movements in Finland threatening the security of Petersburg. An armistice was signed in March, establishing the Danube as the line of demarcation between Russian and Ottoman troops, after Catherine abandoned as impracticable a project to send a naval expedition to Constantinople. Negotiations
began at Fokshany in July, then soon broke down, but resumed in Bucharest in October. They failed again, largely because the Ottomans were not ready to recognize
the independence of the Crimea. War resumed in 1773. By then, the empress was
more determined than ever to override Rumiantsev's objections. In February, he
was instructed to cross the Danube and take Shumla. Deceiving the Ottomans
about his intentions was crucial to success. He ordered Grigorii Potemkin to launch
a flanking movement from Hirsovo to take Silistria from the rear, but Potemkin
failed. However, Alexander Suvorov crossed the Danube downstream from Tur-
kukai in a similar operation and took the fortress in June, allowing Rumiantsev to
cross with his main force, but he returned a few days later, claiming he needed an
army three times larger before he could face the Ottomans in the field. The remainder of the year was spent conducting secondary operations in Dobrudja and a
half-hearted attempt on Varna, provoking anger and consternation in Petersburg. A
second attempt was made in 1774, and Rushchuk and Silistria were blockaded and
neutralized, while the main force defeated the Ottomans at Kozludja in June and
moved on toward Shumla.[22] Ottoman resistance broke down, and peace was signed
at Kuchuk Kainardji (Kainardža) in July: the Crimea became independent, while
the Russians annexed Kerch, Enikale, and Kinburn. The goal of the war had been
reached: the Ottoman hegemony on the Black Sea had been irreparably damaged.
But the war also exposed a serious gap between the objectives of the empire's
strategy in the southern theater and its military capabilities. More disappointments
were in store.

The peace of 1774 could not last. The Russians had gained only a narrow access to the Black Sea and the Ottomans were not ready to accept the independence
of the Tatar nation, which they understood all too well was just a front for the eventual annexation of the peninsula and the Tatar pastures on the mainland. The
khanate, the last remnant of the Chingissid Empire, had lorded over the southern
steppe for three hundred years, giving the Ottoman high command the northern
cover they needed to pursue their traditional strategy along a west-east axis from
Bosnia to Georgia and Baghdad. Civil war broke out between the supporters of two
rivals for the title khan, and Suvorov foiled an Ottoman attempt to land at Sudak
and Kaffa in 1778. Five years later, Petersburg announced the annexation of the
peninsula and the territory between the Don and the Kuban. Two army corps were
deployed in the region, one in the Crimea, the other north of the Kuban, forming,
via the strait of Kerch, a forward perimeter facing the entire northern coast of the
Black Sea. In the bay of Akhtiar, the Russians laid the foundations of Sevastopol,
from which the future Black Sea fleet's mission would be to support land operations
on the lower Danube and along the Bulgarian coast, raid Turkish cities on the coat
of Anatolia, and support attacks against Anapa and Sudzhuk Kale on the Caucasian
shores. Nevertheless, the empire's access to the sea would remain insecure as long
as the Ottomans retained Ochakov and the so-called Ochakov steppe between the
Ingul and the Dniestr, which Rumiantsev had considered in 1773 a worthier

objective than crossing the Danube and Russia had failed to gain in the peace treaty.

The annexation of the Crimea and the Kuban steppe was part of a broad political offensive resulting from the imperial army's deep strategic penetration across the steppe to the Danube and across the Caucasus. Only a few months after the annexation, the governor general of the northern Caucasus signed in Georgievsk a treaty of vassalage with Erekle II, the tsar of eastern Georgia. He had been lukewarm to Totleben's expedition in 1769, in part because it gave priority to western Georgia. The treaty now provided for the stationing of two infantry battalions in Tiflis and the construction of a road across the mountains from a new fort on the Terek to be called Vladikavkaz, "the dominator of the Caucasus."[23] The move pursued a triple objective: to threaten the rear of the mountain peoples in the Kabardas, Chechnia, and Dagestan, who were increasingly restive at the encroachments of the settler and the Cossack on the approaches to the mountains; to challenge the Ottomans' interference in Georgia; and to obliterate Erekle's status as a client of the Persian Empire. Catherine's ostentatious trip to the Crimea in 1787 was an additional challenge, which the Ottomans answered with a declaration of war.

It was a war for which neither the Russians nor the Ottomans were ready, despite the warlike rhetoric. Indeed, the two battalions were withdrawn from Tiflis and the foundations of Vladikavkaz — "the dominator of the Caucasus" — blown up, exposing for all to see the limited capabilities of the empire in Transcaucasia. Nevertheless, Grigorii Potemkin, the imperial proconsul in so-called New Russia and the Crimea, had drawn up in 1785 an operational plan to take Ochakov, then cross the Danube toward the Balkan Mountains and Adrianople, while a separate force would invade Transcaucasia via Derbent, which would have meant war with Persia as well.[24] There was something quite traditional about such a plan: the organic unity of the Black Sea basin dictated that operations against the Ottomans must aim at the Danube and the Caucasus: that had been the case in 1711 and 1769. But an advance on Derbent and Baku meant an invasion of the Caspian basin, Persia's sphere of influence. The expedition of 1796 would show that the empire did not yet have the military capability to fight both powers at the same time from widely separated regional headquarters like Kiev and Astrakhan. Only the establishment of an unchallengeable forward operational base in Tiflis would give it interior lines in Transcaucasia sufficiently short to fight both Ottomans and Persians, either separately or even at the same time. Such a base did not yet exist in 1787.

Once operations in the Caucasus had been ruled out, the objective of this new Russo-Turkish war was once again to reach the Danube and cross into Bulgaria, but not until the Ochakov steppe had been occupied, justifying Rumiantsev's earlier concerns that an advance beyond the river had been premature before its rear was fully secured. Very large forces were again committed to the southern theater for a decisive blow that would "shake the Turkish monarchy to its foundations." Two armies were formed, as in 1768: the Ekaterinoslav Army of 75,000 men under Potemkin, its staging area between the Dniestr and the Bug, and the Ukrainian Army of 48,000 under Rumiantsev in the Kiev area. The Crimean and Kuban Corps remained in place to block any Ottoman attempt to land in the peninsula. Consideration was given to sending another naval expedition around western Europe to the Greek archipelago, but Britain's unfriendly stance made that impossible. Potemkin, who, as president of the College of War, outranked Rumiantsev, assumed the offensive against Ochakov, while Rumiantsev was sent against Khotin to link up with the Austrians in Bukovina and remain on the defensive until the capture of Ochakov. For Potemkin, taking Ochakov and its steppe hinterland had more than strategic value: it would round out his bailiwick in New Russia and facilitate the development of the Kherson naval headquarters and shipyards.[25]

But the war did not begin well and dark clouds were rising over the western theater. Gustav III, in another foolish misunderstanding of Sweden's relative position vis-à-vis the empire, took advantage of the fact that almost the entire strategic force had been sent against the Ottomans to embroil Russia in a naval war in the Gulf of Finland. In Prussia, Frederick II had died in 1786; his nephew and successor chose to believe he was not a client of the empire. Meanwhile Poland was in the throes of a revolution that would bring about the complete partition of the country. In a word, the clients in the western theater were in full revolt, no longer overwhelmed by Russia's awesomeness. Khotin surrendered in August, but Ochakov was not stormed until December. Tensions between Potemkin and Rumiantsev — there was no room for two field marshals in command of large bodies of troops in the same Danubian sector — were resolved by the merger of both armies under Potemkin in 1789. Nevertheless, despite the fact that the single army now exceeded 100,000 men and operated jointly with the Austrian corps moving along the Seret from Bukovina, it scored few successes, besides the capture of Bendery and Akkerman (Belgorod-Dniestrovskii), which controlled the entire lower course of the Dniestr. Peace was made with Sweden in 1790; the "friendly kingdom" then left the war, and Suvorov stormed Izmail in December. After three years of war, and without any of Rumiantsev's victories of 1770 to its credit, the imperial army had barely reached the lower Danube. The following year, 1791, was one of crisis with Prussia and Britain, but it also saw the end of the war. After suffering defeats at Babadag, Machin, and Anapa, the Ottomans sued for peace. Potemkin, who died in October, was spared a final disappointment. Although the Treaty of Jassy gave the Russians Ochakov and its steppe hinterland, it also returned to the Ottomans Akkerman and Izmail. The Dniestr became the empire's new border. This second Russo-Turkish War of Catherine's reign did not produce any deep penetrations into Ottoman territory. It was instead as if the advance had stalled, and indeed it had, for nearly forty years. Only the consolidation of Russian power in the Right-Bank Ukraine and New Russia — the lands of the Tatar nomads now open to colonization and agriculture — could henceforth generate enough surge capability to launch imperial armies across the Danube and the Balkan Mountains on their way to Constantinople.

## Marking Time

The imperial government's determination to impose on Sweden the status of a client state, openly avowed in 1743, only increased after the return of the Caps to power in 1765, but it also created a backlash. There was nostalgia for Sweden's "age of greatness" in the seventeenth century and for Charles XII — after Gustav Adolf, the greatest of the country's kings — even if his misguided strategy and political blindness were largely responsible for defeat in the Northern War. The accession in 1771 of Gustav III, an unsteady individual fond of theatrical gestures, made matters worse when he decided to capitalize on the national mood to stage a coup d'état in the summer of 1772, soon after hearing the news of the first partition of Poland. The coup replaced the constitution of 1720, which had suited Russian interests so well, with a new one giving the royal power preeminence over parliament. It also implied a rejection of Sweden's client status, and only the redeployment of their strategic force to the southern theater kept the Russians from reasserting their claims. The justified expectation that the return of strong royal power would be accompanied by a forward policy explained the signing a year later in Petersburg of a treaty of mutual assistance with Denmark, the latter pledging 12,000 troops and a squadron of fifteen ships, the Russians 20,000 troops and ten warships in the event either country was attacked by Sweden. Gustav III, like Charles XII, would face a war on two fronts and could only hope that a Russo-Turkish war would free his hands in the west and allow him to attack Denmark in Norway; the two countries were then under the same crown. This he vainly hoped to do in 1783, at the time of Russia's annexation of the Crimea. When Russia went to war against the Ottomans in 1788, the king, carried away by delusions of grandeur, attacked both Denmark and Russia. The parallel with Charles XII was striking, but the geopolitical environment had changed radically since then.[26] Nevertheless, the Russians were unable to mount a general offensive against Sweden, which, if past practice in the 1710s and 1743 was any guide, would have involved deep strikes across Finland and an attempt to cross the Bothnian moat to the Swedish coast. There was no choice but to assume a forward defensive stance and wait for a propitious time to impose a final capitulation on Sweden.

The Baltic navy was in poor shape, the Guard was the only organized force, and the 19,000 men who were sent to the front in 1788 consisted of government clerks convicted of misdemeanors, household servants, coachmen, Gypsies, sons of clergy, poor nobles, even hard labor convicts. Orders were sent to recruit Bashkirs, Kalmyks, even Kazakhs. This disorderly mass was placed under the command of Valentin Musin-Pushkin, a "windbag," in Catherine's own words, without any military talents.[27] The Swedish plan called for an army of 36,000 to capture Nyslott and Willmanstrand while the king attacked Frederikshamn. If the two forces were successful, they would then link up and march on Vyborg, while the Swedish navy, from its operational base in Karlskrona, attacked Kronstadt and landed at Krasnaia Gorka for a concerted offensive on Petersburg. It was much too simple. The Swedes could not take Nyslott, and when Finnish soldiers decided to go home, they had to withdraw. They invested Fredrikshamn, but were forced to lift the siege by the Russians, who then moved on Willmanstrand to block the approaches to Vyborg. There were successes at sea. The Kronstadt squadron under Admiral Samuel Greigh defeated the advancing Swedes off Hogland Island, blasting Swedish hopes for a quick and decisive victory at Kronstadt, and blockaded them in Sveaborg, off Helsingfors, where Gustav had built a Gibraltar-like fortress, but Catherine refused to commit more troops to attack it from the landside. After Greigh's untimely death, the Russians allowed the Swedes to retreat to Karlskrona.[28]

The 1788 campaign ended in a stalemate on land and at sea, but for Gustav III, it was a political disaster. The Swedish offensive—disguised as a defensive operation when Swedish soldiers dressed in Russian uniforms crossed the border and fired on their countrymen—brought about the so-called Anjala League, named after a small Finnish town on the Kiumeme River, in which Swedish generals and superior officers accused the king of making war without the approval of parliament and refused to obey his orders.[29] The formation of the league was not only an act of insubordination by members of the aristocracy who resented the king's absolutism; it was also, in part, the expression of a separatist movement, in which those officers betrayed their country in the name of Finnish independence and sought Russian support. In the chaotic political pluralism created by the constitution of 1720, Swedes in Finland had developed a separate identity based on territorial separateness, Finland being cut off from Sweden during the long winter months. Even Lewenhaupt, the Swedish commander in chief in 1742, had entertained the idea of a separate Finland under his own leadership.[30] Gustav, however, was able to rally the country behind his rule by appealing to the peasantry, and Swedish pride was challenged by Catherine's call on the Finns to summon a provincial assembly under Russian protection to expel the Swedes—a reminder to their contemporaries of the confederations that were destroying the Polish Empire. The result was the Act of Union and Security of 1789, which tightened the king's power, but Gustav's fate was sealed. He was assassinated three years later.

The war resumed in 1789, without either side being able to break the stalemate. The Russians, keeping to their strategy of forward defense, captured St. Mikhel (Mikkeli), an important supply base, but could not keep it. Their navy engaged the Swedes off Bornholm Island, forcing them to retreat to Karlskrona. The stalemate did not deter the empress, who called for the occupation of Finland in 1790 and a naval assault on Sweden. Musin-Pushkin was replaced by Ivan Saltykov, who proved unequal to the task. The operational plan called for the army to advance along the coast of the Gulf of Finland, forming the right wing of a broad thrust directed against Åbo, the galley fleet hugging the shore, and the fleet of ships of the line forming the left wing. At the time, the Russians had twenty-nine ships of the line and thirteen frigates, the Swedes twenty-five and twenty, respectively. The Swedish plan was to destroy the Russian fleet at Reval and Kronstadt and try another landing at Krasnaia Gorka. The campaign quickly turned into a naval war. The Swedes failed when Admiral Vasilii Chichagov inflicted on them a crushing defeat in Vyborg Bay, where Gustav barely escaped with his life. Cannon fire was heard in Petersburg and the Court was ready to abandon the capital. But a week later, the Russian galley fleet, which had first bottled up the Swedish galley fleet in Kotka Bay, suffered in turn a crushing defeat off Svensksund (Rochensalm) Island, the Russians losing 10,000 men, including 6,000 prisoners of war.[31] Sweden was exhausted, however, and the king knew he had lost the war, whose success so depended on the element of surprise and a successful strike against Petersburg. Russia's war potential was such that the imperial army would regain the initiative sooner or later and shatter the Swedish hold on Finland. He initiated negotiations and peace was made in August 1790, on the basis of the status quo ante bellum. For the first time in their eighteenth-century wars, the Russians had been unable to carry out a deep strategic force into enemy territory. The commitment of their entire strategic force to the southern theater had destroyed their offensive strategy to keep operations contained beyond the imperial periphery. The Treaty of Jassy a year later confirmed that they were marking time in the southern theater as well.

The Russians were also marking time in Poland, but in a different way, and their grand strategy there was likewise being challenged. They had made clear in 1733 that the election of a new king would require their approval, and the imperial proconsuls in Warsaw, notably Hermann von Keyserling (1733–44, 1749–52), made certain that Poland would remain within the client system. There was no doubt that when Augustus III died in 1763, the new king would also be Russia's candidate. The event prompted Chernyshev, the "war minister," to submit a project of territorial annexation of eastern Bielorussia that showed a certain similarity between his vision and that of Peter I: the expansion of the empire was harmful because it generated an outflow of people who should be kept instead to populate the core (*seredina*).[32] Once borders advanced, he wrote, troops must be deployed to the frontier regions to defend them and maintain order. The revenue collected in the core was spent outside, resulting in an increase of the money supply and of trade in those regions and the equivalent impoverishment of the core. Chernyshvev was willing to compromise this zero-sum conception of economic activity by claiming that Russia needed to find "natural borders" along rivers, which in the western theater were the horizontal roads intersecting the corridors of troop deployment issuing from Moscow and Petersburg, the two great hubs of the empire. Rivers were preferable to land borders because they could easily be defended with a small number of fortresses while regular troops remained kept within the core. Such natural borders were also channels of trade, but trade directed inland to boost the core's economy, making it easier for the population to support a large force of intervention as its well-being increased. Therefore, Russia should round out its western border along the Dvina and the Dniepr, connected by their tributaries the Ulla and the Drut, forming a continuous waterway between the two regional headquarters, Riga and Kiev, "facing Europe" (*k storone Evropy*), to which Russia obviously did not belong.

The fact that the "first" partition of Poland in 1772 would move the imperial periphery to precisely that "natural border" did not make Chernyshev's project one of partition of the Polish Empire, if only because partition implies sharing the spoils with someone else, and the project made no reference to partners. The election of Stanislas Poniatowski, the last Polish king, took place in 1764, with 3,000 Russian troops encamped outside Warsaw and 36,000 deployed along the border. It was thus clear that the Russians were determined to maintain their dominion over the entire Polish Empire with a new proconsul in Warsaw, Nikolai Repnin, the nephew of the imperial "foreign minister," Nikita Panin. Thirty years later, however, the Polish Empire, Russia's major client state, would cease to exist, its eastern marches occupied by the Russians who had been expelled from Poland proper. While the three partitions may be accounted a major political and diplomatic success, they also marked a strategic retreat.

Scholars will continue to debate who was responsible and what the partitions meant, but, as in the famous Japanese garden where no observer can ever see the fifteen stones no matter what position he occupies, they will never reach an agreement. We must limit ourselves here to the geopolitical and military consequences of the empire toward the friendly kingdom and the Prussian state. The partitions were inseparable from the reassignment of strategic priorities to the southern theater at the beginning of Catherine's reign and from the commitment of the strategic force to a massive onslaught on Ottoman hegemony in the Black Sea basin. The Russian occupation of Moldavia and Wallachia and the proclamation of the independence of the Tatar nation revolutionized the situation in a region where the friendly kingdom had vital interests, generating hostility in Vienna and forcing it to assume a posture of active defense against the growing Russian Empire. Similar consequences followed in Berlin, where long-standing territorial ambitions and resentment at the patronizing policy of the empire meshed to create a determination to stand up to Petersburg. The acquisition of West Prussia merged Brandenburg with East Prussia and brought the commercial towns of the lower Vistula under Prussian control, prompting Frederick II to boast that Brandenburg would never again fear hunger. He might have added that those towns had been the supply bases of the imperial Russian army during the Seven Years' War and that their annexation stripped the empire of its ability to make war on Prussia. The Austrian share of Poland, by far the largest in size and population, stretched to the Bug and the Zbruch and expelled the Russians from the approaches to the Carpathians between Silesia and the sources of the Prut, barring their access to Budapest and Vienna.[33] It is hard to believe that Chernyshev, who had fought at Zorndorf in 1758, did not realize the Russians had been had.

A similar conclusion may be reached from the partitions of 1793 and 1795. Once peace had been made with the Ottomans, nearly 100,000 imperial troops, or most of the strategic force, were redeployed for an invasion of Poland from two directions, across Lithuania and from Moldavia. The invasion began in the spring of 1792; the Battle of Dubienka forced the Poles to surrender. In January 1793, Russia and Prussia signed a treaty of partition, the Russian boundary running from Druia on the Dvina past Pinsk to the Zbruch. But Prussia gained much of Great Poland west of a line running from Częstochowa via Rawa to Soldau on the East Prussian border, only 80 kilometers from Warsaw. Two Baltic Germans now ruled in Warsaw: Jakob von Sievers, the new ambassador, and Otto von Igelström, the commander in chief of all imperial troops in Poland. A year later, in March 1794, an uprising broke out in Kraków led by Tadeusz Kościuszko. In April, another caught the Russians by surprise in Warsaw, followed by a third in Vilno. The Russian counteroffensive was delayed by differences in Petersburg, but Vilno was retaken by Repnin at the end of July. Rumiantsev, who commanded imperial troops on both sides of the Dniepr, ordered Suvorov to move into southern Poland and reclaim Warsaw. Suvorov marched from Nemirov to Brest-Litovsk, crushing Polish resistance at Maciejowice in October, where Kościuszko was taken prisoner. Warsaw surrendered three weeks later.[34] The declaration of December 1794 proclaimed the end of the Polish Empire.

But what did these deep strikes by the Russians achieve? In 1794, the Russian Empire, very much against Chernyshev's wishes, reached the Niemen and the Bug, Poland's approximate ethnic boundaries in the east, and ended on the Zbruch. In other words, Russia incorporated the eastern marches of the Polish Empire but was expelled from the Polish core, now divided between Austria and Russia, with Warsaw in the Prussian zone. In 1762, the Russian ambassador had been the empire's proconsul in the entire Polish Empire all the way to the Oder, the Vistula forming the logistical axis for the supply of imperial troops facing Brandenburg, Silesia, and the Carpathians, and Russia basked in its clients' perception of the empire's awesomeness. By 1795, the revolt of the Swedes, the Prussians, and the Austrians had destroyed the client system in the western theater, and Petersburg had been forced to carry out a seven-hundred-kilometer strategic withdrawal from the Oder to the Niemen and the Bug. Even Danzig, Poland's last "spoonful of seawater,"[35] in which the Russians had taken a very special interest, had been lost. Russia, Prussia, and Austria had become immediate neighbors. Any future conflict would have to be fought on the imperial periphery or even behind it, requiring the adoption of a defense-in-depth strategy. But major geopolitical realignments were about to take place in Europe in the wake of the French Revolution; the empire was only marking time.

It was marking time in the Caspian sector as well. After two long wars with the Ottomans and the destruction of the Polish Empire, Catherine revived the Petrine project to gain control of the southern shore of the Caspian. The 1796 expedition was part of a broad offensive across the entire southern theater against both Ottomans and Persians. As early as 1794, the empress was contemplating a war on the Ottomans that would take Russian troops to Constantinople. Her new entourage, led by the Zubov brothers, dreamt of conquests that would outshine those of Rumiantsev and Potemkin.[36] The Russians had withdrawn from Transcaucasia in 1735 and did not resume a forward strategy for nearly fifty years. In 1780, Suvorov was sent to Astrakhan to prepare a large expedition against the khanates of eastern Transcaucasia, all clients of Persia, but nothing came of it, even though Georgia became a client state of the empire three years later. The event was a direct challenge to Persia, where the Zand dynasty was weakening. It was overthrown in 1792 by Aga Muhammad Khan, the chief of the Qajar tribe, who transferred the capital to Tehran. In an effort to reclaim Georgia, he sent a punitive expedition against Tiflis in 1795, challenging Russia to reply in kind.[37] Sometime in the 1790s, a former governor general of the Caucasus, Ivan Iakobi, drew up an ambitious project to make war on Persia and China. It called for the creation of large reserves of provisions in Tsaritsyn and Astrakhan, from which a combined land and naval operation would take Derbent, Baku, and Rasht—this last place providing a convenient bridgehead for a move on Tehran.[38] By then, a consensus had developed in Petersburg that the Caspian sector must be the next object of Catherine's increasing megalomania.

The command of the expedition was first offered to Suvorov, who declined it, then given to Catherine's favorite's brother, Valerian Zubov, who was only a lieutenant general and had neither the talent nor the experience to command such a delicate enterprise. His instructions called for an advance, not across the mountains, but along the coastal route to Baku. He was to restore Erekle on his throne and annex the Ganzha and Erivan Khanates to the Georgian kingdom in order to gain a decisive influence on Ottoman and Persian affairs. An amphibious landing in Enzelinsk (Bandar-e Anzali) and Astrabad (Bandar-e Turkoman) would bring back into the empire the three provinces annexed in 1723 and, with the help of the Turkmens, destroy the new Persian dynasty. Astrabad would lead on to Khiva.

To ensure the loyalty of the Georgians, Zubov would demand hostages from Erekle, including his heir and the favorite sons of his second wife. Provisions would follow from Astrakhan, Kizliar, and the Caucasian Line, by ship and across the mountains.[39]

Zubov took over the command of the Caspian Corps of 30,000 men in February 1796 and left Kizliar in May, already late in the season, before the great summer heat. He took Derbent without resistance and received the keys of the city from a very old man who had given them to Peter in 1722, causing premature enthusiasm in Petersburg. Then Zubov fell victim to his own lack of foresight. The Kizliar magazine was inadequate, and there were almost no provisions or transport ships in Astrakhan. The Georgians had promised to deliver supplies, as they had in 1769, but did so with considerable delays. The country's subsistence agriculture had few ties with the market, grain had to be shipped in open barrels because there were no sacks, and it was impossible to buy enough carts to transport whatever was bought. Harassment by parties descending from the mountains became such a permanent threat that Zubov had to call for more troops to garrison forts and defiles and maintain communications with Kizliar. The men began to suffer from the heat. Nevertheless, Zubov moved on, taking Baku in July and Ganzha in December, but his supply line was becoming dangerously overextended. The amphibious operation failed to achieve its purpose, and Zubov discovered he had reached a dead end. He had not been able to accomplish as much as Peter had seventy years earlier, yet his ambition had been even greater. Not only had he intended to restore Russia's dominion over the southern shores of the Caspian, he had also expected to reach Isfahan, the old capital, by September, and unbelievable as it may sound to the modern reader, Constantinople five years later. But in so doing, the new Alexander the Great, by means of unprecedented strategic penetrations, would have asserted the empire's hegemony within the Heartland along the Taurus and Zagros Mountains. Catherine and her immediate entourage had obviously lost all touch with what was feasible, yet the strategic vision was both grandiose and clear; it still informed Russian foreign policy in 1915.[40] In the meantime, even if Zubov failed and the empire had to mark time on the Kura, the expedition paved the way for the annexation of Georgia five years later and the creation of a base of operations in Transcaucasia from which the Russians would destroy both Ottoman and Persian hegemony in the region.

Megalomania did not reign only at the Court. In distant Irkutsk, Governor General Iakobi (1783–88) was thinking of war with China, but was recalled when Petersburg found out. Such a war would have a triple purpose: to humble the Chinese whose "arrogance" and "unbearable pride" refused to recognize Russia's awesomeness; to establish trade relations with China and Japan and create a client state in Korea; and to annex the entire massif of the Altai, with its great mineral wealth. Iakobi's project provided a good example of Russia's "strategic culture" of deep penetrations across enormous distances toward the enemy's capital. Three corps were assigned to the war. About 30,000 troops would march or be transported on barges from the Moscow region to Kazan, Ekaterinburg, Tobolsk, Tomsk, Krasnoiarsk, and Irkutsk. They would cross Lake Baikal to Verkhne-Udinsk (Ulan-Ude), where they would link up with troops coming from the Dniepr region via Tambov,

Simbirsk, Bashkiria, and Tomsk. In Verkhne-Udinsk, 6,000 kilometers from Moscow, they would split to form two corps, one moving on to Kiakhta on the Mongolian border, the other to Nerchinsk on the Manchurian border. The third corps, consisting of troops coming from the same two regions, would swing southward after reaching Ekaterinburg toward Ust-Kamenogorsk. The first and second corps, supplied from magazines in Irkutsk and Chita, would advance into Mongolia toward Peking, 1,700 kilometers from Kiakhta, while the third, supplied from Kolyvan, would occupy the Altai Massif and Lake Zaisan and build a line along the new periphery of the empire from the lake to the Aral Sea. The new imperial periphery would be moved to the Gobi Desert and follow the Amur to its mouth. From there, Russia would open up Hokkaido and Korea to trade and establish itself in one of the best Korean ports. The project, which bears an uncanny resemblance to Alexei Kuropatkin's recommendations of 1916, had no chance of being accepted at the time, but it also embodied a far-sighted strategic vision that would become official policy after the 1860s.[41]

But by the time of Catherine's death in November 1796, the empire was clearly marking time. In the western and southern theaters, its grand strategy had fallen victim to its emphasis on deep strikes. In the former the Seven Years' War focused on a massive onslaught against the Oder in order to reach Berlin, relegating to second place the main political interest of reducing Prussia to a modest size by establishing a client society in Pomerania; and in Poland, the empire suffered a strategic setback. In the southern theater, the insistence on crossing the Danube on the way to Adrianople obscured the importance of securing the Ochakov steppe, without which the deep strike was doomed to fail; Zubov failed at the gates of Persian Azerbaijan. Moreover, the enormous transformation of the geopolitical environment between 1772 and 1796 had fundamental consequences for the deployment of the strategic force and the operation of the client system.

# 5

# Peripheral Deployment

To trace the evolution of the army's deployment it will be best to take the beginning of Catherine's reign as our starting point; then to examine the changes brought about by the first partition of Poland, the acquisition of a frontage on the northern coast of the Black Sea, and the internal unrest known as the Pugachev Rebellion; and finally, to describe the deployment of the strategic force at the end of the eighteenth century following the other two partitions of Poland and the extension of imperial control over much of the northern shore of the Black Sea. This survey will show how the original policy of concentrated deployment was radically transformed to become one of peripheral deployment in the border regions.

## After the Seven Years' War: 1763

The army that fought Frederick II in the valley of the Oder slowly returned to the empire in the course of 1762 and was deployed in permanent quarters the following year. For the first time, the strategic force was given a quasi-regional organization; it was divided into eight "divisions"—in fact, nine if we include Siberia, where the troops formed a separate "corps." Four divisions were deployed in Russia proper, the largest with seventeen regiments and headquartered in Moscow. Its commander was Marshal Saltykov, the victor at Kunersdorf (1759), and now governor general of Moscow Province (*guberniia*), which incorporated at the time the entire Muscovite center from the Smolensk border to Nizhnii Novgorod. The Petersburg Division, the fourth largest with eleven regiments, was under Kiril Razumovskii, hardly a military man, who had been hetman of Little Russia since 1750 and president of the Academy of Sciences since 1746 and was promoted to field marshal in 1764. His deputy commander was Alexander Golitsyn, who would be given the command of the First Army in 1769 and was promoted to field marshal that same year, when he replaced Razumovskii and became the de facto governor general of the northern capital when the empress was away. The third was the Smolensk Division of nine regiments commanded, in absentia, by Chernyshev, the "war minister"; eight more

## Legend

| | |
|---|---|
| ■ | Regiment headquarters |
| — | Fortification lines |
| ·—·—· | Empire boundaries |
| ▨ | Cossack territories |
| ▨ | Serbo-Hungarian settlements |

Deployment of 1763

regiments constituted the Sevsk Division **under Lt. Gen. Christoph von Stoffeln.**
The other four divisions were in the border **regions, stationed** among some of the
client societies. Three were in the Baltic provinces: the Finland (Vyborg), Estland,
and Livland Divisions, with twenty-seven regiments, thirteen of them in the Livland Division alone—the third largest—under Marshal Alexander Buturlin, the former commander in chief of the army in 1761. Petr Panin, the foreign minister's
brother and future commander of the Second Army, in Vyborg, and Vasilii Dolgorukov, wounded at Küstrin in 1758 and who would lead the attack on the Crimea in
1771, in Reval, were full generals. The fourth was the Ukrainian Division of seventeen regiments commanded by General Rumiantsev, who had taken Kolberg in
1761 and became governor general of Little Russia in 1764 following the abolition of
the hetmanate. His headquarters was in Glukhov. Thus, of the eight divisional commanders only three—in Moscow and Glukhov, and in Petersburg with some reservations—also possessed a regional civil appointment as governors general, but the
three men also commanded most of the strategic force concentrated in the Muscovite center and its two wings, in the Baltic sector and on the Left-Bank Ukraine.

The deployment of 1763 showed a total of one hundred regiments, sixty-two of
them infantry, the other thirty-eight cavalry, and one Cossack regiment (no longer
included among the irregular troops but integrated into strategic force), for a total
strength of about 150,000 men. Garrisons were reorganized in 1764. Their twenty
Baltic (*Ostzeiskie*) and twenty-six internal regiments were broken up to form sixty-
five border battalions (because they were also stationed outside the Baltic provinces) and nineteen internal battalions, comprising about 65,000 men.[1]

None of the seventeen regiments of the Moscow Division was stationed in the
old capital, or in Tver and Iaroslavl. Almost no troops remained east of Moscow:
they had been shifted westward, and individual regimental headquarters became so
many transition points toward the other divisions deployed on the periphery. That
was true especially in the valley of the Oka, which led to the Little Russian border
and the Ukraine of Settlements. North of Moscow, the eleven regiments of the
Peterburg Division guarded the approaches to the northern capital from Livland
and Moscow, forming with the nine regiments of the Smolensk Division a well-
rounded strategic deployment facing the Bielorussian border. The three Guard
regiments (not included in the table) were stationed in Petersburg and its environs.
It was no coincidence that Chernyshev commanded the Smolensk Division: it was
he who drafted in 1763 the project of intervention in Poland in the event of the
king's death in order to impose Russia's candidate on the throne and round out the
empire's periphery along the new "natural borders." Those troops also operated as a
police force, patrolling the border in order to capture the numerous vagrants who
crossed into the Polish Empire. South of Smolensk, and filling the space between
the Moscow and Ukrainian Divisions, was the Sevsk Division of five regiments, deployed along a forward perimeter from which to strike at Gomel on the southern
fringe of Bielorussia or move into northern Little Russia to reinforce the troops of
the Ukrainian Division. There were no other troops in the area save for a garrison
battalion in Belgorod and another in Voronezh. Thus the deployment of 1763 retained the shift already noticeable in 1743 toward a more substantial military presence in the Petersburg area while withdrawing regiments that had been stationed

east of Moscow and even from the Elets-Tambov-Penza corridor in favor of a greater concentration in the valley of the upper Oka above Kaluga. As a result, the deployment in Russia proper created a strategic reserve for the new and massive concentration of troops in the Baltic provinces and the valley of the Dniepr.

A comparison between the deployments of 1725 and 1763 shows clearly their impacts on the local population. In 1725, seventy-one of the seventy-three regiments (excluding the two stationed in Bashkiria and Siberia) were stationed in nineteen of the twenty-six provinces of Russia proper (in their nineteenth-century borders). The number of regiments per province varied from one to nine, the heaviest concentrations in Moscow, Vladimir, Nizhnii Novgorod, Iaroslavl and Kazan—along the Volga axis of Fortress Russia—the lowest in Orel on the fringe of the *odnodvortsy* settlements, which manned the land militia. The burden was thus very unevenly distributed. In Moscow, Valdimir, and Nizhnii Novgorod Provinces there was one regiment (of about 1,500 officers and men) for every 42,000–50,000 (male) inhabitants, in Tula one for every 80,000, and in Orel one for 353,000. In 1763, forty-five regiments were stationed in Russia, the largest concentration in Smolensk Province (nine) and Orel (eight), with only five regiments (instead of eight) in Moscow and four each in Petersburg and Pskov Provinces. The population had risen substantially by then, but the ratios were comparable; one regiment for every 40,000–47,000 inhabitants in Smolensk and Orel Provinces, 36,000 in Petersburg, but 62,000 in Pskov, and 79,000 in Moscow. The westward deployment had brought relief to the inhabitants of Vladimir Province, where one regiment now resided among 391,000 inhabitants. Even if the presence of troops often created frictions with the local population among whom they were quartered, it cannot be claimed that the deployment of the strategic force in Russia proper constituted a heavy burden on the population at the provincial level. In general, it was less heavy than in 1725: at that time, 100 percent of the strategic force had been stationed in Russia proper; in 1743, the number was 64 percent. These units constituted a central strategic reserve designed to maximize the empire's disposable military power kept available for deep penetrations into the western or southern theater. The strategic force still remained unfragmented and freely redeployable, notwithstanding a perceptible shift toward a theater strategy to be carried out by regional armies.

The decision to deploy a substantial number of troops in the Baltic provinces was as evident in 1763 as it had been twenty years earlier, at the conclusion of the war with Sweden. The situation in the Baltic sector remained uncertain, what with France more active than ever in supporting the restoration of the absolute monarchy in Sweden and the worsening health of Augustus III in Poland, whose death was certain to bring about a major succession crisis. And the rapprochement with Prussia did not obviate the need for close supervision of its moves in the aftermath of the Seven Years' War. All these factors combined to make the Baltic provinces one of the empire's most sensitive strategic sectors. Three divisions flanked that of Petersburg, which served as both a wing of a single strategic reserve and a regional reserve in its own right for those three divisions. Four of the six infantry regiments of the Finland Division were stationed in Vyborg, but the divisional headquarters was in Petersburg. Vyborg's massive fortress also housed a four-battalion garrison. The other two infantry regiments were in Fredrikshamn (with a two-battalion garrison) and the carbineer regiment was in **Kexholm on Lake Ladoga**. The deployment formed a triangle guarding the approaches to the capital from the north—Vyborg was about 150 kilometers away—but also a base of operation for immediate intervention in Finland while waiting for reinforcements from the Petersburg Division. The security of the northern capital was inseparable from that of Vyborg, which had once been Sweden's forward base of operations in Karelia, and during the War of 1788–90 both cities and provinces would be placed under a single governor general. The Estland Division flanked the Petersburg Division to the west. Its headquarters was in Reval, 350 kilometers from the capital. The city was also the headquarters of one of the two squadrons forming the Baltic Fleet, the other being in Kronstadt. The Estland Division was deployed inland, notably in Wesenberg (Rakvere), the site of one of the most grandiose castles in the region, with a substantial population of Old Believers in a sea of Lutheran Germans, and in Weissenstein (Paide), the residence of the Stackelbergs. Along the coast, military units carried out the dual responsibility of deterring a possible Swedish landing in the event of war, perhaps facilitated by the presence of Swedish fishermen and farmers in the region, and cracking down on spies and smugglers. A battalion was stationed in Rogervik (Baltiiskii Port, Pildiski), where the Russians were still vainly trying to build, with hard labor convicts, a naval base where the sea almost never froze. Such a port would have a substantial advantage over Reval: the ice broke there later than in Karlskrona, the Swedish naval headquarters, allowing the Swedes to reach the Russian squadron before it could put out to sea.

With thirteen regiments, the Livland Division was much larger. Its headquarters was in Riga, the great port on the Russian Baltic coast after Petersburg, the emporium for German, Swedish, Russian, Polish, and Lithuanian traders: five regiments were stationed there, in addition to a four-battalion garrison with another battalion at Dünamünde on the Dvina's estuary. The others were echeloned along the Riga road, which linked Petersburg with Königsberg and Riga with Kurland and Lithuania. The imperial military presence was much heavier in the Baltic provinces than anywhere else in the empire. In Vyborg province, poor in local resources, there was one regiment for every 11,321 inhabitants; in Estland, one for every 11,890, and in Livland, known for its extensive pastures, one for every 14,690 inhabitants. The westward shift of the strategic force had alleviated the burden in Russia as a whole but increased it tremendously in the Baltic provinces, where no troops had been stationed in 1725. This deployment in Estland and Livland created an infrastructure of regimental headquarters grafted upon the territorial division of the region into districts (*Kreise*), where the Baltic Germanic nobility kept a tight hold on the native peasantry. It helped maintain internal security in the Baltic provinces and facilitated the integration of the Germanic client society into the command structure of the imperial army from the Baltic to the Ural and Irtysh Rivers, where officers with Germanic names were prominent in the administration of the frontier territories. All three divisions—twenty-seven regiments—together with the eleven regiments of the Petersburg Division—a total of thirty-eight—and the Baltic fleet constituted a formidable strategic formation for the defense in depth of the northern capital and the Gulf of Finland. But this same formation, backed by reinforcements from the strategic reserve in the Muscovite center, was also a powerful force of intervention in the affairs of the Polish Empire and a permanent warning to East Prussia to keep the Prussian client state in line. Making up nearly 40 percent of the strategic force—47 percent if we include the Smolensk Division—it already began to look like "the army of the western theater," its own mission confined to a specific geographical space. Much depended on the geopolitical environment. If Sweden, Prussia, and Poland could be kept safely within the client system, and the cooperation of the friendly kingdom retained, these troops would remain mobile and freely redeployable to merge with the strategic reserve in order to maintain a single strategic force in being and available for operations in the southern theater.

The empire's strategic posture there remained offensive as it has been since the deployment of 1743, if not before, since Anna Ivanovna's reign witnessed Münnich's massive attack against the Crimea, followed by an attempt to reach the Danube. With seventeen regiments, the Ukrainian Division was as large as Moscow's and the fact that ten of them were infantry (with six carbineer and one dragoon regiment) showed conclusively that its mission was not to stop nomadic raids into the hetmanate and the Ukraine of Settlements but to stand ready to cross the Dniepr toward the Crimea and the Danube once again. This becomes even more obvious when we realize that most of those troops were the product of a reorganization of the force structure in the region and were added to the strategic force in order to extend the radius of operations in the southern theater, with its immense distances and sparse population. The Ukrainian Line was closed and the Landmilitia abolished.[2] Its twenty regiments were transformed into ten regular infantry regiments and their horse companies were combined to form a new dragoon regiment stationed in Pereiaslav, a short distance from the Dniepr. They were deployed between the Desna, which served as the line of advance for the troops of the Sevsk Division toward the Dniepr, and the Vorksla, beyond which stretched the old Ukrainian Line: near the Desna, on the Sula, on or near the Psël, on or near the Vorksla. All these rivers descended from the Central Upland and flowed into the Dniepr. Some of these locations were trading towns of some importance, especially Nezhin, where a large Greek colony controlled the region's trade with the Black Sea and the Danubian principalities; others were company headquarters of Little Russian Cossack regiments. One regiment was in Valki, where the walls were a reminder that the town stood on the old Tatar invasion route.

This core of infantry regiments was flanked in the west by the six cavalry regiments, former dragoons who had fought in the Seven Years' War. Their deployment straddled the Desna: in Starodub in the north, a very old fortified outpost between Muscovy and Lithuania and by the eighteenth century the chief market for almost all local products on the hetmanate, on the fringe of the Smolensk and Sevsk Divisions; in Chernigov, Sosnitsa, and Kozelets on or near the Desna, and in Priluki and Konotop farther south, adjoining the quarters of the infantry regiments. All these locations were also trading towns and company headquarters, and Priluki was even a regimental Cossack headquarters.

Also included in the Ukrainian Division were five regiments of hussars from the Ukraine of Settlements and four of Trans-Kama Landmilitia, which were slowly being transformed into regular units. The construction of the Ukrainian Line had challenged the raison d'être of the five territorial regiments of Slobodian Cossacks in Sumy, Akhtyrka, Kharkov, Izium, and Ostrogozhsk; this went a long way to explain the disintegration of that Cossack society by the late 1750s. These Cossacks were re-named hussars, and their regimental headquarters became district capitals in the new Kharkov province.[3] All these regiments were stationed in three provinces (in their nineteenth-century borders) — Chernigov, Poltava, and Kharkov — but their presence was much less obvious than in the Baltic provinces, ranging from one regi-ment for 56,226 inhabitants in Kharkov Province to one for every 73,150 in Chernigov Province.

They flanked the core of infantry in the east. At both ends of the Ukrainian Line were the Serb settlements. They went back to the early 1750s, when Colonel Ivan Khorvat reported to the Russian ambassador in Vienna that Orthodox Serbs wanted to emigrate and become subjects of the empire. Khorvat offered to organize the emigrants in two regiments, one of 1,000 hussars, the other of 2,000 infantry (*pandury*). They were settled beyond the Dniepr, along the Polish border on lands that the Zaporozhians considered their own: the hussars along the Vys River, a tributary of the Siniukha that flows into the Bug, the infantry along the lower course of the Tiasmin and the upper Ingulets. These regiments were settled troops and did not belong to the regular army, even though they were subordinated to the commander of the Ukrainian Line. They founded New Serbia. A little ahead of the hussar regiment, Fort St. Elizabeth (Elizavetgrad, Kirovograd) was founded in 1754, manned by some 2,000 Little Russian Cossacks. More Serb emigrants filled another two regiments of "settled hussars" of 1,000 men each, named after their colonels, Johann Shevich and Raiko Depreradovich, at the other end of the Ukrainian Line, between the Bakhmut district and the bend of the Donets below Lugansk. The re-gion was called Slavianoserbia.[4] Regular troops and auxiliary units were supple-mented by a network of garrisons: in Kiev, the largest in the empire (six battalions); in St. Elizabeth, south of the Dniepr, and Bakhmut, south of the Donets, both for-ward outposts exposed to Tatar raids; in Novokhopërsk on the Khopër River, along the ecological boundary between the wooded and the open steppe, on the fringe of the Don Cossack settlements. Farther east, four battalions were stationed in St. Dmitrii on the Don estuary and two in Kizliar on the Terek. Another four battalions were in Astrakhan and one in Tsaritsyn, on the line linking the Don with the Volga.

The deployment of 1763 in the southern theater was clearly offensive and had ominous implications for the client societies, the Crimean Tatars, the Ottomans, and the Poles. The Ukrainian Division, contained behind the Dniepr, was de-ployed in Cossack territory, where the population was increasingly bound to the soil as a result of its internal social evolution and under the impact of immigration from the north. The advance of the strategic force followed the advance of the settler into the frontier and accelerated the transformation of Cossack society. Beyond the Dniepr, the Serb military colonies created a fringe of settlement threatening the way of life of the Zaporozhian Cossacks and implanting a military presence backed by units of the strategic force in the open steppe where the rule of the nomad had been unchallenged. A force of seventeen regular regiments and auxiliary forces, commanded by a governor general whose sway extended over the entire former het-manate and deployed behind a fringe of settlements in the open steppe no longer protected by a defensive line, could have but one mission: to challenge the

Crimean Tatars. And they could not be challenged without provoking the Ottomans. No level of threat from the Tatars could justify a deployment of such magnitude in the valley of the Dniepr.[5] Moreover, the Ukrainian Division also faced across the river the southeastern march of the Polish Empire, that interlocking frontier between Russian, Ottomans, and Poles, the unavoidable line of advance toward the Danube and a rich source of supplies. The Russians faced no substantial threat from that region either. That the spark which set off the Russi-Ottoman conflagration in 1768, which in turn resulted in the Russian advance to the Black Sea littoral and the partition of the Polish Empire, should have been struck there is seen as no coincidence, once we become aware that the deployment of the Ukrainian Division was basically offensive.

In the eastern theater, the deployment of 1763 ignored the Orenburg Territory. No regular troops were stationed there. The four regiments of Trans-Kama Land-militia became part of the Ukrainian Division despite the great distances separating Kiev from Ufa, but they remained auxiliary troops. The Ural Cossacks, about 4,000, continued to police the imperial periphery along the Ural River west of Orenburg, while the Orenburg Cossacks, created officially in 1755 and numbering about 6,000 men, policed the middle and upper courses of the river east of the city.[6] Both Cossack formations were subordinated to the governor of Orenburg, first appointed in 1744. The withdrawal of regular troops resulted both from the absence of high intensity threats in the Caspian basin at the time—their withdrawal from the eastern provinces of Russia proper between the Oka and the Volga reflected similar perceptions—and from the concentration of all regular forces in the theater along the Irtysh, where relations with China had been very tense since the 1750s.

The Manchu offensive of 1755–60 against the Zunghars and its repercussions among the Kazakhs of the Middle Horde threatened to destabilize the entire frontier from the Aral Sea to Mongolia. Three separate Chinese armies of 50,000 men—the equivalent of the entire Russian strategic force—converged on the Ili region, creating panic among Zunghars and Kazakhs, while Chinese patrols appeared on Lake Zaisan and the Irtysh.[7] The precipitant had been the betrayal of the Manchus by a Zunghar chieftain who had fled to the Russians and was given asylum in Tobolsk, where he died of smallpox in 1757. The Manchu determination to exterminate the Zunghars, and the absence of a recognized border between the Manchu and Russian Empires in the area of Lake Zaisan and in the Altai, raised the threat to unprecedented levels and exposed the empire's weakness in the region. Only the recognition by the Manchus that the lake and the Altai represented an optimum of conquest beyond which a farther advance would be counterproductive saved the Russians from a major disaster on the fringe of settlement they had painstakingly built on the approaches to the mountains. Nevertheless, regular troops were sent in 1759 to the Siberian Line to reinforce Cossack outposts. These Siberian Cossacks numbered no more than 4,000 men,[8] scattered along the line and in various towns of the enormous Tobolsk Province. Their military value was nil against a well-organized army. In 1763, eleven regiments formed the so-called Siberian Corps. Four dragoon regiments were stationed in Petropavlovsk on the line linking the Ural River with the Irtysh, in Omsk, Zhelezinsk, and Iamyshev on the Irtysh. Farther up the river, another dragoon and an infantry regiment were in

Ust-Kamenogorsk facing Lake Zaisan, and two more dragoon regiments were in eastern Siberia, in Irkutsk and Selenginsk, which, along with Tobolsk and Tomsk, also had small garrisons. These troops merely showed the flag, served notice on China that the empire's posture in the eastern theater remained defensive, and suggested that an accommodation between the two empires would be of mutual interest.

Three features of the 1763 deployment thus stand out: the continuing expansion of the two wings in the Baltic sector and in Little Russia on the left bank of the Dniepr, the assumption of an offensive posture in the southern theater, and the retention of a defensive posture in the eastern theater even after the Chinese demonstration of strength against the Zunghars.

## The Emerging Force Structure: 1765–1796

Catherine's reign (1762–96) was a time of extraordinary territorial expansion, unseen since the annexation of the Volga Khanates in the 1550s and the "first" partition of the Polish Empire in 1686. The imperial periphery advanced seven hundred kilometers from the Dvina-Dniepr watershed to the Niemen and the Bug, four hundred kilometers from the middle Dniepr to the Black Sea shore, and five hundred to the Dniestr. While the eastern marches of the Polish Empire were settled and required only the establishment of an imperial infrastructure of agencies and regimental headquarters, the steppe was nearly empty and its settlement had a profound impact on the composition of the imperial army in the region. More troops were needed to secure imperial control in the new territories, and the imperial army grew in both size and diversity.

The table of organization of 1763 had called for an army of fifty infantry regiments (forty-six of musketeer and four grenadier regiments) and twenty-five of cavalry, keeping a 2:1 ratio between the two major arms. In fact, there were forty cavalry regiments in 1765 — five cuirassier, nineteen carbineer, nine hussar, and seven dragoon — but not including the Guard, consisting of three infantry regiments and one of cuirassiers. The total strength of the strategic force was estimated at about 150,000 men. The size of the infantry grew by creating new regiments and raising the number of battalions in each regiment. In 1786, there were, in addition to the Guard, seventy-six infantry regiments, including ten of grenadiers (four battalions in each), fifty-nine of musketeers (two battalions in each, save for two with four battalions), and seven "corps" of chasseurs (*Jäger*) of four battalions each, together with twelve so-called field battalions, for a total (with some other units) of 218,400 men. The chasseurs had been created in 1765 at the initiative of Petr Panin, the commander of the Finland Division, to take into account the conditions of warfare in Finland, where cavalry charges were nearly impossible but where quick movement and accurate firing were indispensable. Sixty chasseurs were added to each infantry regiment in the Finland, Estland, Livland, and Smolensk Divisions to form a first "corps" of 1,650 men. By 1786, the complement of each of the seven corps had grown to nearly 4,000 men, five of them in the western and two in the southern theater. The field battalions were at first called cohorts, then field units (*polevye komandy*), an original experiment in combined arms formations begun in 1771, each unit to consist of 532 officers and men, including 320 infantrymen, 57 chasseurs, 75 dragoons, and 34 artillerymen. Embarrassed by the flight of the Kalmyks across the Ural River, which the Ural Cossacks were unable to prevent, the government decided to create small units capable of moving quickly in the steppe to quell emergencies involving the nomads. These units were based in Astrakhan, Orenburg, and near Lake Baikal. The experiment was not a success and was abandoned in 1775, the units being transformed into infantry battalions. By 1795, the number of grenadier regiments had been raised to fifteen and that of chasseur "corps" to ten, bringing the total to eighty-two regiments (eighty-six including the Guard) with twenty field battalions, or 279,000 men, an 86 percent increase over the 1763 level.

The cavalry underwent a bewildering number of changes, largely reflecting Potemkin's imperial ambitions and love of colorful uniforms. By 1786, however, there were still five regiments of cuirassiers and ten of carbineers, but only one of hussars, all of six squadrons each, while the number of dragoon regiments had risen to ten (of ten squadrons each). There were also fifteen so-called light cavalry regiments of six squadrons each, bringing the total to fifty regiments and 62,400 men, a ratio of 1.6 infantry regiment to 1 of cavalry. In 1783, the Little Russian Cossacks had been abolished and their horsemen integrated into the carbineer regiments while the Slobodian Cossacks had become part of the light cavalry regiments. Ten years later, the number of carbineer regiments had been reduced to seventeen and of light cavalry to eleven, but the number of dragoon regiments had been raised to eleven and of hussars to two. Some of the abolished units went into forming one regiment of mounted grenadiers and three regiments of mounted chasseurs, for a total of fifty regiments (fifty-one including the Guard) and about 60,000 men, hardly any change since 1786. Thus, we can estimate the size of the strategic force at 150,000 men in 1763, 280,000 in 1786, and 340,000 in 1796, a 128 percent increase since 1763.[9]

As the empire expanded in fanlike fashion from its old center in Moscow toward the Vistula, the Black Sea coast, and the Caucasus, in the process incorporating client societies, which had permitted the imperial government to practice an economy of force and maximize the surge capability of its strategic force, a question began to be raised in the high command about the expediency of concentrated deployment: should that force not be fragmented into regional armies, adapted to carry out specific missions in separate theaters? As early as 1776, only four years after Kuchuk-Kainarji—the treaty that allowed Russia access to the Black Sea—Rumiantsev, now a field marshal, pointed out that the deployment of the army must be made to depend on political circumstances and correspond to the specific conditions of future theaters of war. He proposed the creation of four armies.[10] One, the Baltic or coastal (*pomorskaia*) army, would be deployed in the three Baltic provinces, and in Petersburg, Novgorod, Pskov, and Polotsk Provinces; it would incorporate the Finland, Petersburg, Estland, Livland, and Smolensk Divisions and would truly be the army of the western theater poised for operations against the Polish Empire. The second, or Ukrainian, army would be deployed in Mogilev, Voronezh, and Belgorod, the Ukraine of Settlements, and Azov province, which at the time included the former Zaporozhian territory, New Serbia, the continental part of the Crimean Khanate, and Kerch and Enikale on the peninsula, both acquired in 1774. Although Rumiantsev inexplicably did not mention them, it would include Little Russia, where he was governor general, as well as the Don Cossack Territory. The area of deployment would thus include all the left-bank tributaries of the Dniepr and the entire basin of the Don. The Ukrainian army would be, in fact, the army of the southern theater, poised to operate against the khanate and the Danube. The third, or eastern (*nizovaia*), army would occupy the eastern provinces of Nizhnii Novgorod, Kazan, Astrakhan, and Orenburg, where no regular troops had been stationed in 1763. The untoward consequence of this neglect had been to facilitate the progress of the Pugachev Rebellion, crushed in 1775. The inclusion of Orenburg Province was justified by the decision made in 1763 to place the Trans-Kama Landmilitia into the Ukrainian Division, but the developing geopolitical situation in the Kazakh steppe would soon restore the importance of Orenburg in the eastern theater. Likewise, the inclusion of Astrakhan Province brought part of the north Caucasian sector within the radius of operation of this eastern army, probably headquartered in Kazan. This decision was justified on historical grounds, but was soon overruled by the necessity to unify that sector under a separate command. The fourth, or reserve, army would be deployed in the Muscovite center; it was a strategic reserve without territorial commitments, but with a mission to reinforce any of the three armies deployed around it in a semicircle from the Baltic to Orenburg.

Rumiantsev's proposal was not acted upon, perhaps because of the ascendancy of his rival Potemkin, the need to consolidate the imperial presence in the steppe and on the coast, the annexation of the Crimea, and the treaty with eastern Georgia in 1783 that kept focusing the government's attention on the southern theater. Nevertheless, Potemkin was ready by 1784 to consider a similar approach for the deployment of the strategic force.[11] There would be three armies, the first directed against Sweden. Relations with that country had been relatively friendly since Gustav III had staged his coup in 1772, but the king had an eye on Norway, united with Denmark under the Danish crown, and Denmark had been a Russian ally since 1773. Russo-Swedish relations cooled during 1783, and Potemkin recommended a declaration of war "at the smallest demonstration" of Swedish intentions against Denmark, the latter tying down large Swedish forces on the Norwegian border while the Russians occupied Finland, destroyed the Swedish fleet for good (*naveki*), and attacked Karlskrona. Against the obstreperous Prussian client, which might cause difficulties in Russia's relations with Sweden and the Ottomans and might use the opportunity to attack Austria, Potemkin positioned an "army of observation" consisting largely of cavalry which would ravage the king's lands, destroy his magazines and logistical support, and deny him total victory over the friendly kingdom. But the major enemy remained the Ottomans, against whom a third army was directed to attack them "in Europe and in Asia," advancing toward the Danube in the west and via Derbent and Erivan to the Anatolian border in the east.

Potemkin thus contemplated the fragmentation of the strategic force into three armies, two of them designed to establish the empire's hegemony in the Baltic and the Black Sea, along the Bothnian and Danubian moats, while shoring up Austria, the friendly kingdom,against any farther attempts to destabilize the client system in central Europe. We know how unrealistic that ambition remained: the second

Turkish War of 1788–92 would require the concentration once again of nearly the entire strategic force in the southern theater, leaving the Baltic sector dangerously exposed to Swedish naval attacks. Nevertheless, these two proposals by the leading figures of the military establishment showed that attitudes toward the deployment of the strategic force were slowly changing, becoming ready to accept the necessity of territorially based deployments with regional missions, overlooking the fact that such dispersion would reduce the surge capability and awesome power of the strategic force. But it would still take a long time before that truth finally became obvious.

Meanwhile, the partition of the Polish Empire of 1772 had realized Chernyshev's ambition of 1763 to move the imperial boundary forward to the Ulla and the Drut, incorporating into the empire the watershed between the Dvina and the Dniepr and presumably giving Russia its "natural borders" in the region. Chernyshev, who remained "war minister," became governor general of the two provinces of Polotsk and Mogilev and commander of a new Bielorussian Division consisting of seven regiments (three of them infantry), deployed on the Dniepr to the forests and swamps separating the territory from Little Russia, on the Dvina, in Polish Livonia (in Rezhitsa/Rezekene), as well as in Russia proper behind the old border as far back as Pskov and Velikie Luki. This deployment reinforced Russia's presence along the eastern marches of the Polish Empire, directly threatening Kurland and Lithuania. Garrison battalions were posted in Dünaburg (Daugavpils), an old fort of the Teutonic Knights at a strategic location on a sharp bend of the Dvina, where Kurland, Polish Livonia, and the lake region of northern Lithuania and eastern Bielorussia all met; in Polotsk and Vitebsk on the Dvina, Rogachev on the Dniepr; and in Bobruisk, another old fort on the Berezina, well ahead of the new imperial border.[12]

Elsewhere in the western theater, the strength of the divisions had been substantially reduced in 1781 from their 1763 levels. Two regiments had been withdrawn from the Finland Division, one from the Estland Division, but six from the Livland Division, and three each from the Smolensk and Petersburg Divisions, a total of fifteen from the forty-eight deployed there in 1763. The importance of the western theater had been downgraded because of the necessity to redeploy more troops elsewhere in the southern theater and the eastern provinces during and after the Pugachev Rebellion. The seventeen regiments of the Moscow Division were reduced to ten, seven of them in the usual semicircle around Moscow, the other three as far away as Nizhnii Novgorod and Kozmodemiansk on the Volga toward Kazan and in Kurmysh on the Sura, considerably extending eastward the deployment of that central division. These regiments were supplemented by the new Voronezh and Kazan Division stationed in those provinces. As a result, the eastern provinces beyond the Moksha and the Oka gained a significant number of infantry regiments operating in concert with garrison battalions in Kazan, Simbirsk, Saratov, and Voronezh, creating at long last a military and police infrastructure in a region becoming rapidly settled by peasants from the central districts. This more even distribution of the army in the Russian core served not so much a strategic purpose as it sought to strengthen internal security against new peasant disorders while the reform of local government was in progress. Begun in late 1775, this reform was completed in the Russian provinces in 1784 and brought about a radical transformation of the territorial grid of administrative, police, judicial, and tax collecting agencies. It streamlined the apparatus of repression, beginning with the land captains and a rudimentary police force at the district level and ending with the divisional commander, required to provide military assistance in emergencies at the request of the governor or governor general, who, in other cases, had to make do with garrison soldiers.[13]

Fifteen years later, when the empress died in 1796, the geopolitical situation in the western theater had changed dramatically; regular troops had been withdrawn from Russia altogether except in the Petersburg region. Following the partitions of 1793 and 1795, the imperial border was moved, about 450 kilometers west of the 1772 partition line and the "natural border" of 1763; almost all the marches of the Polish Empire had been incorporated into the Russian Empire. Only in the Baltic sector had no territorial changes taken place since the peace with Sweden had restored the status quo in 1790. The territorial "divisions" had been abolished in wartime and had not yet been restored. Of the four great formations in existence in 1796, one was concentrated in Petersburg, Novgorod, Tver, and Vyborg provinces, and two were in the southern theater. The fourth was in Lithuania, the Russian zone of occupation after the partitions north of the Pripet marshes. It was under the command of Nikolai Repnin, who resided in Slonim. Repnin combined the governor generalship of Estland and Livland with that of Lithuania, his jurisdiction including the entire Baltic region from the Gulf of Finland to the East Prussian border. He had under his command a large force of twenty-seven regiments: sixteen of infantry and eleven of cavalry, with five smaller Don Cossack regiments.[14] They were deployed in Estland, Livland, and Kurland, annexed in 1795, in what had been the Grand Duchy of Lithuania, including the whole of Bielorussia with Polotsk and Mogilev Provinces. This "western army" was now deployed on the line, facing the troops of the Prussian client, which had acquired more than half of the territory of the Polish core.

The Polish client state had disappeared, forcing the empire to build a costly military and administrative infrastructure and adopt a defense-in-depth strategy where it had been on the offensive for a century. The appearance of Prussian troops on the Niemen raised the level of threat by the very fact of their presence. It could not be forgotten that in 1791 the Prussian king, nephew of Frederick II, forgetting the position assigned to him in the client system, had contemplated war with the empire in Poland. The advance of the friendly kingdom to the Zbruch and Western Bug, even if justified largely by defensive considerations, similarly eliminated any intermediate territory, brought the Russian and Austrian Empires face to face, and raised the possibility of future tensions. The western theater was beginning to acquire its own army with a distinct mission independent of an overall strategic plan for the empire.

Similar developments were taking place in the southern theater. While Rumiantsev was winning victories in Moldavia in 1770, a new line was built across the steppe from Alexandrovsk (near Zaporizhzhia) on the Dniepr to Petrovsk (Berdiansk) on the Sea of Azov, along the course of the two steppe rivers, the Konka and the Berda. Eight fortified outposts were built on it, manned by five garrison battalions and three Cossack regiments, a force of 5,400 men. This so-called Dniepr Line incorporated the entire territory of the Zaporozhian Cossacks east of the Dniepr and advanced the imperial border to that of the Crimean Khanate as it had been defined by the Nissa Convention of 1739. It also transformed those Cossack lands into a forward base of operation against the khanate, which was conquered the following year. The treaty of Kuchuk-Kainardji, however, proclaimed the khanate's independence, while giving the Russians Kerch and Enikale, two forts controlling the strait between the Azov and Black Seas, and a triangular territory formed by the Southern Bug and the Dniepr, which included the remainder of the Zaporozhian lands, west of the Dniepr. In 1775, two new provinces were created, one called New Russia, its capital planned at Ekaterinoslav, bounded by the Bug, the Dniepr, and the Polish border. East of the Dniepr and the Dniepr Line, Azov Province combined the territory of the old Ukrainian Line, Slavianoserbia, the north Caucasus steppe to the Eia River and the upper Manych, with the Don Cossack Territory, recreating a situation similar to that which had prevailed after 1709 when the hetmanate on the left bank of the Dniepr had been included into Kiev Province. Potemkin, who had replaced Chernyshev as "war minister," was appointed governor general over both. His jurisdiction was extended to include Astrakhan Province, bringing the entire north Caucasus and the southern steppe north of the khanate to the Polish border under a single military command. As in Bielorussia, but on a much vaster scale, an imperial frontier would no longer be administered by a client society of Cossacks and Serb settlers but governed by an imperial proconsul who was also the head of the military establishment and, in Potemkin's case, the empress's favorite and close adviser.

Since Potemkin spent most of his time in the newly conquered lands, managing the imperial army from his field chancery nearly 2,000 kilometers from Petersburg, he also commanded the Eleventh or Border (*pogranichnaia*) Division deployed in both provinces. Eight regiments of infantry, two of dragoons, and two battalions of chasseurs were in New Russia, as well as nine regiments of "settled hussars" and "pikemen." These units consisted of Serbs and other immigrants from the Balkans and remained outside the regular army; they operated much like a new kind of Cossack, settled well ahead of the old Cossack zone north of the Dniepr. They were found on the lands of the Zaporozhian Cossacks who were disbanded in 1775. There were fewer troops in Azov Province: two regiments of infantry and one of dragoons, and a smaller "Greek" regiment doing garrison duty in Kerch-Enikale, as well as six regiments of settled hussars and pikemen. Three Don Cossack regiments were attached to the division, and other Don Cossacks remained available in their territory, now part of the province. Farther east, in Astrakhan Province, three infantry and three dragoon regiments with two battalions of chasseurs and one field battalion were stationed chiefly on the Caucasian Line between Mozdok and Kizliar, together with the Greben, Terek, and Astrakhan Cossacks. These troops were not only combat soldiers; they also built fortresses and boats and settlements—the infrastructure of the empire's hegemony in the region and the last challenge to the nomads' own hegemony. Behind the eighteen regiments and other regular and irregular units of Potemkin's division, which placed the "independent" Crimean Khanate in a vise, stood the Ukrainian Division of nineteen regiments, still commanded by Rumiantsev, the governor general of Little Russia who now resided in Kiev. Fifteen of these regiments were deployed in Little Russia and the Ukraine of Settlements, the other four in Kursk and Orel provinces. These two divisions, commanded by Catherine II's most famous field marshals, formed the "army of the southern theater," poised for a general offensive against the Ottomans toward the Danube, in the Crimea, and across the Caucasus.

The annexation of the Crimea and the treaty with Georgia (1783) were the first stage of that general offensive. That same year, in a symbolic move reflecting the change brought about by the final defeat of the khanate whose existence had created the Cossack frontier societies, the Little Russian Cossacks were disbanded and reorganized to form ten carbineer regiments. In 1792, however, the remainder of the Zaporozhian Cossacks who had fought with the Russians during the war with the Ottomans of 1788–92 were resettled under the name of Black Sea Cossacks on a new frontier, the land of the Kuban Tatars. In the meantime, Potemkin had created a Crimean and a Caucasian "corps"—in the unsystematized terminology of the period, a smaller division or even part of one; their commanders were responsible to him. By 1796, imperial troops were deployed along the entire periphery of the southern theater from the Zbruch to the Caspian, along the Black Sea coast, and in the Caucasus. Two of the four formations in existence in 1796 were stationed there. One was commanded by Rumiantsev and consisted of twenty-four regiments, seventeen of them infantry, a "corps" of chasseurs, and twelve regiments of Cossacks. It was still deployed on the left bank of the Dniepr, but also across the river, in Podolia and Volhynia, acquired from Poland in 1793 and 1795.

Within thirty-three years, Rumiantsev's troops, which had been stationed well behind the imperial boundary, with Cossack and Serb settlements separating them from the Crimean Khanate, had moved to the new imperial periphery along the Dniestr, beyond which began Moldavia, the Ottoman client state. From that time on, any move across the Dniestr would bring about instant Ottoman retaliation. These troops also faced Austrian forces in Galicia, adding to the uncertainties created by the Russian advance to the Western Bug in Lithuania. The other formation of twenty regiments, thirteen of them infantry, commanded by Suvorov, was deployed in the Ochakov steppe, New Russia, the Ukraine of Settlements, and the Crimea. The Caucasian corps had become separate in that it no longer depended on a larger army-like formation. Its commander kept his headquarters on the Caucasian Line. The strategic force had been almost entirely deployed on the periphery and divided into two "armies" with specific missions, one facing the Germanic powers, the other poised against the Ottomans.

In the eastern theater, the imperial military presence was so insignificant that its only purpose remained to patrol the border, intercept parties of nomads seeking to cross into settled lands, pursue horse thieves into the steppe, and carry out occasional punitive expeditions against Kazakh *auly*. The Trans-Kama Landmilitia was abolished in the Orenburg Territory but the deployment of 1781 refers to an Orenburg Corps, part of the Kazan Division, consisting of five infantry and two dragoon regiments created, it seems, by transforming the local infantry battalions into full-strength regular units. They and some 10,000 Ural and Orenburg Cossacks were responsible for patrolling a 1,300-kilometer long border from the Caspian to the middle Urals. In Siberia, the very length of the border continued to impose a defensive posture against a Manchu China which had lost its expansionist urge anyway: the Siberian Line was 2,070 kilometers long to Kuznetsk in the Altai and 3,000 kilometers from Kuznetsk to the Amur River. In 1781, there was a Siberian Corps consisting of only one dragoon regiment and ten infantry battalions or about 7,000 men, in addition to about 4,000 Siberian Cossacks. The border with China remained essentially undefended.

The deployment of 1781 marked the temporary reversal of a trend, increasingly noticeable since 1763 and even earlier, to disperse the strategic force from the old Muscovite core. The major cause was the aftermath of the Pugachev Rebellion, which required, especially in the eastern provinces, the provisional implantation of a military infrastructure to back up the police forces being created in the wake of the local government reform.

## The Fragmentation of the Strategic Force: 1796–1801

There remains to examine the deployment of the strategic force at the very end of the eighteenth century, once the conquered territories had been fully integrated into the administrative and military organization of a hegemonic empire and just before the empire was drawn into a titanic struggle with Napoleonic France to maintain that hegemony in the Heartland.

Catherine's reign had been a time of experimentation and diversity, especially in the composition of the cavalry, which emphasized light over heavy units and was used as much as an instrument of colonization in the southern steppe as tactical units on the battlefield. In contrast, Paul's reforms emphasized simplicity and uniformity, and favored the heavy cavalry (cuirassiers) stationed chiefly in the two capitals and in Livonia. The emperor eventually reduced the strength of the infantry from 340,000 men in 1795 to 203,230 men by 1800. No changes were made in the Guard, which continued to consist of four regiments, including one of grenadiers. The grenadier regiments were reduced from fifteen in 1796 to twelve by 1800, each consisting of two instead of four battalions. However, the number of musketeer regiments was raised from fifty-nine to sixty-nine in 1800. The ten "corps" of chasseurs were reorganized first into battalions, then into nineteen regiments in 1798. The infantry thus consisted of 104 regiments and 20 battalions of chasseurs by 1800. The field battalions were abolished. Even the number of garrisons was reduced from 104 in 1795 to 81 in 1800—with barely a change in their strength, however, from 77,663 men to 77,500 men. The cavalry was greatly simplified. The number of Guard regiments was raised from one to three by incorporating into it the so-called Gatchina troops, which had been created by Catherine to serve as Paul's grand ducal guard. The seventeen carbineer regiments were reorganized into cuirassier regiments, reduced to thirteen in 1800. The number of dragoon regiments rose from eleven in 1796 to fifteen in 1800, that of hussars from two to eight, a total of thirty-nine cavalry regiments. The mounted grenadiers and chasseurs and light cavalry regiments were disbanded. By the end of Paul's reign, the strength of the cavalry was down to 41,730

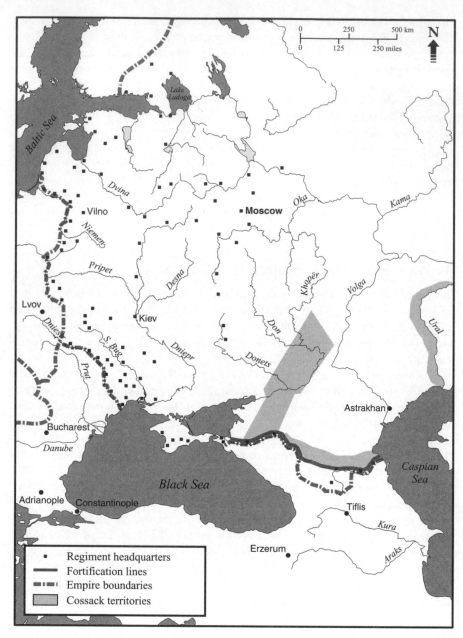

Deployment of 1796

men, and the ratio of infantry to cavalry regiments was 2.8 to 1. The strategic force, including the Guard, consisted by 1800 of 143 regiments with a strength of 244,960 men.[15]

The army was once again deployed in territorial divisions as it had been in 1763 and 1781; the system had been abandoned in wartime, when the strategic force was gathered to form field armies without permanent quarters. Twelve divisions were created in December 1796[16]—immediately after Paul's accession—only two of them in Russia proper: one in Petersburg commanded by Grand Duke Alexander, the future tsar, the other in Moscow under Iurii Dolgorukov, with the title of commander in chief in the old capital, the equivalent of a governor general. By then, however, Moscow province no longer occupied the entire Muscovite center as it had in 1763, but had shrunk to include only Moscow's immediate surrounding territory. The Petersburg Division was small, with only eight regiments, including two of cuirassiers, all stationed in the capital, except for one of infantry in Novgorod and Shlisselburg, guarding the waterway from Lake Ilmen to the Neva. The Moscow Division was much larger, with thirteen regiments, including eight of infantry. Four were stationed in the old capital, the other nine deployed in the usual semicircle around it, in Torzhok, Tver, and Volokolamsk in the west; Kaluga, Tula, and Kolomna in the south; Kostroma in the east; Pereslavl-Zalesskii and Uglich in the north. There were no garrisons in the area of deployment of these two divisions except in Petersburg (two battalions) and Moscow (eight battalions). We may also add here the Smolensk Division, under Alexander Prozorovskii, deployed across the Russian-Bielorussian border. Five of its eleven regiments (all but two infantry) were in Russia: in Smolensk (two), Viazma, Porech'e, and Toropets; the other six in Bielorussia: in Vitebsk and Polotsk on the Dvina, Mogilev and Rogachev at the confluence of the Dniepr and the Drut, and Minsk, acquired in 1793.

There was something very traditional about the deployment in Russia proper, but there was also a striking novelty: the twenty-one regiments deployed in Russia proper (or twenty-eight, if we include the five in Smolensk and two in the Ukrainian Divisions) made up only 18.3 percent (or 24.3 percent) of the 115 regiments listed in the table, much less than the 45 percent stationed there in 1763. This force was much too small to be considered a strategic reserve. Its mission was instead to maintain internal security at a time of turmoil, especially in the two capitals, following the long reign of Catherine II. The spread of peasant revolts in 1798 would soon show that the new government's concern was justified. The sharp reduction in the number of garrisons supports this interpretation. In 1763, the army had sought to be free of the task of policing the country by developing the network of garrisons and creating other, semi-military, police forces. The new tsar looked upon the army in Russia proper as an instrument of direct rule and established a system of governing that resembled a military dictatorship, certainly in spirit, if not completely in practice. This is what Peter I had also done with his network of governors, commandants, and regimental commanders in Fortress Russia. The abolition of the post of governor general and the appointment in a number of provinces of military governors who managed their province directly or watched over the civil governor, went a long way in the direction of a military dictatorship.

The other nine divisions were deployed in another semicircle around Russia proper, from Finland to Orenburg, with a long tail belonging to the Siberian Division under Lt. Gen. Gustav Strandmann. He was the only lieutenant general among the twelve divisional commanders: the others were three field marshals and seven full generals, with Grand Duke Alexander a special case. Another characteristic feature of the 1796 deployment was the complete separation of the regional military administration from the civil administration. None of the divisional commanders, except Dolgorukov in Moscow, had any civilian responsibilities: gone were the days when Chernyshev, and especially Rumiantsev and Potemkin, combined their military command with the civil administration of vast territories, even with the post of "war minister" in the case of Chernyshev and Potemkin. The military dictatorship, incomplete as it was, was exercised at the lower, provincial, level, where some civil governors, themselves former generals in many cases, were subordinated to military governors.

Two divisions were stationed in the Baltic provinces: one in Finland (at Vyborg) under Mikhail Kamenskii, the other in Livland (at Riga) under Johann von Elmpt. The Lithuanian Division, commanded by Field Marshal Repnin, who was also military governor in Vilno, was stationed in the former grand duchy, ahead of the Smolensk Division. Three divisions were thus deployed in the western theater, four if we include the Smolensk Division. There were four in the southern theater: a Ukrainian Division headquartered in Kiev under Field Marshal Rumiantsev who would die shortly afterward, his death followed by the abolition of his governor generalship; another headquartered in Ekaterinoslav under Field Marshal Suvorov; the third in the Crimea under Mikhail Kakhovskii, who had commanded troops in the peninsula since 1787. The fourth was in the Caucasus: the Caucasian Corps, like the Crimean, Orenburg, and Siberian Corps, was finally reorganized into territorial divisions for the sake of administrative uniformity. Its commander, Ivan Gudovich, was military governor of Astrakhan and had been governor general of the northern Caucasus since 1793. A similar situation prevailed in Orenburg, where Otto von Igelström, who had been governor general of Ufa and Simbirsk in the 1780s, was now military governor of Orenburg and divisional commander. Thus, of the eleven divisional commanders outside of Petersburg, only five were also military governors of provincial capitals housing divisional headquarters, and all but one were in the peripheral regions.

The shift to peripheral deployment becomes even more obvious when we turn to the western and southern theaters. In the western theater, the deployment kept advancing with the imperial boundary: there was no more question of pulling back troops toward the Moscow or Petersburg center, leaving the client system to work in the empire's favor. The partitions of Poland destroyed the client state and required a forward positioning of military units by the three partitioning powers, if only because none of the three could afford to keep its troops out of its share of Polish territory if the other two kept theirs under military occupation. And the very fact that the Russians were forced to carry out a substantial strategic withdrawal as a result of the partitions made it imperative for them to establish a strong presence in their zone.

There was still a Finland Division, of three regiments, three chasseur battalions, and six garrisons. Its headquarters was now in Vyborg. Its posture was largely defensive: Paul was determined to restore good relations with Sweden following the stressful years of the 1788–90 war and the rude refusal of the new king to marry his daughter. But the Estonian Division was gone, and no troops remained in that province, save for a cuirassier regiment in Hapsal. Most of the Livland Division was in fact deployed in Kurland. Only six of its fourteen regiments remained in Livland proper. The others were in Kurland. The duchy occupied a narrow strip of land along the Lithuanian border and had been a fief of the Polish crown since 1561. Its two ports, Libava (Liepaja) and Vindava (Ventspils), and its oak forests had attracted Peter I's attention as far back as 1699. It was of course not included into Russia's Baltic acquisitions in 1721, but the tsar had already married off his niece, the future empress Anna Ivanovna, to its duke in 1710. A Russian minister was regularly appointed in Mitava (Jelgava) beginning in 1716: the province became a de facto client society of the empire. Anna imposed her lover, Biron, on the ducal throne in 1739. He would remain Russia's straw man until 1769, when he was replaced by his son Petr. By then, however, the nobles' conflict with their duke had only increased their dependence on the goodwill of Petersburg, a dependence supported by the presence of imperial troops across the Dvina. In 1795, following the third partition of the Polish Empire, the annexation of the duchy was brokered by Otto von der Hoven, one of the duke's bitter enemies.[17]

The Kurland nobility became a client society *within* the empire and joined their brethren in Estland and Livland to become dutiful sons of the imperial fatherland in return for the right to manage their own affairs with minimal imperial supervision. But the inclusion of Kurland into the inner frontier of the empire also brought about the advance of the strategic force—and of the imperial forest administration—into its territory because it stood next door to East Prussia and its major port in Memel (Klaipeda) was only thirty kilometers from the new imperial checkpoint in Polangen. Two of the seven regiments were cuirassiers, near the confluence of the Ewst (Aiviekste) with the Dvina, the key to Polish Lithuania, the other in Goldingen (Kuldiga), the temporary residence of the dukes, and Pilten (Piltene), the ancient see of the Kurland bishops, whose possessions continued to enjoy autonomous status within the duchy. The others were in Libava and Mitava and strung along the border with Lithuania to patrol what was essentially an ethnic border on the approaches to the Samogitian Highland and in the east to Braslav in the lake district, where Kurland met with Lithuania and Bielorussia. Despite the presence of seven regiments in Kurland, the empire's military presence in the Baltic sector was much lower than it had been in 1763: the average ratio was now one regiment for every 40,000 male inhabitants.

The deployment in Kurland, in the valley of the middle and lower Dvina, complemented perfectly the Bielorussian development along the upper Dvina and upper Dniepr, Chernyshev's "natural borders." Both provided a backup force for the Lithuanian Division deployed in the former grand duchy behind the Niemen and the Western Bug, the empire's newly discovered "natural borders," four hundred kilometers west of the old ones. Lithuania, where autonomous tendencies had always been noticeable—against the Polish core as well as within the grand duchy itself—consisted of two major regions.[18] Samogitia (Zhmud) occupied a heavily forested watershed between the valley of the Niemen and that of the Dvina, an old transition zone between the ancient possessions of the Teutonic Knights in Livonia and Prussia, long resistant to Christianization, and not finally forced to submit until the sixteenth century. Of the division's ten regiments, six were stationed there. One of grenadiers was in Kovno (Kaunas), the future provincial capital of Samogitia, once a major source of conflict between the Teutonic Knights and the Lithuanians, and an important trading center on the Niemen, where Napoleon's Grande Armée would begin the invasion of the empire in 1812. The others were distributed across Lithuania between the Niemen and the Dvina. These troops not only maintained a military presence but also functioned as a custom guard along a very porous border just behind Memel, where smuggling was widespread.

The other part of Lithuania was the Vilno-Grodno region or the basin of the upper Niemen descending from the Minsk upland. Regiments were stationed in Slonim where some of the diets (*seims*) had taken place in the seventeenth century: in Vilno, the capital of the grand duchy; in Grodno, its second capital, where a diet had met in 1793 to accept the second partition; in Brest-Litovsk on the Bug, where the Bug-Dniepr waterway began linking Warsaw with Kiev; and on the Smolensk-Warsaw road via Minsk. Brest-Litovsk and Grodno were the most strategic locations on the edge of the eastern marches of the Polish Empire; from there it was only 200 and 280 kilometers to Warsaw respectively, less than a week's march away. The division also included chasseurs stationed along the Niemen from Polangen to Olita (Alytus), near where the roads from Kovno and Vilno merge on their way to Grodno, and between the Niemen and Pripet, where they linked up with the infantry stationed in Grodno and Best-Litovsk to form a cordon along the imperial boundary between those two cities. By stationing units of the strategic force so far west along the periphery, the imperial government assumed immediate responsibility for the security of the region instead of depending on local associations of clients who would do the work for it. It involved the army in local ethnic politics, a mutually harmful relationship. A permanent presence also entailed the construction of fortresses and associated infrastructures of supply magazines and artillery parks and the improvement of the many castles (*zamki*) studding the countryside. They were being transformed into regimental headquarters, all costly undertakings facing the Germanic powers, with which the old client relationship was certain to suffer new strains. At the same time, those associated infrastructures along the imperial periphery indicated the gradual transformation of Fortress Russia into Fortress Empire, as we shall see presently.

In the southern theater, the shift to deployment on the line was even more pronounced. While 33 of the 115 regiments (28.6 percent) were stationed in the western theater, 45 (39.1 percent) were spread along the immense periphery created by the Polish partitions and the two Russo-Turkish wars. The Bug, the Dniestr, the Black Sea coast, the Kuban, and the Terek neatly demarcated the empire from its Austrian and Ottoman neighbors, but also raised the level of risk, because neither the friendly kingdom nor the Ottomans could accept any farther Russian expansion, which would henceforth threaten their most vital interests. At the same time, the imperial advance and the resulting destruction of the client societies required the construction of the same network of administrative, military, and economic infrastructures. In both theaters, the advance brought the empire close to territories where ecology and human geography created insuperable obstacles to any farther expansion of imperial power, be it in Poland, the Danubian Principalities, or Transcaucasia. As Fortress Russia became transformed into Fortress Empire, the shift from a forward defense to a defense-in-depth strategy was becoming a growing necessity. While its wartime strategy remained faithful to the primacy of the offensive and deep penetrations, its peacetime strategy began to rely increasingly on the defensive supported by regional armies well entrenched in the peripheral regions along a political and military "isobar" separating the empire from its Germanic and Ottoman neighbors.

The Ukrainian Division remained the largest of them all with seventeen regiments, but it was no longer deployed on the left bank of the Dniepr, save for three cuirassier regiments in Kharkov, Kursk, and Orel, these last two in Russia proper. There were two grenadier regiments in Kiev (and a two-battalion garrison commanded by the city's military governor) and seven regiments in Volhynia: on the road from Kiev to the Bug; in Lutsk, where that road branched off toward Brest-Litovsk and toward Lwów (Lviv), the capital of Galicia annexed by Austria in 1772; in Kovel, where the road to Brest-Litovsk swerved toward Lublin and Warsaw; and in central Volhynia, in major fairs and trading towns, and on an estate of the Sanguszko princes. Others were in Podolia, including Kamenets-Podolsk (Kam'ianits-Podil'skii), a huge former Polish fortress facing Khotin across the Dniestr, the last of the three great fortresses (with Ochakov and Azov) that had once formed the Ottomans' northern defense perimeter, still in Ottoman hands. Two hussar regiments patrolled the border in Potocki country, one between Kamenets-Podolsk and the Pripet marshes, the other between Mogilev/Dniestr, one of the largest trading towns of Podolia on the commercial track from Moldavia, and Iampol (Jampil), where the deployment of the Ekaterinoslav Division began.

The selection of trading towns and road junctions showed that this peripheral deployment was directed as much against the friendly kingdom as against the Ottomans: one would expect it to be the case in an interlocking frontier, where the agricultural resources of the region had long supported the Russian war effort against southern Poland (now in the Austrian zone of occupation) and the Ottomans. Despite the massive shift of the strategic force to the eastern marches of the Polish Empire, the ratio of regiments to the population remained very low: in Lithuania there was one regiment for every 82,740 inhabitants, and on the Right-Bank Ukraine one for every 95,533. In Podolia, however, along the Ottoman border with Moldavia, it was already higher: one regiment for every 52,770 inhabitants. And in Kherson Province, which belonged to the Ekaterinoslav Division, the ratio was one to 13,358, among the highest ever found in the empire. These regiments were on the empire's front line, ready for intervention against the Ottomans, with whom the empire was in a state of permanent cold war.

The fifteen regiments of that division had indeed a different mission: to operate as a strike force in the event of war and, in peacetime, to give the empire staying power along the Dniestr, on the Moldavian border, which guarded the approaches to the Danube. Only two regiments remained in the old area of settlement of the Right-Bank Ukraine: in Novomirgorod and Elizavetgrad, with two regiments of Chuguev Cossacks in Kharkov Province. Hussars patrolled the Dniestr border from

Iampol to Ovidiopol on the river's estuary, facing the Ottoman fortress of Akkerman. Dragoons and infantry were stationed along the Siniukha, the old border between the Polish Ukraine and the Ochakov steppe, flanked by more infantry in Uman and Olgopol (Ol'hopil). Other regiments were in the Ochakov steppe. Finally, the deployment on the line was completed by staggering six battalions of chasseurs along the lower Dniestr all the way to Kherson. There were also garrisons in Elizavetgrad, Bakhmut, Taganrog, St. Dmitrii, and Azov. Two smaller divisions, with even more clearly defined regional missions, created territorial infrastructures to strengthen the empire's staying power in two highly turbulent regions. The six regiments of the Crimean Division were confined to the peninsula, although one of the two chasseur battalions was in Fanagoria on the Taman peninsula, which the Russians still believed was an island. Beyond Fanagoria began the territory of the Caucasian Division of five infantry and four dragoon regiments, with two battalions of chasseurs standing guard on the Caucasian Line all the way to Kizliar. There were, in addition, garrisons in Astrakhan, Kizliar, and Mozdok.

The eastern theater remained a case apart, where deployment on the line was the characteristic feature of military territorial organization, and where the official posture was always defensive. It is significant that the shift to peripheral deployment in the western and southern theaters also presaged the adoption of a similar defensive posture, although the attraction of the Danubian moat and the lure of Tiflis kept a forward strategy very much alive. Paradoxically, the end of the eighteenth century witnessed the beginning of the Manchu Empire's decline; no danger was any longer expected from there, the Zunghars had been exterminated, and the Kazakh client society was disintegrating. Such geopolitical developments — including Persia's losing its grip on Khiva and Bukhara — invited a shift to a forward strategy in the eastern theater, but with a minimum of force, because the Kazakhs offered little resistance and units of irregular cavalry were adequate to cope with turbulence in the frontier. Nevertheless, regular troops remained stationed east of the Volga, but only nine regiments in the Orenburg and Siberian Divisions, or only 7.8 percent of the strategic force.

The Orenburg Division was essentially the police force of the southern Urals, with three infantry regiments in Orenburg, Ufa, and Ekaterinburg, the administrative capital of the Ural mining region, while one regiment of dragoons, together with the Orenburg Cossacks, patrolled the banks of the Ural River between Orenburg and Troitsk. The jurisdiction of the Orenburg military governor-and-divisional commander extended as far as Kazan, whose commandant and garrison were subordinated to him. Kazan remained the supply base of the territory, its link with Russia proper, west of the Volga. Beyond Troitsk the Siberian Line stretched to Ust-Kamenogorsk. The entire line was patrolled by two dragoon regiments, and three of infantry were stationed in Omsk, Ust-Kamenogorsk, and Kolyvan in the Altai mining district. A number of garrisons provided logistical support for all these units. There were no regular troops in eastern Siberia, but garrisons in Irkutsk and Selenginsk reported to the military governor in Irkutsk, although the overall command of all regular forces in Siberia remained vested in the divisional commander in Omsk.

The deployment of 1796 drew attention to the continued importance of Ust-Kamenogorsk. The fort was one of the gates to the Altai and controlled the approaches to Lake Zaisan on the unofficial Russo-Chinese border. Upstream from the fort, the Bukhtarma descended from the Altai watershed separating the valley of the Irtysh from the Kobdo depression of western Mongolia. In 1763, Petersburg had ordered the construction of a fort at the river's mouth from which to develop trade with the nomads of Mongolia and eastern Turkestan in order to break the Kiakhta monopoly on the Russo-Chinese trade. The long interruptions in that trade during Catherine's reign thwarted the execution of that plan. It was revived by Strand-mann, the divisional commander, in 1796—and Iakobi had implicitly recom-mended it as well. Strandmann pointed out that the fort would be only twelve days from Kobdo and thirty from Peking. His intentions were not only commercial, they also had military implications (forcing the Manchus to renegotiate Russo-Chinese relations), and they contributed to Paul's decision to continue to station a regiment of regulars at Ust-Kamenogorsk. The eastern theater was beginning to stir with new expectations.

The deployment of the strategic force at the very end of the eighteenth century had little in common with the previous deployments of 1725, 1763, and the 1780s. The trend toward its dispersion ever more widely in the frontier zones was unmis-takable. At the same time, however, the mission of that force underwent a subtle change. In the 1720s, the strategic force had been an operational army concentrated at the imperial center and ready to move in any directions, even in more than one direction at once. But it was also a police force with a duty not only to maintain order but also to secure the collection of the capitation on which its pay and provi-sioning depended. From the 1760s on, a clear emphasis was placed on removing the force from police duty in central Russia, while in the peripheral regions the army became both a striking force against potential enemies and a police forma-tion; in the southern theater, it also took up duties of colonizing the newly acquired lands and building there an administrative infrastructure. With the reign of Paul, however, the army reappears in Russia proper as a police force, to maintain order against the rising tide of rural disorders. This renewed combination of military and police responsibilities, coupled with the redeployment of part of the strategic force in the central regions of the empire, marked the gradual transformation of Fortress Russia into Fortress Empire, which reached its completion after 1815.

# 6

# Economy, Culture,
# Client Societies

## The Economy

Russia's rise to hegemony in the Heartland was made possible by the continued strength of its economy within the few parameters set by Peter: while "free" labor made progress in the textile industry concentrated around Moscow, metallurgy remained largely concentrated in the Urals, where the labor force was overwhelmingly servile. The foundation of the military-industrial complex continued to be serfdom, with its accompanying infrastructure of compulsion geared to the production of the weapons of war for the army and the navy and to the construction of fortresses and naval installations in an ever expanding empire. By 1750, the production of iron had reached 36,363 tons; by the end of Paul's reign, in 1800, it had quintupled to reach nearly 181,820 tons, keeping Russia still ahead of England with its 172,730 tons.[1] Russia had overtaken Sweden to become the leading exporter of iron and copper. But Russia's lead over England was narrowing, as the basic flaws of Russian metallurgy began to appear: the exhaustion of the Ural forests and the reliance on serf labor, which discouraged innovation. Serfdom's capabilities were being stretched to the limit, and farther demands would become counterproductive.

The production of muskets reached 30,000 in 1746, and there was a reserve of another 36,000 in Tula, Petersburg, and Sestroretsk. Production became increasingly concentrated in Tula while Sestroretsk specialized in the repair of muskets and the production of pistols and bayonets. The Tula works produced an average of 19,000 muskets a year between the late 1730s and the late 1770s and about 25,000 in the 1780s. The requirements were large, however. The establishment of 1762–63 called for 216,352 muskets and carbines and that of 1785–86 for 227,172 in addition to a reserve equivalent to 75 percent of those totals. Production was barely enough to cover the needs, especially after the long Turkish Wars, which caused much destruction of military equipment. Tula continued to receive its raw materials from the Urals and, for a time in the 1770s, spare parts from a new plant in Briansk. Another new plant at Izhevsk produced guns for the army in the southern theater and for the Black Sea fleet. Production was shipped down the Kama and the Volga and carried overland to the Don.[2]

The production of army cloth was complicated—and stimulated—by changes in uniforms carried out for "ideological" reasons. In the 1740s, the Petrine uniforms were restored; they had been replaced by new ones patterned after Prussian uniforms in the 1730s. Peter III restored the Prussian uniforms, Potemkin abandoned them, and Paul restored them once again. In addition, new formations, like the cuirassiers, the chasseurs, grenadiers, hussars, carbineers, and "light cavalry" units, required new uniforms. In 1743, the college of war placed an order for 357,140 meters of cloth and for another 388,570 to form a reserve, a total of over 745,700 meters, but the existing textile factories could deliver only 571,400. It was not until the outbreak of the Seven Years' War that production reached 785,715 meters. The country was becoming self-sufficient in army uniform production. During the Turkish Wars, orders went out for about 500,000 meters a year. Some factories produced exclusively for the commissary, others sold only part of their production to it. By the end of the century, the industry produced over 1.4 million meters, more than enough to cover the army's needs. Quality increased, and the regular demand encouraged the development of sheep raising, especially in the Ukraine, largely under government auspices, another feature of the command economy geared for the satisfaction of military needs.[3]

While the imperial government had reached by the end of the eighteenth century a level of production adequate to supply the equipment, uniforms, and boots of its strategic force, there were disquieting signs that the shift from concentrated deployment in Russia proper to deployment along the much longer imperial periphery was beginning to tax its fiscal capabilities. The capitation/poll tax was no longer adequate to cover all military expenditures—let alone naval ones—and other sources of revenue had to be diverted to the military budget. By 1765, the capitation was expected to yield 7 million rubles, but military expenditures for 1766 were estimated at 8.1 million. The first Turkish War of 1768–74 created an unprecedented burden. Between 1769 and 1773 the cost of maintaining the army rose to 51.4 million rubles, an average of 10.2 million a year, to which must be added 33.1 million to pay for wartime operations, or an average of 6.6 million a year, and another 2 million a year for the navy. By 1786, the peacetime cost of the army had more than doubled to 19.1 million. Then came the Second Turkish War, during which the regular expenditures for the army alone reached 106.1 million, or 21.2 million a year in addition to 11.3 million for extraordinary expenditures. Civilian expenditures also rose following the local government reform of the 1780s. The inelastic tax base could not cope with such a level of expenditures, but the capitation was not raised until 1794 lest it cause discontent—memories of the Pugachev Rebellion were still fresh. By then, the situation was so critical that the government resorted to in-kind deliveries in order to supply the basic necessities to the army in the southern theater.[1]

A solution was found in the issuance of paper money. This was not a new idea, but earlier experiments in England and France in the 1720s had ended in failure. There was much to recommend it in a country like Russia, where enormous distances and the poor condition of roads greatly impeded the transport of heavy barrels of coins from one end of the realm to another. In 1760, when the Seven Years' War was creating additional difficulties, a special bank was established to issue paper notes called *assignats*, but its operations were curtailed at the accession of Catherine II two years later. It was recreated in 1768, at the outset of the First Turkish War, and the amount of *assignats* in circulation was fixed at 20 million in 1774, or about two-thirds of what it cost to finance the war. Some bonds were also floated in Amsterdam. One may consider these first operations beneficial: Peter and his immediate successors had financed their wars by brutal measures of fiscal compulsion, including the collection of arrears by military force. Catherine II loosened up the management of the economy, encouraging the development of trade and freedom of enterprise, albeit within the narrow confines imposed by serfdom. The reforms of 1775–85 created an administrative framework, an infrastructure of empire, to facilitate this transformation of the economy. But these same reforms, guided by a policy of administrative unification, were expensive and nearly destroyed the autonomy of the client societies, which had cost so little, facing the treasury with demands that could not be met by taxation alone. The lure of the printing press became irresistible. By 1786, in peacetime, the amount of *assignats* had reached 45 million, but with the approach of another Turkish war it was raised to 100 million, with a solemn promise that this ceiling would not be exceeded. By 1796, however, it had reached 156.7 million in addition to the 33 million floated in Amsterdam.[5] In other words, while the cost of domestic management was largely covered by taxation, the expansion of the empire, the growth of the army, and its deployment in faraway lands with few resources were financed by printing paper money. The resulting devaluation of the paper ruble and inflation did much harm to the Russian economy and raised questions about the wisdom of shifting from a policy of concentrated to peripheral deployment with its attendant consequences for the strategic posture of the empire and the management of the client system.

Fortress Russia continued to suffer from poor internal communications, themselves the result of weak economic development. In Peter's time, they had been built around a west-east axis linking Petersburg with the Urals via Moscow by means of the rich hydrographic network of the Baltic and Caspian basins connected by the Vyshnii-Volochek Canal. But the wooded steppe and steppe zones south of the Oka belonged to the Black Sea basin and faced south. It was impossible to link the two regions by canals, so much better adapted to encourage exchanges than poor roads which disappeared under the snow in wintertime, melted into mud in the spring, and choked travelers in summer dust. Even autocratic Russia could not build a "Grand Canal" linking north and south, if only because it lacked China's vibrant commerce. Nevertheless, the economies of the north and south were complementary, the south supplying livestock and grain to the agriculturally poor forest zone. The economy of the valley of the Dniepr had once been part of the Polish Empire, but the secession of the future hetmanate and the resulting civil wars of the seventeenth century had divided it into two regional economies on each side of the river, that of the right bank in Podolia-Volhynia remaining oriented toward the Vistula, that of the left bank moving into Moscow's orbit. The abolition of internal customs duties in 1753 encouraged the creation of a single market supplying the single strategic force deployed from Petersburg to the Dniepr, without abolishing the mutual dependence of the two economies. The south was fated to become the key agricultural region of the empire while the Baltic north was becoming the key strategic region,[6] but the south was also capable of supporting a large force with its own strategic mission. Interdependence thus created unity but also sustained the development of two separate economic regions, exposing the strong correlation between the structure and location of the strategic force and the economy.

The configuration of the empire remained unchanged between 1743 and 1772, and little progress was made in canal building to improve the transportation network. The Vyshnii-Volochek Canal left much to be desired and required a long detour around the Valdai upland to reach Petersburg via Novgorod. An alternative was to link Rybinsk on the sharp bend of the Volga north of Iaroslavl with the northern capital, using the Volga's tributaries and the rivers flowing into Lake Ladoga. Such was the origin of the Tikhvin waterway, better adapted to the transportation of goods to and from Petersburg, as the city began to develop as a major manufacturing center. In 1753, Petr Shuvalov, who that same year submitted the project to abolish internal customs duties and would soon become chief of the artillery and, as such, a key member of the military-industrial complex, proposed building the waterway, but surveying work was interrupted by his death in 1762. It was resumed in 1765 but interrupted again during the Turkish War and not resumed for good until 1800; the waterway was not open for navigation until 1811. It began at the confluence of the Mologa near Rybinsk, followed the river almost to its source, where a canal linked up with the Sias flowing past Tikhvin into Lake Ladoga and merging with the Ladoga Canal on the way to Petersburg. A second waterway called the Mariinskii System was first planned in 1786, but the funds were redirected to improve the Petersburg-Moscow highway first built in the 1740s. Work began in earnest in 1797, and navigation opened in 1810. The waterway started at Rybinsk at the confluence of the Sheksna, which it followed to the White Lake; from there it followed the Kovzha and Vytegra to Lake Onega and the Svir to Lake Ladoga.[7] The two waterways deepened the integration of the Petersburg region with the Muscovite core and the Urals, strengthening the economic unity of Peter's Fortress Russia. But there was no progress in road building, as it required a commitment of resources the imperial government did not have.

Chernyshev's proposal of 1763 to reach Russia's "natural borders" by annexing eastern Bielorussia and linking the Dvina with the Dniepr represented at attempt to connect the north with the south by way of the west and was the first of similar attempts to create a "horizontal" link intersecting the radial roads from Moscow to facilitate troop transfers from one strategic theater to another. In poor and densely wooded country it sought to create a western duplicate of the Volga waterway linking the Urals with Tsaritsyn, from which men and equipment crossed over to the Don and the Sea of Azov. The projected canal never materialized, but the empire's "natural borders" were pushed to the Niemen in 1795, incorporating the extensive river networks and the watersheds of Bielorussia and Lithuania, and reviving the old Polish-Lithuanian dream of an empire from sea to sea, from the Baltic to the Black Sea. The Lithuanian Grand Duchy had never become integrated into the Polish economy, and as late as the second half of the eighteenth century the volume of trade with Poland remained small and exchanges irregular, with only 3.3 percent of the duchy's imports coming from Poland and 6.6 percent of its exports going to it. In 1776, the Polish Diet ordered the dredging of the Mukhavets, which flows into the Western Bug past Brest-Litovsk, and the Pina, a tributary of the Pripet that flows into the Dniepr above Kiev, followed by the building of a connecting canal to be known as the Dniepr-Bug Canal. At the same time, work was begun on a road from Slonim to Pinsk on the Pina, thereby opening the Grand Duchy to Polish and Ukrainian trade from Danzig to Kiev. The canal and the road fell into Russian possession in 1795. Slonim, the headquarters in Lithuania, became the major link in a new north-south trade route from the Prussian port of Memel on the Baltic to Kiev and the Black Sea. The link was strengthened by the so-called Oginskii Canal built in 1784 and rebuilt in 1798, connecting the Shchara flowing through Slonim with the Iaselda, another tributary of the Pripet. Even then, there was renewed interest in the Chernyshev project, and construction began in 1797 of the so-called Berezina canal linking the Ulla no longer with the Drut but with the larger and deeper Berezina, which never became truly navigable and was used only for floating timber.[8]

All these waterways could not become a true duplicate of the powerful Volga in the east, but they served an important purpose. In the new peripheral lands of the empire there also existed a mutual dependence between the north and the south. New Russia (southern Ukraine), acquired in 1775 and 1792, had no forests and depended on timber shipments from Lithuania and Bielorussia to build houses for settlers and ships for the new Black Sea fleet. The canals facilitated these shipments and contributed to the economic reunification of the valley of the Dniepr. The Right-Bank Ukraine, which had gravitated toward the Western Bug, had been turning southeastward since the First Turkish War of 1768–74, when it became the supply base of the imperial army operating in Moldavia and Wallachia. The partition of 1795 completed the process, and Odessa on the Black Sea, which began its phenomenal growth in the first decades of the nineteenth century, would become the main export channel of a Ukraine now almost completely unified within the Russian Empire. The annexation of Poland's eastern marches created a new, western, periphery of the empire, unifying the basin of the eastern Baltic and most of the basin of the Black Sea and connecting them with canals. The annexation also drastically changed the nature of the client system. Imperial troops would be stationed in the periphery, where the introduction of the local government reform created everywhere a uniform infrastructure of provincial, district, and regimental headquarters to enforce imperial rule and bring about the transformation of Fortress Russian into Fortress Empire. It was no coincidence that the emperor Paul, who shut out his empire behind a Chinese wall of prohibitions and censorship, should also have launched the building of canals along the western periphery. They merged to form a wall, connecting the western and southern theaters, behind which the newly deployed strategic force assumed a defensive posture within the new "natural borders" of the empire—the Niemen, the Western Bug, and the Dniestr.

The empire's economic policy, conceived as a part of a grand strategy worked out by the ruling elite and its military-industrial complex, did not neglect foreign trade and the tariff.[9] The tariff of 1731 had relaxed the protectionism that had been the dominant feature of its 1724 predecessor, because it assumed that the strengthening of Fortress Russia by the more widespread use of serfs in the metal industries was more likely than protectionism to encourage their development. In other words, the road to hegemony would be paved with greater servitude for the dependent population. The pattern of Russian foreign trade did not change: Britain remained Russia's main commercial partner, and the balance of trade was favorable to Russia, Britain being dependent on the naval stores, Russia making a substantial profit from the acquisition of bullion in which it had been almost completely deficient until the mining of silver and gold began in the Altai in the 1740s. Internal trade was stimulated by the abolition of internal duties, especially between Russia and the Left-Bank Ukraine. But a high tariff wall was then raised between the empire and the outside world, when Elizabeth's government returned to protectionism with a vengeance: the tariff of 1757 imposed some prohibitive duties that were even higher than the value of the goods. The unification of the domestic market, which coincided with the forward deployment of troops away from the Muscovite center, was thus accompanied by the building of a high tariff wall around the growing empire, with the exception of the Baltic provinces, where the century-old Swedish tariff remained in effect. Thus began the transformation of Fortress Russia into Fortress Empire. At the same time, some members of the military-industrial complex, notably Shuvalov, were favored with lucrative monopolies and could have no interest in opening the domestic market to foreign competitors.

This tariff was published in wartime, when Britain was subsidizing the king of Prussia, with whom Russia was at war. With the end of the war and the accession of Catherine a change of policy became apparent. The new empress subscribed to free trade ideas borrowed from the philosophies of the European Enlightenment. One of her first moves was the abolition of monopolies, facilitated by the reshuffling of some key personnel within the elite and the drafting of a new tariff. It took effect in 1767, except in the Baltic provinces, the Orenburg Territory, and Siberia, and reduced export and import duties across the board, with some notable exceptions reaching 200 percent ad valorem. The new tariff was obviously not a true free trade document. It was followed, immediately after the conclusion of peace with the Ottomans in 1774, with a loosening of requirements for starting businesses in order to encourage domestic production and trade. But serfdom's harshness was not lessened. Indeed, Catherine's early tariff policy marked in many ways a return to the 1730s, with duties remaining too high and widespread smuggling the inevitable result. Nevertheless, free traders remained on the ascendancy. The annexation of part of the Black Sea littoral in 1774, the local government reform that encouraged local enterprise, and the administrative unification it imposed across the empire convinced the government to review the 1767 tariff under the leadership of Alexander Vorontsov, a strong believer in free trade: he was convinced that lower tariffs would encourage both exports and imports. The new tariff of 1782 was noteworthy on two counts: it reduced duties to an average of 10 percent ad valorem on imported goods, a very considerable concession to the Physiocratic ideas that formed the economic ideology of Catherine's reign. It was also extended to include the Baltic provinces, where the old average duty had been about 12 percent. Thus it did for those provinces what the 1757 tariff had done for the Left-Bank Ukraine. The empire of 1782, with the exception of the Orenburg and Siberian trade, which followed its own rules, had become a common market, but one also more open than the emerging Fortress Empire had ever been. In the Black Sea ports, duties were even lowered by 25 percent in order to encourage their development. The new tariff also regulated the transit trade with Poland, Lithuania, and Kurland via Riga and with the Black Sea and Mediterranean via Kherson.

Free trade is for the strong, and Catherine's reign was marked by self-confidence and a passion for fame, both in accord with a determination to impose hegemony. An expansion of foreign trade driven by the costs of "Westernization" and conspicuous consumption would produce enough wealth to raise government revenue and satisfy the needs of a ruling class looking on foreign trade as a means to exchange the products from its estates for foreign luxuries. It has rightly been pointed out that the "custom revenue in the Russian financial system was the only important article of the revenue budget not collected directly from the lower classes,"[10] but it was just as true that in a capital-poor country expenditures on foreign-made luxuries only deferred essential investments in economic infrastructure and productivity. Like the printing of paper money in excess of economic growth, they mortgaged the future. The 1782 tariff was barely ten years old when new dangers on the political horizon required substantial modifications. Trade relations were broken with France in 1793 following the execution of Louis XVI, affecting the importation of large amounts of luxury goods. With the partitions of Poland of 1793–95 incorporating the Right-Bank Ukraine, Lithuania, and Kurland into the empire, Prussia and Austria became its immediate neighbors. A review was in order, yet the 1796 tariff was the heir to that of 1782, although with a slight tilt toward protectionism.

As the empire expanded as it never had since 1710 and redeployed its strategic force in the new territories, the imperial government carried out a tariff unification of unprecedented scope. It seemed as if the empire might not become a fortress after all, but a huge common market and the dominant economic power in the basin of the Baltic and the Black Sea. But the annexations began to expose the market's major flaw: it was a colonial market, Lithuania and Bielorussia with their timber and flax only duplicating the raw material base of northern Russia, while the Right-Bank Ukraine and New Russia with their grain were a continuation of the grain fields of Orel, Kursk, and Voronezh. These raw materials were exported to the European Coastland powers, which were about to radically transform their economies based on manufacturing while the Silesian mining and textile industries were about to challenge Russia's own. The empire's hegemony could not be based on an agrarian market unless the empire became a fortress once again capable of warding off economic penetration and political subversion.

The tariff of 1796 never took effect: the empress died before it could, and Paul had different economic views. A new one was promulgated in 1797, which retained the major principles of that of 1782 but also the restrictions imposed in 1793. In addition, it introduced some disturbing novelties, restricting imports to a small number of "staple towns" and raising a wall around the imperial periphery. Fortress Empire was becoming a reality once again.

## The Ideology of Russia's Grand Strategy

Russia's emerging grand strategy also produced its own ideology. The tremendous outburst of energy that went into the country's transformation during Peter's reign and the necessity to cultivate old relations and create new ones with the outside world—chiefly within the Heartland—left its mark on the creation of an ideological foundation for the empire's new power position. The impact of Peter's personality and achievements on contemporaries and their descendants in the eighteenth century, together with Catherine II's own striking achievements in dismantling the Polish Empire and dealing a major blow to the Ottoman Empire, aroused the elite and its clients in the church and among the writers to fashion a vision of empire and elucidate the end purpose of striving for hegemony within the Heartland.

The ruling house, together with its ruling elite, believed that it ruled by virtue of conquest. Its assumption of Byzantine and later Western trappings of power was linked with a determination to emphasize its separateness from the conquered population of Russians and non-Russians alike.[11] Conquest did not require consent, or make it irrelevant at the outset of the relationship, but it generated an ubiquitous and pervasive cult of power, of awesomeness, to rationalize the subservience of the population. Conquest as the foundation of a political system would subsequently be taken for granted and its legitimacy would never be challenged. Peter's personality and the brutality of his methods in the name of a Westernization inspired by foreign models, and the exaltation of his power to an unprecedented degree, enhanced the importance of awesomeness in the perception of imperial power, not unlike that of God himself, so that its very existence and acceptance among the population within the empire's borders and among peoples beyond its periphery would be sufficient to impose obedience, precluding a need to resort to physical actions certain to bring about disastrous results for those bold enough to challenge the system.[12] Awesomeness would also find its expression in a new capital arising as if by magic out of the swamps of Karelia and designed eventually to outshine Stockholm, Warsaw, and the nomadic capital of Persia, if not Vienna and Constantinople, all within the Heartland. Peter's city, Petersburg, would develop a gravitational pull and redirect the allegiance of the local elites in Russia's frontiers from the Swedish, Polish, Ottoman, and Persian Empires toward the northern capital, floating on a cluster of islands off the coast of Eurasia.[13] And awesomeness also found its expression in the concentration of a mobile strategic force in the geographical center of the empire—leaving out the eastern theater—in the Muscovite core, from which it could strike in any direction to impose Russia's will, as it did in the Northern War and in 1711 and 1722 against the Ottomans and the Persians. If those deep strategic penetrations were not always successful, they nevertheless created everywhere in the Heartland a perception of Russia's overwhelming strength that could no longer be ignored, as they raised the possibility that subsequent interventions, especially against the Ottomans, would upset the balance of power in the frontiers.

The myth of conquest and the reality of the ruler's awesome power—even if that power derived in fact from his membership in a ruling elite comprising the politicians and the high command of the army—implied an equality in servitude of

Russians and non-Russians alike among the dependent population. The lot of sub-jugated Russians was serfdom. It was not the only paradox that this ruthless monar-chy found inspiration in the Western monarchies at the very same time it system-atized and generalized serfdom as the foundation of the sociopolitical order. The lot of the non-Russians was also serfdom, whether for the small peoples of the valley of the Volga, or in the Left-Bank Ukraine, where hetman Mazepa, in collusion with the imperial government, was beginning to introduce it among the Cossacks, or in the Baltic provinces, where the association of the Germans with the empire was purchased at the price of tightening the servitude of Estonians and Latvians. Serf-dom was a system of power in which the master knew no limits to the exercise of his authority. In a pre-industrial society, such a system was well designed to extract a maximum of resources from the dependent population in the form of men, taxes, and in-kind services.[14] It created a command economy to give the military es-tablishment the wherewithal to make war. Such was the system that Feofan Prokopovich, a Ukrainian from Kiev who became archbishop of Novgorod, glori-fied in his sermons and other writings: the awesomeness of the tsar-emperor toward his subjects, the awesomeness of Russia toward its enemies. The Pole Adam Czarto-ryski, sent as a hostage to Petersburg after the partition of 1795, who later became imperial foreign minister, noted in his memoirs that "every demonstration of power, even if unjust, pleases the Russians," that "to dominate, command, crush is a need for their national pride," and that they profess an "affectation of insulting superi-ority, (a) manner of wrenching from the weak a thing of no value which is taken only in order to humiliate him."[15]

The cult of awesomeness, of arbitrary and overwhelming power, remained fashionable after Peter's death. Vasilii Trediakovskii, the son of a priest from As-trakhan, studied in Western Europe like Prokopovich, and in 1728 sang the praises of Russia, "a world that has no ends," but where the Orthodox warriors are known for their bravery. He also wrote an ode in 1737 to celebrate the surrender of Danzig to the Russians, glorifying the empress as "the beautiful and favorable sun of the European and Asian sky," whose name inspired fear in a world where "entire na-tions submit themselves of their own free will without a battle," but also who, if need be, "is always able to conquer those who dare oppose her."[16] Interestingly, Trediakovskii appropriated the conviction among the Chinese elite—great practi-tioners of "victory by means of awesomeness"[17]—that foreign peoples must bring presents to the emperor to express their submission to his rule. He boasted that the Chinese rulers had brought tribute to the empress on two occasions, in 1731 and 1732. But it was for Mikhail Lomonosov from Arkhangelsk, who left such a deep im-print on Russian literature, history, and science, to resort to more martial language to praise Russia's awesomeness in his "Ode on the Seizure of Khotin" by the forces of Marshal Münnich in 1739, written in blissful disregard of the costs and difficul-ties of the campaign. Tatars who threatened the Russians fell "headlong and soul-less," and there were no obstacles to the flight of Russian eagles, "wherever the wind freely blows." The entire world would fear Russia because its feats of arms pro-claimed how "terrible" Russia's power was. The Khotin victory was only the first of many, when Russia would strike terror in Aleppo and Cairo and the Russian fleet would darken the Euphrates with the blood of Russia's enemies, establishing the

Russian empress as "the goddess of the shores washed by the seven wide seas." Anna's name was revered even in China.[18]

The modern reader will smile at the hyperbolic language—and marvel at Lomonosov's interest in deep strategic penetrations!—but he will also be sensitive to the imagery it seeks to convey. It was still too early to boast of the superiority of Russian civilization whose separateness was fiercely guarded by the Orthodox establishment. The role of Orthodoxy, and of moral principles in general, in the formulation of a grand strategy is very difficult to assess. Czartoryski recalls that as soon as he mentioned to his colleagues in the ministry the obligations supremacy imposed on the imperial government—principles of justice and the rights of others—he encountered a cold silence. Their only interest was to impose the empire's supremacy in Europe and Asia.[19] But there is no doubt that the liberation of the Orthodox lands supplied a handy ex post facto justification of Russian actions and afforded what ideology usually provides: a rationalization of political, strategic, or economic policies with which a power elite can feel at ease. What we see is a cult of raw power as an end in itself, a cult of the centrality of military might, of Russia's invincibility. Nowhere do we find the awareness of a larger goal, a statement of purpose behind the use of military power, although the empire's grand strategy contained a preoccupation with controlling overland trade routes between east and west. But access to trade routes was designed to increase the elite's revenue in order to farther expand military power. The correlation between the concentrated deployment of a mobile strategic force and the glorification of military power was so obvious that the determination to project Russia's awesomeness everywhere within the Heartland must be seen as one of the major components of its grand strategy.

Elizabeth's reign (1741–61) and the early years of Catherine's, from 1762 to the first Russo-Turkish War of 1768–74, built upon the Petrine legacy and raised Russian national self-consciousness to new heights. A return to Moscow after Peter's death seemed to threaten the abandonment of the new capital, but Anna Ivanovna's return to Petersburg marked the final commitment to develop a new political center to outrank Moscow, and to ground the political and military headquarters of the empire on the Baltic shore. Petersburg was still a ramshackle collection of buildings, constantly threatened by the growth of the surrounding forests, but once the final commitment had been made to conquer nature and build the new capital in a Finnish swamp, it remained for Elizabeth, with her passion for Baroque exuberance, to make it not only a political and military center but also a work of art, beckoning across a vast empire to its conquered peoples and beyond them to its client societies. The building of Petersburg was an act of conquest over nature that relegated Moscow to a purely administrative capital and cozy retirement nest for great families. The monarch's return to Moscow for her coronation was also an act of conquest, a glorification of force.[20] The continuing cult of power affected the government's attitudes in other ways: it was also under Elizabeth that the Baltic lands acquired in 1721 began to be called the "conquered provinces," as if to emphasize everywhere that conquest and the glorification of power were the defining factors in the governing of the empire by the Romanov house and its ruling elite.

The emergence of Petersburg as both an imperial capital and a regional one in the eastern Baltic transformed it and its hinterland into the main base of operations in the western theater and explained the redeployment of a substantial part of the strategic force from Moscow for eventual operations against Swedes and Prussians. The redeployment must also be related to a changing perception of "Germans" in general. They had been too prominent for their own good during Anna's reign and suffered from the backlash that brought Elizabeth to the throne, not only by losing their lucrative positions within the ruling elite but also by finding themselves exposed to the first manifestations of Russian nationalism. The famous Norman controversy began in 1749, pitting the German Gerhard Müller in the Academy of Sciences against his colleague Lomonosov who had so glorified the awesomeness of Russian power a decade earlier.[21] Even if the Scandinavian Varangians who had come to rule over Novgorod and Rus' were not German, they were associated with the Swedes who had been Peter's and Elizabeth's enemies. The 1740s and 1750s were pervaded by constant rivalry between Russians and Germans in the Academy and elsewhere, including the army. The creation in 1755 of Russia's first university in Moscow, the building of the Winter Palace in Petersburg, together with the systematic conquest of the marsh with a geometric grid of imposing avenues and the construction of majestic palaces in Peterhof and Tsarskoe Selo by Bartolomeo Rastrelli, were so many expressions of a will to power and a striving for hegemony.[22] The strong support of Orthodoxy by a pious (but also fun-loving) Elizabeth and the political necessity for Catherine to appear more Orthodox than the native Russians reinforced the traditional fusion of religion and national identity for the greater encouragement of both.

The culmination of these developments in architecture, in religious life, in perceptions of the German "other," was the rising antagonism toward Prussia and the Seven Years' War that nearly destroyed the Prussian dynasty. The war produced a new generation of generals, born in the 1720s, who would lead the empire to its greatest victories against the Ottomans during Catherine's reign. Its purpose was to reassert Russia's awesomeness over a Prussia in full transformation under the leadership of Frederick II, who challenged Russian hegemony and had to be compelled to understand that the empire's awesome power could be translated into overwhelming force. The king learned his lesson and in the process gave the Rumiantsevs, the Chernyshevs, and the Suvorovs a belief in Russia's invincibility that soon after the war motivated a redeployment of the strategic force with greater emphasis on the southern theater in preparation for an all-out offensive against the Ottoman infidels. The war ushered in the classicism of Catherine's reign, with its passion no longer for the shimmering variety of forms, but for the cold uniformity of an imperial vision across the entire continent from the Baltic to the Sea of Okhotsk. It also clarified the geographical outline of the empire's grand strategy. The Heartland's periphery had remained vague until then. By the late 1760s, the discovery of the Heartland was in full swing, with the Elbe, the Dinaric Alps—visited by Iurii Dolgorukov's mission to Montenegro in 1769—the approaches to Constantinople and the mountains of Transcaucasia looming as the empire's permanent political horizon. The extensive geographical work done during Catherine's reign would only strengthen that perception.

We remember that the redeployment of the strategic force in the 1740s and early 1760s created two wings for the Muscovite center, one in the Petersburg region as a base of operation in the western theater, the other in the Dniepr-Khopër corridor and Little Russia to the middle Dniepr as a base of operations against the Crimean Tatars and the Ottomans. The integration of Little Russia had proceeded apace since hetman Mazepa's treason in 1708, with the incorporation of the territory into the large Kiev Province administered by a governor from one of the great families of the empire. Later, the territory became a separate province but with its own form of government. The restoration of the hetmanate in 1750 with the appointment as hetman of Kirill Razumovskii, a native Cossack whose brother was Elizabeth's morganatic husband, was not, despite appearances, a step toward greater self-rule. The new hetman had gone a long way from the Cossack *khutor* to the imperial palaces of Petersburg, from the simple life on the frontier to the elaborate etiquette of the imperial capital. He had already become president of the Academy of Sciences and count of the empire and would become a field marshal, in his case a purely honorary title, but one that gave him the privileges restricted to a very select group at the top of the military establishment. The Razumovskiis and their relatives became integrated into the ruling elite, especially in the Naryshkin-Trubetskoi network, laying the foundations of what would become the Black Sea network, while a profound social transformation was bringing serfdom to the territory with the hetman's 1760 order forbidding the peasants to move.[23] This "conquest" of the hetmanate by one of its own members endowed with the awesome civil and military attributes of the imperial power was sealed by the abolition of the hetmanate and the appointment of Rumiantsev as governor general in 1764. The conquest was also a victory for Orthodoxy since the cossacks professed that religion; they became "Russians speaking Ukrainian"—in the same way the Bulgarian flock of the Greek Patriarch of Constantinople was considered "Greeks speaking Bulgarian"[24]—and equal in servitude with their Russian brethren. The conquest was also a challenge to Catholicism and Islam, and it required a permanent headquarters. It would have to be Kiev, with its glittering churches including St. Andrew, built between 1748 and 1767 by the same Rastrelli, the architect of Elizabeth's Petersburg. Thus, the redeployment of troops in the Baltic hinterland and in the valley of the Dniepr was also governed by ideological factors that were an intrinsic consequence of the empire's grand strategy: the formulation of a national identity vis-à-vis the Lutheran Germans, Catholic Poles, Islamic Tatars, and Ottomans, demanding the creation of forward headquarters staking a claim for hegemony within the Heartland's periphery: Riga, Vilno, Kiev, Ekaterinograd, Vladikavkaz, and even Orenburg.

The military victories over the Ottomans in two long and bloody wars were also victories of Orthodoxy over Islam. The annexation of the Crimea gave the empire for the first time a patrimony with deep roots in antiquity—Greek ruins—and the beginnings of Orthodoxy among the eastern Slavs—the site of Vladimir's baptism. The double connection with ancient Greece and Orthodoxy stimulated the ambition to bring about the final defeat of the Ottomans and recreate an eastern empire to be governed, if not from Constantinople, at least from the new city of Ekaterinoslav built, like Petersburg, out of nowhere along the banks of the Dniepr.[25] The return to antiquity could not ignore ancient Rome, especially in an empire where the army, like the Roman army, built and colonized as much as it fought. The regular army built fortresses and ports and shipyards; its irregular units settled the empty steppe together with colonists from the interior or from abroad. And the interest in ancient Rome could not but encourage a transition to peripheral deployment, as the Romans had once done at the height of their power along the Rhine and the Danube.

The growing interest in antiquity accelerated the transition from the Baroque to neoclassicism, especially prominent in architecture, the art of conquest, which in its monumental forms creates an image of power and awesomeness. Russia's eighteenth century "lived under the magic spell of architecture."[26] Catherine II naturally had a strong interest in it, and her architects, notably Charles Cameron and Giacomo Quarenghi, were students of ancient Rome and of the Roman imperial style of Louis XIV, Quarenghi creating "the most austere forms of Petersburg's Roman classicism."[27] If austerity, coldness, and uniformity were not enough to convey the image of Fortress Empire, Catherine chose to express the continuity of her rule with that of Peter, the founder of Fortress Russia, by commissioning a statue of the first tsar-emperor, facing the Neva on his rearing horse, the very image of conquest and awesomeness, which would once lead to madness Pushkin's creation in the "Bronze Horseman."[28] Classicism, with its belief in the uniformity of human nature and in making disparate customs conform to a "rational" order, eventually degenerated into the "paradomania" that began with the accession of Paul in 1796. Public values during Catherine's reign had been predominantly civilian, focused on the "general good" and the improvement of civilian government, following the introduction of the local government reform of 1775, geared toward the greater good of the elite and its clients in the ruling class all over the empire. These values did not exclude the continued glorification of arbitrary power and awesomeness, as when Repnin threatened during the Polish Diet of 1766 to destroy Warsaw "stone by stone" if it carried out a reform of its government[29]—not a vain threat in view of the fact that the Russians would massacre 20,000 Poles in the storming of Praga in 1794, three years after visiting the same awesome power over the Ottomans at Izmail on the Danube. Paul imposed military values on Russian society itself: a rigid sense of hierarchy, unconditional obedience, and rule by generals and traveling inspectors. The theatricality of the monarchy found its expression less in balls and artistic evenings in a relaxed atmosphere than in impressive, awesome parades in Petersburg and Moscow, where men were quickly promoted and just as quickly demoted. The parade became the ultimate degeneration of the classical ideal—the reduction of human beings to the uniform level of automata, marching, turning, and shouting at a single command.

One of the manifestations of Russian classicism was the administrative-territorial reform that began with the local government statute of 1775 and continued with the charters of 1785. In the name of reason and geometry, the existing empire was divided into provinces and districts, with the same number of peasant "souls" placed under the same set of provincial agencies everywhere. The result was the abolition of the client system within the imperial periphery. As the empire expanded following the partitions of 1793–95 and the Turkish War of 1788–92, the same organization was introduced in the frontier regions, whether the nearly empty Ochakov steppe or the eastern marches of the Polish Empire, abolishing the client system there as well as creating an enormous space without internal distinctions and automatically transforming Fortress Russia into Fortress Empire. The process required a redeployment of the strategic force along the imperial periphery, much in the same way as Fortress Russia had deployed it along the periphery of the Muscovite center. The empire's grand strategy possessed its own logic and ideological justification, even as it gradually evolved to replace much of the client system everywhere with direct rule in an ever increasing geopolitical space.

The Germanophilia of the 1730s had been replaced by a wave of Francophilia that crested between 1755 and 1775 and exercised a powerful influence on the development of Russian art, literature, and the writing of history. The challenge posed by this influence created a backlash and accelerated the process of self-examination which had begun in the late 1730s as a response to the growth of German influence.[30] The French Revolution, with its rejection of classical values, cosmopolitanism, and assault on the ancien régime, was a threat to the established order in the empire. Even before its outbreak, the Orthodox Church had raised the alarm at the progress of secular ideas driving a wedge in the association between religion and national consciousness. The great expansion of the empire took place when Russian values were being glorified once again, alongside a religious revival identifying Russia with Orthodoxy and the faith with Russia. The advance completed the conquest, which had been so long in the making, of Catholicism in Poland's frontier territories and launched the conquest of Islam toward the Danube and in Transcaucasia. Everywhere, the ruling elite sought to obliterate the distinctions between Russians and Estonians, Latvians, Lithuanians, Bielorussians, Ukrainians, and Crimean Tatars by making them into "Russians," subject to the same laws, until, like the Ukrainians and Bielorussians, they would become Orthodox as well. The transformation required the presence of the imperial army to enforce it along the new periphery and to protect it against threats from the outside. Fortress Russia became Fortress Empire by combining classicism with an emerging Russian-Orthodox nationalism.

## Client States and Societies

The concept of Fortress Russia was inseparable from a client system managed at a distance by the imperial power with the help of local elites for the advantage of both. It enabled the imperial government to practice an economy of force by relying on those elites for the security and internal administration of their territories and binding them to the interests of the empire as a whole. Mutual interest and a perception of Russia's awesomeness held the system together. But this client system was shaken to its foundations between the 1740s and the end of the century, in the western theater by the ambitions of Frederick II of Prussia, in the southern theater by Russia's own ambitions. It survived, however, and, if some clients disappeared, new ones were found.

The king made no secret of his determination to upset the balance with the friendly kingdom by annexing Silesia and gaining an industrial base that could support his military machine. In so doing, he violated a cardinal rule of the client system according to which no client could take independent action without the approval of the grand patron. He also raised the specter of a client gaining sufficient strength to develop its own client system, compounding these two errors by refusing to recognize Russia's awesomeness and predicting that the Russians would soon be forced to return to their old borders, to the darkness and "extreme barbarism" from which Peter had sought to extricate them.[31] The imperial government's overreaction to the rise of Prussia showed the strength of the assumption that Prussia was a client state and expected to behave as such. What was written about Russia's relations with Poland applies equally well here: that Russia looked on its treaties "not so much as agreements between equals or near-equals—-*traktaty*—but as pledges of allegiance—*sherti*—of the sort it had routinely imposed on the Tatars, Bashkirs, Kazakhs and other non-Orthodox peoples on its periphery."[32] It was feared as early as 1744 that Prussia, following its victory over Austria, would impose its candidate on the Polish throne and revive Polish claims to Livonia, Smolensk, and the Left-Bank Ukraine and might even change patrons by seeking an alliance with France, Russia's and Austria's enemy.[33] The so-called Diplomatic Revolution—when Prussia allied with England and France with Austria—ensured that this would not take place and brought about the Seven Years' War, which severely damaged Prussia's economy and army and strengthened Russia's determination to reassert its dominion over a wayward client. A much chastened Frederick did form an alliance with Russia in 1764, but one in which Catherine showed little interest. The persistence of the Austro-Prussian hatred subordinated the two Germanic powers to Russia's will; hatred also created resentment of Russia's growing power during the Turkish Wars, and Poland became a victim, partitioned to provide those two powers with "compensations" and keep them within the system.

But Russia's policy did not change. It remained anchored in the friendly kingdom and looked on Prussia as a client state. Frederick had already complained in 1766 of the Russian "yoke," that he was not a Syrian king to whom a praetor came to impose the will of Rome; he was not Russia's "slave,"[34] but there was little he could do to alter the unequal relationship with the dominant power in the Heartland. In 1780, after the Teschen Agreement recognized Russia as one of the guarantors of the Peace of Westphalia in the Holy Roman Empire, he had to send his nephew and heir to Petersburg, where he was received as "a repentant subordinate."[35] When Frederick died in 1786, the Russian ambassador, who happened to be the son of Marshal Rumiantsev, the destroyer of Ottoman hegemony in the southern theater, refused to attend his funeral and proceeded to "treat Prussian ministers like chancery clerks." He explained his haughty behavior by saying that "the Prussian Court must not be able to stand up to us [*nous tenir tête*] without fearing in all cases the consequences of our enmity" and, paraphrasing a Russian proverb, that not only must the pike be dead, its teeth must be removed.[36] By the time of his death, the king had become obsessed with Russia's dynamism, that of a power more "Asiatic" than European. He would have been right if he had only changed his adjective to look on Russia as a great Eurasian power approaching hegemony to which all powers from the Baltic to Mongolia were expected to submit, manipulating the European state system as it manipulated the system of client societies in the steppe, and seeking everywhere to win its victories by means of awesomeness.

Following the election of Stanislaw Poniatowski to the Polish throne in 1764, the disintegration of the Polish Empire had been accelerating and its eastern marches were in full rebellion. The Russians encouraged the creation of client societies within a client state. This came to a climax in 1792 with the Confederation of Targowica, led by a group of magnates of the Right-Bank Ukraine who resented, like the Russian government, the promulgation of the Constitution of May 3, 1791, inspired by French Revolutionary ideas.[37] They were bound together by their hatred of the royal power in Warsaw: their revolt was one of the frontier against the core. But, by its very existence, a frontier needs to gravitate toward another core. It turned east toward the rising empire, a move facilitated by the reorientation of the Right-Bank economy toward the Black Sea, and the subsequent partitions consolidated Russia's hegemony in the western theater. Similar developments were taking place in Kurland, whose duke, Anna Ivanovna's lover, had been imposed by the Russians in 1739, banished to Siberia in 1742, and returned in 1763. He died in 1772. His son made himself unacceptable to Petersburg, but there were Kurland nobles who, like the magnates of the Right Bank, were ready to change their allegiance, even if it meant abolishing the contractual relationship between the duchy and the Polish Empire and placing themselves at the mercy of the all-powerful and all-merciful imperial ruler who recognized no contractual obligations. The leader of those nobles was Otto von der Hoven, an intelligent master of intrigues and a personal enemy of the duke; in return for bringing the nobles over to Russia's side he became a privy councilor and senator—and immensely rich.[38]

These client societies beyond the empire's nominal periphery were to discover that the disruptive game they had played with such ruthlessness had become a crime of treason against the ruling elite they had just joined, with all the attendant consequences. Others were becoming systematically integrated into the administrative infrastructure of the empire. The reform of 1783 in the Baltic provinces sought to break the hold of the "matriculated" nobility and diversify the social composition of the local ruling class by bringing in outsiders, including Russians, and canceling some of the old privileges, many of them restored by Paul. Nevertheless, the Baltic Germans would continue to administer their territories in the name of the imperial power, and their importance in the high command of the army would only grow during the reign of his two sons. Across the Gulf of Finland, a new client society was emerging. In Finland, secession had been in the air since the 1740s, but a Finland separated from Sweden would have to gravitate toward Russia. Gustav III's determination to restore royal absolutism in 1772 only stimulated secessionist yearnings. The Russo-Swedish War of 1788–90 created a situation very similar to that which had been developing in the Polish Empire, when nobles, also bound together by their hatred of the royal power, revolted against the king and put out feelers to Petersburg for Russian support.[39] The Sprengtportens, Armfelts, Klicks, and Jägerhorns, among others, some of them related to families in the Baltic provinces, were the true brethren of the Lubomirskis, Potockis, and Rzewuskis of the Right-Bank Ukraine in offering their services to the empire and in their willingness to translate its desires into reality within the larger framework of Fortress Empire.

The advance to the Niemen, the Western Bug, and the Dniestr, and the sharing of a common border with Prussia and Austria were followed by a methodical demarcation of the imperial periphery, eliminating the invisible frontier and destroying the old client system in the Polish Empire. The administration of the new territories remained in the hands of the Polish nobility, but they were profoundly distrusted in Petersburg because they were less inclined than the Baltic Germans to cooperate with the empire. While the Baltic frontier had become secure by 1743, the Polish periphery and the immediate proximity of the Germanic powers created a high level of insecurity, requiring a substantial deployment of the strategic force for the dual purpose of a fixed frontier defense and a forward strategy.

In the southern theater, military successes, rather than political developments, eliminated the Crimean Khanate and brought the empire to the Black Sea littoral from the Dniestr to the Kuban. Nature, here the coastline, began to demarcate neatly the imperial periphery in this region as well, requiring a similar forward deployment. The result of this process was the elimination of the Cossack societies as clients of the empire. The Cossack social and political order had been disintegrating for some time. Elizabeth had put off the day of reckoning, but it had become unavoidable by the 1780s. Back in 1765, the Cossacks of the Ukraine of Settlements had been reorganized to form five hussar regiments that became part of the strategic force, while their former territories became districts administered by *voevody* subordinate to a new governor in Kharkov. Once the imperial periphery began to follow the Black Sea shore after 1774, the Cossack frontier societies became an anachronism. Their purpose since the days of Polish rule had been to guard the border against Tatar raids, to do what the Poles and later the Russians could not do with their regular troops in such forward positions. There was no longer any need for them, but only for cossack-like detachments, highly mobile but without a territorial base, to carry out reconnaissance and patrolling missions along the coastline and the peripheral rivers.

Internal developments also destroyed their raison d'être. Cossack societies imploded. As they settled down during the first half of the eighteenth century, they began to split three ways, with the process reaching completion in the 1780s. An upper layer of *starshiny* and rich landowners, originating among the rank-and-file Cossacks, grew to become a new elite. Influenced as they inevitably had to be by the serfdom prevailing in neighboring Poland and Russia, they too sought to enserf the population, including their own Cossacks, and thereby destroyed the legitimacy of their claim to represent the old Cossack world with its "rights and privileges." This elite was an eager client of the Russians because it needed a patron, beyond whom there was no appeal, to recognize and confirm their newly won status as well as land deeds they had acquired by hook and by crook. They also needed the empire because it was a source of lucrative careers in the army, the civil establishment, and the Orthodox Church. Most of the rank-and-file Cossacks were transformed into serfs and state peasants, the collective property of the elite and the ruling class. Finally, those who refused to accept their fate joined the new Cossack regiments that became part of the regular army. The local government reform introduced on the Left Bank in 1783—not coincidentally the year of the annexation of the Crimean Khanate, whose existence had justified the creation of Cossack forces two hundred years earlier—made that transition easier for them.[40] The territorial regiments of the old hetmanate were regrouped to form three provinces and the Cossacks were incorporated into ten carbineer regiments. Farther south, the

Zaporozhian Host, subordinated to Razumovskii in 1750, and to Rumiantsev in 1764, was abolished in 1775, the opposition banished to distant monasteries, its territory becoming Ekaterinoslav Province. The host was partly restored in 1783 under the name of Black Sea Cossacks, transferred to the North Caucasus in 1792, and settled along the right bank of the Kuban to the confluence of the Laba. There, as well as along the Terek, Cossack forces were still needed. Even the Don Cossacks began to feel the pressure, as they ceased to be a frontier society with the elimination of the Kuban horde in the 1780s.

The advance of the periphery, followed by the redeployment of the strategic force behind it, projected among the peoples of the Caucasus a perception of Russia's awesomeness in the wake of Kuchuk Kainardji: the Ottoman Empire with its Crimean client had been the hegemon in the Black Sea basin for five hundred years, and its defeat was an extraordinary event. There had been a Georgian lobby in Petersburg and Moscow ever since Tsar Wakhtang VI had moved to Russia in 1725, and there were Georgian colonies in Kizliar and Astrakhan. The tsar of eastern Georgia, Erekle, had supported, if not facilitated, the Russian military expedition across the mountains into western Georgia in 1769. He sought to use the Russians to consolidate the position of his house and expand his power westward into Ottoman-controlled Transcaucasia and eastward to Azerbaijan, where the khans looked to Persia for protection. There, the usual roles were reversed: the client used his patron to pursue his agenda. But the Russian advance into mountain country and Erekle's machinations brought about an increase of Ottoman activity along the eastern coast of the Black Sea, including the storage of supplies at Sudzhuk Kale (Novorossiisk) and the building of new ports at Anapa and Gelendzhik. From the coast, the Ottomans strengthened their hold on the mountain peoples, known collectively as the Circassians. They used their old ties with the leading Abkhazian families to stir up the latent antagonism between Abkhazia and Mingrelia, the birthplace of Erekle's third wife. The client found himself hemmed in between the growing Ottoman counteroffensive and the ambitions of the Azerbaijan khans. He turned to the empire for protection in 1783, offering to become its vassal: he would continue to govern his country but would supply troops to the imperial army; the Russians would have a minister in Tiflis, and the imperial ruler would bestow on every new Georgian tsar the regalia of his office. But Erekle incurred the wrath of the Persian shah and received none of the expected protection during the sack of Tiflis in 1795. The perception of Russia's awesomeness in the region was damaged, as it had been in part following the poor results of the second Turkish War. The invasion of Azerbaijan in 1796 was a grandiose although poorly planned attempt to restore it, but the empire was by then marking time and nothing was accomplished. The deterioration of the internal situation in Georgia after Erekle's death in 1798 finally induced his son to propose the annexation of his kingdom to the emperor Paul, who accepted it shortly before his death in 1801.[41] The Georgian case clearly showed that the maintenance of the client system depended on the continued perception of Russia's awesomeness. When that perception ceased or was dimmed by the inability to project overwhelming force successfully, the client relationship collapsed. The empire was forced to resort to a forward deployment in the territory of the client state, thereby creating a highly ambivalent situation vis-à-vis its former patron and compelling the client's integration into the administrative and military infrastructure of the imperial state. The economy of force gave way to on-line deployment, a development that did not necessarily serve the empire's best interests.

Beyond the Volga and the Caspian, in the eastern theater, the strategic picture had always been radically different, because the empire never faced the resistance of powerful core areas (like Sweden, Prussia, and the Ottomans) to its striving for hegemony within the Heartland, and because Manchu China possessed a complementary spatial vision of its security interests: the crushing of the Zunghars in the 1750s and indeed the entire course of Russo-Chinese relations in the eighteenth century showed that China conceded Russia's hegemony on the periphery of the Heartland.[42]

A major turning point in the history of the client system in the eastern theater was the appointment in 1744 of Ivan Nepliuev as the first governor of Orenburg Province, where he remained until 1759. He was a great believer in the necessity to impress Bashkirs, Kalmyks, and Kazakhs with Russia's awesomeness, and he succeeded in the end, being partly responsible for encouraging the incipient political disintegration of the Small and Middle Hordes. Other factors also played a role in the changing situation in the region. The progress of colonization and the development of industry in the southern Urals aroused a strong reaction among the Bashkirs, who rebelled in 1755 and were crushed mercilessly, many of them fleeing into the Kazakh steppe. At the same time, however, Kazan Tatars, skilled in agriculture and trade, moved into Bashkiria and became the empire's agents in its relations with the Central Asian khanates. Bashkirs who chose to expiate their disloyalty to the empire became intermediaries between the imperial authorities and the Kazakh clan leaders. As the empire expanded, it brought along its own clients from the interior to develop and strengthen new client relationships along the edge of settlement. As in the Chinese Empire, where nomadic peoples on the periphery of the settled core paid tribute by bringing products typical of their economy, the Ural Cossacks sent fresh fish and caviar;[43] the Kazakhs and Kalmyks sent fine horses and richly decorated saddles on their periodic visits to the imperial capital and received rich presents in return. They delivered hostages to Orenburg, who were sons, brothers, or nephews of khans, and replaced them every few years with new ones.[44] As the fringe of settlement kept advancing in the latter part of the century, the Ural and Orenburg Cossacks were integrated into the administrative infrastructure of the empire and became just another constituent part of a frontier society, eager to seize the land and expel the nomad.

The Kalmyks had been "disciplined" in the 1730s; in the 1770s, they were domesticated. The inexorable advance of the settler and the activities of the Ural Cossacks, together with the usual internal squabbles among clan leaders, convinced the imperial government that the Kalmyks had outlived their usefulness as a frontier society. The decision taken in Petersburg, following the death of Khan Donduk in 1761, to open up the governing council (zargo) to clans other than the khan's led Ubashi, the new khan, to leave the empire and rejoin the Zunghar homeland in 1771. By then, however, Zungharia had passed under Manchu control, and the Kalmyks who were not massacred along the way by the Kazakhs, their old enemies, were resettled by the Manchus in present-day Sinkiang. Only about 5,000 *kibitki* (25,000 Kalmyks) remained under Russian jurisdiction. The Russians too resettled them, but across the Volga, in a nearly deserted region between the Caspian, the Manych, and the Kuma under the authority of the Astrakhan governor.[45] They had ceased to be a frontier society. Only the Kazakhs remained.

Abul Khayr of the Small Horde had become a client of the empire in 1731, but his relations with Nepliuev were tense, because he aspired to reunite the three hordes under his authority, that of a single khan, and the proconsul could not accept a client's becoming so powerful that he would develop his own client system in the steppe that would not depend on the Orenburg headquarters directly. Abul Khayr's major rival was Sultan Barak of the Middle Horde, who "protected" the territory of the Karakalpaks on the shores of the Aral Sea and killed him in 1748 after Abul Khayr laid claims to his pastures. The khan was succeeded by his son Nur Ali, who would reign over the Small Horde until 1786, after receiving the regalia of his office from Nepliuev in Orenburg in the presence of representatives of the three hordes, but without the title of khan over all the Kazakhs. Nur Ali did not have his father's political skills and found himself under attack by the Zunghars; he could not stop the fleeing Kalmyks in 1771, had to deal with the flood of Bashkir refugees during the crushing of the Pugachev Rebellion, and could not cope with a rebellion in the steppe against his own authority. The Russians eventually banished him to Ufa, where he died in 1790. They had worked all the while to undermine his authority because a khan, even if his powers were at times nominal, could become a symbol of resistance to the encroachments of the settler. With the disappearance of the Zunghar danger in the 1750s, the client society of the Kazakhs, like that of the Cossacks, had become an anachronism. Nur Ali was succeeded by his brother Er Ali, who died in 1794, by his son Ishim, who died in 1797, and then by another brother, Ayshuak, who died in 1800. All received their investiture and patent of office from the imperial authority in Orenburg, but the prestige of the office of khan was gone. In the Middle Horde, Abul Muhammad reigned until 1771, but the leading figure there after Barak's assassination in 1750 was Sultan Ablai, who succeeded Abul and died ten years later, in 1781. With the horde's pastures at a much greater distance from the lines, the settler had not yet become a power factor, and the long arm of the Orenburg administration did not reach the khan's tent with the same force. Ablai sought Manchu friendship in order to obtain additional pastures in what had been Zunghar territory. Then he turned friendlier to the Russians, but refused to come to Orenburg to take the oath of loyalty and receive his investiture.[46] Time was working against him, however, and his balancing game between Russia and China appeared increasingly meaningless. After his death, the Middle Horde disappeared as a client society, his son Vali ruling over only the northern clans, those to the east maintaining their rule with Chinese support, while the southern clans were absorbed by the Great Horde, which gave its allegiance to China.

By the end of the eighteenth century, the client system had undergone major changes. Sweden, which had refused to accept its position in it, ended up taking Russian subsidies and producing a secessionist movement in Finland, which brought closer the final day of reckoning. Prussia was brought low, and the disintegration of its military position became obvious. Both powers remained clients of an empire that fulfilled its striving for hegemony by agreeing to the partitions of the Polish client. Its elimination necessitated a peripheral deployment that rendered the empire, the friendly kingdom, and Prussia uneasy neighbors in Polish territory, a situation fraught with potential dangers. In the south, the annexation of the Crimean Khanate and the advance to the Black Sea littoral destroyed the client societies in the steppe but also brought about the formal creation of a client state in Georgia. In the eastern theater, the destruction of the client system was nearly complete. Fortress Russia, which had depended on the maintenance of such a system, had been transformed into Fortress Empire.

# PART III

# THE TERRITORIALIZATION OF THE EMPIRE, 1797–1831

# 7

# Strategic Penetration

## Italy, Holland, Sweden, and Turkey, 1799–1812

We now turn to the third period in our history of Russia's grand strategy, that of the French Revolutionary wars, when the empire consolidated its hegemony in the Heartland, a hegemony it would retain until the unification of Germany in 1871. It was then that what may be called the cold war with France during much of the eighteenth century turned into an open conflict, when Napoleon challenged that hegemony and struck at the Muscovite core itself. The counteroffensive stirred Russia's determination to resort to deep strategic penetrations once again in order to destroy French hegemony on the continent. It took the form of unprecedented offensive operations in Austria, Switzerland, Italy, and Holland, going far beyond those of 1735 and 1748, and ended with the occupation of Paris in 1814. Once French hegemony had been destroyed, the empire found itself facing a maritime British Empire claiming global hegemony, but forced to concede Russia's hegemony in the Heartland as long as its periphery was neutralized.

The strategic implications of the French Revolution did not become clear in Petersburg until Prussia was forced out of the First Coalition against France in 1795. The subsequent defeat in Austria in northern Italy in 1797 made matters worse. Such was the background of Suvorov's expedition of 1799 and the landing in Holland that same year. Following the French annexation of Belgium, the left bank of the Rhine, and northern Italy to the Po River, the imperial government committed 65,000 troops to a joint Austro-Russian army that would recapture northern Italy, invade France from the south, and topple the revolutionary government in Paris.

The expeditionary force consisted of three corps. One left Brest-Litovsk and followed in the footsteps of Lacy in 1735, marching via Opole, across the Moravian Gate to Prague, beyond the Danube west of Regensburg, and entering Switzerland to face a French force near Zürich. It planned to move on across a weakly defended border into France itself. The second corps also left Brest-Litovsk but marched farther south via Kraków and Krems to Vienna, where Suvorov assumed the overall command of the army. From Vienna, it crossed the Alps and entered Italy via the

Brenner Pass, descending into the valley of the Po at Brescia on the way to Milan, which it captured in April 1799, 1,650 kilometers from Moscow. The base of operations of the third corps was Kamenets-Podolsk, from which it marched to Lwów, crossed the Carpathian Mountains to Budapest, and reached the Po Valley at Verona on the way to Turin. The bloodiest battle was fought at Novi in August; it earned Suvorov the title of prince of Italy. The French had already surrendered Turin in June. But coalition warfare was often governed more by politics than by strategic planning, and the Russians fell victim, as they had during the Seven Years' War, to the jealousy of the ever cautious Austrians, who resented Suvorov's impetuosity. In addition, the British were not eager to see a possibly permanent Russian presence in Genoa, a major port which could become a base of operations for the Russian squadron in the Mediterranean.[1] Instead of moving on into southern France, Suvorov was induced to move northward into Switzerland. The first corps had been defeated by the French outside Zürich. To reassert the allied presence in the area, Suvorov, by forced marches—and despite the lack of supplies promised by the Austrians, who had pledged responsibility for the logistics of the entire operation—crossed the St. Gotthard Pass into Switzerland in September and followed the valley of the Reuss River to Altdorf, where he discovered there was no farther road leading to Zürich. The Russians had become trapped in the mountains and were pursued by the French. They managed to escape across desolate terrain, roadless even today, and reached the upper Rhine (Vorderrhein) at Ilanz in October, "where even the French would not venture to follow them."[2] What was left of the Russian expeditionary force took up winter quarters in Bavaria.

While Suvorov was fighting his way across the mountains of Switzerland, Russian transports were ferrying more than 10,000 troops from the Baltic ports to Holland in a joint Anglo-Russian expedition inspired by the British. Its purpose was to establish a foothold on the Coastland from which Russian troops would move toward Amsterdam, the main city of the so-called Batavian Republic, a French protectorate since 1795. The expedition failed, partly because the strength of the French had been underestimated.[3] Nevertheless, there was something grandiose in this deep strategic penetration by the Russians, no longer merely within the Heartland, but beyond it into the continental Coastland. In an immense enveloping movement from bases of operations in the western theater, directed against northern and southern France, two invasion forces intended to converge on Paris. This went far beyond the precedents of 1735 and 1748; it anticipated the campaigns of 1813–14. Suvorov had barely returned to Russia in 1800 when Paul sent 22,000 Don Cossacks to the Indus River via Khiva and Bukhara in order to strike at British power in India.[4] His death in March 1801 put an end to this senseless expedition, but in the unlikely event it would have succeeded, imperial troops would have reached an objective 5,000 kilometers from Moscow. Not unlike the Mongols who had once planned a simultaneous invasion of Poland and Korea, the Russians could plan deep strikes from one end of the Eurasian continent to another.

Compared with those ambitious undertakings, the campaign of 1805 was a more limited projection of power, but it involved a larger number of troops commanded, at least nominally, by the tsar in person. The Russians committed a "Podolian army" of 30,000 under Friedrich von Buxhöwden and a corps of 20,000 under

Magnus von Essen forming a reserve. The Podolian army crossed the imperial border at Radzivillov and marched via Teschen (Cieszyn), Brunn (Brno), Krems, and Braunau toward Ulm, where the Austrians were awaiting Napoleon. Mikhail Kutuzov advanced slowly at twenty kilometers a day, then by forced marches of sixty kilometers per day, but was unable to link up with the Austrians before their defeat in October, when he suddenly found himself the only obstacle between Napoleon and Vienna. Rather than facing Napoleon's 220,000 men, he chose to retreat—one of the most difficult strategic maneuvers—facing a constant danger of encirclement, and forced to fight a number of bloody engagements with the French avant-garde. After the French bypassed him and took Vienna at the end of October, Kutuzov retreated farther into Moravia to Wischau (Vyshkov) between Brunn and Olmütz (Olomouc), where he linked up with Buxhöwden. There, Kutuzov wanted to wait while the other Austrian forces returned from northern Italy and Prussia entered the war. Instead, the tsar and his young advisers chose to go on the offensive. Assuming the French army was exhausted, they engaged it at the famous battle of Austerlitz (Slavkov) near Brunn in December.[5] It became Napoleon's most famous victory. Austria was forced to leave the war, and the Russian army marched back to Brody, where it re-entered the empire a few weeks later. If the 1799 campaign was a precedent for the campaigns of 1813–14, the retreat from Braunau to Brunn was a precedent for the retreat of 1812 from the Niemen to Moscow.

Russia remained in the war, but on the defensive. The French advance continued, directed against Prussia, which was forced out of the war when Napoleon entered Berlin in October 1806. Russia was now alone on the Continent and had to make peace after the battles of Eylau and Friedland fought in East Prussia. The two emperors met at Tilsit on the Niemen in June 1807. For the first time since 1708, Russia found the enemy at its border, but an enemy ready to make peace. An outcome of that peace, however, was a return to a forward strategy against Sweden and the Ottoman Empire, whose relations with Russia had become friendly in the wake of the international upheaval brought about by the French Revolution but had turned hostile again after Russia's defeat at Austerlitz because the sultan had become convinced Napoleon was invincible. The Prussian client had become a French satellite; the Polish core area, partly restored as the Duchy of Warsaw, a French protectorate. It was agreed at Tilsit that Russia, defeated outside but not within its empire, would annex Finland, but would withdraw its troops from Moldavia and Wallachia, keeping the empire away from its moat on the Danube.

The fourth and last Russo-Swedish War of 1808–9 was a direct result of the third (1788–90), but, unlike the third, it was not a defensive but an offensive operation in which Alexander, like Peter in the 1710s, was determined to strike at Sweden itself. The Russians would combine forces with Napoleon, who had decided to force Sweden to join the Continental System and planned an invasion of the country's southern provinces across the Sound similar to Peter's plan in 1716. Alexander's determination was strengthened by the necessity to restore the prestige of the imperial army and the unjustified assumption that the Finnish peasantry was ready to welcome the Russians in order to overthrow Swedish domination. There were also memories of 1788, when the sound of Swedish cannon was heard in Petersburg, and fears that an invasion of Sweden would give Napoleon, already established in

Poland, strategic control of the eastern Baltic.[6] But this time, the Russians were determined to wrest Finland from Sweden for good and establish themselves along the Bothnian moat, thereby consolidating their influence over Sweden to the Heartland's periphery.

The invasion of Finland began without a declaration of war in February 1808 in three directions under the command of the same Buxhöwden who had reinforced Kutuzov before the battle of Austerlitz. The invasion force consisted of only 24,000 men, much smaller than the forces committed against the French or the Turks. One column moved along the coast of the Gulf of Finland toward Helsingfors and the huge fortress of Sveaborg, "the Gibraltar of the North," with its two hundred guns and enormous supplies, which surrendered in April. From there, the Russians moved on to Hangö and Åbo and occupied the Åland Islands, coming within thirty kilometers of the Swedish shore.[7] They were forced to retreat, however, by a Swedish counterattack to defend the approaches to Sweden. Another column moved north toward St. Mikhel on the way to Björneborg (Pori) and Vasa. These last two columns were at first very successful. The second took Björneborg in March and advanced along the coast toward Vasa, converging on Uleåborg, where it hoped to link up with the third advancing from Kuopio. But the retreating Swedes began to put up stiff resistance, as the narrowing of the front always favors the defensive. The Russians' columns had moved along too far north too quickly and were now cut off from their reserves by six hundred kilometers of difficult terrain, freezing temperatures, inadequate supplies, and a Finnish partisan war. Nevertheless, they had forced the Swedes by September to retreat farther north and occupied Karleby (Kokkola), where Buxhöwden moved his headquarters from Åbo.

The Swedish commander in chief, now convinced the Swedes had no chance to recapture southern Finland following the failure of a number of Swedish landings and the control of the coast by the Russians, offered an armistice, which the Russians accepted. But the tsar ordered Buxhöwden to break the truce and resume the offensive. In November, the Swedes were forced to abandon Uleåborg Province and withdrew behind the Kem (Kemijoki) River, one hundred kilometers north of the city. The whole of Finland was in Russian hands. But the Russians had not yet gained staying power. Their total forces now numbered 48,000 men, including 38,000 infantry and 4,000 cavalry, but it was scattered across an enormous territory: Uleåborg was 750 kilometers from Helsingfors, Vasa 500 from Joensuu. Buxhöwden estimated Russia needed at least 50,000 troops to garrison Finland and another 50,000 to invade Sweden.[8] These reminders did not sit well with the tsar and his entourage and Buxhöwden had powerful enemies. He was recalled in December and replaced by Gotthard von Knorring, who had been chief of staff in the 1788–90 war.

There were disagreements in the high command about future operations since Finland had been occupied and annexed to the Russian Empire, a political and strategic decision the Russians had avoided in 1714 and 1743. One option was to assume a defensive posture, wait for the Swedes to invade Finland, and force them to negotiate the peace, but this would require maintaining a strong Russian presence in the country as Buxhöwden had warned, creating considerable logistical difficulties in a poor country and at great distances from the base of operations. The other option was to force the Swedes to capitulate by invading their country. This had been Peter's policy, and Alexander was equally determined. He confirmed a plan of operations submitted by Michael Barclay de Tolly, who would later win fame in the 1812 war. Imperial troops would invade Sweden from three directions: across the Åland archipelago, across the Kvarken between Vasa and Umeå, and around the northern end of the Gulf of Bothnia from the Kem River to Umeå, where they would join forces and advance on Stockholm after linking up with the force crossing from the archipelago.

At the beginning of 1809 the Russians had 48,000 men and 127 guns in Finland deployed among four corps headquartered in Helsingfors, Åbo (under Petr Bagration), Vasa (under Barclay), and Uleåborg (under Pavel Shuvalov). The winter was the most propitious time, when the Gulf of Bothnia froze over, but it was a treacherous moat, where the ice was known to break up in sudden storms, leaving cracks and fissures disguised under a deep snow cover. Although the campaign did not begin until March 1, Bagration's troops hopped across the archipelago and landed on Swedish soil, while Barclay crossed the one hundred kilometers of the Kvarken in an epic march among mountains of ice, the soldiers walking in snow up to their knees.[9] Umeå was taken, but the two forces were now separated by five hundred kilometers of coast without any hope of resupply because Russian transports were seized by a British naval squadron that patrolled the sea on Sweden's side. At this juncture, a coup in Stockholm overthrew the king (and eventually the dynasty). The regent offered an armistice that Knorring, who did not support the expedition he commanded, accepted, recalling Bagration and Barclay to Finland a mere two weeks after the start of the campaign. Shuvalov, meanwhile, had not gone very far: after taking Tornio he signed an armistice with the Swedes at Kalix. The tsar, however, disavowed Knorring and replaced him with Barclay with orders to renew the offensive, but it was now too late to cross the Kvarken again. A new landing from the Åland Islands was prepared, while another force advanced from Tornio toward Umeå with inadequate supplies and ammunition, reaching Piteå in August. But negotiations were already going on and peace was made in September: Sweden ceded not only Finland but also the Åland archipelago, bringing the Russians to within 120 kilometers of Stockholm.

At the time of Catherine's death in 1796, the empire was marking time in the western and southern theaters. By 1809, despite its defeats in Central Europe, the empire was on the offensive again and had reached the Bothnian moat, placing Sweden at its mercy and consolidating its hegemony in the Heartland's Baltic sector. The agreement with Napoleon, who encouraged a resumption of Russo-Ottoman hostilities in 1806 but would also abandon Moldavia and Wallachia to the Russians in return for a peace that would deflect Russian power southward for a war of attrition, challenged the empire to renew the offensive toward the Danubian moat as well, while launching strikes in Transcaucasia against Ottomans and Persians in an attempt to reach the Araks, the third moat on the Heartland's periphery.

After the annexation of the Crimea in 1783, the imperial strategy in the southern theater faced an intriguing dilemma. The building of a Black Sea fleet in Kherson and the development of a naval headquarters in Sevastopol created a naval capability for operations either against the Ottomans in battles for hegemony in that sea, or, in cooperation with them, for penetrations into the eastern Mediterranean in search of naval bases in the Greek archipelago. In the event of war, the imperial navy would support overland operations toward the Danube and Constantinople; imperial forces would eventually invest the capital by land and sea, forcing it to capitulate. Such an ambitious strategy was also the more conservative, however, because it assumed that the Ottomans would close the Straits to Russian commercial and naval shipping, keeping the empire's ships bottled up in the Black Sea, or would find an ally to do it for them. On the other hand, cooperation with the Ottomans in certain favorable circumstances would allow the empire to send warships into the Mediterranean and keep them there to defend Ottoman interests and create Russia's own, beyond the Heartland's periphery. But such cooperation assumed the abandonment of Russia's traditional policy of seeking to destabilize Ottoman rule in the Balkans with the help of client societies. In fact, the leadership's perception of its grand strategic ambitions—hegemony within the great space between the Baltic and the Black Sea—settled the dilemma, save in a very few instances, in favor of continued hostility toward Constantinople and the reluctant acceptance of the principle imposed by Britain in 1809 that the Straits must be closed to all but Ottoman warships. The short-lived Russo-Ottoman cooperation that began in 1798, during which imperial troops landed on the Ionian islands occupied by the French, ended in December 1806, when the Porte, annoyed at Russian claims in Moldavia and Wallachia and incited by the French with whom it was again at peace, declared war, thereby automatically closing the Straits to Russian warships. By then, the imperial government had ten ships of the line and four frigates and some twenty-four smaller ships with 7,900 men in the eastern Mediterranean.[10]

The declaration of war was untimely because the empire was still at war with France and could commit only 35,000 men to the so-called Moldavian Army. Yet by the end of 1806 imperial troops were already in Khotin and Jassy in Bessarabia, Kilia on the delta of the Danube, and Akkerman on the estuary of the Dniestr, but had failed to take Izmail and Brailov on the left bank of the Danube, which would have given them control of the lower course of the river.[11] After Tilsit in June 1807, additional troops were transferred to the southern theater and the empire went on the offensive. The navy won a major victory over the Ottomans in the archipelago after blockading the Dardanelles, and the troops of the Caucasian Corps defeated the Ottomans in Western Georgia. The left bank of the Danube was cleared of Ottoman troops, and assistance was sent to the Serbs who were in full revolt against their Ottoman overlords. But no further progress was made. In 1808–9, Russia was at war in Finland and even with Austria for a short time in 1809. For the first time, the empire was committed on three fronts at the same time and had to keep substantial forces facing the Duchy of Warsaw, where Napoleon's intentions were unclear. It had been assumed until then—and this had certainly been the case during Catherine's reign—that the army operated as a single strategic formation and would be committed to a single theater at a time, with some units kept in reserve and assuming a defensive posture along the imperial border. Between 1808 and 1812, the ruling elite was forced to elaborate a multi-theater strategy in which the army ceased to operate as a single mass and was broken up into regional formations with independent missions. The dispersion of the empire's wartime deployment continued to take shape.

There was peace on the Danube in 1808, as the Russians consolidated their positions in preparation for offensive operations in Bulgaria, which alone could compel the Porte to sue for peace and cede Moldavia and Wallachia. In October, the Franco-Russian agreement at Erfurt recognized that the river must be the boundary of the empire in return for Russia's recognizing the territorial integrity of the remainder of the Ottoman Empire. When war resumed in 1809, Prozorovskii, the commander in chief of the "Army of the Danube," was instructed to secure from the Porte not only the Danube as the new imperial boundary, but also the right to send warships through the Straits into the Mediterranean. The indecisive commander was averse to taking the substantial risk, which even Rumiantsev had been reluctant to take in 1773, of crossing the Danube and carrying the war into Bulgaria against Ottoman fortresses from which cavalry could cut off the Russians' communications with their bases on the river's bank. Alexander insisted on taking chances and launching a daring raid against Constantinople without first investing the Bulgarian fortresses, but to no avail: his impetuosity, which had led to the Austerlitz disaster, was all too well known. Nevertheless, the end of the war with Sweden and rising tensions with France convinced the leadership that the war had to be prosecuted more vigorously. In 1810, the army's strength was raised to 80,000 men. It finally crossed the Danube, took Turtukai and Silistria, and advanced toward Varna, taking Bazardzhik, which continued to threaten the Russians' rear. But gains were made on the eastern coast of the Black Sea: Sukhum Kale was taken in January, and Abkhazia, one of the Ottomans' most reliable clients in the region, was annexed to the empire. Poti had fallen in November 1809, and Sudzhuk Kale fell in December 1810. Only Anapa and Batum remained in Ottoman hands, but Russian ships patrolled the coastal waters to interdict their communications with Constantinople.

The decisive year was 1811. Kutuzov, who had been commander in chief in 1805, but had fought at Austerlitz against his better judgment, took command of the army in April: he focused on Rushchuk, which capitulated in July. Two more divisions joined the army, giving the Russians a substantial preponderance. When the grand vizier crossed the Danube near the fortress, his 40,000 men were trapped by a Russian counterattack at Slobodzeia (Slobozia), the exact replica of the maneuver the Ottoman had hoped to carry out against the Russians in Bulgaria. An armistice was signed in November, but it was broken on the tsar's orders. A general offensive began in January 1812, the Russians crossing the Danube in four places, while preparations were made in Petersburg for a landing in Constantinople; they were interrupted by the news of an outbreak of plague in the Ottoman capital. This was sufficient to force the enemy to capitulate. Peace was made at Bucharest in May and ratified by the tsar on the eve of Napoleon's invasion of Russia. Not the Danube but the Prut became the new imperial boundary, the site of Peter's defeat one hundred years earlier. Bessarabia, a part of Moldavia, was annexed to the empire, which reached the northern branch of the Danube delta with Izmail and Kilia. Nevertheless, the war had been a strategic failure: it warned the Russians they would never establish themselves on the Danubian moat along the Bulgarian border.

## The War with France, 1812–15

The Franco-Russian peace of 1807–8 was only a lull before the inevitable storm. It seemed to create a neat territorial division between the French and the Russian Empires, the latter established on the Gulf of Bothnia and the Danube, the former on the Niemen and the Bug, the eastern borders of the Polish core. But the very partitioning of eastern Europe could be seen in Petersburg only as a threat to the empire's vital interests. It destroyed the client system on which the security of the Russian core had depended for a century, and, in the Duchy of Warsaw, brought France's unsettling influence to bear on the very periphery of the empire. The partitions of Poland and the territorial propinquity they created among "the three black eagle powers" had been acceptable in Petersburg so long as the Germanic powers that acquired the Polish core remained within Russia's orbit and amenable to its pressures. Napoleonic France was inherently hostile, overpowering the friendly kingdom and humiliating Prussia, supporting the Ottomans and the Persians in the southern theater. Indeed, France had been Russia's avowed enemy during most of the eighteenth century, determined to keep it out of the affairs of continental Europe, where France and Austria had vied for hegemony and France had now won supremacy. But an empire that had been on the offensive since 1700 with remarkable success could not accept defeat at the hands of its hereditary enemy and its expulsion within the Heartland from a European state system it had manipulated to serve its geopolitical interests. There would have to be a final showdown on imperial soil, which had remained inviolate until then. French and Russian expectations were irreconcilable, as it quickly appeared from the dispatches of the French and Russian ambassadors reporting the positions of their respective masters. Fundamental political and strategic disagreements were aggravated by commercial rivalry. Napoleon's goal was to create a French Fortress Empire, excluding Britain from the continent in order to force it to capitulate and accept French hegemony. This Continental System could not succeed unless the Russian Empire became a member, but the empire could not join without damaging its commercial position, which depended on a continuing high level of trade with Britain, a source of prosperity for the landed members of its ruling class and of hard currency for the treasury. Tensions began to rise in 1810. By 1811 it was assumed that war was inevitable, and preparations began for the expected showdown.

Should the empire go on the offensive or assume a defensive posture against Napoleon's invasion? Parallels came to mind with the Northern War, when Russia had gone on the offensive against Swedish hegemony in the Baltic, and had retreated eight years later before the Swedish advance toward Smolensk—which turned into the Left-Bank Ukraine to face disaster at Poltava, followed by a general offensive that eventually destroyed the Swedish Empire. An offensive strategy, advocated by Bagration and even the cautious Barclay at first, was in fact impossible. A preemptive strike against the Duchy of Warsaw served no purpose because it was certain to provoke Napoleon's massive retaliation and could not be followed up by a general offensive against the French Empire: the legend of Napoleon's invincibility had not yet been broken. The Russians, mesmerized by the French emperor, would not believe in the imminence of the attack. Alexander refused to build border defenses and position artillery on the right bank of the Niemen and ordered his local commanders to avoid provocative actions against the French[12]—a behavior uncannily similar to that of Stalin before the German invasion of 1941.

The only alternative was a defense-in-depth "Fabian" strategy hoping to wear down the enemy until he was found weak enough for the empire to resume the offensive. Barclay had supported such a strategy in 1807 in expectation of a French invasion after the Battle of Friedland. Its major advocate in 1812 was Karl von Phull, a Prussian general in imperial service, who enjoyed the tsar's support but later became an object of derision in many quarters and was immortalized in Tolstoy's *War and Peace*. Three armies were in the field, numbering 230,000 men: the first and largest, of 130,000 men, was commanded by Barclay and covered the Petersburg direction; the second, of 45,000 commanded by Bagration, blocked the advance on Moscow; the third, of 46,000 under Alexander Tormasov, guarded the approaches to Kiev. Facing the three armies was Napoleon's Grand Army of 675,000 men deployed along the Niemen, with an additional 225,000 reserves in Poland. Phull assumed Napoleon would move against Petersburg and not Moscow. His plan consisted in building a huge fortified camp around the core of First Army at Drissa on the Dvina toward which Napoleon was expected to move after crossing the Niemen at Kovno, barring his farther advance toward Riga and Petersburg. When the Grand Army stalled before the Dvina, the Second Army would attack its flank and rear, and the two armies would crush it in a vise. The plan's major flaw was to leave a gap between the First and Second Armies, which Napoleon, a past master at dividing his opponents and beating them separately, was quick to use to his own advantage when he marched on Moscow, not Petersburg.

Napoleon did cross the Niemen near Kovno on June 24 but directed his main thrust against Bagration, while trying to pin down Barclay in his fortified camp, but Barclay escaped and reached Vitebsk ahead of him, hoping to march on toward Smolensk to link up with Bagration in full retreat to form a single mass capable of stemming Napoleon's advance toward Moscow. The two armies met in Smolensk on August 3, pursued by the Grand Army, which crossed the Dniepr on pontoon bridges at Rasasna and cut them off from Tormasov's Third Army. They did not merge, however. Although Bagration was subordinated to Barclay, with whom he was on bad terms, he retained direct access to the emperor, who remained commander in chief. Despite the resulting command problems, the retreat soon gave the Russians an advantage over Napoleon. The Grand Army had marched over six hundred kilometers in forty days and had already lost 100,000 men to heat, sickness, hunger, and sheer exhaustion. The battle of Smolensk on August 16 caused it another 20,000 casualties. Nevertheless, Barclay ordered the evacuation of the town, encountering a storm of opposition because it left the road to Moscow, four hundred kilometers away, open to the invader. There had been much hostility against the "Germans" since the outbreak of the war, and the seemingly endless retreat sealed Barclay's fate: he was dismissed on August 27 and replaced by Kutuzov who, as a native Russian, was expected to restore morale and stand up to the French. He was also given full powers as commander in chief of the army in the field. It had been assumed that the army would retreat across what had been the eastern marches of the Polish Empire, but that a final stand would be taken at Smolensk, which, located on the watershed between the Dvina and the Dniepr, guarded the entrance to the Russian core.

But Kutuzov was already known for two major feats: the retreat from Braunau to Wischau over a distance of five hundred kilometers in 1805, and the envelopment of the grand vizier's army at Slobodzeia in 1811. He too, like Phull and Barclay, believed that the defensive must precede the offensive and that the time had not yet come to turn against Napoleon. Nevertheless, he was under great pressure, political as well as psychological, as he had been before Austerlitz, to challenge Napoleon: it would be the last chance to save Moscow. After quickly dismissing a plan to take a stand at Tsarevo Zaimishche east of Viazma, he chose to face Napoleon at Borodino, near Mozhaisk, 130 kilometers from the old capital, on September 7. By then, Napoleon had a disposable force of only 135,000 men, while Kutuzov had already lined up 126,000. The famous battle's outcome was at first uncertain. It dealt the French cavalry a blow from which it could not recover and inflicted 58,000 casualties, which could not be replaced. Even if Borodino did not stop the advance, it was a Russian strategic victory because it left the Grand Army, now 1,130 kilometers from its base of operations in Warsaw, at the mercy of the Russians. It also made politically acceptable the abandonment of Moscow—because there was no longer any choice—in preparation for an enveloping strategy which, if successfully carried out, might trap the Grand Army on Russian soil. The decision to abandon Moscow was made on September 13, and the imperial army pulled back through Podolsk to Tarutino. The move checkmated Napoleon, now unable to take the risk of marching southward to the richer agricultural regions to replenish his ambulatory stores and to the Tula arsenal to replace his ammunition. It would force the Grand Army to retreat in winter along the same invasion route across territory where the Russians had carried out a scorched earth policy. The remnants of the Grand Army entered Moscow the next day. The prestige of the city was so great that Napoleon had forgotten that the political capital of the empire was no longer there but in Petersburg. Moscow was not Berlin or Vienna, and Petersburg was more like London, beyond the reach of his army. When he entered a deserted Moscow, he won a tactical victory but he lost the war. Time was not on his side.

The retreat began on October 19. Kutuzov's strategy paid off when the attempt to reach Kaluga was blocked at the bloody Battle of Maloiaroslavets on October 23, leaving Napoleon no choice but to return to the Moscow-Smolensk road, pursued by Cossacks, who had played a major role at Borodino and now harassed the retreating army. By the time he reached Smolensk, he had only 60,000 men left, and his army was an army in full disintegration. Since crossing a river is one of the most dangerous operations in warfare, especially for a retreating army, Kutuzov hoped "to do a Slobodzeia" at the crossing of the Berezina, the first significant river barring the retreat. But Napoleon outfoxed Kutuzov and crossed on November 28 where he was not expected, nevertheless suffering additional losses. By the time he reached Smorgon, east of Vilno, where he abandoned his army and left for Paris, he had only 9,000 men left. When the imperial army reached Vilno on December 10, it had gone full circle and the enemy had been expelled from imperial territory.

The imperial leadership now faced a momentous decision. The great losses in men and resources suffered during the invasion, the general exhaustion following marches over 2,000 kilometers in six months, the difficult financial situation, and the uncertain state of British subsidies, dictated caution and a pause to allow the troops to rest, obtain new uniforms and boots, and await the arrival of new recruits to bring the regiments to full strength. But higher imperatives prevailed immediately. The determination to resort once again to deep strategic penetrations and to restore the client system—the two major factors in the empire's grand strategy— reasserted itself. While Barclay and Kutusov supported the more cautious approach, the tsar insisted on an immediate offensive at the very onset of winter, a general offensive that would take the imperial army across the Germanies all the way to Paris, three thousand kilometers from Moscow, and defeat the hereditary enemy once and for all. Prussia had been forced to side with France but did not take an active part in the invasion; Austria had contributed an army corps commanded by the soldier-diplomat Karl von Schwartzenberg. Both countries had to be brought back into the Russian orbit in order to consolidate the empire's hegemony in the western periphery of the Heartland.

The geography of the western theater created a succession of rivers flowing northward into the Baltic and intersecting horizontal roads or corridors of expansion between the Elbe and the Niemen. This grid of rivers and roads determined the goal of each consecutive campaign. The Russians crossed the Niemen two weeks after reaching Vilno. In January 1813, an army corps that had been kept in reserve to block a possible advance toward Riga entered Königsberg, where the Prussian king had taken refuge after the French occupation of Berlin, and moved on to Danzig to blockade its 30,000-man garrison. A second corps moved to Blomberg (Bydogoszcz) and besieged Thorn, while a third invested Plock, all four towns on the Vistula. Schwartzenberg abandoned Warsaw to avoid encirclement. The Russians were now fully established on the river, for the first time since 1795. The advance continued toward the Oder. After leaving enough troops to keep Danzig blockaded, the Russians marched through Poznan to Küstrin at the confluence of the Wartha and the Oder. Schwartzenberg retreated to Częstochowa, and the Saxons, Napoleon's allies, were beaten in February at Kalisz, where Menshikov had won his battle with the Swedes in 1706. There, the ever cautious Prussian king finally went over to the Russians, and the Swedish crown prince, a former French marshal elected in 1810, joined them in March. When the allies reached Glogau (Głogów) in March, the Oder passed under their control. The Russians occupied not only the Duchy of Warsaw but also the Prussian and Austrian shares of the Polish partitions. The entire former Polish Empire had become a single Russian zone of occupation.[13]

Meanwhile, Napoleon in Paris had been busy levying a new army of 225,000 men with which he reached Erfurt in April, while 150,000 Russians and 80,000 Prussians advanced beyond the Oder on the way to the Elbe. Kutuzov, who had been ill for some time, died of exhaustion in Silesia at the end of the month. After a short interlude, he was replaced by Barclay as commander in chief of all Russian forces; the overall command was assumed by the tsar and the Prussian king. The Russians had never crossed the Elbe before, although Lacy had crossed one of its tributaries in 1735 on his way to Heidelberg. The Elbe and the Saale, which had been the westernmost boundary of the advance of the Slavs in the Middle Ages, formed a triangle resting on the Erz Mountains. Beyond it to the south began the Bohemian upland, and to the west the Thurigian Mountains announced the continuous upland leading beyond the Rhine into northern France. If Napoleon lost control of this strategic region, he would invite a Russo-Prussian advance into the Coastland; if he won a decisive victory, nothing would stop him from returning to Berlin and pushing on to Warsaw. The two key cities were Dresden, the Saxon capital, and Leipzig. After taking Berlin on March 4, the allies reached Leipzig on April 3 and engaged the French at the Battle of Lützen south of the city on May 2. Despite heavy losses, it was a French victory. The Russians retreated beyond the Elbe, pursued by Napoleon, who fought them at Bautzen, east of Dresden, on May 20. These two battles were not decisive, and from his headquarters in Dresden, Napoleon proposed an armistice on June 4 that would last until August 10.

The armistice was a mistake because it allowed the Russians to recoup their losses with troops deployed in Poland for this purpose in the so-called Reserve Army. The army withdrew almost to the Oder, to Reichenbach, east of the fortress of Schweidnitz, which had been with Kolberg the great strategic object of the campaign of 1761. There, on June 27, Austria pledged to enter the war against Napoleon with 150,000 men. Soon afterward, in September, the three black eagle powers formed a political alliance at Toplitz (Teplice) and signed a convention for the provisioning of the Russian army. The now once again friendly kingdom gained a dominant voice in allied strategy when Schwartzenberg, accomplished courtier, diplomat, and commander, was given the command of the allied armies, causing much bad blood with Barclay, and the Austrian emperor joined the tsar and the Prussian king on the political committee responsible for shaping a common strategy to destroy Napoleon. The allies now had half a million men in three armies: a Bohemian army covering Vienna, a northern army covering Berlin, and a Silesian army blocking a move against Warsaw. Napoleon faced a threat of encirclement. At the Battle of Dresden on August 26–27, the allies took advantage of another error of Napoleon, who had divided his army into two parts, and forced him to retreat across the Elbe. Two days later, half a French corps, including its commander, was forced to surrender at Kulm, a major psychological blow. As Napoleon retreated, the allies converged on Leipzig and fought him at the famous Battle of Nations outside the city on October 16–18. It was symbolic and not entirely coincidental that all these battles of 1813 were fought on the Heartland's periphery: their objective was to settle the fate of a Russian Empire hegemonic in the Heartland and a French Empire hegemonic in the continental Coastland. When Napoleon lost the battle at Leipzig, he opened the gates of the Coastland to the Russians and invited their pursuit via Erfurt and Hanau near Frankfurt, where an attempt was made to repeat the Berezina operations, which also failed. The allies reached Mainz on the Rhine on November 4.

But all was not well in the allied coalition. The tsar's refusal to assume the supreme leadership of the coalition—a role to which he was entitled by the fact that he alone had never surrendered to Napoleon—was a shrewd move: it made it easier for Prussia and Austria to accept his role as the arbiter of their inevitable rivalry among the German states. Austria was determined to reassert its primacy,

Prussia more than ever to challenge it. Austria was still willing to reach an accommodation with France—Napoleon was, after all, the Austrian emperor's son-in-law—while both the tsar and the Prussians would not stop until Napoleon's final overthrow. More disturbing to the Austrians were the logistical implications of a crossing of the Rhine in the direction of Paris. Russian troops would move south of the Main toward the Danube, the trip wire in Austrian strategic thinking: the monarchy called itself Danubian, as if the great river was its exclusive property all the way to its delta, where the Russians had established themselves in 1812, past Serbia and Wallachia, where they had old ambitions. Nevertheless, the allied advance had gained its own momentum; Napoleon's intransigence only made it irreversible, and the Austrian Empire, by its geographical location, legitimist policies, and fear of nationalism, had no choice but to remain the friendly kingdom.

The final allied offensive began in January 1814.[14] It had taken exactly one year for the Russians to advance from the Niemen to the Rhine, 1,500 kilometers away, via Warsaw, Leipzig, and Mainz. They and the Austrians crossed the river at Strasbourg and on the upper Rhine at Basel, Laufenburg, and Schaffhausen. All these forces were to converge on Troyes, about four hundred kilometers to the west and only two hundred from Paris, then follow the valley of the Seine to the French capital. Other Russian forces and the Prussians crossed much farther north at Koblenz and Mannheim—near Heidelberg where Lacy had met the Austrians in 1735—and advanced on Nancy, then followed the Marne in the direction of Paris. Napoleon won a number of tactical victories but was unable to stem the advance. The allies had committed an enormous force of 600,000 men, including 280,000 Russians, to defeat him. The main army under Schwartzenberg consisted of 200,000 troops including 64,000 Russians, and the Silesian army under Gebhard von Blücher numbered 75,000, including 56,000 Russians. Napoleon had only 130,000 men at his disposal. The allies entered Paris on March 31, and he abdicated on April 16. The peace of June 11 restored France within its 1792 borders and paved the way for the allies to leave French territory. By August, the Russians had returned to Poland, and the strategic force was divided into two armies, the first and largest consisting of six army corps under Barclay, the second of three army corps under Bennigsen. But Napoleon escaped from Elba and returned to Paris in March 1815. Barclay was given the command of an army of 200,000 with which he marched back to France, reaching the Rhine in June, only to learn of Napoleon's final defeat at Waterloo. It was during this rapid march across Europe that Barclay created a military police called gendarmes, soon to acquire a reputation far beyond the army.

Napoleon's "Hundred Days" cost France dearly. The country lost the left bank of the Rhine and had to pay an indemnity of 700 million francs at the peace treaty of November 20, signed by Richelieu, who in the days of emigration had been governor general of Odessa and New Russia. Until the indemnity was paid, 150,000 allied troops would remain in France, including a Russian corps of 27,000 men commanded by Mikhail Vorontsov, later to become one of Richelieu's successors in Odessa. Its headquarters was in Maubeuge near the (future) Belgian border. It would remain in France until the settlement of October 1818, when Vorontsov returned to Russia.

Never before had the empire carried out such deep strategic penetrations in the western theater, and never again would it be able to cross the Heartland's periphery during the imperial (or Soviet) period, let alone carry out operations in northern Italy and Holland. It marked the culmination of a long series of strategic thrusts directed against the empire's enemies—Sweden in 1716, Poland in 1734, Prussia in 1756–61, and France itself in 1735, 1748, and 1799. The defeat of France called for magnanimity, because its humiliation would block the establishment of a durable peace, and Alexander showed it by defending the former hereditary enemy against the harsh demands of a Prussia thirsting for revenge for the humiliation of 1806. The defeat of France also brought the history of those deep thrusts to an end. The alliance forged among the three black eagle powers in 1813–15 would continue for more than a generation, but it was not an alliance of equals, at least in Russian eyes. Prussia and Austria, turned outward toward the Rhineland and northern Italy by the settlement of 1815,[15] would protect Fortress Empire against the subversive ideas and possible resurgence of France, while the empire would help the friendly kingdom and the Prussian client maintain the new conservative order in their own lands, in Poland and in Hungary. The new international order, based on the maintenance of the status quo, paved the way for the final dispersion of the strategic force.

## Persia, Turkey, and Poland, 1815–31

While the empire was fighting bloody battles with Revolutionary France and committing the bulk of its strategic force to the western theater, important developments were taking place in Transcaucasia. The expedition of 1796, launched in response to the Persian offensive on Tiflis, announced Russia's return to a forward strategy in the region for the first time since 1735, when the empire retroceded Derbent and Baku to Persian suzerainty. The consequence of the new interest in facing up to the Persians was the annexation of eastern Georgia in 1801 and the appointment of a military governor in Tiflis with the powers of a commander in chief over the Caucasian Line and all imperial forces in the North Caucasus and Transcaucasia. The decision was not made without much hesitation among the ruling elite, because the move had momentous implications. The Persians could not accept without war the establishment of the Russians in an area where they had been dominant since at least 1639. The Russians were committing themselves to operate with limited forces in a highly complex political environment consisting of half a dozen khanates, Muslim in religion, generally faithful to Tehran but treacherous in their dealings with the Christian empire, which counted, however, on the support of the Georgians and Armenians.

The logistics of warfare in Transcaucasia presented serious problems. The troops could not depend for their supplies on the local population, which had little to spare in an essentially subsistence economy: provisions had to be brought from the North Caucasus steppe along a single and dangerous road across the mountains that could be cut at any time.[16] The distance from Tiflis to Erevan was 250 kilometers, but it was 570 kilometers to Baku and another 270 to Lenkoran at the gates of Persia. From Lenkoran to Tehran, which became the Persian capital in 1788, the distance was another 560 kilometers. The terrain was mountainous except in the

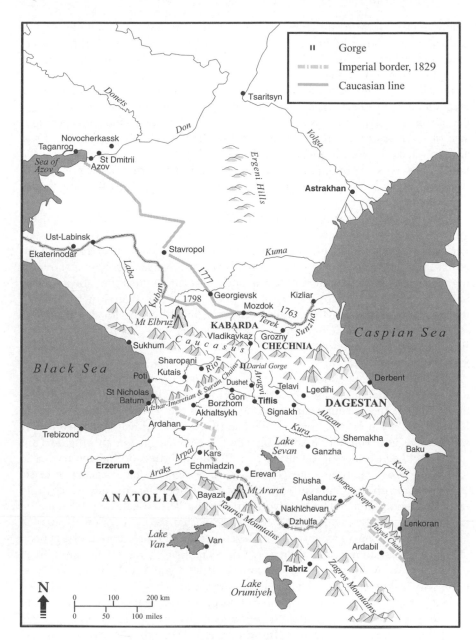

The Caucasian Sector

nearly impassable Murgan steppe, so hot that the Russians could not adjust to it, and exposed to nomadic raids. To complicate matters, Tiflis was also the natural base of operations against the Ottomans. Poti on the Black Sea was 365 kilometers away, but western Georgia was heavily wooded and unhealthy, and the Ottomans were solidly established at Akhaltsykh, their forward base against Georgia for the great Ottoman headquarters at Erzerum. Although a permanent deployment of imperial troops in Tiflis was justified by the necessity to launch punitive expeditions against the rear of the mountain peoples threatening the Caucasian Line, it was also an offensive move in preparation for deep thrusts across Georgia against the Persian and Turkish cores, against Tehran and against Erzerum at the entrance of Anatolia, while the empire's main forces operated in Bulgaria in the direction of Constantinople.

War broke out in 1804 over the control of Erivan, whose khan resented the growing Russian influence. He called on the shah for help and by June, 20,000 Persians were already deployed near Echmiadzin, the ecclesiastical capital of Armenia. But they were routed on the Arpai River by a Russian force of 4,300 moving down from Tiflis. The siege of Erivan failed for want of provisions and ammunition, and the Russians retreated in August.[17] The shah tried again in 1805, sending his capable son, Abbas Mirza, against Georgia, but he met with defeat at Shemakha, the great trade emporium of Transcaucasia. The Russians failed before Baku, however, in spite of combined land and amphibious operations mounted from Astrakhan.

Desultory warfare continued for the next four years, without any decisive victory on either side, but in 1810, Persians and Ottomans joined forces against Russia, not without some encouragement by the French: the Tiflis headquarters would have to fight a war on two fronts for the first time. Abbas Mirza penetrated deeply into Georgia and would have linked up with the Ottomans before moving on Tiflis had he not been beaten at Akhalkalaki, an Ottoman fortress on the approaches to the Georgian capital. In 1812, the Russians were as eager to make peace with Persia as they were with the Ottomans, and the Peace of Bucharest in May left them to face the Persians alone. The decisive event was the Persian defeat at Aslanduz on the Araks in October, where 4,000 Russians defeated 30,000 Persians. It was followed by the storming of Lenkoran in December and the preparation of a general offensive against Tehran, this at the very time Napoleon's Grand Army was retreating from Moscow. The offensive was conceived on a grand scale, using the Turkmens who had been raiding the domains of the Qajar dynasty in a joint enveloping movement against the Persian capital. But peace was made at Gulistan in October 1813, four days before the great Battle of the Nations at Leipzig. The treaty recognized the empire's suzerainty over Transcaucasia between the Caucasus chain and the lower course of the Araks and over the Salian range to Lenkoran, as well as its exclusive right to maintain warships in the Caspian. This striking victory enabled the high command to move its base of operations to the Persian border, within striking distance of Ardabil and especially Tabriz, both old capitals of Persia, threatening its communications with Erevan. They also reached the approaches to the rugged mountain region where the Taurus chain of Anatolia gradually merged into the Zagros Mountains of Persia, both forming the Heartland's periphery. Erevan remained the prize: its capture would make the moat along the Araks the natural, "scientific," border of the empire.

For the next twelve years, repeated warnings by Alexei Ermolov, the commander in chief in Tiflis, that the Persians had not accepted their defeat and would try to reassert their supremacy in the region were ignored. Nevertheless, even he was taken by surprise by the Persian offensive in July 1826. Abbas Mirza had 60,000 men and called a holy war to rally more warriors from the mountains of Daghestan, where the Russians had been fighting since 1817 a guerrilla war that stretched their resources. The resulting need to keep garrisons in increasingly scattered fortresses meant Ermolov had no more than 15,000 troops available for operations in the field. Abbas Mirza launched a general offensive against Shusha, Lenkoran, and Baku and advanced toward Ganzha on his way to Tiflis, while the Erivan khan, reinforced by Kurdish cavalry, also moved toward Tiflis. Despite such a concerted advance with overwhelmingly superior forces, he was stopped at Ganzha in September, and a Russian counteroffensive forced him to retreat behind the Araks. Ermolov, suspected of Decembrist sympathies, was replaced by Ivan Paskievich in March 1827. Coming from general headquarters in Petersburg, he, even more than Ermolov, accepted the general principle of imperial grand strategy that the war must be taken to the enemy's capital. Erivan was stormed in September after the fall of Nakhichevan in June. Imperial forces then crossed the Araks at Dzhulfa, reached Tabriz in October. After the shah refused to accept a preliminary treaty, Paskievich moved on with 27,000 men to occupy Ardebil and begin the march on Tehran. The shah then yielded, and peace was made at Turkmanchai in February 1828. The new border reached the Araks and the Astara River below Lenkoran, bringing the Talysh upland into the empire. Persia had lost the war over Transcaucasia. This new border has remained unchanged up to the present day. In the eyes of some members of the high command, it also meant the completion of one of Peter the Great's projects. Twelve years earlier, in 1816, General Filippo Paulucci had submitted a memorandum discussing the empire's optimal boundary in the Transcaucasia. It must run along the Araks—the moat, even if he did not use the term—to the Arpai River, bringing eastern Armenia into the empire, including Echmiadzin, the residence of its patriarch; from there began the highway running via Kars, Erzerum, and Amasya to Scutari facing Constantinople across the Bosphorus, the ideal line of operations to attack the Turks from "Asia."[18]

Peace had been made just in time on the Danubian front in 1812, showing once again how difficult it had always been for the empire's opponents to coordinate their operations, whether during the Northern War of 1700–21, the Crimean War of 1735–39, or the War of 1788–90. It was as if the western and southern theaters were completely autonomous for all belligerents, the Russians succeeding in separating their enemies by assuming an essentially permanent offensive posture from their interior lines stretching via Moscow from Petersburg to Kiev. The return of peace in 1815 renewed the pressure the empire had been exerting on the Ottomans since the peace of Kuchuk Kainarji (1774). The time was opportune, because the French Revolution had made a deep impact on the peoples of the Balkans and eastern Mediterranean. Nationalist stirrings were beginning to destabilize the Ottoman Empire, and nowhere more so than in Greece. A Greek secret society sought Russian support for an uprising and was encouraged to act when Alexander Ipsilanti, a general in the Russian army, aide-de-camp of the tsar, and the son of a former *hospodar* of Wallachia, agreed to join it and made careless promises in 1820. The society's headquarters was in Kishinev, in Bessarabia, from which Ipsilanti invaded Moldavia in March 1821. He found no support there or in Wallachia, where his supporters were crushed at Craiova in western Wallachia in June. He fled to Austria and was disavowed by the tsar.[19] Nevertheless, the uprising had in the meantime become the signal for a general uprising in the Morea. The murder of the Orthodox patriarch of Constantinople in April aroused sympathy even among the maritime powers and threatened to engulf the Ottomans in a general war.

The Russians were caught in a dilemma, however. The uprising provided an excellent opportunity to stand up for the rights of the Orthodox Christians and crush the Ottomans while their forces were occupied in the Morea. On the other hand, the Christians were the lawful subjects of the sultan, and the settlement of 1815 had called for a repression of popular uprisings against legitimate rulers. While the tsar hesitated, the chief of staff of the First Army, Hans von Diebitsch, submitted to him in July 1821 a plan of blitzkrieg against Constantinople designed to destroy once and for all the political and military capabilities of the Ottomans, as had just been done with France six years earlier.[20]

Diebitsch's operational plan was extremely ambitious, but overly optimistic about the Ottomans' weakness. The goal was clear: to launch a swift and decisive in-depth penetration of Bulgaria and reach Constantinople. The Greek Uprising would be only a pretext, and must play no role in Russia's planning. The Second Army, stationed in Podolia, supported by the III and IV Corps of the First Army, from Kremenchug and Kiev respectively, the IV Reserve Cavalry Corps from Voronezh, and even the I, attached to the Guard in Petersburg, would march quickly to the Danube and invest Brailov. They would then move to Varna, while some of the troops would follow the Danube to Rushchuk and Turno. The entire operation aimed at an envelopment of Shumla, still the most important fortress in Bulgaria and often the grand vizier's headquarters. Even if the fortress resisted, the army would continue to Burgas, the finest port on the Bulgarian coast.

Diebitsch also envisaged a secondary operation along the Danube all the way to Serbia. After the surrender of Shumla, the army would cross the Balkan Mountains and engage the Ottomans in a general battle for Adrianople, the sultan's summer capital, and continue toward Constantinople, where it would link up with the Black Sea fleet for a general assault on the city. Diebitsch expected to complete the war in two campaigns, in 1822 and 1823, an unprecedented achievement. The wars of 1812–15 had given the high command an operational confidence it had never possessed before. Diebitsch's vision was in other ways very traditional. The empire's strategy had assumed since 1711 that the Ottomans must be threatened by another enveloping movement, along both sides of the Black Sea, in the Balkans and the Caucasus. The creation of the Tiflis headquarters now provided an opportunity from the south, in Transcaucasia. Diebitsch knew the logistical difficulties inherent to Caucasian warfare and called for only a diversion in western Georgia in alliance with the Persians, with whom the empire was now at peace. They would be encouraged to launch their own diversion toward Baghdad and the upper Euphrates.

Diebitsch gave precedence to the Balkan subtheater because the decisive battle for Constantinople would have to be fought there.

War did not break out in 1821, but relations with the Ottomans continued to deteriorate with the progress of the Greek Uprising and the intervention of the pasha of Egypt in 1825. The new tsar, Nicholas I, did not share his brother's hesitations, although he had no sympathy for the Greek insurgents. Diebitsch's plan was certain to appeal to him. In July 1827, Britain, France, and Russia called on the sultan to settle the Greek question by peaceful means, but in October, their squadrons sank the pasha's fleet at Navarino in southern Greece. The sultan retaliated with a declaration of holy war. Hostilities with Russia began in April 1828, two months after peace was made with the Persians, thus relieving the empire of the burden of a two-front war in Transcaucasia.

Diebitsch, who had become chief of staff of the army in 1823, was responsible for planning this war.[21] He was even more optimistic than in 1821, and even assumed that the war would be over in one campaign, with imperial forces crossing the Danube in April and May and reaching Constantinople in September. He continued to downgrade the importance of operations in Transcaucasia. He would be proved wrong on both counts. By now relying on a deep thrust not across Bulgaria but along the Bulgarian coast, he would depend for the provisioning of the army on the Black Sea fleet—very much as warfare against Persia depended on the assistance of the Caspian flotilla based in Astrakhan. Everything was made to depend on the capture of Varna whence the army and fleet would advance on Constantinople. But in order to reach Varna as fast as possible, the army would have to cross Dobrudja (Dobrogea), a wooded and sparsely populated country with hardly any roads. It was very risky to emphasize speed across such inhospitable terrain.

Imperial forces, 115,000 men strong, crossed the Danube in June 1828 at Isachka, where Peter I had tried to head off the Ottomans in 1711, but found themselves caught in the narrow corridor between the Danube and the sea, exposed to flanking attacks from Brailov, Machin, and Hirsovo, old battlegrounds of past wars with the Ottomans. The three fortresses were soon taken, and the army advanced toward Varna and Shumla, still exposed to flanking attacks from Silistria. Then the plague, the usual visitor of Ottoman and Russian camps in the region, struck; it forced the lifting of the siege of Shumla, but Varna surrendered in October. At the end of 1828, the Russians were bogged down once again in positional warfare, their advance paralyzed by the threat to their communications from Ottoman fortresses. More serious was the shortage of supplies and muskets following the crashing of the dam at the Tula works: the army received 195,000 recruits in 1828, but only 45,000 muskets were produced.[22] The Russians had a choice: to follow in the footsteps of Rumiantsev and set up a string of secure operational bases along the Danube before advancing deeper into Bulgaria, or to launch a deep thrust against Constantinople. Faithful to their doctrine of the offensive, they chose to advance at any cost against the Ottoman capital. Diebitsch's gamble paid off. At the Battle of Kulevcha near Shumla, the Ottomans seeking to relieve the fortress suffered a major defeat, and Silistria was taken in June 1829. Diebitsch, who had been appointed commander in chief in February, now felt strong enough to advance on Adrianople, which he reached in August, while a parallel offensive across the Shipka Pass of the Balkan

Mountains took imperial forces to Enos (Enez) on the Aegean coast, establishing communications with the Russian squadron in that sea and preparing for a naval blockade of Constantinople. Meanwhile, Diebitsch took Midia (Kiyiköy) and Viza (Vize), within two hundred kilometers of the Ottoman capital.

The unexpected major contribution to the eventual victory was made by Paskievich in Transcaucasia with his 40,000 men. After taking Erivan from Persia in September 1827 he was free to concentrate all his available forces against the Ottomans toward Anatolia, while the Black Sea fleet received the mission to take Anapa and Poti. He stormed the great fortress of Kars in June 1828, Akhaltsykh in August. The capture of these two fortresses put Ardahan in a vise: it was taken soon afterward, as well as Bayazit (Dogubayazit), near Mount Ararat. Paskievich had opened a broad two-hundred-kilometer-long front facing Erzerum and Trebizond (Trabzond), raising the prospect of an occupation of western Armenia and a seizure of the famous caravan route linking Trebizond on the Black Sea with Tehran via Lake Van and Tabriz. Anatolia, the Turkish core, would then be defenseless. Nicholas I, true to his predecessors' vision of imperial invincibility, kept insisting on moving on, and Paskievich asked for a naval demonstration before Samsun. Erzerum was taken in June 1829, and the Ottomans suffered another defeat at Bayburt, opening the road to Trebizond.[23] By then, however, the sultan was ready to negotiate.

At the peace of Adrianople in September, the Russians retroceded the pashaliks of Kars, Bayazit, and Erzerum but kept Akhaltsykh and annexed the entire Black Sea coast from the mouth of the Kuban to Fort St. Nicholas including Anapa and Poti, cutting off Ottoman communications with the mountain peoples in the basin of the Kuban. The treaty also confirmed Russia's right to send merchantmen through the Straits. But Petersburg had to restore Silistria, Hirsovo, Machin, Isachka, and Tulcha, the fortresses that had always slowed the Russian advance. Moldavia and Wallachia became a virtual Russian protectorate with a constitution ("organic statute") drawn up by Pavel Kiselev, the chief of staff of the Second Army. Only the opposition of Austria and the maritime powers prevented their outright annexation, and imperial troops later withdrew behind the Prut in 1834: they had failed to establish themselves permanently along the Danubian moat.[24] It was a paradox that while Diebitsch had emphasized the primacy of the Balkan subtheater and downgraded the importance of the Caucasus, the empire's greatest gains were in Transcaucasia.

The army had not yet fully returned to its quarters when the Polish Rebellion shook the foundations of the empire's security in the western theater. The incorporation of the Duchy of Warsaw and additional Polish territory in 1815 had been a mistake: Poland was not Finland, but an irreducible core area, yearning for its past greatness and proud of its civilization that continued to exercise, despite the partitions, a powerful influence on the eastern marches of its former empire. That Russian policy and behavior between 1815 and 1830 reflected the considerable ambiguity felt in Petersburg toward Polish autonomy did not help matters. In November 1830, an uprising took place in Warsaw that soon spread to Lithuania and the Right-Bank Ukraine, and the Polish parliament deposed Nicholas I as king of Poland in January 1831, challenging the imperial power to restore its hegemony in the region.

There were two ways of invading Poland: from the northeast, as Lacy had done in 1734, or from the southeast, as Suvorov did sixty years later. The Second Army, which had borne the brunt of the fighting in the Russo-Turkish War, had been disbanded in July 1830, but its troops were still deployed on the Danubian front. Diebitsch, now a field marshal, was appointed commander in chief of an invading army of more than 180,000 men drawn largely from the First Army, although the actual numbers available on the battlefield were much lower. Although Diebitsch was a Saxon educated in Berlin who married Barclay's niece, his views were faithful to his belief, rooted in Russian strategic doctrine, that the imperial army must carry out deep thrusts to reach the enemy capital and dictate the peace. He vowed to put down the rebellion at one blow.[25] A week after the tsar's deposition, the army was already deployed along the line from Grodno-Bialystock-Brest-Litovsk, forming the base of a triangle formed by the Narew and Western Bug Rivers. It was a wooded, swampy, and sparsely populated region that the Prussians had not wanted at the time of the third partition. Diebitsch counted on the ground remaining frozen during the winter months and neglected the logistics of his offensive. When his troops crossed into Poland in January, they had provisions for only fifteen days and their horses for only twelve; Bialystock and Brest-Litovsk were 185 and 200 kilometers respectively from Warsaw. The Poles assumed a defensive stance from the beginning, determined, if they could not stop the Russian advance, to give battle at Grochów on the outskirts of Warsaw. They nevertheless suffered a major defeat there in February, three weeks after the invasion began, and the Russians were ready to storm Praga (which Suvorov had so mercilessly treated in 1794) and occupy the city across the river.

The weather now turned against Diebitsch. A sudden and intense thaw set in, turning the swamps and roads into quagmires and thinning the ice on the Vistula. The neglect of logistical support caught up with him. The troops had finished their rations; requisitioning food from the population only increased local enmity against the Russians. Diebitsch was forced to halt the advance and wait for provisions from Russia carried on carts that sank into the proverbial Polish mud. He retreated along the Warsaw-Brest-Litovsk road to the Siedelts (Siedice) area, but allowed a gap to form between his troops and the Guard deployed around Ostrołęnka, 125 kilometers to the north. The Poles took advantage of this oversight to try to defeat the Guard, commanded by Grand Duke Mikhail, in an attempt to break through and carry the war into Lithuania. But Diebitsch managed to link up in time with the grand duke, and in February inflicted on the Poles the catastrophic defeat of Ostrołęnka, forcing them to withdraw once more to Warsaw. He refused to pursue them, however, failing to end the war at one blow as he had promised. A long period of inaction followed. Before he could resume the offensive, he died of cholera at the end of May. Paskievich was recalled from the Caucasus and arrived at Pultusk in June. He looked for a place to cross the Vistula but did not find one until Osiek, some twenty kilometers from Thorn, near the Prussian border. From there, he marched back to Warsaw, over two hundred kilometers away, and stormed the city in August. It had taken Lacy and Suvorov about two months to reach the Polish capital. This Polish campaign had lasted nearly eight months.

Looking back upon these first thirty years of the nineteenth century confirms that deep strategic penetrations remained a cardinal element in the empire's grand strategy. The thrusts toward Stockholm and Warsaw as well as the advance to the Danube were not new; they went back to Peter's reign. But the Russians also for the first (and last) time occupied Paris, 2,970 kilometers from Moscow via Leipzig, Mainz, and Troyes; they reached the approaches to Constantinople via Kiev, Kishinev, Bucharest, and Adrianople, 2,660 kilometers away; and they marched on Tehran via Tiflis and Tabriz, 3,240 kilometers from the old capital and 4,000 from Petersburg, the empire's nerve center. Such projections of power had been unthinkable in the eighteenth century. What was important was not the delays, the poorly managed logistics, the corruption, or even the shortage of weapons, but the determination to carry the war at any cost to the enemy capital in order to dictate the peace. Napoleon too crisscrossed Europe and eventually reached Moscow, but the remarkable fact was that the empire's strategy remained very traditional, while Napoleon's was not. At the same time, however, the expansion of the empire in the wake of the revolutionary wars affected its grand strategy in a fundamental way: it nearly destroyed the client system and paved the way for the dispersion of the strategic force by fragmenting it in the form of regional deployments. Fortress Empire began to assume a defensive posture for the first time since the 1650s.

# 8

# Dispersion of the Strategic Force

### Growth of the Army and Deployment, 1801–12

The reign of Alexander I was certain to bring about an enormous increase in the size of the strategic force. The wars against Napoleon and against Sweden in Finland in order to assert the empire's hegemony in the western theater, as well as those against the Ottomans and Persians in Bulgaria and Transcaucasia to round out its hegemony in the Heartland, imposed tremendous demands on the empire's military capabilities. The imperial army of the late 1820s had changed beyond recognition.

At the outset of the reign, in 1801, the infantry consisted of thirteen grenadier, sixty-nine musketeer, and fifteen chasseur regiments; by 1803, there were eight more musketeer and five more chasseur regiments, in addition to the three of Guard infantry, for a total of 113 regiments and 235,122 troops, including 8,099 in the Guard. The cavalry consisted of thirteen cuirassier, fifteen dragoon, and eight hussar regiments, a total of thirty-six raised to thirty-seven in 1803, in addition to four of Guard cavalry. By then, the importance of the cuirassiers so favored by Paul had been downgraded in favor of the dragoons in twenty-two regiments, in accordance with the recommendation of the Military Commission of 1801, which looked on the dragoons as a form of mounted infantry capable of moving easily over long distances to convoy the infantry's train. In 1803, the cavalry numbered 49,900 horsemen, including 3,612 in the Guard. The ratio of infantry to cavalry regiments was now 2.7 to 1, only slightly lower than at the end of Paul's reign. The strategic force, including the Guard, consisted of 285,022 troops in 154 regiments.[1] This force level was about the same as in 1786 but still lower than it had been in 1796. It would soon rise very sharply, however, as we shall see presently. Garrison troops numbered 74,500 officers and men.

In peacetime, the strategic force continued to be deployed in territorial "inspections," the new name for the old "divisions." There had been eight of them in 1763 — nine if we include the so-called Siberian Corps — and twelve in 1796. In 1801, there were fourteen, listing 140 regiments.[2] As in 1796, only three were in Russia proper, in Petersburg, Moscow, and Smolensk. Another three were deployed, as in 1796, in the western theater, in Vyborg province, Livonia, and Lithuania, and there was a new one in Brest-Litovsk. In the southern theater, there were still a Ukrainian and Crimean Inspection, but Kiev had replaced Ekaterinoslav as the headquarters of a third. A new one was in the valley of the Dniestr. The fifth was still in the Caucasus, and there were another two in the Orenburg Territory and in Siberia. The outward deployment of the strategic force had become more evident in 1801: only 31 of the 140 regiments, including the 6 of the Smolensk Inspection and 4 of the Kiev Inspection, or 21.4 percent, were still deployed in Russia proper, against 24.3 percent in 1796 and 45 percent in 1763.

In Russia proper, the Petersburg Inspection consisted of only eight regiments, as in 1796, two of them grenadiers in the capital, the others at the Staraia Rusa and on the roads to the Baltic provinces, Bielorussia and Lithuania. The inspection thus filled the space between the Petersburg-Moscow corridor and the Baltic provinces. Supporting this deployment were the eight garrison battalions, four of them in Kronstadt, others in Novgorod, Pskov, Narva, and Schlüsselburg. None was stationed in the capital itself. The Moscow Inspection was much larger, with twelve regiments, against thirteen in 1796, but all stationed outside the old capital. Several were in their old locations forming the usual semicircle around the city, from Tver on the Petersburg-Moscow corridor via Kaluga, Tula, and Riazan to Vladimir Province, with others on the Volga at Iaroslavl and Kostroma guarding the approaches to Rybinsk, the increasingly important grain procurement center, where the waterways to Lake Ladoga began. Four were in the valley of the Oka, once along the old line that had once defined Moscow against the Crimean Tatars.

This deployment of regular troops formed the core of a much larger military region studded with garrisons located far apart; four battalions in Moscow, one each in Tver, Vladimir, and Nizhnii Novgorod, but also Voronezh and Tambov, and even Saratov and Arkhangelsk. The third inspection, that of Smolensk, continued to straddle the Russo-Bielorussian border. Most of its ten regiments were in the province: the deployment closely resembled that of 1763. Those in Bielorussia were chiefly stationed in Mogilev Province. As in 1796, the troops deployed in the Smolensk region linked the Moscow core with Livonia and Lithuania, but also Livonia with the Left-Bank Ukraine, facilitating strategic transfers from one theater to another. The thirty-one regiments deployed in Russia proper were thus concentrated in the same two wings that over the years had distended the original concentrated deployment in the Muscovite center: nine were in the Petersburg-Pskov-Novgorod triangle and six in Smolensk province alone. South of Moscow, there were ten in Kaluga, Tula, Riazan, Orel, Kursk, and Voronezh Provinces, a very light military force in the wooded steppe zone. Altogether they had ceased to be a concentrated force in order to become a rear formation, keeping open communications between the two capitals and supporting the much heavier deployment along the imperial periphery.

The other inspections were deployed, as they had been in 1796, along a huge outer semicircle stretching from the Gulf of Finland to the Volga, its more distant segment even farther away from the old capital, as the deployment followed the imperial periphery closer than ever before. Deployment there remained the policy, incorporating client societies more tightly into the administrative and military infrastructure of the empire. The strategic force ceased to be a tool of political suasion to become a police force to secure tranquility in the border regions and to map out the border of Fortress Empire. It began to assume a defensive posture to protect what had recently been acquired and was being integrated into a unified empire, while retaining an offensive capability toward those regions of the Russo-Swedish and Russo-Turkish frontier that remained beyond Russia's grasp. Vis-à-vis Prussia and Austria, a forward deployment served as a warning that a client state and even the friendly kingdom must not be allowed to develop a military capability along the imperial periphery exceeding the empire's own ability to project force. It also served notice that the empire would come to the aid of both powers in the event of a Napoleonic offensive in Central Europe that threatened their vital interests. In both cases, it sustained a perception of Russia's awesomeness, which even Napoleon would eventually have to recognize.

The Finland Inspection remained confined to Vyborg Province, but there was a strong garrison force: three battalions in Rochensalm, where the decisive battle had been fought with the Swedes in 1790, two each in Vyborg and Fredrikshamn, and a single battalion in Willmanstrand, Kexholm, and Nyslott. This inspection was obviously no more than an extension of the Petersburg military region, guarding the approaches to the northern capital in peacetime. The Livland Inspection, with only ten regiments, was much smaller than in 1796, but it was distributed more evenly in Reval and Wesenberg in Estland, on the road from Narva to Revel. Three musketeer regiments were spread across Livonia in Derpt, Fellin, and Pernau. There was also a garrison battalion on Ösel Island, at Arensburg (Kuressaare). But three more musketeer regiments were stationed in Kurland. Livonia, except at Polangen, was no longer on the land periphery of the empire. It had become an inner frontier of the empire where the strategic force maintained a largely nominal presence supported by large garrisons in the major towns. The downgrading of the Baltic provinces had been steady since 1763: at that time, there were 27 regiments (out of 100) in those provinces (including Vyborg); in 1796 and again in 1801 there were only 17 (out of the 140).

By contrast, the Lithuanian Inspection, which included no garrisons, was larger than in 1796. Its fourteen regiments made it the third largest after the Dniestr and Kiev Inspections. It stood guard behind the Niemen facing East Prussia and Prussia's possessions in Poland. It was chiefly an infantry inspection, comprising eleven regiments, with only three of cavalry. The inspection was as much an army of occupation—its commanding general in 1801, Levin von Bennigsen, was also the military governor of Vilno with jurisdiction over the whole of Lithuania—as a force of intervention: in 1805, Bennigsen would carry out a military demonstration along the Prussian border when it was suspected that Prussia might side with Napoleon, at a time when Kutuzov, who replaced him in 1810, was leading a Russian army against Napoleon in Austria. The new Brest-Litovsk Inspection completed the linear deployment in the western theater. Its eleven regiments were equally divided between cavalry (cuirassier) and infantry regiments, and it had no garrisons. Like the Lithuanian Inspection, it fulfilled the dual role of army of occupation in the territories acquired as a result of the third partition, and of force of intervention, here against Austrian possessions in Poland. Brest-Litovsk was a major strategic location where the Moscow-Smolensk-Minsk-Warsaw and Vilno-Slonim roads crossed the Western Bug, the imperial border since 1795, less than two hundred kilometers from the Polish capital. To sum up, 45 of the 140 regiments, or 32.1 percent, were deployed in the western theater, against 32.3 percent in 1796 and 47 percent in 1763. In fact, the share of the western theater had been higher in 1796 (39 percent) because seven regiments deployed in Volhynia belonged to the Ukrainian Division, which focused the southern theater. As the empire kept expanding, the old concentrated deployment was giving way to an increasingly thin peripheral deployment on the line. However, the deployment of 1801 also showed that primary consideration was still given to the southern theater, where 58 of the 140 regiments, or 41.4 percent, were stationed.

The reasons were clear. The empire had abandoned, temporarily, its traditional hostility toward the Ottomans, and by the treaty of 1799 had gained permission to send warships through the Straits. The treaty was a response to Napoleon's 1798 expedition to Egypt, the seizure of Malta, and the occupation of the Ionian Islands: Russian warships would help the Ottomans reassert their position in the eastern Mediterranean.[3] But the alliance also raised the possibility of additional troops being sent to man garrisons, to "defend" Constantinople against the growing threat of Revolutionary France to Ottoman possessions on the Adriatic coast and in the archipelago. The deployment would also make it possible to invade Moldavia and Wallachia quickly in the event of renewed hostility with the Ottomans.

There were five inspections in the southern theater. The Ukrainian Inspection, which had once been the largest, was now one of the smallest, with only six regiments, in part because the regiments deployed farther west along the Austro-Polish border were now part of the new Brest-Litovsk Inspection. Its creation illustrated the progression of the strategic force's fragmentation into a larger number of regional commands stationed on the periphery, with missions defined in increasingly territorial terms, combining those of an occupation force, defense in depth, and forward defense against the other powers already established in the frontier zones beyond the imperial periphery. This Ukrainian Inspection of four to six regiments was deployed in parts of Podolia and Volhynia, in towns that had been the scene of bitter fights between Poles, Cossacks, Tatars, and Russians, the typical fate of border towns; some were also important grain trade centers. They now became district centers with a civilian infrastructure complementing that of the regimental headquarters. To the south, in what used to be the Ochakov steppe, there was a new Dniestr Inspection, the largest of all, with eighteen regiments. As the name indicates, its deployment was peripheral, facing Moldavia and a short distance from the Danube delta. Its chasseur regiments were stationed at various crossings on the river from Dubossary to Ovidiopol and in the interior near Balta close to the old Polish-Ottoman border. The infantry was in Kherson, Nikolaev, and Odessa, all major towns on the Black Sea coast, the estuaries of the Dniepr and the Southern Bug, centers of the growing grain trade of New Russia, naval headquarters and shipyards for the new Black Sea fleet. There was also a two-battalion garrison in Kherson and another in Ochakov. Three more infantry regiments were in Kamenets-Podolsk, the huge Polish fortress facing Khotin on the other side of the Dniestr; in

Mogilev-on-the-Dniestr, where they linked up with the chasseurs to form a thin line along the river; the third in Tiraspol, facing Bendery which had been another major Ottoman fortress on the Khotin-Ochakov-Azov forward perimeter of the Ottoman Empire. Others were in Nemirov and Tulchin, on the road from Vinnitsa to Iampol on the Dniestr, and in Uman on the road from Belaia Tserkov to Odessa. The cavalry was kept inland, in the old lands of New Russia: in Novomirgorod, Elizavetgrad, Boguslav, and Olviopol (Pervomaisk). This Dniestr Inspection was thus overwhelmingly infantry, and it was poised for operations in Moldavia-Wallachia, either for or against the Ottomans depending on the circumstances. Some of these regimental headquarters were former Potocki properties and important grain trade centers, providing a convenient source of provisioning for the troops. The heaviest concentrations were in this region: ten regiments each in Volhynia and Podolia and nine in Kherson province, even higher than in 1796.

The peripheral development of the strategic force in the southern theater continued eastward, as it had in 1796, with the seven regiments of the Crimean Inspection. It was also an almost exclusively infantry inspection with garrisons in Akhtiar (Sevastopol) and Perekop. The only change was that the inspection stretched beyond Fanagoria to Ekaterinodar on the Kuban, where a chasseur regiment was stationed. There, on the Kuban, began the Caucasian Inspection now including not only the Caucasian Line but also eastern Georgia, annexed de facto the preceding year, in 1800. Four of its eleven regiments were dragoon, stationed by squadrons from Fort Ust-Labinsk, where the territory of the Black Sea Cossacks ended. There Cossacks remained under the jurisdiction of the military governor of Kherson, later Odessa, who operated as the governor general of New Russia and the Crimea. From there, the regiments were deployed all the way to Stavropol and, in Georgia, in Tiflis, Telavi, Signakh, Lori, and Gori to the east and west of the Georgian capital, facing the Azerbaijan Khanates and Ottoman western Georgia, in forts once built by the Georgian tsars. There dragoons formed the supporting arm of the infantry deployed by companies along the Caucasian Line in the same places or between them, but extending as far as Kizliar, as well as in Tiflis and Dushet (Duseti), on the mountain road descending from the Darial Pass. The deployment of the Caucasian Inspection completed the peripheral deployment of the strategic force in the southern theater. It also included the old garrison towns of Astrakhan and Tsaritsyn and, on the Sea of Azov, St. Dmitrii, Azov, and Taganrog.

Behind this linear deployment along the Dniestr, the Crimea, the Kuban, and the Kura stood another inspection, that of Kiev, with sixteen regiments the second largest after the Dniestr Inspection. It was in fact the successor of the Ukrainian Division of 1763, but now deployed well inland in what had become the inner frontier of the empire. Half of its complement consisted of cavalry, cuirassiers, dragoons, and hussars, and two regiments in Voronezh and Ostrogozhsk in Russia proper. The regular Cossack regiment remained in its hometown, Chuguev. This was the old land of the Little Russian and Slobodian Cossacks, now part of the regular cavalry. The infantry was in Kiev (with a two-battalion garrison), in the old hetmanate on the left bank of the Dniepr, as well as in Kursk and Briansk. This inspection formed the strategic reserve of the southern theater for the Dniestr and Crimea and even the Brest-Litovsk inspections, reflecting the major importance of

Kiev as the region's great military headquarters, comparable to Brest-Litovsk, which had eclipsed Riga, and to Tiflis, which had replaced Astrakhan.

The eastern theater had always been of secondary importance because threats from the steppe nomads could easily be contained, and only in the 1750s had the appearance of Manchu troops at the entrance of the Kazakh steppe raised alarm in Petersburg. The Orenburg Inspection, still commanded by the military governor, was even smaller than in 1796 with only four regiments, three of them in Bashkiria, the other in Ekaterinburg and some of the metallurgical plants. The Kazan (and Simbirsk) garrisons were under his command; the others were stationed in various forts along the Orenburg Line. In Siberia, the imperial government's major preoccupation was with the development of trade with China. Military concerns were limited to tightening the defensive perimeter against Kazakh pressures while facilitating at the same time the creation of small bases of operation from which to launch punitive expeditions into the steppe. The two dragoon, three musketeer, and two chasseur regiments were all stationed on the Irtysh Line and in the Altai, including the musketeer regiment, which Paul had insisted must remain at Ust-Kamenogorsk. Garrisons were stationed on the line and in the Altai as well as in Tobolsk, Irkutsk, and Selenginsk, with a new one on Kamchatka.

In conclusion, the deployment of 1801, on the eve of the protracted conflict with Napoleonic France, accentuated the dispersion of the strategic force and accelerated its peripheral deployment to complete the transformation of Fortress Russia into Fortress Empire. These regional commands created an infrastructure of regimental headquarters and logistical support bases to consolidate the imperial government's hold on those territories, where client societies had only recently helped the empire practice an economy of force by working at no cost to support its ambitions. At the same time, this peripheral deployment assumed an offensive posture maximizing the threat of immediate action against both recalcitrant clients and enemies across the border, backed by support of a strategic reserve in the form of a Lithuanian Inspection in the western theater and a Ukrainian Inspection in the southern theater. Both theaters were becoming autonomous, as Rumiantsev and Potemkin had once suggested they should become, bringing about a fragmentation of the strategic force and the consolidation of regional commands. This, however, could not take final shape until the "hereditary enemy" had been finally crushed.

The size of the strategic force began to rise very rapidly after 1803. In 1805, there were already 123 regiments of infantry and 50 of cavalry, for a total strength of 12,620 men in the Guard and 326,380 in the regular army. By 1812, on the eve of Napoleon's invasion, the strength of the infantry had risen to 172 regiments, including 6 in the Guard, 14 of grenadiers, 98 of musketeers, 50 of chasseurs, and 4 of naval infantry, for a total complement of 15,000 Guardsmen and 390,000 regular infantrymen. The cavalry included 76,165 horsemen in sixty-five regiments, five of them in the Guard.[4] The importance of the cuirassiers as shock cavalry continued to be downgraded in favor of the dragoons and hussars used in reconnaissance missions, in pursuing the enemy, and in protecting the wounded and the baggage train. The growth of the Guard was significant for reasons that went beyond the rise in numbers. It was increasingly becoming the foundation of the Romanov house's legitimacy, the instrument by which the empire projected the awesomeness of its power onto those who came to the capital, the formation around which a new cult of the autocratic tsar-emperor was being nurtured within the ruling elite.[5] Its regiments had risen from seven in 1801 to eleven by 1812, its strength from 11,700 to over 20,000 men, and it would continue to grow in the ensuing years.

While the size of the strategic force kept growing, its internal organization began to change. In June 1806, the forces that had gone to the assistance of Austria the preceding year and were retreating toward the Niemen were reorganized into thirteen divisions, no longer the old peacetime territorial divisions, but tactical formations. The move announced the abolition of the inspections. By July, there were already eighteen divisions. In 1807, the Crimean and Caucasian Inspections became the Nineteenth and Twentieth Divisions, two more divisions were created from scratch, and even the Orenburg and Siberian Inspection were renamed divisions, bringing the total number to twenty-four. By 1811, there were twenty-seven, each consisting of 18,000 to 20,000 men in three cavalry and six or seven infantry regiments (with an artillery brigade).[6] Divisions were grouped into corps and armies according to circumstances, without any uniform organization yet being established. But in October 1810, fifteen divisions were grouped into corps deployed in the western theater, each consisting of from two to three divisions.[7] The term was not new in Russian military organization and had often been used in the eighteenth century, but mostly in the sense of a formation operating separately from the main forces, or in a distant region: this is the meaning that would be given to the "separate corps" during and after the War of 1812, formations that were not administratively integrated into the structure of the field army. The use of the term remained very confused: the force sent into Finland, called a corps, was subsequently divided into several corps of 2,000 to 6,000 men each! Their creation was very much the result of the growing size of the strategic force and of the necessity to create an intermediate command between a commander in chief and the divisional commanders. Napoleon seems to have been the first to use corps in this sense during his 1805 campaign; they were in fact "small armies."[8]

The creation of divisions or corps, and armies operating in widely separated sectors—in Finland, along the Austrian border, on the Danube, and in the Caucasus—reflected two trends, apparently contradictory. One was to maximize flexibility and mobility while keeping the strategic force administratively unified in the tsar-emperor's headquarters in wartime, making it possible to move substantial forces from one sector to another with a minimum of logistical disruption, since divisions and corps were given their commissary and provision infrastructure. But the same flexibility in wartime announced the dispersion in both location and responsibilities of the strategic force in peacetime. In several instances corps headquarters became authorities combining military and civilian responsibilities for the administration of a border region. The reorganization of the army reached completion with the publication in January 1812 of the Statute of the "Grand Active Army," the first such document since 1716.[9] It assumed the consolidation of nearly the entire strategic force under the leadership of a single commander in chief serving as the emperor's military deputy, describing at length the lines of command and the responsibilities and powers at each level. Such a Grand Army was not created until the appointment of Kutuzov in August 1812, just in time to coordinate the retreat beyond Moscow, launch a counteroffensive against Napoleon, and then lay the foundations of a military infrastructure on a continental scale to sustain the empire's hegemony in the Heartland.

The years 1809–12 were marked by incessant troop movements avidly followed by the French ambassador in Petersburg in an attempt to fathom Russian intentions or simply to obtain Russian assistance in pursuing French interests.[10] His purpose was to commit the Russians to war in Finland in order to force Sweden to join the Continental System, and to a war of attrition on the Danube to relieve the pressure on the Duchy of Warsaw, whose central location made it an ideal place for a strategic thrust along the fault line between the western and southern theaters. Much of the growing antagonism between Alexander I and Napoleon revolved around the tsar's unwillingness to play the French game, winning quickly in Finland and refusing fully to join the Continental System; fighting what was essentially a holding operation on the Danube; refusing to join in Napoleon's attack of the friendly kingdom in 1809; and concentrating by March 1811 over 250,000 men between the Baltic and the Dniestr. In anticipation of the great war that everyone considered inevitable, the strategic force was increasingly deployed along the western periphery of the empire. As Caulaincourt, the French ambassador, reported that same month, the interior was denuded of troops and "tout est sur les frontières."

## War and Peace, 1812–1831

It is a measure of the imperial government's refusal to be bound by its own legislation that no single commander in chief was appointed in the spring of 1812, but three, for three armies of very different sizes. The eight infantry corps and the four of cavalry were unevenly distributed among them. When Napoleon crossed the Niemen, Alexander I was in Vilno, at the headquarters of the First Army commanded by Barclay. The statute provided that the sovereign exercised the powers of a commander in chief when he was with the army; only in his absence did the commander in chief issue orders having the force of imperial commands, to be obeyed unconditionally. But Alexander I had neither the training nor the qualities required of a commander in chief. His interference in battlefield strategy had been pernicious enough in 1805. He now knew, and so did the high command, that his presence was essential in Petersburg while his generals squared off with Napoleon for the decisive battles that would decide the fate of the empire. The monarch's role was to formulate the grand strategy for the war once Napoleon had been checkmated on the battlefield, without risking his reputation and the awesomeness of the dynasty by suffering defeat in battle, let alone being taken prisoner by the swift-moving Napoleon.

The strong mutual dislike between Barclay and Bagration, the commander in chief of the Second Army—one a taciturn German, the other a fiery Georgian, made it even more imperative that the tsar cease to be associated with one of the armies and leave the theater of operations altogether. But when he finally did, after the First and Second Armies met at Smolensk and began to retreat toward Moscow, and after he was forced by his entourage to appoint Kutuzov, whom he disliked and distrusted, as commander in chief of both armies, he gave him no instructions, as if the statute of January had not been created for this very purpose.[11] The ensuing situation was awkward in the extreme. The two armies remained separate, each under its commander in chief, with Dmitrii Dokhturov replacing Bagration, who was killed at Borodino in September. Barclay could only resent the humiliation of having to receive orders from the new commander in chief and his chief of staff, the same Bennigsen who had commanded the imperial troops at the Battle of Friedland in June 1807 and lost the field to Napoleon. The withdrawal of Alexander, who seems to have been out of his depth among these high-powered and rival army commanders, threatened to paralyze the effectiveness of the high command. After the abandonment of Moscow—which Barclay supported and Bennigsen opposed—the First and Second Armies were finally merged to form a single Main Army. Barclay resigned for reasons of health, and Kutuzov assumed the full powers of a commander in chief. There were still a Third Army, commanded by Admiral Pavel Chichagov, and two separate corps under Fabian von Osten-Sacken and Peter von Essen, all three operating south of the main line of operations, as well as another separate corps under Peter von Wittgenstein north of it. By the end of 1812, all these forces, despite their retaining much operational authority, had been placed under Kutuzov's supreme command.

Barclay returned to the army in February 1813 to become commander in chief of the Third Army, replacing the incompetent Chichagov, but did not succeed Kutuzov when the latter died in April. Wittgenstein became the new commander in chief of the Main Army, but at the Battle of Bautzen at the end of May Barclay showed his superior talents and became, at last, commander in chief, taking Diebitsch as his chief of staff. At the same time, an "Army of Poland" was being created in the duchy under Bennigsen; it caught up with the Main Army and was sent to blockade Hamburg. A third, called the Reserve Army, replaced it in Poland under Dmitrii Lobanov-Rostovskii.[12] To coordinate the operations of all these armies and corps, a unified central command under Karl von Toll was established at the tsar's headquarters.

The entry of the friendly kingdom into the war on the allied side in June complicated the situation even farther. Russian, Prussian, and Austrian (and Swedish) troops were combined to create under the overall command of Schwartzenberg four armies that would be responsible to the political committee consisting of the Russian and Austrian emperors and the Prussian king. The Northern Army of 156,000 men was commanded by Jean-Baptiste Bernadotte, a former French marshal, chosen in 1810 to found a new Swedish dynasty. It consisted of a Swedish and a Russian corps, three Prussian corps, and a mixed one of Prussian, Mecklenburg, and Swedish troops. The Silesian Army under the Prussian Blücher was also a combined force of 99,000 men, consisting of five Russian corps (44,000 men), a Prussian corps, and a right wing of four Russian infantry divisions. The second largest of the four armies was the Main Army, commanded by Barclay with instructions to merge with the Austrian or Bohemian Army of 110,000 men. Its 125,000 troops included the Prussian Guard and a Prussian corps, the other seven infantry corps, and a hussar division of Russian troops. Bennigsen's army of 60,000 remained a separate army, directly responsible to the political committee.[13] From then on, the major components of the allied force were in place, commanded under Schwartzenberg by Bernadotte, Blücher, and Barclay, with the Bohemian Army renamed the Main Army as it prepared to cross the Rhine into France at the end of 1813. After the occupation of Paris in March 1814, Barclay was made a field marshal.

In October, while the strategic force was returning to its home base, it was divided into two armies, the First under Barclay, the Second under Bennigsen, each commander invested with the powers of a commander in chief in accordance with the 1812 statute. The return of Napoleon from Elba delayed their deployment until the following year. By 1815, the First Army consisted of seven infantry corps, six corps of cavalry, and four of reserve cavalry, the much smaller Second Army of two infantry corps and one of cavalry. There were in addition several separate corps outside the armies' chain of command, including one remaining in France until the final settlement. The Second Army was abolished in July 1830, when its troops were integrated into the First Army, the latter five years later, in the wake of a major reorganization of the military establishment.[14]

In the meantime, a similar major reform of the high command had taken place in December 1815. The War Ministry, which had become in 1802 the central administrative agency for the entire army, was stripped of its responsibilities for the line to remain the army's central supply organization. Responsibilities for personnel, deployment, and military planning were vested in His Majesty's Main Staff—to distinguish it from the Main Staffs of the two armies—headed by Petr Volkonskii, replaced by Diebitsch in 1823. Commanders in chief and separate corps commanders reported to Volkonskii and no longer to the War Minister. Their powers were curtailed in accordance with peacetime circumstances.[15] After the war a number of changes took place in the structure of the strategic force that pointed to its eventual transformation into a huge garrison establishment for Fortress Empire. By 1825, the infantry consisted of 179 regiments, including 10 Guard regiments, 15 of grenadiers, 8 of carbineers (now considered infantry), 96 of "infantry" (the new name of the musketeers), and 50 of chasseurs, for a total strength of 526,512 men, or 124 percent more than in 1801. The increase in the size of the cavalry was hardly less dramatic. There were now 77 regiments, including 10 Guard regiments, 9 of cuirassiers, 18 of dragoons, 12 of hussars, 20 of uhlans, and 8 of mounted chasseurs, for a total strength of 106,726 men and an increase of 114 percent. The ratio of infantry to cavalry regiments was now 2.2 to 1, slightly less than it had been in 1763 and 1801. The strength of the strategic force now exceeded 633,000 men in 256 regiments.[16]

The most striking change had taken place in the size of the Guard. Its eleven regiments in 1812 had nearly doubled to twenty in 1825; it was now so large that it was divided in 1813 into the old and the new or young Guard, to distinguish the latter from the regiments created much earlier, including the three most famous: Preobrazhenskii (1694), Semenovskii (1694), and Izmailovskii (1730). The comte de Langeron, a French émigré who served in the Russian army, reached the rank of full general, and was governor general of Odessa and New Russia, estimated the strength of the Guard at 60,000 men (including artillery units) and at 90,000 men if fourteen of the grenadier and cuirassier regiments were added, because they were granted privileges similar to those of the Guard. Those Guard regiments were courageous and disciplined, he writes, the cream but also the scourge of the army, as they had always been: some three-fourths of the regimental commanders were officers parachuted from Petersburg,[17] the mini-fortress, the *kazenny gorod*, of Fortress Empire.[18]

A second change concerned the policing of Fortress Empire. In the 1760s, local units called provincial companies had been created to serve as a mobile police force to convoy recruits, prisoners, and funds from one place to another within each province before turning them over to small detachments of the neighboring provincial company. In addition, there were garrisons in some of the most important provincial capitals, as previously noted, which functioned as logistical bases for the regular army and were responsible for putting down peasant disorders in emergencies. In 1811, the companies and garrisons were combined to form an Internal Guard distributed among eight regions, consisting of provincial battalions of 554 men each. Regions were headed by major generals who reported to the war minister. Three regional headquarters north of Moscow were in Novgorod, Tver, and Iaroslavl; another four were in central Russia, in Kaluga, Orel, Kursk, and Voronezh; the eighth was in Ekaterinoslav with jurisdiction over New Russia, Podolia, and Volhynia. As a rule, regions straddled the border between Russia and its borderlands: the Baltic provinces were divided between the Novgorod and Tver regions, Bielorussia and Lithuania between the Kaluga and Orel regions, the remainder of Ukraine between the Kursk and Orel regions. In the Caucasus, garrisons remained subordinated to the military governor in Tiflis.[19]

The Internal Guard had little time to take shape before the Napoleonic invasion, and it was transformed in 1816 into a "separate corps" commanded by an "inspector," Lt. Gen. Evgraf Komarovskii, who served as deputy war minister. By 1829, there were nine regions with a much clearer distinction between Russia and its borderlands: the Iaroslavl, Kazan, and Tambov regions included only Russian provinces; Petersburg and Pskov belonged to the Riga region, Vyborg and Sveaborg to the Petrozavodsk region. The Grodno, Kiev, and Kherson regions had no Russian provinces. In the Caucasus and Siberia, the Internal Guard reported to the respective separate corps commanders.[20]

Another militarized police force was the gendarmes, created in 1815 by transforming a regiment of dragoons into one of gendarmes, who were at first a purely military police. In 1817, however, the small dragoon detachments, which had been attached to the provincial companies since the 1760s to form a mounted police subordinated to the civilian authority in the person of the governor, were integrated into a separate force called "gendarmes of the Internal Guard," each detachment of thirty gendarmes attached to the provincial battalion. Finally, these gendarme units were consolidated in 1827 to form another "separate corps," whose commander (*shef*), General Alexander von Benckendorff, was also in charge of the Imperial Headquarters (the suite) and the Third Section, the political police of the empire created the preceding year.[21] Since the gendarmes were mounted troops and the Internal Guard consisted of infantry, the two separate corps were complementary and together formed a new militarized police force for Fortress Empire, whose commanders were responsible to the emperor, like the army commanders in chief and other separate corps commanders.

This gendarme separate corps was also given a regional organization. Five regions were created in 1827, each headed by a major or lieutenant general. The en-

tire north, including parts of Finland and the Baltic provinces, formed the Petersburg region; Moscow was the headquarters of eleven central provinces; Lithuania
and Bielorussia, Podolsk and Volhynia depended on Vitebsk; Little and New Russia
on Kiev. The huge fifth region based in Kazan included the eastern provinces with
the Caucasus and the Orenburg Territory. By 1836, there were seven regions, following the creation of a separate one for Siberia and another for eastern Ukraine
and the Caucasus.[22] These gendarme and Internal Guard regions overlapped with
the deployment of the strategic force in armies and separate corps, as we shall see
presently, creating an imperial police infrastructure with jurisdiction over both the
army and the civilian administration.

The third major change was the creation of the military settlements, certainly
one of the most controversial reforms in the history of the imperial army. The idea
went back to 1810, when an infantry battalion was "settled" in Mogilev Province.
The experiment was intended to show that army units could live off the land without requiring support from the imperial treasury, but it was interrupted by the war.
In 1815, Alexei Arakcheev, who had been director of the tsar's chancery since 1812
and would become the de facto prime minister of the empire, worked out a project
of settling more army units in various parts of the country, in Novgorod and again
in Mogilev, in Kharkov and Kherson Provinces. The troops would engage in agriculture while continuing to train and would draw their recruits from their area of
settlement, an important factor that, it was held, would mitigate the horrors of the
recruiting system, where young men in their teens were brutally taken from their
native villages and died in droves on the way to their units. In other words, this "settled" army would become self-sufficient. Detractors would point out that the settlements would also create a military caste, dangerous to the security of the empire, as
the uprisings of 1831 would eventually show. It cannot be excluded either that
Arakcheev, a former war minister, was seeking to create his own bailiwick like that
of the current war minister, who until 1826 commanded the Internal Guard and the
gendarmes. Be that as it may, the military settlements were combined in 1821 to
form yet another separate corps commanded by Arackcheev himself. By 1827, it had
grown to become an enormous enterprise consisting of nearly 160,000 men.[23]

We now turn to the deployment of the strategic force after its return from the
Napoleonic wars, using a document probably acquired by the French embassy in
Petersburg and entitled "Composition of the Russian Army in 1819." Not only does
it contain a comprehensive list of corps, divisions, and regiments, it also locates
their headquarters, even though some personal and place names became garbled
beyond recognition in transliterating the Cyrillic alphabet.[24]

At the time the strategic force consisted at the time of a corps of Guard troops
commanded by Grand Duke Constantine, the tsar's brother (who resided in Warsaw), with the title of commander in chief; a First Army, with headquarters in
Mogilev (Bielorussia) and commanded by Osten Sacken (Barclay had died in 1818),
of six corps of infantry (including one of grenadiers) and four corps of reserve cavalry; a Second Army, with headquarters in Tulchin (Podolia) and commanded by
Wittgenstein (Bennigsen had returned to his native Hanover that same year), consisting of two corps of infantry and one corps of reserve cavalry; and five separate
corps in Finland, Lithuania, Georgia, the Orenburg Territory, and Siberia. These

armies and separate corps combined divisions of infantry and cavalry, of which there were now fifty. Divisions, except in the eastern theater, consisted in turn of regiments: 253 are listed in the document. As a rule, army corps consisted of four divisions and twenty-two regiments, those of reserve cavalry of two divisions and eight regiments; separate corps of only one or at most two smaller divisions.

The Guard was stationed in Petersburg and its immediate environs, in Sofia, Peterhof, and Krasnoe Selo, but one regiment of dragoons was in Novgorod and one of carbineers in Kexholm. To this corps of Guard troops, commanded (under Constantine) by Illarion Vasil'chikov, was attached the I Corps of reserve cavalry under Nikolai Depreradovich (a descendant of Serbs who had settled in New Russia), deployed along the Petersburg-Tver waterway in Novaia Ladoga, Borovichi, Vyshnii Volochek, Torzhok, and Tver. The twenty-seven regiments of these two corps were the descendants of those that had formed the Petersburg Division and Inspection in 1763, 1796, and 1801. They enhanced the majesty of the ruling house and guarded the palaces, and their uhlans patrolled the vital waterway linking Petersburg with Moscow.

The establishment of the First Army's headquarters in distant Mogilev on the Dniepr illustrated in the most graphic manner the extent to which the territorialization of the army had taken place. Moscow was no longer the command center from which the strategic force had surged toward the periphery of the empire at the beginning of the eighteenth century, nor did it any longer provide the essential strategic reserve for the divisions deployed in the outer semicircle facing the western and southern theaters. In fact, the V Corps stationed there was among the smallest. Commanded by Petr Tolstoi (who had been ambassador to France in 1807 after Tilsit), it consisted of three divisions and eighteen regiments: the Twenty-Third Division stationed in Moscow; the Tenth in Kolomna with units in Bronnitsy and Egorevsk straddling the Riazan-Tambov corridor, the old invasion route from the southeast; the Eighth in Iurev-Polskii, its six regiments in Vladimir Province, from which another two major radial roads led to Iaroslavl and Vladimir, and beyond them to Rybinsk and Nizhnii Novgorod. The Moscow deployment had been given a more limited eastern orientation: it both guarded the approaches to the old capital from the east and created a backup force for the II Corps, headquartered in Vladimir and commanded by Dmitrii Golitsyn. It consisted of three divisions of infantry and one of hussars. The Second Hussar Division and the Fourth Infantry Division were stationed in Tambov and Riazan respectively, planting a military presence in sleepy provincial towns where the memory of Tatar raids was still very much alive. The Sixth and Seventeenth Infantry Divisions were in Iaroslavl and Vladimir, filling the space between the two great bends of the Volga from Uglich to Nizhnii-Novgorod.

The deployment of a substantial number of troops east of Moscow marked a return to the situation of the 1740s and 1780s, when regular troops were considered essential to maintain security in areas of recent settlement. In 1819, the deployment embodied a policy of using the army, backed by the Internal Guard and the gendarmes, as an instrument of rule by an imperial government turning increasingly conservative and determined to crush any manifestation of "liberalism," whether in the universities (as in Kazan) or in the countryside. The (unnumbered) Grenadier

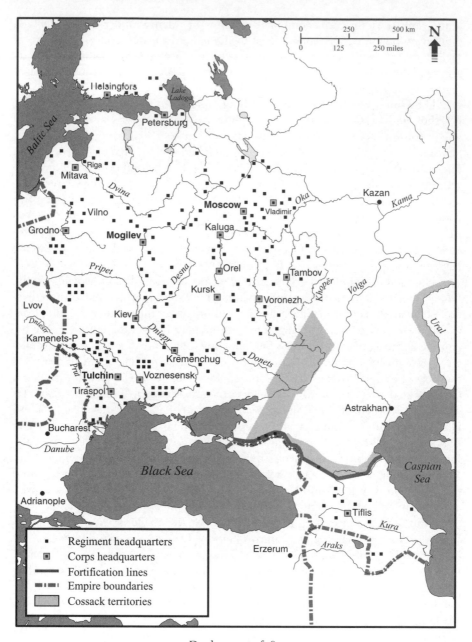

Deployment of 1819

Corps commanded by Osterman-Tolstoi was based in Kaluga and deployed south and west of Moscow. It was a smaller corps of only two divisions. One was in Kaluga, its six regiments deployed in the province and in Mozhaisk; the other in Viazma, its grenadiers in Smolensk Province and one regiment in Staritsa in Tver Province, from where the grenadier corps linked up with the corps of reserve cavalry attached to the Guard.

The southern wing of the deployment within Russia was formed by the four corps of reserve cavalry. The II Corps was in Orel, commanded by Fedor Korf. Like the more prestigious Grenadier Corps, these corps were even smaller, consisting of only two divisions and eight regiments, and were commanded not by full but by lieutenant generals. Its Second Cuirassier Division was stationed in Orel and Kursk Provinces, and its Second Uhland Division "settled" in the environs of Livny. The town had once been the junction of the invasion routes from which the Crimean Tatars had attempted their final push on Moscow. The area south of the Orel-Livny line had also been the territory where the eighteenth-century *odnodvortsy* had been required to contribute service to the Landmilitia set up to cope with the threats from the steppe. The geographical-historical background of the military settlements is often overlooked. Most of the troops deployed in the south did not become part of them, but those who did were settled in areas where a tradition of combining agricultural pursuits with military service belonged to the recent past. The III Corps of reserve cavalry was in Kursk under Alexander Voinov. Its Third Cuirassier Division was deployed in the province and its Third Uhlan Division (four regiments) was in Kharkov Province, the old land of the Slobodian Cossacks, who had once also combined military service with work on the land. The IV Corps was in Voronezh under Nikolai Borozdin, its First Dragoon Division deployed in the province and its First Horse Chasseur Division in neighboring Voronezh, Orel, and Tambov provinces. The V Corps in Tambov under Karl Lambert (Charles de Lambert, a French émigré) consisted of the Second Dragoon Division in Voronezh Province and the Second Chasseur Division in Tambov.

The deployment of the strategic force in Russia proper suggests a number of conclusions. The First Army, including its three other corps deployed in the borderlands, was spread across an enormous area stretching from Lithuania to Nizhnii-Novgorod and from Tver to the Ukrainian border. If we include the Guard deployed between Tver and Petersburg, the old division between the Muscovite center and its two wings had reappeared, one in the north, the other in the south. There were no troops in the provinces east of Nizhnii-Novgorod or north of Iaroslavl. The strategic force was now deployed substantially in Russia proper despite the much greater length of the imperial periphery—108 of its 253 regiments or 42.6 percent, a situation similar to that of 1763. They were stationed in fourteen of the twenty-six provinces, and the concentration was exceptionally high: twenty-one regiments in Petersburg province, fifteen in Moscow, ten each in Vladimir and Kursk. Each of these provinces were nodal areas from which troops could easily be dispatched to any place in European Russia, especially the east between Nizhnii-Novgorod and the Volga.

The deployment amounted to a relative withdrawal from the periphery and a renewed concentration of the strategic force in the Russian core. In First Army's area of deployment, eight provincial capitals and two district centers became divisional as well as corps headquarters, commanded by full or lieutenant generals, while divisional commanders were majors general. Each provincial capital had a governor who was also a major general (unless he was a civilian) and had at his disposal a battalion of the Internal Guard commanded by a lieutenant colonel or colonel. Beginning in 1826, a gendarme unit was added, commanded by a colonel. These four or five officers made up the provincial and police staff of Fortress Empire, responsible each in his separate way to the chief of staff, the ministers of war and interior, and the head of the Third Section. The result was an unprecedented dispersion of the strategic force, in which each infantry and cavalry division was transformed into a provincial army for the maintenance of internal security, and the strategic force became the foundation of the imperial ruler's dictatorship, a trend that would reach its completion during the reign of Nicholas I.

## Peripheral Deployment

The remainder of the force was deployed in the border regions, from the Gulf of Finland to the Caucasus. The annexation of Finland in 1809 and the reintegration of Vyborg province into it two years later created a new geopolitical situation in the eastern Baltic. The grand duchy, with the tsar-emperor as its grand duke, was given a degree of autonomy unparalleled anywhere else in the empire, largely because this last zone of the old Russo-Swedish frontier was now considered a buffer zone guaranteeing lasting peace between the two great Baltic powers that had engaged in a struggle for hegemony for over a century—a struggle Sweden had irretrievably lost. From a military point of view, Petersburg's interest focused on the channel formed by the Gulf of Finland and its approaches between the Åland archipelago and the islands controlling the entrance to the Gulf of Riga. A separate corps was stationed there, commanded by Lt. Gen. Fabian von Steinheil from the Estland nobility, who had spent his entire career in the so-called general staff, the topographical service of the army, and had been appointed governor general of Finland in 1810.[25] This separate corps was in fact no more than the Twenty-First Infantry Division, headquartered in Åbo, the capital of the grand duchy until 1819, when it was moved to Helsingfors. Its six regiments were deployed along the coast of the Gulf. The Internal Guard maintained a brigade for Vyborg and Kuopio in the lake district, and a commandant was appointed in a number of fortresses. The maintenance of internal security in the interior was essentially left to the Finns. In 1823, Steinheil was replaced by Arsenii Zakrevskii, who had been closely associated with Volkonskii on His Majesty's Main Staff. His appointment amounted to a demotion following Volkonskii's dismissal that year. He moved his residence to Petersburg, abandoning Finland altogether. Beginning in 1826, he would combine the posts of governor general and separate corps commander with that of minister of the interior. His successor, Alexander Menshikov, would remain for twenty-four years both governor general and chief of the naval staff, showing how closely military units in Finland had become associated with logistical support for the Baltic Fleet based in Kronstadt and Reval.

Across the Gulf, in the Baltic provinces, began the deployment of the three army corps belonging to the First Army, only one of them in the western theater. The headquarters of this I Corps was in Mitava, under the command of Eugen von Württemberg, a cousin of Alexander I. His relative was at the time governor general of Vitebsk and Mogilev. Württemberg, however, did not have any regional civilian responsibilities; only certain separate corps commanders could also be governors general over a number of provinces. The Piedmontese Filippo Paulucci was governor general of the three Baltic provinces in Riga, and he had no military command. Riga was also the headquarters of a region of Internal Guard troops that included Pskov Province as well. The corps was one of the largest, consisting of four divisions and twenty-two regiments, larger than only a few of the old inspections. The divisional headquarters were in Riga, Mitava, Jakobstadt (Jekabpils), and Vitebsk. The deployment of this I Corps thus formed a thin line stretching along the left bank of the Dvina from the Baltic coast to the upper Dniepr, the first of three zones connecting the Russian core with the Prussian possessions in Poland.

The second echelon in the deployment of the strategic force was constituted by the so-called Lithuanian Corps in Bialystock commanded by Lt. Gen. D'Oeuvray (Fedor Dovre), a French Protestant émigré. The corps was created in 1817 and consisted of two infantry divisions in Bialystock District, annexed after Tilsit—a sliver of land between the Narew and the Niemen whence Diebitsch would launch his offensive against Warsaw in 1831—and in Dubno in Volhynia.[26] This deployment across the Pripet marshes resembled that of the Brest-Litovsk Inspection in 1801. If Bialystock led to Warsaw from the north, Dubno led to Zamość, the Wieprz, and the Vistula toward Warsaw from the south, the old invasion route taken by Suvorov in 1794. The Lithuanian Corps was as much a force of occupation in the territories acquired as a result of the third partition as a force of intervention in the Polish Kingdom in the event of an emergency. Indeed, it was considered in 1819 as "attached" to the Polish Army commanded by Grand Duke Constantine, the de facto viceroy of the kingdom, with the title of commander in chief. This Polish Army formed the third echelon. Created following the Vienna Settlement, which enlarged the Duchy of Warsaw and transformed it into a Polish Kingdom united with Russia under the Romanov scepter, it consisted of Polish troops who had fought in Napoleon's army, even during the recent invasion of Russia, and it was not entirely reliable. Nor was the Lithuanian Corps, which consisted of native soldiers from the eastern marches of the former Polish Empire. These two formations made up in 1823 a force of 69,000 troops, including 53,000 in the infantry and 13,000 in the cavalry.[27] Nevertheless, their existence confirmed Alexander's determination to recreate in some form a Polish Empire within the Russian Empire, a very risky undertaking that would eventually fail. There were no Internal Guard units in Poland, but the eastern marches were combined to form a single region with headquarters in Vilno, where a governor general (called, as in Riga, military governor) exercised jurisdiction over the whole of Lithuania, while Podolia and Volhynia depended on the military governor of Kamenets-Podolsk.

A total of forty regiments, or a mere 15.8 percent of the strategic force, were stationed in the western theater. This deployment was both defensive and offensive. The Baltic and Polish sectors had become completely separated. The six regiments of the Finland Separate Corps had the purely defensive mission of supporting the

Baltic Fleet, whose own defensive mission was to protect the approaches to Petersburg. The remaining thirty-four regiments were in the Polish sector and belonged to two different formations, one reporting to the commander in chief in Warsaw, the other to the commander in chief of the First Army in Mogilev. Three of the four regional deployments along the imperial periphery were given ethnic names (Finland and Lithuanian Corps, Polish Army), the expression of a commitment to territorial defense in which deployment served to secure the tranquility of the border regions. As in Russia proper, the force had become dispersed, its mission defined no longer as the projection of power far beyond a base of operations but as the application of brute force to maintain order and build a military, administrative, and police infrastructure in conquered territories. Viewed from this perspective, this peripheral deployment complemented the more concentrated deployment of the strategic force in Russia proper to complete its transformation into the Romanovs' and the elite's instrument of rule within Fortress Empire.

On the other hand, the deployment of 1819 also had offensive implications. It marked a return, within limits and in very different circumstances, to the deployment of 1725, in which the strategic force was concentrated, if no longer in the Muscovite center, at least in the Russian core, and kept ready for a massive projection of power into Poland—as Diebitsch would do in 1831—and beyond Poland as well, against the Prussian client state and even the friendly kingdom. The annexation of the Duchy of Warsaw in 1815 gave the empire a strategic salient between Brandenburg and Austria, and a Polish-Lithuanian army in a restored but truncated Polish Empire created a potential danger for the two Germanic powers. The Polish border crossed the Vistula near Thorn, while Danzig was only 220 kilometers away; it ran past Kalisz, only 130 kilometers from Poznan and less than 300 from the Oder. By 1914, when the growth of German power had placed Russia on the defensive, the salient had become a liability. A century earlier, it gave the empire a sword of Damocles suspended over Berlin and Vienna. If the association between the Polish and Russian Empires had become as fruitful as Alexander hoped it would, Polish irredentism would have posed a major threat to Prussia's and Austria's possessions in prepartition Poland. The threat represented by the salient was not a vain one: when Austria hinted in 1828 that it might oppose a Russian advance toward the Danube, Nicholas I warned that he would send three army corps across Poland in the direction of Vienna via Olmütz and Brunn.[28] In 1849, Paskievich, by then the imperial viceroy in Poland, would invade Hungary from southern Poland to save the Habsburg dynasty, while the imperial envoy to Berlin cautioned the king his government might intervene in Berlin across Poland if he granted a constitution to his people. Thus the deployment of 1819 in the western theater can be seen as a combination of a light peripheral deployment in border regions—to maintain order where client societies had been unable to create a stable political system favorable to the interests of the empire—with a concentrated deployment in the Russian core from which the strategic force would operate, as it had in the past, by deep thrusts against hostile activities beyond the periphery.

Similar conclusions can be reached about the deployment in the southern theater. The remaining two of the First Army's ten corps were stationed there. The IV Corps was commanded by Nikolai Raevskii in Kiev, which also functioned as the headquarters of its Seventh Infantry Division located in the province on the right bank of the Dniepr. The province stood in the central segment of a linear deployment stretching from Bielorussia to the eastern end of Little Russia. A second divisional headquarters was in Cherikov (Cerikau) on the Sozh at a major crossing of roads leading westward to Bobruisk and Minsk, southward to Gomel, Chernigov, and Kiev. A third was in Chernigov on the Desna, 150 kilometers north of Kiev at the very entrance of Little Russia on the river's left bank, and the fourth was in Priluki, a district center in Poltava Province about 170 kilometers south of Chernigov and 150 east of Kiev. The headquarters of the III Corps, commanded by Andrei Gorchakov, was in Kremenchug, where the river is easily forded, and its four divisions straddled the course of the river. Three were in Poltava, Romny, and Novomoskovsk, making five divisions stationed on the left bank of the Dniepr, one of the heaviest concentrations in the empire. There too, the regional and military commands were kept separate: the governor general of Poltava and Chernigov, who resided in Poltava, had no military command. The fourth was based in Elizavetgrad, the old fortress that had once been the capital of New Serbia. Parts of these divisions were "settled," others retained their regular organization. These settled troops were planted in areas that had once been the "military settlements" of Serbs, Hungarians, and Macedonians in the latter half of the eighteenth century.

The I, III, and IV Corps thus formed a thin peripheral deployment on both sides of the Dniepr between the Russian core and the two regional armies, the Polish Army (including here the Lithuanian Corps), and the Second Army. With only forty-two regiments, the latter was much smaller than the First Army, but its mission was more clearly defined. Its headquarters, Tulchin, was a former Potocki estate, ninety-six kilometers from the Moldavian border on the Dniestr. It consisted of three corps. The headquarters of the VI Corps was in Tiraspol, and its two divisions straddled the river: one on the left bank; the other in Bessarabia, annexed in 1812. The VII Corps with four divisions was twice as large. Based in Kamenets-Podolsk, it was commanded by Alexander Rudzevich.[29] It was a largely "Podolian" corps, with most of its troops stationed in that province between Mezhibozh'e and Mogilev on the Dniestr, a second zone of heavy concentration. They faced northern Moldavia across the river and the Carpathian passes. Finally, the VII Corps of reserve cavalry, consisting of two uhlan divisions, was "settled" in the Ochakov steppe, facing the Budzhak, the lowland steppe of Bessarabia, which led to the Danube delta. In this entire region, from the southern fringes of the Russian core to the Prut, garrisons were combined to form two regions with headquarters in Kiev and Kherson. There were no longer any regular troops in the Crimea.

The deployment of the strategic force in the southern theater clearly pointed to the Danube. Troops of the First and Second Armies, many of them "settled" in still sparsely populated territory, functioned as an occupation force in the southeastern marches of the former Polish Empire which had served as a source of provisions for the imperial army operating along the Danube since the War of 1768–74. The military settlements in the Ochakov steppe performed the same function as their Serb and other ancestors in New Serbia and Slavianoserbia: they created nuclei of agricultural settlements in a nearly empty steppe, where the settler had not yet established his ascendancy against the occasional nomad. But the deployment was also offensive. The Second Army could just as well have been called the Moldavian Army or the Army on the Danube, as its predecessors had indeed been called during the War of 1806–12. Its mission was to move quickly into Moldavia and Wallachia, occupy Bucharest and deploy along the lower Danube in preparation for a deep thrust into Bulgaria that would take the imperial army to Adrianople and even Constantinople. That army would be reinforced by troops from Little Russia and the southern provinces of the Russian core: four of the five corps of reserve cavalry were stationed there. This is what Diebitsch's operational plan of 1821 had called for: to send the entire Second Army together with the III and IV Corps as well as the Guard and its own reserve cavalry in a massive thrust against the Ottoman army in Bulgaria. The deployment was also directed against Austria across the Carpathians. A road from Jassy in northern Bessarabia through the Tihutu Pass led to Cluj in central Transylvania, another from southern Bessarabia via Bucharest led through the Turno Rosu (Red Gate) Pass to Sibiu. This potential threat against the friendly kingdom—should it decide to oppose a Russian advance toward the Danube—also served, paradoxically, as a guarantee of its survival: imperial troops taking Hungary-Transylvania in a vise in 1849 would use these two roads in conjunction with those coming from southern Poland to save the dynasty from internal disintegration.[30]

The Caucasian sector of the southern theater was becoming more autonomous than ever. The occupation of eastern Georgia in 1801 and the spread of Russian influence across western Georgia, together with the treaty of Gulistan (1813), transformed Tiflis into a major regional military headquarters, with its own interests, its own ambitions, and its own needs. The "Caucasus" was no longer merely the Caucasian Line seeking to pen in the mountain peoples in their deep mountain valleys. It had become a zone of operations against the Persians and the Ottomans. Within a decade the imperial army had achieved hegemony in Transcaucasia. The Georgian Separate Corps (renamed the Caucasian Separate Corps in 1820) was commanded by Alexei Ermolov, who also functioned as the de facto governor general of the North Caucasus and Transcaucasia. It consisted of two infantry divisions, the Nineteenth in Georgievsk on the Caucasian Line and Twentieth in Tiflis, and one regiment of dragoons. In 1817, the corps had a total strength of 50,000 men. Attached to it were three Cossack formations: 5,000 North Caucasian Cossacks, 5,200 Don Cossacks, and 1,600 Astrakhan Cossacks.[31] There were few troops in western Georgia; most were deployed east of Tiflis as far as Shusha, within striking distance of Aslanduz, where the Persians would be expected to cross the Araks in the event of war. An important change since 1801 was the forward deployment in Lezgin country around Telavi and Lgedihi, east of the Alazani River: this deployment to the foothills of the broad Daghestan highland reflected the offensive strategy against the mountain peoples pursued by Ermolov since his arrival in 1816. Nowhere else in the empire did a deployment of the strategic force serve so clearly the functions of an occupying army to maintain order along a sector of Fortress Empire's periphery with an offensive mission against neighboring powers: the wars with Persia (1826–28) and with the Ottomans (1828–29) would demonstrate this convincingly.

The concentration of the strategic force in the western and southern theaters became even more marked than it had ever been since the days of Peter I, resulting in a farther downgrading of the importance of the eastern theater. All regular troops were withdrawn from there in 1809.[32] There were no Internal Guard units in the Orenburg Territory, where the military governor, Peter von Essen, also commanded the Orenburg Separate Corps, which was no more than the Twenty-Ninth Infantry Division. Despite the name, it consisted of only twelve garrison battalions strung along the Orenburg Line. In Siberia, Internal Guard units were part of the Siberian Separate Corps commanded by Petr Kaptsevich. Like the Orenburg Corps, it consisted of only one division, the Thirtieth Infantry, with headquarters in Omsk, consisting also of twelve garrison battalions. Beginning in 1822, when Kaptsevich became governor general of Western Siberia, the command of the corps and the post of governor general were combined in the same officer. Thus, in Helsingfors, Tiflis, Orenburg, and Omsk, the regional delegate of the ruling elite was given responsibility for both military and civilian administration.

By the end of Alexander's reign, the strategic force had become almost evenly distributed across the empire west of a line Nizhnii-Novgorod-Tambov-Voronezh, leaving the rest of the empire east of it policed by Internal Guard units placed at the disposal of the provincial governors. West of that line, where most of the population still resided, infantry and cavalry divisions had been deployed in almost every province, and in cooperation with the Internal Guard constituted a powerful force to maintain internal security in the service of an autocracy about to reach the apogee of its power. The effect was to integrate the strategic force into a military-police infrastructure to uphold the status quo and cope with any resistance to bureaucratic rule from an increasingly distant Petersburg. The purpose of such a deployment was even more in evidence in the frontier regions, where the strategic force operated as an army of occupation in territories that had once been the lands of client societies. At the same time, the expansion of the empire in fanlike fashion from the old Muscovite center had considerably lengthened the periphery, resulting in the creation of regional "armies" with regional missions unrelated to an overall strategic plan. Such was the case in Finland, in the old Polish Empire, and in the Caucausus. There, regional theaters began to develop a life of their own. Garrison duties brought about fragmentation, even though the troops of the First Army deployed in the Russian core were intended also to serve as a strategic reserve. After the Polish Revolt of 1830–31, conservatism and retrenchment won the day, and the main mission of the strategic force became to garrison Fortress Empire.

# 9

# Fortress Empire

## The Economy

The consolidation of Fortress Empire took place against the background of an economy entering a period of retrenchment. The Napoleonic Wars, the Continental System, and the devastation caused by the invasion of 1812 dealt it a blow from which it would not recover. Skyrocketing expenditures were covered by printing paper money and, in part, by British subsidies to keep the army in the field in 1813–15. The economy began to retrench at the very time Britain, followed by France and Prussia, was being transformed by the Industrial Revolution, which caused a qualitative chasm to split the imperial economy from that of the European Coastland. Economic retrenchment became the foundation of Fortress Empire, sustaining the basically defensive deployment of the strategic force, despite the implicitly offensive posture assumed by some of its regional components. The mobilization of a servile labor force to work in heavy industries had reached a point of diminishing returns, reducing as it did the pressure to re-equip and restructure those industries. The destruction of forests was causing a progressively debilitating shortage of charcoal, insoluble for a lack of coal within acceptable distances. Nicholas I and his finance minister, Egor Kankrin, former quartermaster general (*general-intendant*) of the army in 1813, did not believe in the usefulness of steam power and railroads,[1] these two symbols of the Industrial Revolution, because they saw in them threats to the social order and the internal security of the empire.

In 1800, the production of iron had reached nearly 180,000 tons, just a bit ahead of Britain's 173,000. It remained stable during the first decade of the nineteenth century, despite the tremendous demands generated by the wars. During the 1820s, it reached an annual average of only 218,000; by 1850, the empire produced a mere 382,000 tons, while production in Britain had climbed to 2.5 million tons.[2] The Continental System that Russia was forced to join in 1807 sustained the vision of Fortress Empire and for a time stimulated production by shielding the imperial market from competition. Interior Minister Osip Kozodavlev (1810–19) made a reputation for "factorymania," but the reopening of the market after the wars had disastrous consequences for these recent factories. Landowners, especially great ones, were uniquely capable of mobilizing an adequate labor force to operate factories because of their ownership of serf labor, at a time when the old policy of letting merchants buy more serfs for their enterprises was restricted in 1802 and abolished in 1816. The number of factories more than doubled from 2,423 in 1804 to 5,200 in 1825, and so did the number of their workers from 95,000 to 190,000, but these were small numbers for such a large country.[3] The position of the landed nobility as the core of the empire's ruling class and the key support of the throne at a time of great turmoil militated in favor of developing cottage industries rather than encouraging the growth of towns, so necessary to the stimulation of agricultural and industrial production. Conservatism did the rest: Alexander Shakhovskoi satirized in an 1818 play progressive landowners who ruined themselves by attempting new agricultural and industrial techniques.[4]

The economic landscape remained a constellation of self-sufficient production islands, isolated by the absence of roads where navigable rivers were not available. It is sometimes claimed that markets do not grow in the absence of roads; in fact, it is often the opposite. Before the construction of hard surface roads, roads were merely paths that carts had traveled over and over again. Necessity being the mother of invention, incipient markets would create their own roads. The laggard state of the imperial economy, which became increasingly marked by the end of the 1820s, must be blamed on the persistence of this continent-wide archipelago of self-sufficient territorial units of production. The government's intention to build hard-surface roads (*shosse*, Fr. *chaussée*) after 1815 did not extend beyond the Petersburg area. The major roads linking Petersburg with Grodno, and Moscow with Smolensk and Kiev, were no more than improved postal roads, unusable in the spring and fall. New canals were cut, but they only integrated Petersburg more deeply with its hinterland along the Volga axis, the only place where an "other Russia" of commercial cities had a chance to grow, had its development not been held back by the preponderant weight of the market towns in central Russia, where peasants sold some grain and spent the money on hard liquor.

As previously mentioned, three canals began operations in 1810–11—the Tikhvin, Mariinskii, and Svirskii canals—facilitating the transportation of goods from the middle and lower Volga to the northern capital, supplementing rather than bypassing the Vyshnii Volochek canal, but also shortening considerably the distance from the river to Lake Ladoga. These canals contributed to the better integration of Peter I's Fortress Russia, but not that of Fortress Empire, where the army and the police were called upon beginning in the 1820s to uphold the integrity of an overwhelmingly agrarian sociopolitical order. The deployment of the strategic force over much of the territory of the Russian core and the western and southern borderlands thus sought to recreate a situation similar to that which Peter had intended to create in Fortress Russia: corps, divisional, and regimental headquarters would function as "towns" and centers of consumption stimulating production for the market in an otherwise self-sufficient economy, but this combination of the militarization of the economy and autarky would prove lethal to Russian economic development.

The production of weapons and the improvement of their quality suffered from the inability of the imperial economy to grow at the rate of industrializing economies. The troops used muskets of different calibers and of different origins, some being Swedish and Prussian relics from the Seven Years' War. The iron produced in the Urals was too soft for barrels to handle greater explosive charges. On occasion, production could not cover all the needs, and muskets had to be imported: at the beginning of 1812, 50,000 were bought from England. Musket production remained concentrated in three places: Tula, Sestroretsk, and Izhevsk, the last two on the Petersburg-Volga-Kama-Urals economic and commercial axis of northern Russia. Tula produced an average of 40,000 to 45,000 muskets a year until 1810, when the war ministry raised its quota to 146,000—a quota that could not be met, although production reached nearly 123,000 in 1813, following colossal efforts made by the plant management. By 1825, it was down to 25,000 muskets a year, and the dam was about to break, putting the plant out of commission on the eve of the Persian-Ottoman Wars of 1826–29. Sestroretsk was much smaller and engaged chiefly in the repair, rather than the production, of muskets; nevertheless, it produced 18,040 of them in 1810 and 15,100 in 1825. The Izhevsk plant, which had practically ceased to operate by the end of the eighteenth century, was rebuilt in 1807 to supplement the insufficient capacity of the Tula works but could produce only 1,285 muskets in 1810 and 15,181 in 1825. Tula obviously remained the main center of musket production for the imperial army.[5] Production in "normal" years was thus about 75,000 muskets, hardly enough to supply the needs of a strategic force of 633,000 and an Internal Guard of some 80,000 troops. We must assume that many of them had only old and obsolete weapons, perhaps none at all, and shortages were already in evidence during the Turkish War of 1828–29. To make matters worse, conditions at the three plants were appalling: rundown equipment, shortages of charcoal at Tula, a disgruntled labor force. Re-equipment was out of the question in view of the sorry state of imperial finances. In such conditions, there was hardly an alternative to the consolidation of Fortress Empire. That the production of army cloth fared better does not change this gloomy assessment. Production rose from 192,857 meters in 1802 to 328,570 in 1812, and 535,714 in 1825. Much of it was produced in the so-called possessional factories—those owned by nonnobles, who bought serfs who did not become their personal property but were tied to the enterprise—but it was not enough during the war years of 1812–15, and the government had to buy 385,714 meters from Britain in 1815. By 1825, the needs of the army were estimated at 528,570 meters and they were fully covered by current production.[6]

The financial situation of the empire also called for retrenchment and retreat behind the walls of Fortress Empire. Until 1772, the empire had consisted of the Russian core, the Baltic provinces (including Vyborg), and the Left-Bank Ukraine; the annexation of eastern Bielorussia that year added little to its size and population. But the acquisition of the Black Sea littoral between 1774 and 1792, the second and third partitions of the Polish Empire in 1793 and 1795, and the annexation of Georgia, Finland, and the Duchy of Warsaw between 1801 and 1815 enlarged the empire almost beyond recognition and radically transformed its internal composition. They also sounded disturbing warnings. It could not have been a coincidence that the sustained commitment to take advantage of favorable circumstances in order to pursue a forward strategy seeking to incorporate the Russo-Swedish, Russo-Polish, most of the Russo-Turkish, and Russo-Persian frontiers took place at the very same time the imperial government resorted to the printing of paper money, at first with caution, then increasingly with abandon. The reason was the persistence of an economic structure that remained fundamentally unchanged during the entire period from the end of the seventeenth century to the reign of Nicholas I: quantitative expansion was not followed by qualitative transformation; the tax base remained inelastic and proved incapable of supporting the growth of the empire's political and military responsibilities.

The capitation and the quitrent remained major sources of revenue, but their growth was limited by the natural increase of the male population and the acquisition of new territories to which they could be extended. This fiscal system, so fundamental to the social constitution of an overwhelmingly agrarian empire, was applied to the Baltic provinces and the Left-Bank Ukraine in 1783, and to the provinces of the former Polish Empire after the partitions, but never to Finland, the Duchy of Warsaw, or Transcaucasia. It was followed by the extension of the recruitment system to those territories, resulting in a dramatic change in the ethnic composition of the strategic force. The total population grew from 18.1 million males in 1795 to 25.5 million in 1833, an increase of 40.9 percent,[7] while the receipts from the capitation and the quitrent rose more than five times from 24.7 million rubles in 1796 to 126.1 million in 1825: the rates that had been fairly stable in the eighteenth century began to climb steadily in the 1790s. Typical of the same unchanging socioeconomic order was the growth of other revenue from the sale of vodka. The low level of urbanization in the market towns of the core and border provinces restricted the marketing of grain, which was recycled into vodka on the estates of the landowners, a situation the deployment of the strategic force across much of the western and southern theaters was intended to correct by creating an artificial demand for grain in the regimental headquarters. Nevertheless, the revenue from the sale of vodka rose nearly 600 percent, from 22 million rubles in 1796 to 128.4 million in 1825. These two sources made up 62.6 percent of the revenue from taxation in 1796, 64.7 percent in 1825—the situation had gotten slightly worse in thirty years. The share of other sources barely changed, even though the revenue from trade increased from 8.7 percent in 1796 to 12.2 percent in 1825.[8] These figures, which are not adjusted to account for inflation, show that the ability of the imperial government to raise additional revenue was limited by its determination to stretch serfdom to its limits, and the limits had already been crossed toward the end of Alexander's reign. Pushing farther would raise the specter of popular discontent and even uprisings. The overstretch of the fiscal system was thus closely related to the deployment of a military and police infrastructure designed to cope with its anticipated consequences.

While the total revenue from taxation rose over five times, from 74.6 million rubles in 1796 to 393 million in 1825, expenditures rose much faster. It is more difficult to determine their level accurately because of the practice of keeping an ordinary budget, which was usually balanced, and an extraordinary one containing items of expenditures that had to be covered from other sources. The rise of ordinary expenditures paralleled that of the ordinary revenue, from 78.2 million in 1796 to 393 million in 1825. The share of military expenditures rose from 27.7 million (35.4 percent) to 173.8 million (44.2 percent). But military expenditures were in fact much higher. The extraordinary budget owed its origin to the discrepancy between the fixed prices that the government had set for the purchase of grain, meat, and salt by the Provision Department, of cloth by the Commissary, of metals by the Artillery Department, and the real prices these agencies had to pay at the time of purchase. During the wars of 1812–15, actual military expenditures reached an average of 230 million a year, and in 1820 still amounted to 197.5 million. During the wars of 1826–29, they reached 832.8 million, or an average of 208.2 million a year, and in 1830, 219.4 million, or over 60 percent of the total expenditure budget.[9]

In order to pay for expenditures far exceeding the revenue available to pay for them, the imperial government continued to resort to the printing of paper money, the simplest way to create artificial revenue. The amount of paper money (*assignats*) in circulation in 1796 was 156.7 million rubles; by 1817, it had peaked at 836 million and by 1825, it was down to 595 million, after the institution of a program of debt redemption. The domestic debt of 15.6 million rose to 371 million and the foreign debt from 33 to 257 million. The burden of debt had become overwhelming because the rigid tax base of an agrarian economy gave no hope that the government would be able to cope productively with the rising responsibilities of empire. The Russian Empire staked its claim to hegemony in the western and southern theaters by printing paper money and borrowing: by 1830, when it had consolidated its hegemony, it could no longer afford to take risks. Faced with the choice between industrializing with its attendant dangers for the stability of the empire and the security of its ruling class and retrenching behind the walls of Fortress Empire, it chose the latter course, which promised stability in the short run. Little did the ruling elite anticipate that by choosing security and creating a garrison state on a continent-wide basis, it was digging a moat between the economy of the empire and that of the Coastland powers already setting off into the uncharted waters of the Industrial Revolution, until the empire would become, despite its pretensions to hegemony, the sick man of Eurasia.

In the meantime, the unrestrained resort to the printing press had generated a devastating inflation that attacked the fabric of the imperial economy and society. It disturbed the operation of the law of supply and demand by raising demand to a level far above the ability of the economy to respond adequately. It encouraged bribery and corruption in all kinds of economic transactions. It devalued savings and assets while raising the cost of borrowing, and it damaged, if not entirely destroyed, the prospects of the new factories that sprouted like mushrooms after the empire joined the Continental System. Money lost its value, the *assignat* ruble being worth no more than twenty-five silver kopecks. The widespread counterfeiting of *assignats* added to the problem. Excessive depreciation became a major factor hindering economic development. Inflation was also socially disruptive, because it struck hardest at those with fixed incomes, who were many in an empire where laggard urbanization and an insufficiently differentiated economy had generated little private enterprise—there were hardly any private banks. Such people perforce depended on government salaries, government contracts, or government pensions. Inflation provoked a flight from money, broke down trade networks, and encouraged localized autarkies in the economy. The inflation of 1787–1830 truly laid the economic foundations of Fortress Empire.

The imperial government's trade policy fluctuated during Alexander I's reign between experiments with free trade and a return to across-the-board protectionism. The new and very young tsar and his circle of friends, all inexperienced in the complexities of managing a huge empire, were attracted to the liberal ideas they saw as a useful guide, not only in their projected reorganization of the central government but also in the improvement of the empire's economic condition. The new tsar had been taught the value of free trade by Heinrich Storch, who had written a treatise of Russian statistics and was a disciple of Adam Smith.[10] He was also willing to continue, in the name of a general peace the empire badly needed after the campaigns of 1799, a cooperation with France, whose own imperial ambitions were not yet clear. Consequently, Alexander was ready to abandon the restrictive provisions of 1793 and 1797 and return to the more liberal tariff of 1796. Although some duties were raised between 1803 and 1807, the import of machinery and instruments became duty-free because the new government felt the need to encourage large-scale industrial production, a departure from Catherine's more physiocratic policies. However, the new policy brought about little change in the overall value and composition of commercial exchanges: in 1801, imports were valued at 52.2 million rubles, in 1806, at 51.6 million, with exports at 67.2 and 67.4 million respectively. The main articles of the export trade remained grain, animal fats, raw hemp, and raw flax (55 percent of the total) and metals (7.5 percent), while imports were dominated by cottons, woolens, and dyes (39.5 percent), as well as food products and colonial goods consumed by the ruling elite and ruling class showing off their commitment to "Westernization."

But trade policy was also seen as a means to help the empire gain economic independence from the constraints imposed by Britain's domination of the seas and determination to impose its will on the neutral trade. The exuberance and self-confidence of Catherine's government was slowly giving way to a realization that free trade would deliver the imperial economy into the hands of British merchants who could not but see that the Russian and British economies were complementary: Britain would supply finished products, the empire would remain a huge colonial market of raw materials. While the tsar's "young friends" preached Adam Smith, Nikolai Rumiantsev, a son of the field marshal and minister of commerce (1802–10) and foreign affairs (1807–14), elaborated a vast program, based on the protection of the imperial economy and the promotion of commerce, designed to make the empire a great economic power. But Rumiantsev could only fall back on very traditional assumptions which had also been those of Peter I and even antedated his reign: that Russia could become the great intermediary between the trade of the East and that of the West, as if it had not already become obvious that seaborne trade, even if controlled by Britain, was far cheaper than overland trade across Eurasia subject to the whims of local imperial officials.

The Tilsit Agreement of June 1807 required the empire to join the Continental System directed against Britain, and the new policy suited Rumiantsev, who became one of the strongest supporters of the alliance with France. But the drive toward autarky failed, because the borders of Europe could not be sealed off to British trade, because France could not replace Britain as the supplier of manufactured and colonial goods, and because autarky only contributed to the transformation of the enemy into the dominant world power operating from a growing network of naval bases and commercial outposts. The Continental System became unacceptable to the empire when Napoleon insisted that the neutral trade be banned on the ground that it was only British trade under another name: it meant prohibiting the import of sugar, coffee, cotton, and dyes, the major articles of Russian imports. If neutral ships were barred access to the ports of the empire, its exports would be crippled because it did not have a merchant marine worthy of the name. The break with France came with the tariff of 1810: while restrictive, it opened Russian ports to neutral ships, chiefly American, and to the products of British colonies. In the meantime, however, the Continental System had stimulated the development of native industries in an attempt to produce the goods that could no longer be imported, but production could not keep up with the demand. It also encouraged protectionist sentiment among the native merchants who had never welcomed foreign competition, and protectionism became linked with patriotism. Despite the change in policy, the value of imports rose little, to 67.3 million rubles in 1812, but the value of exports climbed to 139.2 million. By 1815, when peace returned, the value of both imports and exports had skyrocketed to 122 and 221 million respectively.

Protectionist sentiment remained strong after the war. The tariff of 1816 retained half of the prohibitions of its predecessor and imposed relatively high duties on many other products. Later, however, the government had to make some concessions, chiefly under Prussian pressure to open up the imperial market to textiles from Silesia, and the tariff of 1819 cancelled all the prohibitions but retained some of the restrictions of the 1816 tariff. It opened the gates to foreign imports: an enormous amount of foreign goods flooded the country, forcing the closure of many native manufactures, dealing a major blow to the nascent industries, and destroying the confidence of the merchants. By 1821, the value of imports had risen to 210 million, but that of exports had declined to 208 million: for the first time, exports trailed behind imports. The resulting backlash brought about a sharp turn away from the experiment with "free trade" and led to the prohibitive tariff of 1822. It was drawn up with the participation of Kankrin, who became finance minister the following year, imposed exorbitant duties, and prohibited many imports. Both he and Nicholas I—who kept him in office until 1844—were strong believers in protectionism. They saw the world becoming increasingly divided between the industrial and agricultural powers and felt the empire would be more secure by remaining a chiefly agricultural power. Their emphasis on the primacy of agriculture placed them squarely in the tradition of the Physiocrats, who had dominated Russian economic thinking during Catherine's reign, but the world had greatly changed since then. In their rejection of what was being called the Industrial Revolution and of the emerging international economy, they were proclaiming their belief in Fortress Empire as the foundation of domestic peace and security. The value of imports began to fall; that of exports kept rising, but metals disappeared, to be replaced by more agricultural products. In 1825, the value of imports had fallen to 185.6 million rubles, that of exports had risen to 236.8 million, but more significant was the stagnation of shipping in the empire's ports: between 1802 and 1804, an average of 7,530 ships had visited them; by 1824–26, the average had fallen to 7415. The economic policy of the imperial government had gone full circle: the 1822 tariff resembled in many ways that of 1724, which had laid the foundation of Fortress Russia. But by focusing on the Petersburg-Moscow-Ekaterinburg axis Peter had sought to create an "other Russia" of commercial cities that would become sources of capital; by denigrating the contribution of railroads, Kankrin's main concern was to leave undisturbed the network of market towns that guaranteed the stability of an agrarian society. His was a policy of retrenchment behind the economic curtain of Fortress Empire.

## Client States and Societies, Old and New

The wars of Alexander I, the emergence of the empire as the great continental victor over Napoleon, and the post-1815 deployment of the strategic force had radical consequences for the old client system. Catherine's policy had been to replace dependence on client states and societies with direct rule by members of the elite dispatched to border regions to take over their management and integrate them immediately into the empire. Paul sought a compromise between the old and new policies by recognizing the regional identity of border territories based on their history, religion, economy and customs; Alexander followed in his footsteps after the annexation of Finland and the Duchy of Warsaw. In the end, the imperial government found itself pursuing a policy of relying on client societies increasingly domesticated and integrated into the political and domestic infrastructure of Fortress Empire.

Sweden's political and military capabilities were destroyed in 1809—the country lost 26 percent of its population and 40 percent of its territory. A new dynasty was founded by a former French marshal about to desert Napoleon, who found himself dependent on Russia's good intentions. Petersburg had long maintained that the Baltic must be a closed sea in which the empire would obviously be the dominant power, even if that claim could not be accepted by Britain, which quickly became Russia's enemy after 1815. Alexander showed generosity in 1809 by agreeing to let the Finnish border run along the Tornio rather than the Kalix River—the territory between them included some of Sweden's richest mines. But the annexation of Finland and the Åland Islands made it clear that in the event of another Russo-Swedish war it would be fought not in Finland as in the past, but in Sweden, where Stockholm had become very vulnerable. Sweden remained more than ever a true client state of the empire, dependent for its stability and well-being on friendly relations with the empire. The old commercial ties with Finland could not easily be broken, and Sweden continued to depend on imports of Livonian grain to help stabilize the price of basic commodities. Bernadotte, the French marshal, elected crown prince in 1810, became king in 1818 and would rule until 1844, but he had to live with the fear that the Russians might openly support the sons of the last Vasa king, Gustav IV Adolf, deposed in 1809, his heirs barred from the succession. Bernadotte's compliance was bought with Russian support for the annexation of Norway in 1814. It turned Sweden outward and westward, a departure from its traditional orientation, and quashed whatever irredentist ambitions remained in the Swedish elite. For the next thirty years, Russia would look on the Baltic as a friendly frontier and closed sea beyond the Bothnian moat of Fortress Empire.[11]

At first glance, it would seem that relations with the Prussian client state had changed radically. Unlike his mother, Paul was very pro-Prussian, as were his sons. Western historiography has treated generations of readers to the spectacle of a deep personal friendship between Alexander I and Frederick William III, whose daughter married the tsar's younger brother, the future Nicholas I. But the empire's policy was merely transformed into one of the iron fist in a velvet glove. Alexander believed, before relations deteriorated into an open conflict that ended with the Tilsit Agreement in 1807, that it would be possible for Russia and France "to dictate the laws" to Prussia and Austria, that a Franco-Russian alliance would keep Prussia within the Russian orbit and prevent it from expanding into northern Germany and escaping Russian tutelage. On the other hand, if the alliance proved impossible and French hegemonic expansionism threatened Russia's own within the Heartland, Prussia (and Austria) would perforce assume the classic responsibilities of a client state: to defeat French ambitions in the German Coastland and interpose their own forces between Russia and France in order to provide geographical depth, so that military operations would remain confined well beyond the imperial periphery.

Prussia remained what it had always been, a recalcitrant client state, obsessively aware of its vulnerability. Faced with the growing threat of Napoleonic France, it hesitated in the summer of 1805 to grant imperial troops the right to passage on their way to Mecklenburg to fight the French in northern Germany, prompting the Russians to threaten to use all their forces to "reduce Prussia," language reminiscent of the 1740s. But at the end of October, when imperial forces led by Kutuzov had gone to the help of Austria, Alexander used a visit to Potsdam to take part in a midnight candlelight ceremony before the grave of Frederick II, where he took the hand of the king and his beautiful queen to swear eternal friendship. A year later, Napoleon was in Berlin, where he imposed a draconian peace on the Prussian kingdom, and in June 1807, he met the tsar at Tilsit. There, the Prussian king was openly snubbed, was not invited to dinner, and was excluded from the negotiations. Napoleon told the Prussian minister of foreign affairs that his king owed everything to the tsar's "knightly support," without which he would have overthrown the dynasty as he had done with other royal houses elsewhere in Europe. Alexander Kurakin, about to become ambassador to France, wrote to the tsar's mother that Russia had become the "guardian angel" of the king, who had found his savior in the emperor.[12] By taking such a harsh stand against Prussia, Napoleon had made it a more obedient client of the Russian Empire.

The defeat of Prussia served Russia's interests as well. While the humiliation of Prussia generated a backlash that would stimulate the growth of Prussian and later German nationalism, it also stirred Russia's arrogance and sense of superiority over its recalcitrant client. In 1812, some members of the ruling elite, like their ancestors in 1760, were calling for the annexation of East Prussia, while the high command demanded that the border of the empire be advanced to the Vistula, incorporating Memel, Königsberg, and Danzig. The following year, in 1813, Petersburg declared that Prussia must become the "avant-garde of Russia," and its anchor in northern Europe (*en l'attachant au poids du Nord dans l'équilibre général*). When Prussia acquired the Rhineland at the Congress of Vienna, it was turned westward to fulfill its duty as a client state in the event of French revanchism.

The professed friendship between emperor and king could not conceal the true nature of the relationship between the two countries: outsiders noted that despite Prussia's role in the War of 1813–14, "it remains under a king of control by Russia," and that the "distance (*espèce d'éloignement*) that always subsisted between Prussians and Russians exists today even more, when Russian officers emboldened by their successes are little disposed to accept that others try to rise to their level, and when the nobility finds a source of vanity in the high position to which the sovereign has raised his empire." The traditional historian, blinded by memories of a powerful and aggressive Germany, will shudder at the thought of Prussia being a client state of the Russian Empire. However, he would do well to ponder the words of Adam Czartoryski, who was well placed to know: relations with Prussia were purely personal; the Russian army and the Petersburg salons were hostile to it. But Alexander I remained faithful to his friendship for the king, and his perserverance succeeded in binding Prussia and making it "a kind of satellite."[13]

While Prussia was to become the anchor of the imperial policy in northern Europe, a first line of defense for Fortress Empire against the subversive activities of a revanchist France, the friendly kingdom would become its anchor in southern Europe. The outlook of the friendly kingdom was changing, however. The Italian and Swiss campaigns of 1799 had exposed a fault line in Austro-Russian relations. Austria became convinced of Russia's striving for hegemony, a hegemony certain to eventually reduce the friendly kingdom to the status of a client state. Austria now had a vested interest in maintaining the territorial integrity of the Ottoman Empire, but Russia had ambitions in Moldavia-Wallachia and even Serbia, and its activities in the Adriatic were but a prelude to an active intervention designed to upset the status quo in the Balkans.

As if to confirm Vienna's fears, Russia's attitude was becoming more protective. Alexander announced in 1801 that "one of the bases of my political system will always be to contribute with all the means at my disposal to the conservation of a state whose weakness and bad administration are precious guarantees of security," and Kurakin would write in 1808 that the integrity of the Austrian dominions was a useful and necessary guarantee of the empire's security. Indeed, much of the antagonism with France continued to revolve around the Austrian anchor, as it had during most of the eighteenth century. In 1805, the empire fought to preserve the Austrian monarchy, but in 1809, when Vienna challenged Napoleon against Alexander's advice, Russia did not move to save the friendly kingdom. In a perverse way, its defeat, like that of Prussia, served the empire's interests: Austria would become a more responsive client and would learn that rejecting Russia's advice had its price. Yet, Austria refused to be convinced and adopted a pro-French policy, prompting Rumiantsev to tell the French ambassador in 1812 that it was not in Austria's interest to be on bad terms with the empire because "we have a common border and we can do the country great harm."

Placing much of the Russian army under Austrian command in 1813 was a master stroke of diplomacy, a sop to Vienna's pride, but relations quickly soured after Napoleon's defeat over the annexation of the Duchy of Warsaw and the Eastern Question. In 1817, some members of the high command were itching for a war on Austria. In 1818, the imperial ambassador to France, Carlo Pozzo di Borgo, wrote to his government that Austria wanted to be "the center of a general system and the planet around which the other powers gravitate like satellites." In fact, it was the other way around. Prussia and Austria had become satellites of the Russian Empire, and the occupation of the Polish salient placed them at the mercy of a Russian offensive, as Nicholas I made clear to Austria in 1828. Austria too was turned outward and enlarged its dominions in northern Italy, there to defend the post-1815 conservative reaction in its own interest, but also in the interest of the Russian Empire. Metternich's petulance and bluster were a mark of weakness; they only exposed the vulnerability of the Austrian empire, the "precious guarantee" of the Russian Empire's security.[14]

A true measure of the imperial government's attitude toward its two Germanic clients was a little-known event that took place on the anniversary of the Battle of Borodino, on August 26/September 7, 1815. In the plain of Champagne, east of Paris, 150,000 Russian troops with their 540 guns gathered to form a huge square awaiting review by Alexander, the Austrian emperor, the Prussian king, and other dignitaries, including Wellington. It was symbolic that the emperor and the king were dressed in Russian uniforms. The tsar called out to them the names of each corps, divisional, and brigade commander, the number of each corps and each division. A few days later, Alexander expressed his gratitude to his army which "had marched quickly from the Dniepr and the Dvina to the Seine to show that the peace of Europe was not a matter of indifference to Russia, which, no matter how great the distance, would always be ready at the call of the fatherland and the tsar to march wherever the truth must prevail." Diplomats attending the review were said to have seen in it great political significance; Wellington was observed to be "pensive."[15] What impression it made on the emperor and the king was not recorded, but one may well imagine that this display of Russia's awesomeness reminded them of the role they were expected to play in the defense of the empire's interests. The tsar was not only celebrating victory over France but also demanding from Berlin and Vienna the recognition of Russia's hegemony in the Heartland.[16]

A similar expectation was in evidence in the Caspian basin, where Persia was being transformed into a new client state. Relations had been hostile since the introduction of direct rule in eastern Georgia in 1801, and the imperial government would not rest until it had found a "scientific" boundary on the Araks, the third moat after the Gulf of Bothnia and the Danube, behind which Fortress Empire would be definitely secure. Persia was much weaker than the Ottoman Empire, toward which a deep and relentless hostility would remain the major factor in Russia's southern strategy. The Treaty of Gulistan (1813), confirmed by that of Turkmanchai (1828), provided that the imperial government, meaning the Tiflis headquarters, would give aid to the crown prince who, in accordance with Persian custom, resided in Tabriz, only 130 kilometers from the new border, should he ask for it to suppress opposition: the empire thus became the guarantor of the Persian "constitution," as it had become in Sweden in 1721, when the Treaty of Nystadt had transformed the country into a client state of the empire. From then on, it became official policy to overwhelm the Persian court with the empire's awesomeness. The choice of Ermolov to command the Caucasian Separate Corps was a judicious one: the proconsul believed, not unlike Repnin in the Poland of the 1760s, in the necessity and readiness to use any means to reach its political ends. Ermolov's harsh treatment of the mountain peoples and his declaration, when he visited the Persian court in 1817, that his family descended from Genghis Khan were designed to propagate a myth of irresistible and invincible power before which the only alternative to submission was destruction on the battlefield. That became quite obvious when Paskievich wiped out the Persian army in 1828. Persia, like Prussia and Austria, was turned outward, here eastward, to translate imperial desires into reality, the chief function of a client state: it would become the empire's "avant-garde" toward Afghanistan, where Russian ambitions were becoming increasingly clear.

The new relationship began inauspiciously enough. A Russian mission sent to Tehran was massacred by a mob that attacked the embassy in January 1829. But the humiliation also offered an opportunity. Instead of threatening military action (which it most likely would not have been able to carry out because of the war with the Ottomans), the imperial government declared it would be satisfied if the shah would send a delegation led by one of his sons to apologize. The delegation was in fact led by a sixteen-year-old son of Abbas Mirza, himself a son of the shah and his designated successor, who had commanded the Persian army during the recent war. Instead of receiving the young prince coldly as would befit an injured party, the Russians made an ostentatious show of power, and Petersburg society went out of its way to charm him. He brought extremely rich presents, including a huge diamond Nadir Shah had taken from India, rare manuscripts, and Kashmir rugs. He was given an extensive tour of the capital and its environs and later a reception in Moscow. He left in tears, overwhelmed by the majesty and munificence of the empire, while a Persian poet in his suite sang the praise of Nicholas I as "the Suleiman of our times."[17] The tsar had truly won "a victory by means of awesomeness," one likely to impress at a distance a shah well known in his day for his 360 wives; after his death in 1834, every one of his successors would reign in fear of Russian power.

Behind the protective barrier formed by the client states, Fortress Empire underwent an internal transformation aiming at integrating the old client societies into a uniform administrative structure that would also preserve the diversity of its regions, peoples, and customs. That transformation was modeled in part on the regional deployment of the strategic force in army and separate corps; its purpose was to generate centripetal forces strong enough to change the outward orientation of the border regions and make them gravitate toward the two capitals, Petersburg and Moscow. Turning the client states outward and the old client societies inward would delineate more forcefully the singularity of Fortress Empire, placed after 1815 in the grip of a military and police infrastructure to preserve a status quo presumably sanctified by the victory over revolutionary France.

The autonomous movement in Finland reached its completion with the annexation of the country in 1809. While the peasantry was hardly pro-Russian, because it feared the introduction of serfdom and perhaps a more repressive fiscal system, the nobility and the Lutheran Church welcomed the transfer of suzerainty because it promised them a better deal under Russian rule: the experience of the Baltic Germans since 1710 was there to justify their expectations. Moreover the empire, huge, mighty, and awesome, offered the ambitious greater prospects of brilliant careers. The "Finnish" nobility—many of them Swedes—formed a closed group with a strong esprit de corps, and the leading military families—the Jäger-horns, Klicks, Knorrings, and Mannerheims among others—had been active in the movement to secede from Sweden. They dominated the Senate, which adminis-tered the grand duchy, and some noble families had already entered imperial ser-vice. Magnus Orräus was governor of Vyborg (1799–1804), and Johan would be-come deputy finance minister under Nicholas I. The Alopäus family, which included the bishop of Borgô at the time of the annexation, was already well repre-sented: Magnus was the imperial ambassador to Berlin (1789–96 and 1802–7), and his son David was resident minister in Sweden (1803–8) and ambassador to Prussia (1813–31). Natives were found at the highest level in Petersburg in the Committee for Finnish Affairs: Robert Rehbinder and Knut von Troil. The most famous was Gustaf Mauritz Armfelt, who had been a favorite of Gustav III and Swedish com-mander in chief in 1806 before he transferred his allegiance to the Russian Empire and became a passionate defender of Finnish interests. He ended his career in the State Council.[18] In the Polish Kingdom, the entire administration was Polish—even though Grand Duke Constantine and Novosiltsev, the imperial commis-sioner, played a decisive role. The state secretary representing the kingdom in Petersburg was also Polish. The dominant figures among these Poles who were play-ing the imperial card was Adam Czartoryski, Repnin's illegitimate son, who was taken to Petersburg as a hostage in 1795, to be raised in the company of the young Alexander and converted to the cause of the empire.[19] He was foreign minister from 1804 to 1806 and remained director of the Vilno educational district for twenty years (1803–23). The scion of another great Polish magnate family, which had been at loggerheads with the Czartoryskis during much of the eighteenth century, Sev-erin Potocki, served as director of the Kharkov educational district from 1803 to 1817. The Polish Army was truly Polish and the Lithuanian Corps was largely Lithuanian and Polish.

While the imperial government was laying the foundations of a Finnish state where none had existed before, it was recreating a Polish Empire within the Russian Empire, surely one of the most original experiments in imperial management any-where. In both territories, the indigenous nobility was expected to play the traditional role of client societies, but now within the imperial periphery—within Fortress Em-pire. This was a role which the Baltic nobility had played to perfection for nearly a century: to administer on behalf of the ruling elite, to send their sons to Petersburg to get the feel of the empire's might, and to marry into the elite if possible. Not all were convinced, however: Czartoryski would become the best example and the Polish Re-volt the symbol of a failed patron-client relationship. The Baltic Germans made a major contribution to the war effort, notably, Buxhöwden, Michelsohnen, Osten-Sacken, Toll, and especially Barclay. The governors general came for the most part from the provinces, and the nobility remained in charge of their administration. Oth-ers, who made great careers in the empire, came from the "invisible frontier" of the Germanic world: Diebitsch, Wittgenstein, Kankrin, and Nesselrode.

In the southern theater, the integration of the Cossack client societies was com-plete, except in the Don Territory, where the struggle between the new nobility and the rank-and-file Cossacks was the last stage in the old conflict that had destroyed the other traditional Cossack societies the preceding generation. There too, the consolidation of the imperial power in Transcaucasia and the creation of a powerful political and military headquarters in Tiflis brought to an end the role of the Don Cossacks as a frontier society. The impact of imperial rule was more severe in Georgia than in Finland, Poland, and the Baltic provinces, because Transcaucasia was a theater of war and Georgian society did not have the resources to fulfill the empire's expectations. Direct rule was not so much the consequence of the empire's expansionist drive as of the inability of a client society to continue to function as one for a variety of reasons. But there were enough Georgians eager to contribute to the challenging task of imperial construction. Petr Bagration, married to a Skavronskaia, was the best known, but another Bagration also fought in the imperial army; so did a Gangeblishvilvi, a Gureli, a Panchulidze, a Shalikoshvili, a Lashkarashvili (Lashkarev—the son of Sergei sent to the Crimean khan in 1782, later chargé d'affaires in Persia from 1786 to 1796, and administrator of Moldavia and Wallachia in 1807), a Madatov (who was Armenian), two Iashvilis, and three Dzavakhishvilis.[20] To the west, Alexander Rudzevich, the chief of staff of the Second Army, was the son of a Crimean Tatar who had sided with the Russians in the 1770s. The role of the Greeks in the Balkan "invisible frontier" was exceptional: Johannes Capo d'Istria served as imperial foreign minister from 1816 to 1821; Constantine Rodofinikin succeeded Lashkarev as director of the Asiatic Department. Other Greeks, like the Ipsilantis and Mavrocordatos, invited Russian expansion as *hospodars* (or relatives of *hospodars*) of Moldavia and Wallachia.

As the empire expanded to include the near totality of the old frontiers, Alexander I toyed with a number of political and administrative schemes to transform the empire into an association of large regions headed by governors general with extensive powers and assisted by regional agencies, either appointed or even elected. The experiment began in 1816 and ended ten years later when Nicholas I rejected its assumptions.[21] The imperial government, obsessed as ever since the 1780s with the determination to create a uniform administrative infrastructure from one end of the empire to another, faced a choice between either extending the system existing in the Russian core to the frontier territories or extending to the Russian core the regional administration existing in Poland and Finland. The originality of the latter experiment consisted in using the Polish Charter of 1815 and the organization of the Finnish central administration as models for carving out large regions everywhere else, creating a uniform grid for the whole empire commanded by governors general responsible to the emperor alone.

It is impossible not to see here a parallel with the territorial deployment of the strategic force in which governors general would be the equivalent of corps commanders and in some cases were corps commanders as well. The tsar, as commander in chief of the entire empire, assisted by a chief of staff for the military establishment and the chief of his chancery for the civil administration, would govern his empire with the help of about twelve governors general and a dozen corps commanders, or twenty-four generals. Each region, once it had been given a civil constitution, would develop a sense of community with the other regions and the sense of a common imperial destiny. The experiment reminds us of the use Catherine II had made of the institutions of the Baltic provinces to carry out the reforms of 1775–1785, but Alexander's vision was truly revolutionary. A constitutional charter and regional agencies would cement the unity of Fortress Empire and give each region a stake in the stability of the empire. Much of all this was utopian, of course, although progress had been made by 1825 in carrying out the program. It is not surprising that the sober-minded Nicholas I should have returned to the more traditional policy of maintaining the distinction between the Russian core and the frontier regions, while gradually seeking to deprive them of their autonomy. His vision of empire was that of a garrison state. The police and the army were adequate instruments to impose it everywhere.

## Army, Police, Ideology

The deployment of the strategic force in both the Russian core and the peripheral regions, economic retrenchment caused in large part by the inability to stretch the servile economy beyond its natural limits, the return to a highly protective and prohibitive tariff, and the creation of a uniform infrastructure of administrative, military, and police agencies—all these factors contributed to the emergence of a Fortress Empire consolidating its hegemony in the Heartland and determined to maintain the status quo by essentially repressive measures within the empire and by the threat of force beyond its periphery.

The transformation of the empire into an armed camp, the growing size of its administrative machinery, and the inability of its old ruling elite to supply all the cadres needed to manage it, necessitated the creation of universities in which Fortress Russia had been notoriously deficient. Until 1802, there had been only one university in the empire, in Moscow, founded in 1755, with a research institution, the Academy of Sciences, opened in Petersburg in 1725. Gustav II Adolf had founded Dorpat University in 1632: it had attracted chiefly sons of burghers and parsons, the nobles preferring to get their education in Åbo or Lund, even Königsberg and Rostock. Its avowed purpose was to train local young men for the royal administration in an attempt to Swedify Livonia and incorporate it fully into the Swedish Empire. It was closed in 1656 during the Thirteen Years' War, reopened in 1690, and was closed again in 1710.[22] In Vilno, there had been since 1578 an "academy" run by the Jesuit Order until its abolition in 1773. It had been an instrument of polonization and Catholic proselytizing, and it was reopened, paradoxically enough, by Governor General Repnin immediately after the third partition of the Polish Empire, a gesture that earned him the praise of being "the most energetic defender of the Polish nation."[23] In 1801, it had 256 students, most of them nobles. At the beginning of the eighteenth century, there was also an "academy" in Kiev, founded in 1632, to teach the children of Cossack *starshina*, Polish gentry, local clergy, and members of client societies of Moldavia and Wallachia as well as those from the "invisible frontier" in Serbia, Bulgaria, and Greece. It was an Orthodox institution that fought Polonization and trained some of the leaders of the Russian church, including Feofan Prokopovich.[24] Its importance was partly eclipsed by Moscow University, beginning in the 1760s, even though the university remained for decades a pitiful travesty of an institution of higher education.[25] Nevertheless, its location and close association with the political elite established it as a major center of imperial education.

The situation changed radically during Alexander's reign. Dorpat University was reopened in 1802, and the Vilno Academy became a university in 1803. The following year, two more universities were opened in Kharkov and Kazan, and a third in Petersburg in 1819, following the reorganization of the Pedagogical Institute created in 1803. By 1825, there were thus six universities (including Moscow) in the empire, three of them in the frontier regions, even four if Kazan, on the eastern rim of the Russian core, is added. There were also a number of institutions not officially called universities but enjoying the status of institutions of higher learning, two of them in the Russian core (Iaroslavl, founded in 1803, Tsarskoe Selo in 1810), and four in the periphery (the Åbo Academy in Finland; Kremenets in Volhynia, Nezhin in Chernigov Province, both founded in 1805; and Odessa, founded in 1817).[26] Of these twelve institutions of higher learning, eight (with Kazan) were in the frontier regions, the other four in Russia proper.

The "deployment" of the universities mirrored that of the army. Three of those "universities" were in the western theater, four in the southern theater, and Kazan was in the east. They formed a ring of regional deployments, each institution with its own regional mission. The general purpose of the universities was to train civil servants and doctors for the empire, just as it was the responsibility of army corps to transform recruits into soldiers. Each university was the center of an administrative region headed by a curator responsible to the minister of education. There were six regions, not including Finland and the Polish Kingdom, that remained outside the system. That of Moscow was the second largest, with ten provinces forming a ring around the old capital; the Petersburg region had only three, in the northwest and far north. The Dorpat region included the three Baltic provinces, that of Vilno the eight provinces forming the eastern marches of the old Polish Empire annexed in 1793–95. The Kharkov region incorporated the old hetmanate, the Ukraine of Settlements, the adjacent core provinces of Orel, Kursk and Voronezh, New Russia, and the lands of the Don and Black Sea Cossacks. The Kazan region was the largest, with eight core provinces east of Nizhnii Novgorod, as well as Astrakhan and the Caucasus, the Orenburg Territory, western and eastern Siberia. Of the six curators appointed in 1803, two were Russian, two Polish, and two German. As a rule, they were privy councilors, the civilian equivalent of a lieutenant general and corps commander. In 1818, Kiev Province, which had been part of the Vilno region, was transferred to the Kharkov region; in 1824, Vitebsk and Mogilev Provinces were incorporated into the Petersburg region. After the crushing of the Polish Revolt in 1832, Vilno University was closed and a new university opened in Kiev.[27]

These regional deployments were primarily defensive. In addition to the general mission to train young men to take their part in the management of a multiethnic empire, each university also taught local languages and the history, geography, and literature of its region. Kazan and Odessa also taught the languages that were used in relations with neighboring states—Mongol and Chinese, Turkish and Persian—and Kazan University became the largest depository of oriental manuscripts sent from China by the Ecclesiastical Mission in Beijing. But these universities, like their predecessors in the Polish and Swedish Empires, were intended to facilitate the integration of their students and future managers of the empire into the political, social, and intellectual world of the imperial power. They were intended

to face inward toward Petersburg and Moscow, to accelerate the centripetal movements that had affected the frontier regions during the eighteenth century away
from the old imperial centers toward Moscow and increasingly toward Petersburg.

Diversity within unity was not an impossible goal; the duty of the new universities was to strengthen the ideological unity of Fortress Empire. Such a policy was
not without some inner contradictions, however: the rise of regional consciousness,
which was fated to follow from the regional missions of the universities, would be
difficult to reconcile within such a large multinational empire with an insistence
on uniformity. The primacy of the Orthodox religion would inevitably create tensions with the Lutherans and above all the Catholics, for whom religion was inseparable from memories of the Polish Empire. The administrative and military reunification of most of that empire under Constantine in the mid-1820s was inseparable
from the recreation of the old world of Polish culture with which Orthodox Russia
always found itself in a state of perpetual hostility. The closing of Vilno University
in 1832 only strengthened the determination of the imperial government to insist
that the deployment of the universities, like that of the strategic force, must contribute to the consolidation of Fortress Empire and the protection of the status quo.

The development of the universities took place against an evolving political
and intellectual background. The accession of Paul changed radically the tone of
Russian politics. There was a new emphasis on "order." Not that order had been
unknown during Catherine's reign. Indeed, her reforms had gone a long way toward establishing it in the administration of the empire, where there had been only
chaos for so long. But Catherine's order had chiefly meant uniformity and the
streamlining of procedures in order to simplify and facilitate the work of managing
such a large and expanding empire. Her style of rule had placed a premium on decentralization and regional administration, while the strategic force was being increasingly redeployed on the advancing periphery to lay the foundations of direct
imperial rule on the territory of former client societies. With Paul, order meant
hierarchy and centralization, the rejection of regional intermediaries between
Petersburg and the provinces, while at the same time, paradoxically, recognizing
once again regional laws and privileges, a policy that had the effect of diluting
Catherine's policy of administrative Russification. The new emphasis on order
and the intolerance of dissent also reflected a change in the social foundation
of the ruler's power. Catherine's rule had relied not so much on the army as on the
nobility—the great families in the capitals, the rank-and-file nobility in the
provinces. Civilian values had dominated her government. The foundation of
the ruler's power during the next three reigns—of Paul and his two sons, Alexander
I and Nicholas I—was the army, and, within the army, the vastly expanded Guard.
Although the officer corps was still largely of noble origin, it also included a large
percentage of men promoted from outside the nobility, especially after the great
battles with their high level of casualties. The reappearance of men on the imperial
throne—after seventy-five years of rule by women whose values were hardly
martial—and their search for a power base to sustain their claim to autocratic rule
created a centripetal pull toward Petersburg, the Court, and the high command; it
largely cancelled certain strivings for autonomy that had marked the long governor-
generalships of men like Rumiantsev and Potemkin.

During Paul's reign, which set the tone of imperial rule for the next fifty years, the Winter Palace began to resemble barracks, and the Mikhailovskii Palace the tsar built for his own safety—where he was eventually assassinated!—looked more like a fortress than the political headquarters of an imperial dynasty. It was necessary to eradicate "the spirit of Potemkin," who had incarnated the Catherinian style of imperial rule as much as the empress herself, and who had in his free-wheeling ways given that rule a human face it had seldom had and would never recover. And Potemkin had stood for the interests of the periphery and the decentralization of the high command far away from the capital on the Neva. With Paul and Alexander, the officer became the tsar's principal image of power. Alexander's first understanding of state service was military service, and Nicholas I grew up with "a respect for force, authority, and punishment."[28] Militarization became a principle of government for Paul, a necessity for Alexander, and a principle once again for Nicholas. It reconciled regional diversity with centralization, and even the civilian ministries began to operate along military lines. Civilians were in uniforms like their military colleagues.

Militarization created a garrison state, and the garrison state was a Fortress Empire, where the preoccupations of everyone in a position of authority were drawn inward and upward. Militarization did not create an expansionist state but, on the contrary, stifled initiative, demanding unconditional obedience and respect for the status quo. The status quo could have been embodied in the formula "Orthodoxy, Autocracy, and Serfdom" if Sergei Uvarov had not chosen to include "Nationality" instead of "Serfdom," overlooking the fact that "Nationality" was certain to destroy the political unity of an empire whose greatest strength had been the ability to forge a conglomerate of regional ethnic elites into a multinational imperial ruling class.[29] Serfdom, even if it had been abolished in the Baltic provinces in the 1810s, continued to be the foundation of the empire's sociopolitical order and would remain unchallenged until the 1840s. The dynamism and self-confidence of the Petrine and Catherinian army was giving way to pessimism and anxiety, exemplified by the brooding figure of Paskievich in Warsaw. Paul had already tried to build a Chinese Wall around the empire with his censorship of foreign publications. The purge of the universities in Kazan and Petersburg in the 1820s cast a pall of gloom over intellectual discourse, and the 230 articles of the 1826 censorship statute, even if amended in the letter but not the spirit two years later, only reinforced the feeling of imprisonment behind the high walls of Fortress Empire.[30]

The major political entertainment of Fortress Empire was the military parade. Great cultures portray themselves through their rituals and the objects of contemplation they inspire. Daily parades before the Winter Palace began with the accession of Paul and were used by the ruler as an opportunity to issue executive orders bearing on any activity of government. They symbolized the "sordid and brutal exercise of power,"[31] when soldiers were punished and officers cashiered for the smallest infraction and at the ruler's whim. In a centralized system, where provincial authorities take their cue from the capital and where military governors began to appear in ever greater numbers, the parade became the major entertainment in the garrison towns, each the microcosm of the garrison state. They became such a typical event that Paul and, later, Alexander were described as suffering from "paradomania." Excellence on the parade ground began to supersede talent in the art of war, as if it were assumed that the mission of the strategic force was no longer to make war but to maintain domestic order by a show of awesomeness toward the empire's population. The most grandiose manifestations of paradomania were Paul's review of 23,000 troops in Moscow in 1798, Alexander's review of 150,000 men in Champagne in 1815, and the parade of 120,000 troops in 1834 to dedicate Montferrand's column to Alexander I in Petersburg. That parade, it was said, gave an impression of "a force that was at once invincible and obedient." The great space facing the Winter Palace was finally enclosed with the completion of the Main (General) Staff building (1819–29) and transformed into an ideal parade ground, extending from the building's great arch to the Senate-Synod building at the other end, with the statue of Tsar Peter on his rearing horse projecting raw and irresistible power. The parade "became the principal ceremony of the Russian monarchy and the role of parade commander the principal persona of the Russian emperor" during the reigns of Paul and Alexander and "the epitome of Nicholas I's.[32]

But the parade was more than "the dominating spectacle"; it also began to symbolize the closing of a world. The subtext was that troops trained to excel on the parade ground must not be spoiled in real combat, that drill commanders were not expected to become successful field commanders let alone strategic leaders, unless war was seen as an opportunity "to win victory by means of awesomeness." To view the strategic force as an army drilled to please the vanity of its commanders and the ruling dynasty was inseparable from the new perceptions emerging after 1815 that the army was primarily the garrison of Fortress Empire and that its mission was to maintain the internal status quo. The logical consequence of this new and growing perception was the closing of the Main Staff in 1832 and the inclusion of its personnel into the War Ministry. During the wars of 1812–15, the creation of a high-level staff directly subordinated to the emperor had served the needs of operational planning, while the war ministry remained responsible for logistics. Closing the staff implied that there was no longer any need for planning those deep strategic penetrations that had been such a major factor in the empire's grand strategy, that the army had now become a huge camp deployed across much of the empire and needed only to parade its strength. Paradomania became a symptom of retrenchment, of the assumption of an essentially defensive posture. Even the military settlements embodied the new strategic vision. Like that of their eighteenth-century predecessors in the Ukrainian steppe, their mission was defensive, and they were not fundamentally different from garrisons, only implanted into a rural environment. That their chief and commandant was Arakcheev was no coincidence: he, more than anyone else, was imbued with the values of paradomania. When Nicholas dismissed him, the tsar-emperor himself became the commandant of Fortress Empire.

The victory of 1815 contributed to a mood of conservative triumphalism: it seemed to consecrate the traditional sociopolitical order and the new autocracy resting on a foundation of military power. The artistic embodiment of the new pride in the empire's achievements was neoclassicism, with its memories of ancient Greece and particularly of imperial Rome. "The pathos of neo-classical imagery exemplified society's idealization of the heroism of military service," and it is significant that neoclassicism would be called in the mid-1850s, after the humiliation of Fortress Empire in the Crimea, another form of "barracks architecture."[33] Buildings sprouted everywhere, in the capitals and the provinces, with rows of columns and Doric, Ionic, and Corinthian capitals, even in faraway Kazan, where the university was built in neoclassical style in the 1820s. The geometry of buildings and public spaces enhanced perceptions of majesty and provided a uniform physical setting for exhibitions of paradomania. Petersburg had to have its imperial church: the Cathedral of the Kazan Mother of God, designed by Andrei Voronikhin, an emancipated serf, to be larger than St. Peter's in Rome, austere in appearance, its interior decorated with captured French trophies, giving the cathedral the aura of a national military shrine,[34] where Orthodoxy and military might combined to project a conviction of self-righteous hegemony.

This conviction that the victory of 1815 had given the empire hegemony in the Heartland was palpable in other ways. Alexander Pushkin in his *Bronze Horseman* (1833) imagined Peter contemplating the banks of the Neva, where he would build a city to "strike terror in the Swede" and "gall our haughty neighbor," but it was Alexander who marched in the footsteps of ancient Rome to complete the transformation of the northern city into the capital of a mighty empire, and Nicholas who galled the haughty Persian neighbor. Two years earlier, Pushkin had bitterly attacked the Polish Rebellion, calling it "a family affair, an old, hereditary, quarrel,"[35] knowing full well that Poland, even under Prussian rule, still extended to the Oder. In a similar frame of mind, Karl Nesselrode had written soon after the great victory, in 1816, that in "Asia"—which at the time meant for Petersburg the lands under the jurisdiction of the Asiatic Department, from Bosnia to Mongolia—"fear is the only guarantee, the sanctity of treaties is meaningless, and relationships with those lands belong to the empire's domestic affairs."[36] Nesselrode's perception was of crucial importance: he headed the foreign ministry under various titles from 1814 to 1856. The shadow of Fortress Empire extended to the Heartland's periphery, beyond which Britain's hegemony held sway.

Conservative triumphalism could also be found in the writings of the Slavophiles, who came into their own in the 1830s. Their "greatest single contribution," according to Michael Petrovich, "was the concept that Russia possessed a separate, original, independent, and self-contained culture based on a Slavic way of life different and incompatible with the Romano-Germanic world."[37] Their perception was inseparable from the vision of a young and rising Russia in opposition to the decaying world of the Coastland ("the West"), corrupted to the core by its individualism, its "arrogant rationalism," its "fondness for the coherence of ideas," its legalistic spirit, its attachment to private property, and its capitalism[38]—in other words, those very principles, assumptions, procedures, and practices that gave the Coastland its dynamism, resilience, and greatness.

The Slavophiles were ill at ease with Nicholas I's government for its increasing reliance on "legalisms" and its "German" bureaucracy, but they nevertheless tapped an important source of popular concern for the definition of a national identity that gradually merged with an incipient Russian nationalism. In its early stages, Slavophilism remained a nationalism of elites transcending ethnic foundations, an "imperial nationalism," not yet the oxymoron it came to be, in which a Barclay and a Bagration could fight together under a Kutuzov at Borodino for the salvation and greatness of a common Fatherland. In the 1830s, when our story ends, the conflict between an imperial identity and separate national identities was not yet deeply felt, and the elite could still rally behind similar slogans. But these slogans combined to create a deep antagonism toward the civilization of the Coastland, not an aggressive but a defensive antagonism seeking protection behind the high walls of Fortress Empire with an enormous strategic force and its police apparatus. One can only agree with the assessment that "Nicholas's scenario [of power] had condemned [Western ideals] as alien to the Russian body politic." Only "a ruthless, unforgiving, and draconian"[39] tsar-emperor, who nurtured a cult of awesomeness both in his person and his empire, could keep the empire secure and maintain its hegemony in the Heartland.

In conclusion, the first third of the nineteenth century witnessed some major changes in the factors that combined to form Russia's grand strategy. The empire's strategic force carried out penetrations that were deeper than any of their predecessors, to Paris, Adrianople, and Tabriz, and grew to unprecedented size, to become larger than the armies of any other state in the Heartland. This alone gave the empire an undisputed hegemony, and its final victory over Napoleon followed by substantial victories over the Turks and Persians gave it an aura of invincibility with which it could hope to maintain that hegemony "by means of awesomeness." But the Napoleonic wars brought about the annexation of Finland and most of the Polish core, transforming the old frontier between Russia on the one hand and Sweden, Poland, and even Turkey on the other, into an inner frontier of the empire where there was no alternative to direct rule. These developments brought to an end much of the old client system as it had existed since Peter's reign. Yet the assumption remained in Petersburg that Sweden and Prussia must remain client states; that the friendship of Austria must be retained; and that Persia must be brought into the system to help the empire maintain its hegemony within the Heartland. A new factor crept in, however: the burden of empire had become too great for the traditional economy, which could no longer generate enough resources while the Coastland economies were entering a new phase: it would leave that economy far behind and expose the empire's feet of clay. Fortress Empire would conceal for another generation the inner rot that must follow the irresponsible stretching of a country's resources beyond their natural limits.

# Conclusion

L ooking back over more than a century and a half of Russian imperial grand strategy, we can now reach a deeper understanding of its constituent elements. One thing must be clear: grand strategy was not simply strategy on a grand scale, a military policy to defeat the enemy on the battlefield and to conquer territorial space. It was a comprehensive, multifaceted policy of an essentially political nature, reflecting a ruling elite's vision of Russia's place in the Heartland. It involved the mobilization of resources and the creation of a military-industrial complex, the forging of an industrial and commercial policy, the elaboration of a foreign policy to create and maintain a network of client states, and the cultivation of a cult of raw power and invincibility to maintain the hegemony of the ruling elite, both at home in the Russian core and in the frontier regions surrounding it. Russia was a warrior state, what the Germans called a *Militärstaat*, one in which the military members of the elite operated by consensus with the political elite headed by the Romanov house and never challenged its ultimate hegemony. In return, the empire's grand strategy gave inordinate weight to military interests in defining political objectives and the elaboration of economic policy.

Periods of expansion often follow great domestic crises. That was the case in France after the religious wars of the sixteenth century, in England after the civil war of the seventeenth century, even in the United States after the Civil War. Such crises generate an enormous amount of energy, channeled, once peace returns, into domestic reconstruction and foreign expansion. Russia underwent its Time of Trouble, and the new Romanov dynasty, slowly but with determination, worked out a long-range policy of domestic reforms in order to lay the foundations for continental expansion. That expansion would steadily continue until the Russians crossed the Heartland's periphery and suffered a crushing defeat at sea—the Russo-Japanese War—which precipitated the first revolution of 1905 and announced the second, which finally toppled the dynasty in 1917.

In what directions would that expansion take place? The Russian core, its back against the interminable and almost impenetrable taiga and the desolate tundra to the north, faced the basins of three seas, two of them beginning on the very edge of the Muscovite center. The rivers that shaped those basins were channels of communication and trade routes. They led across the Russo-Swedish frontier to the Baltic and the Gulf of Bothnia, across the Russo-Turkish frontier to the Black Sea and the Danube. In Siberia, they flowed into the wastes of the Arctic Ocean, but their sources led across the Kazakh steppe to Central Asia and across the Altai to Mongolia and China. They were natural corridors of expansion that determined its direction. However, they flowed across territories still controlled almost entirely by rival powers—Sweden, Poland, and the Ottoman Turks—thereby creating geopolitical frontiers. Geography predetermined that those three powers would be the dynasty's enemies because they alone, by their existence and location, could resist the new expenditure of energy emanating from Moscow. Its location in the Volga-Oka mesopotamia gave the city an eastern orientation, and Ivan IV founded the Russian Empire by destroying the Kazan and Astrakhan Khanates that barred the way to the Volga's estuary on the Caspian. But Astrakhan led to eastern Transcaucasia, Persia's sphere of influence, transforming Persia into Russia's fourth natural enemy, until Russia's energy had spent itself along the Taurus and Zagros chains, the nearly uncrossable periphery of the Heartland. These four geopolitical frontiers formed a huge and continuous semicircle facing Moscow, stretching from the Gulf of Bothnia to the Caspian, and interlocked in two places: in the corridor between the Dniepr and the Dniestr—the Right-Bank Ukraine—and in the Caucasus. On the outer periphery of this uninterrupted geopolitical frontier, nature had created three moats against which the expenditure of Russian energy had to rest—the Gulf of Bothnia, the Danube, and the Araks. Beyond them, the Russians, not unlike the Romans along the Rhine, the Danube, the Euphrates, and the Atlas Mountains of North Africa, would encounter a combination of rugged terrain, hostile religions, incompatible civilizations, higher population densities, and the countervailing ambitions of rival powers that rendered farther expansion counterproductive. The basins of the Baltic and Black Seas thus created two large operational theaters, the western and the southern, in which Russian forces would fight, especially in the southern theater, a long series of wars to destroy Swedish, Polish, and Turkish hegemony and replace it with Russia's own. The Persian sector can justifiably be included into the southern theater, because operations there were often directed against both Turks and Persians.

The eastern theater was a case apart. The eastward expansion across Siberia encountered no significant resistance, but the Irtysh, the Ob, and the tributaries of the Amur led upstream into what would become a Russo-Chinese frontier, where the Manchu dynasty, which had seized power in 1644, called a halt to Russia's advance into the outer periphery of the Heartland.[1] The result was a curious paradox. While the semicircular frontier in the western and southern theaters remained a zone of high-level insecurity during the eighteenth century, until Russia's hegemony became incontestable following the defeat of powers whose potential was not commensurate with Russia's own, the Russo-Chinese frontier became a zone of peace while the Chinese Empire rose to unprecedented heights of power. The reason must be found in the low density of the frontier's population and China's recognition of a line of optimum conquest along the Heartland's periphery. Russia's grand strategy therefore focused on the expenditure of energy in the western and southern theaters in a quest for hegemony. The quest would reach its completion in the wars of Alexander I and Nicholas I, with which our story ended.

How did the Russians proceed to establish their hegemony in those two theaters and in the Heartland as a whole? By means of deep strategic penetrations from the Muscovite center seeking not only to destroy the enemy in the field but also to reach its capital, forcing it to capitulate on Russia's terms. These deep penetrations maximized the surge capability of the empire's strategic force, emphasizing overwhelmingly offensive operations of enormous scale and scope in order to upset the enemy's operational strategy and keep its troops permanently on the defensive. A comparison has been drawn between the Russian emphasis on the offensive and Mongol strategic thinking also based on the offensive and on sweeping enveloping movements to trap the enemy in a vise from which it could not escape. The Muscovites, who had to learn the art of warfare from their neighbors and overlords, tested their growing strength against the nomad whose hegemony in the steppe had been uncontested for centuries. It is logical to assume, even if it cannot be proved, that basic principles of steppe warfare should have become the foundation of Russian overall strategy in the Heartland, even in the forest zone. In every war over long periods of time, the application of overwhelming force to specific geographical objectives served to create a perception of Russia's awesomeness and invincibility and facilitated the success of subsequent operations. It may seem inappropriate to speak of sweeping movements across enormous distances at a time when the cavalry seldom rode more than ninety kilometers a day and the infantry covered about forty, while ox-drawn heavy supply carts advanced at about eight kilometers a day and kept a permanent drag on the advance of the troops. But speed is relative to the times: in World War II, fuel trucks could no more keep up with Rommel's tanks in North Africa. Diebitsch's plan to destroy the Ottoman army and reach Constantinople in three campaigns can properly be called a plan of blitzkrieg long before the term was used.

The empire went on the offensive in the 1650s in order to reverse the unfavorable settlements that coincided with the end of the Time of Troubles. From then on there would be no respite until Sweden's and Poland's military and political capabilities had been destroyed. The Thirteen Years' War was fought for limited objectives and without resorting to deep strategic penetrations. A generation later, however, the campaign against the Crimea had the far more ambitious objective of carrying the war deep into nomadic country and completing the destruction of the khanates that had become the successor states of the Golden Horde. It failed largely for logistical reasons. Infantry troops were the armed embodiment of the settler, who had barely reached the edge of the steppe zone, and the settler was not yet ready to face the nomad in his own universe.

The fixation with the Crimea would continue to occupy the high command for a long time, but a new strategic vision was emerging at the very end of the seventeenth century that informed Peter's planning: the main enemy was not the Crimean Tatar but the Turk. Peter fought the Turks at Azov, 2,400 kilometers from Moscow, in 1696; on the Prut, 1,400 kilometers away, in 1711; and a diversion was carried out on the Kuban, 2,700 kilometers away. The elements of a two-prong strategy were in place: advance along both ends of the Black Sea toward Anatolia to take in a vise Constantinople and the Straits. The campaign of 1711 was a failure but it pointed to the future, although the continued existence of the Crimean Khanate would remain an enduring threat to the operational advance toward the Danube and the Caucasus. To the east, the Russians reached Rasht on the southern coast of the Caspian and Khiva, both more than 3,000 kilometers away. These were imposing penetrations, in unknown and inhospitable territory, even if they were eventually doomed to fail. In the 1730s, the Russians occupied the Crimea but could secure no staying power, again for logistical reasons.

By the 1760s, however, the growth of the empire's potential, the advance of colonization toward the Dniepr, and the deployment of a substantial part of the strategic force in the Left-Bank Ukraine had given the Russians preponderance in the southern theater. Rumiantsev would impose in 1774 a peace settlement on the Ottomans south of the Danube, eliminating the Crimean Khanate as a power factor in the process and creating an interest in Transcaucasia that the passage of time would only strengthen. The war also destabilized the Polish Empire by transforming its eastern march in the Right-Bank Ukraine into a supply base for the Russian army, paving the way for its annexation in the 1790s. It cannot be overlooked that in one Turkish war after another, it was the ruler—whether Catherine II, Alexander I, or Nicholas I—who kept prodding the more cautious commanders to move faster and deeper into the frontier on the way to Constantinople. The annexation of eastern Georgia in 1801 capped the elaboration of the two-prong strategy by creating a powerful military headquarters in Tiflis that complemented the Kiev headquarters and relegated Astrakhan to the position of an auxiliary naval base. In 1829, the Russians occupied Adrianople and Erzerum, springing the trap on the Turks, who were forced to capitulate. By then, Russian strategic penetrations had reached their greatest extent: Adrianople, 235 kilometers from Constantinople, was 2,400 kilometers from Moscow, and Tabriz, reached by Paskievich, 600 kilometers from Tehran, was 2,650 kilometers from the old capital.

The depth of strategic penetration in the western theater was similar. The wars with Sweden were fought for the limited objective of gaining access to the Gulf of Finland, but with unlimited means seeking the eventual destruction of Sweden's hegemony and of its war-making capability. The occupation of southern Finland in 1714 took the Russians to Åbo, 1,260 kilometers from Moscow, but the exceptionally ambitious plan to send an expeditionary corps across the Sound in 1716 took them to Copenhagen, 2,500 kilometers from the capital. In 1743, they reached Uleåborg, 1,830 kilometers away. But it was in 1808–9 that the scope of Russian operations became truly staggering, considering the geographical environment of the eastern Baltic and the difficulties of supply. The three-pronged offensive against Stockholm—along the Åland Islands, across the Kvarken, and around the Gulf of Bothnia—brought Sweden to its knees. The result was the annexation of Finland and the establishment of Russian power along the Bothnian moat, twenty years before the Russians stopped along the Araks moat, but they never quite succeeded in pushing the imperial periphery to the Danube.

Between the Baltic and the Balkan sectors, projections of power were no less impressive. An expeditionary corps reached Heidelberg, 2,500 kilometers from

Moscow in 1735, and another was on its way in 1748. The Seven Years' War was fought along the Oder, which might have become another moat, had it not been for the partitions of the Polish Empire, and the Russians briefly seized Berlin in 1760, 1,800 kilometers from Moscow. In 1799, they fought in northern Italy and Switzerland and landed in Holland, in another huge pincer movement directed against Revolutionary France, which had been Russia's main continental enemy throughout the eighteenth century. They occupied Paris in 1814, 3,000 kilometers away. It thus appears that the radius of operations for the empire's strategic force was about 2,000 kilometers while some penetrations in exceptional circumstances reached 3,000 kilometers. No other power in continental Europe could project effective power over such long distances, the short-lived Napoleonic experiment (1796–1814) being the exception that confirmed the rule. For eighteenth-century France, comparable to Russia in the size of its population, it would have meant sending large forces (between 50,000 and 100,000 men) into Bielorussia—a proposition as unthinkable as it was impracticable. After 1815, however, such penetrations would be impossible, because Finland and Poland had become part of the Russian Empire, and because Russia's hegemony in the western and southern theaters was creating a backlash that would place the empire on the defensive after nearly two hundred years of continuous expansion.

Empires are not always at war. Their armies must be redeployed in peacetime in such a way that they will serve domestic objectives and help realize the government's aspirations beyond the imperial periphery. The strategic force, shaped and hardened by nearly twenty-five years of continuous war, was withdrawn in 1725 from the newly acquired Baltic provinces and the Left-Bank Ukraine to be concentrated in the Muscovite core between Tver and Kazan in the forest zone and along the edge of the wooded steppe. These 100,000 men in seventy-three regiments, only a few of them stationed farther north in the Tver-Novgorod-Petersburg corridor and farther east beyond Kazan in the Urals and Bashkiria, remained in the area of original settlement where most of the population continued to live. Deploying the troops in the region would facilitate their maintenance and provisioning by binding each regiment to a group of towns and villages, where they would collect the capitation introduced specially to cover the needs of the army. The troops would also police the region in their own interest and guard the axis of Fortress Russia linking the Urals via Moscow and Tver with the new capital on the Gulf of Finland.

Fortress Russia never again was a *Militärstaat* to the extent that it had been during Peter's reign, when the extraordinary demands of war and the union of the autocratic power with that of a commander in chief in the field established for all practical purposes a military dictatorship. The strategic force, not tied down to territorial defense, remained single and mobile, at the disposal of the leadership for immediate operation against Sweden and Poland in the Baltic basin, and against Tatars and Turks in the Black Sea basin. Only in the Caspian sector did a separate force gain a regional mission: to defend, at a considerable distance from the Muscovite core, the occupied provinces on the southern coast of the Caspian and to keep an eye on the Turks in eastern Transcaucasia. The effect of this concentrated deployment was to maximize the empire's disposable military power. The pattern of Peter's wars showed how quickly troops were redeployed from one theater to another, either to meet threats or to carry out deep strikes in pursuit of foreign policy objectives.[2]

However, the concentrated deployment of the strategic force was not a viable option in the long run for at least two reasons. The growth of Petersburg and the incipient threat it represented for Sweden in Finland considerably increased the strategic importance of the Gulf of Finland and necessitated the stationing of larger forces on the periphery, both to police the capital and to launch operations from Vyborg into southern Finland. The growing importance of the Swedish sector reverberated in Estonia and Livonia, which protected Petersburg from the west, but were also bases of operations against East Prussia and the Polish Empire, more easily reached from Riga than from Moscow. In the southern theater, the steady growth of the population transformed the wooded steppe into the provisioning base of the strategic force. These two phenomena inevitably caused a distention of the concentrated deployment of the 1720s and the creation of two wings along the imperial periphery, toward which more and more troops had to be withdrawn from the Muscovite core. No longer the core but the periphery became a base for tactically offensive operations within the framework of a strategy that appeared defensive against Swedish revanchism and Tatar raids, but was in fact fundamentally offensive. By 1743, 64 percent of the strategic force was deployed in Russia proper beyond the original Muscovite core; twenty years later, it was 45 percent, even though the force had grown to about 150,000 in one hundred regiments. The geopolitical environment was beginning to dictate the creation of regional armies, each army assigned to one of the three basins—the Baltic, Black Sea, and the Caspian—while troops remaining in the Russian core would become a reserve to support in the event of need, with the regional armies carrying out their missions. The strategic force was becoming tied down to territorial defense, profoundly modifying the Petrine strategy based on the economy of force. As the empire expanded in fanlike fashion into the semicircular frontier facing Moscow, each geographical sector began to impose a specific force structure, including naval support, a specific infrastructure to sustain the operations of each army, and specific goals. These separate goals would have eventually ceased to be integrated into an overall strategic plan had it not been for the fact that they remained inseparable from the permanent objective since Peter's day: gaining hegemony in the Heartland. The annexation of the eastern marches of the Polish Empire and the extension of imperial rule along the Black Sea littoral went a long way toward reaching this objective. They also distended the deployment of the strategic force to an unprecedented extent: by 1796, only 24.3 percent of the 115 regiments were left in Russia proper.

In order to counter these centrifugal tendencies inherent to peripheral deployment, however, the imperial government carried out a systematic territorial reform across the entire empire to create a uniform administrative infrastructure of provinces and districts for the exercise of civilian power everywhere. After the accession of Paul and with the increasing militarization of public life, this administrative uniformity paved the way for the transformation of Fortress Russia into Fortress Empire during the reign of his two sons, Alexander I and Nicholas I. One of the similarities between Alexander's and Peter's reigns was the intensity of warfare in the defense of the monarch's very existence and the exhaustion that followed those wars;

Alexander's reign also brought about an enormous increase in the size of the strategic force, which reached 600,000 men in 253 regiments in 1819. The most original feature of the new deployment was the reconstitution of a large strategic reserve in Russia proper, where 68 percent of the regiments were now stationed, a proportion unheard of since the 1740s, despite the much larger size of the empire. With the onset of the conservative reaction east of the Elbe, the major objective was no longer external but internal security. A large number of provincial capitals became headquarters of army divisions and in some cases corps headquarters as well. A battalion of garrisoned troops was stationed in all of them with a complement of military police, which became independent in 1826. In the border regions, separate armies and corps fulfilled the same combination of functions: the preservation of the conservative order within the imperial periphery and the creation of regional offensive deployments to preserve it everywhere within the Heartland. The new empire-wide military and police infrastructure meshed with the civilian network of provincial agencies to constitute the garrison force of Fortress Empire. Russian history may have been, as Kiuchevskii claimed, a process of colonization, but it was also a process of garrisoning itself at every new stage of imperial aggrandizement within an ever expanding political and economic space.

But what had been the imperial government's aspirations during the earlier period, when Peter opted for concentrated deployment in the Muscovite center? At that time, the security of the empire was held to depend on a network of client states and societies kept together by a perception of the strategic force's awesomeness and invincibility, making it possible to maintain an economy of force and avoid direct rule in territories already considered to be within the imperial periphery. It is not easy to find a common definition of client status applicable to all cases, especially in an empire as vast as the Russian, with peoples in the frontier so different from one another. It is certainly essential that there be a great disparity of power and resources between patron and clients and that there exist a common interest without which the nature of the relationship would have to be settled by force of arms. The client has his own interest, which must be compatible with the overall objectives of his patron's policy, although the defense of that interest may sometimes draw the patron into territory where he would have preferred not to tread. But a client must also be willing to translate imperial desires into policy. A client system must be constantly managed by the imperial power in order to be kept in a state of equilibrium, without which direct intervention would be required, undermining the entire system. All clients were not equal, and the Russian Empire's client system was a hierarchy of states, with Poland at the top, Sweden in the middle, and Prussia at the bottom. Below the states, because they were much less important, were the client societies of Cossacks, Baltic Germans, Moldavians and Wallachians, Georgians and Armenians. And immediately beyond the imperial periphery there stretched an "invisible frontier" of Germans and Greeks, Kalmyks and Cossacks.

The withdrawal of the strategic force to Fortress Russia in the 1720s created a geopolitical universe of two complementary parts: mobile armies and client states and societies. One must not underestimate the fact that of all the wars in which the empire was engaged between 1700 and 1831 the Russians lost only three: the Prut expedition of 1711, Austerlitz in 1805, and Friedland in 1807. The memory of Russian victories nurtured a perception of the new empire's awesomeness and the conviction that any challenge would be met with overwhelming retribution. At the end of the eighteenth century, the newly arrived Czartoryski was struck in Petersburg by the conviction among Russian officers that nothing could resist their glorious army, "which could cross the entire universe without encountering resistence."[3] Such conviction was even stronger in 1814. Client societies were instruments of strategic control by administering their territories on behalf of the empire—the Baltic Germans in their provinces, the Cossacks between the Dniepr and the Volga and along the Terek, the Kalmyks beyond the Volga, and more Cossacks along the Irtysh. They also contributed auxiliary troops (and officers in the case of the Baltic Germans) to the imperial army, chiefly light cavalry; Cossacks and Kalmyks were often combined to give that army in the eyes of non-Russians an "Asiatic" and awesome appearance. They also supplied provisions and guides to the imperial army on the march. They helped manage the client system: the Baltic Germans were instrumental in maintaining proconsular rule in Poland and the Kazan Tatars—another client society within the empire—were active on its behalf in Bashkiria and the Kazakh steppe. Some interposed themselves between the empire and potential and real enemies to provide geographical depth—the Cossacks against the Crimean Tatars, the Kazakhs against the Zunghars, and the Chinese behind them. Their role was crucial to the preservation of the empire's economy of military force. In the western theater, the imperial government had to play a complex game to balance Sweden, Poland, Prussia, and Austria against one another, the prize being hegemony in that part of the Heartland. The Swedish constitution gave the Russians a lever to interfere in the country's domestic affairs; Prussia relied on Russia against Austria and Poland; the friendly kingdom depended on Russian support of its ambitions in southern Germany and the Balkans; the vulnerability of the Polish Empire made it dependent on imperial benevolence. Across the vast expanse of that geopolitical universe patron-client relationships were often cemented by marital alliances, which already formed the foundation of the empire's political "constitution." Many of the great families had once come from Lithuania and the Golden Horde, and this multi-ethnic ruling elite naturally expanded by bringing in Baltic Germans, Cossacks and Moldavians, Georgians and Armenians, and even an occasional Kalmyk.

But the client system, which constituted such an important factor in the empire's grand strategy, was inherently unstable. Its evolution was conditioned by certain major developments. One was the steady demographic shift in the Black Sea basin as Russian colonization expanded in the direction of the Dniepr and the lower Volga, distending the concentrated deployment of the 1720s. Another was the growth of the empire's industrial and military power and the adoption of an offensive strategy in the western theater, the objective being the establishment of the empire's hegemony in the Baltic basin, which led to the Atlantic. The Seven Years' War confirmed that hegemony. The adoption of an offensive strategy in the Black Sea basin, which led to the Mediterranean, was a natural corollary, feeding the empire's determination to gain hegemony in the Heartland. The third development was a consequence of the first two, but it also had its own inner logic. Client societies were by definition frontier societies: the advance of the empire to the shores of the Black Sea destroyed their raison d'être and transformed them into internal provinces. But they had been decaying from within for some time, as a native process of social differentiation created an elite of men of power whose interests were inseparable from those of the imperial elite. This was especially the case in the Cossack zone. The fourth was the emergence of Prussia, which, in violation of the cardinal rule that a client may not aggrandize itself without the sanction of the imperial power, seized Silesia from the friendly kingdom. The resulting Seven Years' War marked the beginning of a long train of events culminating in the partitions of Poland and the annexation of the Black Sea littoral. In the annexed territories, the old client societies were no longer expected to provide the services that had justified their existence.

The maintenance of the empire's security required the creation of an infrastructure of fortresses, communications, ports, and naval installations that had to depend on the active involvement of the imperial government; it alone could finance their construction and maintenance. The permanent stationing of imperial troops brought to an end the old client system. Direct rule within the new Fortress Empire, however, did not exclude the continuation of collaboration between the local men of power and the imperial elite with which they increasingly became identified, while continuing to manage their territories under the watchful eyes of a police and military apparatus determined to maintain the status quo. The empire continued to insist on the maintenance of client relationships with Sweden, Prussia, and Austria, but one in which the old mutual interest was replaced by the not so subtle threat of using force to keep them in line and maintain the conservative order behind the Heartland's periphery. In the Caspian basin, the disintegration of the Georgian ruling house and the Kazakh Small Horde also brought about the introduction of direct rule in association with local men of power. And everywhere — from the Gulf of Finland to the Urals and the Caspian — paradomania became the theatrical entertainment of the garrison state, the new expression of a cult of raw military power that had always been a central feature of the empire's grand strategy. That cult became associated with a glorification of ancient Rome, which had once drawn a line along the Rhine and the Danube to protect itself against the inroads of alien values. It was less certain that it also brought to mind the Great Wall of China behind which the dynasties of the Celestial Empire had found an illusion of security.

The pursuance of a grand strategy was inseparable from the formulation of an economic policy designed to provide the means of sustaining a fundamentally offensive strategy on a continental scale. Eli Heckscher, the eminent Swedish economic historian, remarked that the early Vasa kings, instead of laying the foundations of a new economy, sought "to preserve and reinforce" the medieval economic system that they inherited and built a strong authority on the foundation of a natural economy. He called the Swedish sixteenth century "the age of maturity of the medieval economy."[4] No better characterization could be made of the Russian eighteenth century. While the economies of the European Coastland were moving toward more open economic systems and a freer labor market, the seventeenth century prepared for Peter a legacy of monopolistic enterprise by the ruling elite and

servile labor. Peter, who was much more of a traditionalist than is usually recognized, streamlined that legacy to make it serve the ambitious goals of a grand
strategy seeking hegemony in the Heartland. Serfdom was extended and made
harsher, and almost the entire population was subjected in 1723 to the poll tax created for the specific purpose of paying and provisioning the troops making up the
strategic force.

The Russian defeat at the first battle of Narva (1700) served as the catalyst for
the launching of a vast industrial program to build the economic foundation of
Fortress Russia. Tula and the Lake Onega region were no longer sufficient to produce the iron needed for muskets and sabers, guns, cannonballs, and anchors, and
the center of imperial metallurgy shifted eastward to the Urals where the ore was
of high quality and charcoal abundant. Since the region was deficient in human resources, serf labor was conscripted to operate the foundries and smelters, to prepare
and deliver the charcoal. The textile industry, less dependent on serf labor, developed around Moscow, Vladimir, and Voronezh. These six regions, together with
the immediate environs of Petersburg, became the pillars of the new imperial
economy. But they were at first largely artificial creations, serving only the greater
good of the new military-industrial complex consisting of members of the ruling
elite in the civil administration or the high command, and sometimes in both.
Heckscher has pointed out that "the more self-sufficient a country is, the more deci-
sively all economic activity will be determined by consumption."[5] Internal self-
sufficiency, however, assumes the existence of a low level of consumption, rather
than a rising demand in the civilian economy. If consumers had to be found for the
new metallurgical industries, they would have to be the army and navy. The few
new captains of industry, whether they remained private "industrialists" or were co-
opted into the ruling elite, were largely dependent on government orders and
government credit. The chronic shortage of capital that was the most characteristic
feature of the imperial economy during the eighteenth and early nineteenth century was due to the absence of a substantial nonmilitary market in which rising
demand would stimulate production and raise profits. The incestuous relationship
between the military and industry based on the services of compulsory labor explains why it could be said that Peter's industrial enterprises were not very different
from penal institutions.[6]

Rivers connected the pillars of the imperial economy, and a canal was cut at
Vyshnii Volochek to connect the Baltic with the Caspian, creating a continuous
waterway linking Petersburg with the Urals and Astrakhan and integrating the
Petersburg hinterland with the valley of the Volga. The waterway became the axis of
Fortress Russia, and it was on it that Peter built his dream of hegemony in the
Heartland. Cut off from direct access to the Atlantic sea routes that brought wealth
to the Coastland economies, the empire would become the intermediary between
the trade of the East and that of the West, linking overland the wealth of India with
the markets of Amsterdam and London. Tapping the wealth of that trade would
yield revenue in specie and create influence over the client states and societies,
eventually drawing the basin of the Black Sea into the Muscovite orbit, all the way
to the Danube and the Araks. It would enhance Russian military capabilities and
awesomeness everywhere in the Heartland. The vision was grandiose but utopian, if

only because overland trade could not compete with seaborne trade and because "another Russia" of commercial cities was incompatible with a militarized economy bent on maximizing military power. Far from being able to become a pole of commercial wealth in the Heartland, Russia was becoming instead a raw materials supplier for the Coastland economies. The fearful recognition of that unpleasant truth lay behind the prohibitive tariff of 1724, which destroyed all prospects of modernization of the imperial economy and guaranteed that it would remain a command economy operating by stretching to the limits the finite potentialities of servile labor.

While the economy continued to expand quantitatively throughout the eighteenth century, the empire's fiscal health began to deteriorate. The tax base remained inelastic, dependent as it was on direct revenue, with a limited market incapable of raising the yield from indirect taxes. The Seven Years' War, an operational success even if its political outcome was disappointing, left the empire's finances in a dismal state: in 1761, the immediate liabilities of the treasury amounted to 2.5 million rubles, its assets to 121,000 rubles.[7] Wages and provisions had to be paid for in goods, and the empire's hegemonic ambitions came to rest on an essentially natural economy. The nearly fifty years between the first Turkish War of 1768 and the victory of 1815, during which the empire reached its nearly final shape and gained its long-sought hegemony in the Heartland, were a time when the imperial government financed its power drive by creating paper wealth. The treasury initially issued 1 million paper rubles convertible on demand; by 1774, their amount reached 20 million; by 1785, 100 million; by 1800, 213 million and by 1817, 836 million. By then, they had ceased to be convertible, leaving the population awash in a sea of depreciated currency and prey to rampant inflation, damaging the government's credit and the manufacturers' confidence.

The increasing dependence on paper money (and on foreign loans and on British subsidies) showed that the limits of the servile economy had been reached, but serfdom was not politically negotiable at the end of Alexander's reign. At that very same time, the introduction of the puddling process in England in the 1780s to convert pig iron into malleable wrought iron with mineral fuel was dealing a major blow to the Russian (and Swedish) iron industry already suffering from a shortage of charcoal. The imperial economy, unable to make the transition to the Industrial Revolution, which was radically transforming the Coastland economies, began to retrench again behind a tariff wall. The tariff of 1822 had much in common with that of 1724: one had protected Fortress Russia, the other would protect Fortress Empire. In an entire century, the composition of the revenue from taxation had remained unchanged, and the continued emphasis on raw material extraction for the military-industrial complex and for exports kept delaying economic modernization.

Fortress Russia had been intended to rely on a military and industrial foundation concentrated in the Muscovite core linking the Baltic with the Caspian. That foundation was inseparable from a grand vision that the transit trade would transform that core into a pole of attraction for the commerce of the Baltic, Black Sea, and Caspian basins. Such was the ambition of the new empire's grand strategy at the beginning of the eighteenth century. However, domestic developments distended the original core; hegemonic ambitions developed their own momentum, farther encouraged by the internal evolution of the frontier regions; and Prussian ambitions created turbulence in the client system. The eventual result was the re-deployment of the strategic force and the establishment of direct rule within the new imperial periphery. After 1815, the strategic force was deployed once again in the Russian core as well as in the western and southern theaters to defend the new conservatism grounded in the preservation of the political status quo, censorship, and economic retrenchment behind the Great Wall of Fortress Empire.

Russia's grand strategy had not changed fundamentally in the course of a century: only its theater of operation had expanded, from the Russian core seeking hegemony to a hegemonic empire incorporating the greater part of the Heartland. In the 1720s, it was expected that a powerful Fortress Russia would overwhelm a network of client states and societies and gain hegemony in the Heartland, while practicing an economy of force that would minimize direct intervention by the strategic force and preserve for it a considerable freedom of action. By the 1820s, the integration of the client societies (and of the Polish client state) into the infrastructure of empire had deprived the strategic force of its inherent elasticity by creating regional deployment tied to the pursuit of regional missions that were both offensive and defensive. But it continued to assume that Fortress Empire could keep managing the client state system by projecting an image of awesome power. Nicholas I would become the embodiment of that assumption, but it overlooked the fact that a projection of awesomeness only created a facade behind which economic retrenchment and financial weakness were slowly destroying the very effectiveness of that grand strategy.

The day of reckoning came forty years after the great victory of 1815. The reign of Nicholas I was not a time of economic stagnation: retrenchment only meant that the persistence of the traditional economy, together with political conservatism and changes in the geopolitical environment, induced the empire to withdraw from the great current of economic change sweeping the Coastland, including the new Rhineland possessions of Prussia, the recalcitrant client state. The reform of 1839 stabilized the currency, restored the convertibility of paper rubles, and accelerated their withdrawal, leaving only 170 million in circulation. However, the Crimean War would be financed by printing more: by 1858, 733 million were in circulation, and these rubles were, again, not convertible. Industry continued to expand behind the tariff wall of 1822, but the retention of serfdom in the metal industries and the increasing shortage of charcoal severely damaged the Urals economy. The only railroad in existence on the eve of the Crimean War linked Petersburg with Moscow, but not the two capitals with the periphery. Despite its quantitative increase, the empire's foreign trade remained stationary in relative terms, making up about 3.6 percent of world trade during the entire first half of the nineteenth century,[8] still the trade of an essentially raw materials market for the Coastland economies. Nevertheless, the strategic force, the garrison of Fortress Empire, grew from 633,000 men in 1825 to 1 million in 1853, on the eve of the Crimean War.

The causes of that war, like those of the Polish partitions, will remain a source of disagreements among historians. If it is placed within the context of the empire's grand strategy, the war represented a general offensive by the Coastland powers and the client states against Russian hegemony in the Heartland. Since the death of

Bernadotte in 1844, Sweden was no longer awed by Russian power; Prussia under Frederick William IV, angered by Russia's determination to maintain the client system in equilibrium against Berlin's ambitions, opposed the war; Austria, once the friendly kingdom, whose friendliness had gradually turned to hostility since the Russian occupation of the Danube delta in 1829 and to resentment since the humiliation of 1849 when Nicholas I saved the Habsburg monarchy, was set on opposing a Russian occupation of the Danubian principalities. Austria has been described in these pages as the anchor of the Russian imperial client system; never before had its pivotal position been so decisive, to the point that Russia's failure in the Crimea was attributable to the obsessive fears of Paskievich, the imperial viceroy in Warsaw since 1832, that Austria might attack in Poland and cut off imperial troops along the Danube from their Ukrainian bases.[9] In 1828, similar fears had been stilled by the tsar's determination to carry the war into Austria. By 1853–56, the situation had been reversed, and the empire's field strategy had become hostage to Vienna's resentment.

Nicholas I's vaunting of Russia's awesomeness had earned him the nickname of "gendarme of Europe," but France and Britain only waited for an opportunity to expose his bluff. By then, the gap between the imperial and Coastland economies had become so great that the allied superiority in communications and weaponry was decisive. The revolt of the client system, encouraged by the conviction of the Anglo-French allies that the weakness of the empire must be exposed, paralyzed imperial strategy: most of the strategic force was kept waiting in Poland and the Baltic sector for a ground assault that never came, while the troops in the Crimea, experiencing shortages of powder, ammunition, and even provisions, especially for their 100,000 horses and oxen, which the absence of railroads could not remedy, held out until they were forced to surrender. The Russians had always depended on horse-and-oxen-drawn wagons to transport their supplies and pull their guns. In the past, so had their enemies, but the enemies now had steamships and railroads. The speed differential, together with technological backwardness, doomed Russian efforts in the Crimea. The surrender of Sevastopol did not defeat the imperial army; it only meant the loss of a bastion of Fortress Empire, but once the bluff of Russia's awesomeness had been called, the entire fortress shook to its foundations, ushering in a new era calling for a thorough reappraisal of the empire's grand strategy for the first time since Peter's reign.

After 1855, when the implications of the Industrial Revolution had become obvious, "anxiety and pessimism"[10] replaced the old self-confidence, nay, exuberance, of the eighteenth century and the period between 1815 and 1831: equipment would remain inferior, even to that of the Ottoman armies, and the railroad gap would be impossible to fill, because of the distances involved, laggard steel production, and high costs. The transformation of Prussia into a powerful German Empire—and a leader in production and technology—together with its alliance with the old friendly kingdom in 1879 transformed a security glacis into a zone of high insecurity. The empire could no longer carry out deep strikes in the western theater, because the frontier had ceased to exist and the Central Powers barred the way. In the southern theater, the Russo-Turkish War of 1877–78 was almost an exact replica of that of 1827–29, with the difference that Plevna replaced Shumla as the major obstacle to the Russian advance. The Russians threatened Constantinople once again, but they had to give up their political gains in Bulgaria as a result of Bismarck's intervention, in which a congress of European states caused Russia to lose the peace. On the other hand, the conquest of Central Asia succeeded, in the form of a traditional pincer movement directed from Tiflis in Georgia and Semipalatinsk on the Irtysh. It completed the incorporation, which had long been in the making, of the Caspian basin into the empire. The third deep strategic penetration—and the longest in Russian history—was the Russo-Japanese war, fought in Manchuria, some 8,000 kilometers from Moscow. It combined, like the Turkish War of 1768–74, overland operations with an ambitious projection of naval power over enormous distances. The war was a failure with major negative political implications for Russia's geopolitical position in the Far East.[11] Certainly by 1905, deep strategic penetrations could no longer remain an article of Russia's grand strategy as they had been from the end of the seventeenth century to 1831.

The alliance of the Central Powers—Germany and Austria—and the rising discontent among the national minorities along the empire's periphery had a profound effect on the deployment of the strategic force. The increasing speed of communications required a maximum concentration in the western theater because speedy reinforcements were not a viable option. The creation of military districts in the 1860s, and the subsequent reforms, built upon the old division of the strategic force into separate corps deployed along the periphery but also created a territorial structure in which the commanders of the Vilno, Warsaw, and the Kiev districts automatically became commanders in chief of three armies in the event of war with the Central Powers.[12] The consolidation of Fortress Empire, followed by an attack upon it at the time of the Crimean War, and then by the emergence of the Teutonic threat, combined to bring about a gradual change in policy: from concentrated deployment in the Muscovite center in the 1720s to peripheral deployment in the border regions in the 1790s, and finally to concentrated deployment in the western theater a century later in order to cope with what had become a single overwhelming threat.[13] Despite the determination of some members of the high command to fight an offensive war—especially after the Franco-Russian convention of 1892 required the imperial army to attack Germany in the event of a war with France—the strategic posture of the empire became basically defensive; Petersburg had become mesmerized by the threat to the Polish salient, with its highly developed industry and 16 million people, which had once given the empire a strategic advantage and had now turned into a liability. That defensive posture reflected the "sense of military inferiority"[14] in the high command, as Fortress Empire began to crumble under the impact of industrialization and the accompanying social disorders.

Despite the rapid industrialization that began in the 1860s, the empire could not catch up with the continental economies. The chronic shortage of capital had to be compensated by an increasing penetration of the imperial economy by foreign capital, including that of Germany, creating a potentially disastrous situation in wartime. The revenue from taxation could not cope with rising expenditures, despite the fact that the treasury depended more and more on the yield of indirect taxes: their success presupposed the existence of a far more advanced economy than was the case in Russia. The Crimean War and the Turkish War were financed by issuing more paper money; the Russo-Japanese war, which cost a staggering 2.9 billion rubles, or three times that of the Turkish War, was financed by seven foreign loans.[15]

By the early twentieth century, Russia's grand strategy, as it had developed in the eighteenth century, had disintegrated, leaving behind a combination of poorly coordinated policies and ambitions. Concentrated deployment in a single theater had turned Peter's policy on its head. Financial weakness and laggard economic performance presented a sad contrast to the strength of the Russian economy in the eighteenth century. Political dreams in the Far East, Persia, and the Turkish Straits had become totally disconnected from military capabilities and economic realities. The disintegration of its grand strategy mirrored the empire's decomposition, which would take place after four years of war, during which Germany did not even consider the Russian theater the primary object of its offensives. The history of the Soviet Union would mirror that of the empire: an ideology of conquest, the restoration of Russia's hegemony in the Heartland; a new Fortress Empire with its unprecedented military and police apparatus and overwhelming military-industrial complex; the creation of client states between the Russian core and the Heartland's periphery in the western and southern theaters; and finally, collapse from within under the impact of a failure to reconcile military and political ambitions with continued economic backwardness.

# Notes

*Preface*

1. Virtual history, by contrast, is "what might have taken place, if." See N. Ferguson, *Virtual History: Alternatives and Counterfactuals* (London, 1997).
2. I. Ševčenko "Two Varieties of Historical Writing," *History and Theory* 8 (1969): 332–45.
3. W. Walsh, *Philosophy of History* (New York, 1967), 109.
4. See D. Ostrowski, "The Historian and the Virtual Past," *Historian* 51 (1989): 220. See also his "Essai de typologie des théories de l'histoire," *Diogène* 129 (1985): 130–50, esp. 138–39.

*Introduction*

1. Some may argue that the war against the mountain peoples of the Caucasus would absorb much of Russia's expansionist drive for another generation, but this war was in fact only a police operation, albeit one of considerable magnitude in view of the substantial number of troops committed to the enterprise. But it had nothing to do with farther territorial expansion. Once the Russians had reached the Araks River and gained recognition of their hold on the Black Sea coast from Anapa to Poti, the fate of the mountain peoples was sealed, and only the forbidding terrain of Dagestan explains why it took so long to impose Russia's overlordship in the region. The war did not so much bring about farther territorial expansion as it allowed the Russians to consolidate their rule in a mountain massif of which they already controlled all the exits. The second phase of imperial expansion began with the annexation of the left bank of the Amur and the Maritime Province in 1858–60, followed shortly thereafter by the invasion of Central Asia that began in 1864. It is of course beyond the time frame of this book.
2. Luttwak, *Grand Strategy of the Roman Empire*, 4–5, 18–19, 46–50, 191–94. See also his *Grand Strategy of the Soviet Union*, 75–77. I have used some of Luttwak's concepts and vocabulary, but I will make no direct reference in the text. Luttwak's book caused much controversy, but it was also called "this century's best book on Roman history by a nonspecialist." See A. Ferrill, "The Grand Strategy of the Roman Empire," in Kennedy, *Grand Strategies*, 71. B. Isaac challenged Luttwak's conclusions in his *Limits of Empire: The Roman Army in*

*the East* (Oxford, 1990). The essence of the criticism was that the Romans did not think in terms of a grand strategy, that the empire's posture was offensive and not defensive, that the empire had no well-defined borders, and that there was no defense in depth and no mobile army. It is for historians of ancient Rome to debate the validity of these objections. They are irrelevant to this study of Russia's grand strategy, and it is certainly ridiculous to claim that because the Luttwak model has supposedly been discredited, it cannot be used to work out a theory of Russian grand strategy.

I have in fact been inspired by both Luttwak and Isaac. I see the empire's policy as essentially offensive during the eighteenth and the first quarter of the nineteenth century. I am convinced there was a perception of a grand strategy. Isaac makes the curious statement that Luttwak wrongly assumed that "the Romans were capable of realizing in practice what they could not verbally define" (170). If we follow him, we cannot say that the British pursued in the nineteenth century a policy of containment of Russian expansion because they did not use the term, and that they were not aware of the existence of a basic antagonism between the Heartland and the Coastlands until Mackinder opened their eyes in 1904. What I found most useful in Luttwak's book are the concepts of concentrated and peripheral deployment, of mobile army, and of a relationship between deployment and the client system. If Russian historians disagree, the debate will refine our understanding of the empire's grand strategy, which also includes economic and cultural factors to which both Luttwak and Isaac paid little attention, perhaps because of lack of sources.

3. LeDonne, "Frontier Governors-General, 1772–1825." On ancient Rome, see Dyson, *The Creation of the Roman Frontier*, 27, 38, 55, 197, 273–76.

4. Castex, *Strategic Theories*, 10, 44; Hart, *Strategy*, 321–22.

5. On logistics, see VanCreveld's classic work, *Supplying War*.

6. *Heartland* is Sir Halford Mackinder's term. See LeDonne, *Russian Empire and the World*, 1–3.

7. Bellamy, "Heirs of Genghis Khan," 53. One may object that the Mongols and Russians did not have a concept of Heartland and did not use the term. It is doubtful, however, that Peter, who sent troops to Denmark, to the Danube (even if he failed to reach it), and to the southern coast of the Caspian, did not have a clear concept of the definite geographical space I call the Heartland (after Mackinder). Should we refrain from using the term *geopolitics* in eighteenth-century history because it was not coined until 1918?

8. After the Revolution it became again a combined elite. See Odom, *The Collapse of the Soviet Military*, 218–22.

9. Frederick I of Prussia spoke of the tsar's "vast and ambitious designs" as early as 1713. LeDonne, *Russian Empire*, 231; Czartoryski, *Mémoires*, 1:368. For a discussion of Peter's Testament, see H. Ragsdale, "Russian Projects of Conquest in the Eighteenth Century," in *Imperial Russian Foreign Policy*, 75–102.

10. The term is Alastair Johnston's describing China's policy of "victory by means of awesomeness." Johnston, *Cultural Realism*, 81. I will make much of this concept. Awesomeness was achieved by maximizing military power and enhancing the majesty of the Court in order to create in the visitor a perception of invincibility and overwhelming power. This was particularly effective among the nomads (who sent representatives to the capital), but the reputation of Petersburg as the city built in a marsh by the indomitable will of a powerful ruler (who cultivated his own personal awesomeness) and as a military and naval headquarters was no less effective with the Swedes, Poles, and Prussians. The maximization of power reduced the need to resort to force. Deep strategic penetrations also enhanced Russia's reputation as an invincible military power capable of striking terror at enormous distances from the Muscovite core. See chap. 6.

11. Riasanovsky, *The Image of Peter the Great*, 45, 64.

12. Czartoryski, *Mémoires*, 1:369; *AKAK*, 5:983.

13. Got'e, *Time of Troubles*, 45.

14. Lukowski, *Partitions of Poland*, 67. The myth of Russian defensiveness and backwardness was largely the work of historians reflecting on the post-emancipation (1861) period, which witnessed a growing gap between the Russian and Western economies and Russia's relative loss of power vis-à-vis a rising Germany and Japan. The perception of an expanding and determined Russia was very much in evidence in the eighteenth century among the continental powers and in Britain after 1815: see especially J. Gleason, *The Genesis of Russophobia in Great Britain* (New York, 1972), 42–44, 50–56. The British perceived a Russian determination to "conquer the world."

15. Ostrowski, *Muscovy and the Mongols*, 52, 97, 165–66, 176–77.

16. Doyle, *Empires*, 19.

17. For a theory seeking to explain the energy behind imperial expansion, see Parker, *The Geopolitics of Domination*, 64–75.


## 1. The Geopolitical Background

1. By Heartland, I mean (following Mackinder) the territory bounded in the west by the Norwegian Alps and the Elbe River; in the south, by the Dinaric Alps, the Taurus and Zagros Mountains; in the east, by the Hindu Kush, the Saian, and Iablonoi Mountains. It is flanked by two coastlands, one in western Europe, the other in Asia. LeDonne, *Russian Empire*, 1–6.

2. Ordyn, *Pokorenie Finlandii*, 1:18–27.

3. Brunhes and Vallaux, *Géographie de l'histoire*, 539–41; Christiansen, *Northern Crusades*, 11.

4. Ancel, *Géographie des frontières*, 55.

5. Christiansen, *Northern Crusades*, 38.

6. Martonne, *Europe centrale*, 623–24.

7. Berg, *Régions naturelles*, 33, 76. The term *Polish Empire* is seldom used, and regrettably so. It is assumed that there was no Polish Empire because Poland was a republic and a "commonwealth." A republic is a form of internal political organization, an empire a form of "international" organization. There is no connection between the two terms. Russia and Turkey were autocracies and had empires; so had the British constitutional monarchy and the French republic. An empire results from the imposition by a given ethnicity of its rule over other ethnicities: Poland systematically polonized the Lithuanians, Bielorussians, and the Ukrainians. I do not see why they did not create an empire in the process. Its eastern marches refer to Lithuania, Bielorussia, and the Right-Bank Ukraine.

8. Ordyn, *Pokorenie Finlandii*, 1:28–44; Christiansen, 177–82.

9. Scott, *Sweden*, 118–24, 141–45.

10. Ordyn, *Pokorenie Finlandii*, 1:51–52; see Roberts, *Swedish Imperial Experience*, 10–13, 33.

11. Boockmann, *Der Deutsche Orden*, 12, 178–79.

12. Kirby, *Northern Europe*, 174–75.

13. Beauvois, *Histoire de la Pologne*, 51–55, 90–96.

14. Sobieski, *Kampf um die Ostsee*, 132–45.

15. Wójcik, "Separatist Tendencies," 58–59.

16. Scott, *Sweden*, 207–20; Beauvois, *Histoire de la Pologne*, 107–36; *Istoriia vneshnei politiki Rossii*, 299–311.

17. Martonne, *Europe centrale*, 621.

18. Beauvois, *Histoire de la Pologne*, 109–18, 124–28.

19. Lord, *Second Partition*, 17–20.

20. Solov'ev, *Istoriia Rossii*, 7:550–51; Schulze Wessel, *Russlands Blick*, 33–37; Kaminski, *Republic vs Autocracy*, 256–75.

21. Heckscher, *Economic History of Sweden*, 127–28; Nordmann, *Grandeur et liberté de la Suède*, 77–80; Roberts, *Swedish Imperial Experience*, 110–15,

22. Astrom, "The Role of Finland," 135–36.

23. Nordmann, *Grandeur et liberté de la Suède*, 147–49.

24. Berg, *Régions naturelles*, 76–78, 83, 98, 123, 220. For a general introduction, see Shaw, "Southern Frontiers," 117–42.

25. Camena d'Almeida, *Etats*, 93.

26. An excellent introduction to the military geography of Transcaucasia is Allen and Muratoff, *Caucasian Battlefields*, 3–9.

27. Kinross, *Ottoman Centuries*, 123–38, 173–205, 217–36, 243–55; Jelavich, *History of the Balkans*, 1:30–36.

28. The image of the moat comes from General Douglas McArthur's 1951 speech before Congress, in which he likened the Pacific Ocean to a moat beyond which the United States established a new strategic frontier after World War II, quoted in Collins, *Grand Strategy*, 141.

29. Fischer, *Crimean Tatars*, 1–16, 24–25, 42–47.

30. Hrushevsky, *History of Ukraine*, 152–64, 221–32; Subtelny, *Ukraine*, 105–18; Longworth, *Cossacks*, 11–46. See also "Kazaki," in *Entsiklopedicheskii slovar'*, ed. F. Brokgaus and J. Efron (Petersburg), 12 (1894), 275–79; 15 (1895), 583–86, 590–91; 24 (1898), 345; and Vernadsky, *History of Russia*, 1:8–12; and, more recently, Plokhii, *Cossacks and Religion*, 16–32, 35–44.

31. Zagorovskii, *Belgorodskaia cherta*, 85–113; Shaw, "Southern Frontiers," 126–31.

32. Zasedateleva, *Terskie kazaki*, 185–96; Barrett, *At the Edge*, 13–23.

33. Subtelny, *Ukraine*, 123–37; Vernadsky, *History of Russia*, 1:432–81.

34. Lattimore, *Studies in Frontier History*, 117.

35. Kerner, *Urge to the Sea*, 64–66; Shaw, "Southern Frontiers," 129–31.

36. Solov'ev, *Istoriia Rossii*, 7:391–94, 403–10; Stevens, *Soldiers on the Steppe*, 111–21.

37. Solov'ev, *Istoriia Rossii*, 7:528–35, 538–40.

38. Donnelly, *Russian Conquest*, 6–8; Eversmann, "Estestvennaia Istoriia Orenburgskogo Kraia," in *Orenburgskie Stepi*, 219–64; *Ural'i Priural'e*, 29–43; *Kirgizskii krai*, 1–44.

39. Mackinder, *Democratic Ideals*, 93.

40. *Kirgizskii krai*, 1–44, 72–73.

41. Berg, *Régions naturelles*, 33, 76, 98, 121–22, 297, 302, 311–12; Camena d'Almeida, *Etats de la Baltique*, 268, 272–75.

42. Bakhrushin, *Nauchnye trudy*, 3:111–13, 129–36; Kerner, *Urge to the Sea*, 172–75.

43. Vernadsky, *History of Russia*, 1:292–306; "Kratkaia khronologiia," 204–7; Lantzeff and Pierce, *Eastward to Empire*, 141–54.

44. Donnelly, *Russian Conquest*, 8–17, 30.

45. *Mezhdunarodnye otnosheniia*, 1:31–117, 321–32; Shatina, "Altyn-khany," 383–95.

46. Barfield, *Perilous Frontier*, 278–79.

47. Olcott, *Kazakhs*, xx, 3–9.

48. Wakeman, *Fall of Imperial China*, 75–86; Chen, *Sino-Russian Relations*, 20–21.

49. Pokrovsky, *Chinese-Russian Relations*, 13–14, 123; Barfield, *Perilous Frontier*, 279–82; Blanchard, *Russia's "Age of Silver,"* 65; Chen, *Sino-Russian Relations*, 44–45, 64–75; Cahen, *Histoire des relations de la Russie avec la Chine*, 25, 137.

50. Cahen, *Histoire des relations de la Russie avec la Chine*, 41–44; Barfield, *Perilous Frontier*, 282–83; Pavlovsky, *Chinese-Russian Relations*, 14–18; Chen, *Sino-Russian Relations*, 90–93.

51. Bergholz, *Partition of the Steppe*, 243–77.

52. Donnelly, *Russian Conquest*, 19–26.

53. Ordin-Nashchokin's activities are the object of Y. Kurskov's Ph.D. dissertation, "Sotsial 'no-ekonomicheskie vzgliady i gosudarstvennaia deiatel'nost A. L. Ordina-Naschokina," Leningrad, 1962. See especially 69, 125–25, 307, 336, 340, 456, 470, 494. I thank Jarmo Kotilaine for loaning me his copy. See also Y. Kurskov, *Vedushchee napravlenie obshchestvennoi mysli i proekty gosudarstvennykh preobrazovanii Rossii 40–60kh godov XVII veka* (Chita, 1973), which is largely a summary of the dissertation.

## 2. Mobile Armies

1. Clausewitz, *Campaign of 1812*, 253.

2. Beskrovny, *Russkaia armii i flot*, 1:183–235; Hatton, *Charles XII*, 148–58, 161–67, 192–93, 200–216, 231–52, 261–312, 423–27; Kersnovskii, *Istoriia russkoi armii*, 1:22–41, 45–46. On Poltava, the most recent work is Konstam, *Poltava, 1709*. On the aborted operation across the sound, see Haxlund, "When the Tsar Changed His Mind," 5–17.

3. See "Zhurnal o voennykh operatsiiakh" for a very detailed description of the march; see also Manstein, *Contemporary Memoirs*, 67–84.

4. Beskrovny, *Russkaia armiia*, 1:218–22; Kersnovskii, *Istoriia russkoi armii*, 1:47–48; Duffy, *Russia's Military Way*, 27; Hatton, *Charles XII*, 331–36; Myshlaevskii, "Rossiia," 1–6, 38–52.

5. Brandenburg, "Kubanskii pokhod," 29–42.

6. For various views on this issue, see Beskrovny, *Russkaia armiia*, 1:242–43; Kiniapina, *Kavkaz i Sredniaia Aziia*, 17–18; Solov'ev, *Istoriia Rossii*, 9:391–403; Hekmat, *Essai sur l'histoire*, 141–66.

7. The only book-size study of the war is Lystsov, *Persidskii pokhod*; see also Beskrovny, *Russkaia armiia*, 1:239–43 and Kersnovskii, *Istoriia russkoi armii*, 1:47–48.

8. Beskrovny, *Russkaia armiia*, 1:244–58; Kersnovskii, *Istoriia russkoi armii*, 1:76–82; Solov'ev, *Istoriia Rossii*, 10: 400–404, 407–15, 421–30, 450–56; Manstein, *Contemporary Memoirs*, 90–131, 136–96, 198–246; Kostomarov, "Fel'dmarshal Minikh," 528–51. The logistical problems are discussed in "Turetskaia voina." See also Duffy, *Russia's Military Way*, 49–53. Official documents include Münnich's own reports in *SVIM* 2:10–11, and the "protocols" of the Cabinet ("Bumagi Kabineta ministrov") in *SIRIO*, vols. 114, 117, 120, 124, and 126. They focus on the conduct of the war, not its planning.

9. The Russians reached Jassy (Iasi) in August 1739 while peace was being negotiated in Belgrade. The gains were too small to compensate for the 100,000 casualties of the war.

10. Blanchard, *Russia's "Age of Silver,"* 70–71.

11. Kasymbaev, "Ekspeditsiia." See also Barfield, *Perilous Frontier*, 287–88, 290; Perdue, "Military Mobilization," 758–59; and *Mezhdunarodnye otnosheniia*, 1:231–32, 239–40.

12. Solov'ev, *Istoriia Rossii*, 9:349–50.

13. The fullest treatment of the expedition is Golosov, "Pokhod."

14. Beskrovny, *Russkaia armiia*, 1:39–42. In order to stick to the essentials in this broad synthesis of Russia's grand strategy, I included in the strategic force only the infantry and cavalry regiments and left out the artillery and the navy. Except for the expedition of 1768–70 to the Greek archipelago, the Russian navy did not play any strategic role; its role was almost ex-

clusively tactical, carrying out amphibious operations in the Baltic and Black Seas in support of ground forces.

15. This deployment of troops is based on Kirilov, *Tsvetushchee sostoianie*, first published in 1733 and reprinted in 1977. Its statistics were those available in 1724–26: 7, 18, 20. The location of regiments is on 368–84. Unfortunately, it is not always possible to distinguish between regular and garrison regiments. I have identified seventy-three regiments, a figure close to the seventy-five in existence in 1725.

16. Bogoslovskii, *Oblastnaia reforma*, 360–64, 376–78; Miliukov, *Gosudarstvennoe khoziaistvo*, 1:295–303, 2:517–18; Anisimov, *Podatnaia reforma*, 232–46.

17. Solov'ev, *Istoriia Rossii*, 11:58. See also Parker, *Historical Geography*, 112–20.

18. Johnston, *Cultural Realism*, 81.

19. Auerbach, *Besiedelung der Südukraine*, 12–14; *Entsiklopedicheskii slovar'*, 17:324–25.

20. *Entsiklopedicheskii slovar'*, 37:804.

21. Donnelly, *Russian Conquest*, 21, 56, 147–48, 161–62, and maps.

22. For a complete list of fortresses and outpost dated August 1744, see "Kratkaia khronologiia," 217–18.

23. Esper, "Odnodvortsy."

24. *PSZ*, vol. 43 (*shtaty po voennoi chasti*), 1736, no. 6925.

25. *Entsiklopedicheskii slovar'*, 12:157.

26. "Report gosudaryne," 97, annex.

27. See 85–87.

28. *PSZ*, 11:1743, no. 8798.

29. Rousset, *Recueil historique*, 18:64–83.

30. Hurewitz, *Middle East*, 1:71–74.

31. Solov'ev, *Istoriia Rossii*, 11:197–99; Lang, *Last Years*, 142–43.

32. Fuhrmann, *Origins*, 91–98, 184–92, 262–63; Kotilaine, "In Defense of the Realm," 29.

33. Strumilin, *Ocherki ekonomicheskoi*, 323. Beskrovny, *Russkaia armiia*, 1:94, gives slightly different figures: 1.9 million *pudi* for 1740, 1.4 million of them from the Urals. On the Urals industry, see Portal's classic *L'Oural au XVIII siècle*. For an original discussion of the relationship between serfdom and military power, see Fuller, *Strategy and Power*, 83–84.

34. Beskrovny, *Russkaia armiia*, 1:75, 86–87.

35. Ibid., 1:74–85, 88–90, 93–98. Graf's early study is still useful.

36. Ibid., 1:98–104.

37. Fleury de Saint-Charles, "Un attaché," 270, quoting the Marquis de Montalembert, French military attaché to the Russian headquarters in Poland in 1759–60. Montalembert of course did not use the terms *heartland* and *coastland* and refers only to German and Polish roads.

38. This section is based on Istomina, *Vodnye puti*, 98–167.

39. See, for example, Fox, *History in Geographic Perspective*, 14–15, which develops the concept of "another France" based on this distinction between commerce and trade. See also Wallerstein, *Modern World System*, 318–24, and Pipes, *Russia*, 5–13.

40. Fuller, *Strategy and Power*, 84.

41. Schulze Wessel, *Russlands Blick*, 47–49; Mediger, *Moskaus Weg*, 598–604.

42. Lodyzhenskii, *Istoriia russkogo tamozhennogo tarifa*, 47–52, 55–64; Semenov, *Izuchenie istoricheskikh*, 1:70–73, 134–38.

43. *SIRIO*, 15: 245–46.

44. Lodyzhenskii, *Istoriia russkogo tamozhennogo tarifa*, 78–79 and Semenov, *Izuchenie istoricheskikh*, 1:134–38.

## 3. Client States and Societies

1. The term appears in Braund, *Rome and the Friendly Kingdom*. He does not distinguish between a friendly kingdom and a client state. As the subsequent discussion shows, one can be made in the Russian case.

2. Solov'ev, *Istoriia Rossii*, 10:341, 628–29, 636–37; Lerer, *Politique française en Pologne*, 39–41, 62–64. For a discussion of the networks, see LeDonne, "Ruling Families in the Russian Political Order, 1689–1825."

3. *SIRIO*, 40:xxviii, 189; Solov'ev, *Istoriia Rossii*, 9:433–35, 10:610–13. On the Hats and Caps, see Kirby, *Northern Europe*, 347; and Nordmann, *Grandeur et liberté de la Suède*, 252–53.

4. Solov'ev, *Istoriia Rossii*, 11:180–81.

5. Kirby, *Northern Europe*, 328.

6. LeDonne, *Russian Empire*, 27–28, 31.

7. Koch, *History of Prussia*, 68.

8. Solov'ev, *Istoriia Rossii*, 9:16.

9. Schulze Wessel, *Russlands Blick*, 46.

10. Ibid., 53–55.

11. Solov'ev, *Istoriia Rossii*, 10:38–40.

12. See 23.

13. Nordmann, *Grandeur et liberté de la Suède*, 147–49; Lukowski, *Partitions of Poland*, 128; Kirby, *Northern Europe*, 299; Hatton, *Charles XII*, 105–107.

14. Kirby, *Northern Europe*, 222, 224.

15. Eckhardt, "Livländische Landtag," 138; and see "Zur livländischen," 249.

16. *PSZ*, 7:1725, no. 4782; 8:1728, no. 5332.

17. *PSZ*, 11:1742, no. 8574; Kirby, *Northern Europe*, 357–58.

18. "Zur livländischen," 283–86; Eckhardt, "Livländische Landtag," 140–43; Kappeler, *Russland Als Vielvölkerreich*, 68–69.

19. *PSZ*, 1:1669, no. 447. For the agreement of 1654, see Plokhii, *The Cossacks and Religion*, 58–61, 318–28.

20. *Entsiklopedicheskii slovar'*, 15:590–91; Kohut, *Russian Centralism and Ukrainian Autonomy*, 33–35, 37–38, 91–92.

21. *Zapiski of slobodskikh polkakh*, 32–47; *Entsiklopedicheskii slovar'*, 15:591. Duffy, *Russia's Military Way*, 159, traces the formation of the Chuguev Cossack regiment to the 1730s, but the article in *Entsiklopedicheskii slovar'* (38:958) dates it 1749.

22. *Entsiklopedicheskii slovar'*, 12:277–79; Strumilin, *Ocherki ekonomicheskoi*, 538–40.

23. Lang, *Last Years*, 115, 117, 119–20, 141–41; Solov'ev, *Istoriia Rossii*, 9:390–91; Khakhanov, "Iz istorii," 111–12.

24. *RBS*, 22:177–83.

25. LeDonne, "Frontier Governors General," 169–83.

26. *RBS*, 8:468–73; Amburger, *Geschichte der Behördenorganisation Russlands*, 514, 516; Meurs, "Dimitrie Cantemir as Strategist," 35.

27. On this, see Bergholz, *Partition of the Steppe*

28. See, for example, Sergei Aksakov's "Semeinaia Khronika," in *Sobranie sochinenii*, 5 vols. (Moscow, 1966), 1:57–260, here 57–69.

29. The text of the recommendations is in *PSZ*, 9:1734, no. 6571.

30. Karatanaev, "Istoricheskii ocherk," 42–44, 50–55.

31. Donnelly, *Russian Conquest*, 165; "Orenburgskoe kazach'e voisko," 99–100.

32. Vitevskii, "Iaitskoe voisko," 284, 288, 293–95, 299–304.

33. Khodarkovsky, *Where Two Worlds Met*, 2, 26–28, 32, 55–56.

34. *PSZ*, 4:1710, no. 2298, art. 11.

35. This section is based on Khodarkovskii, *Where Two Worlds Met*, 140–206; and "Kalmyki," *Entsiklopedicheskii slovar'*, 27:58–60. See also *Ocherki istorii Kalmytskoi ASSR*, 143–51, 158–95.

36. Olcott, *Kazakhs*, 10–15, 31–34, 39–40; Kasymbaev, *Gosudarstvennye deiateli*, 15–26, 68–70, 142–43, 172–74; Erofeeva, *Khan Abulkhair*, 210–32.


*4. Deep Strikes*

1. Duffy, *Russia's Military Way*, 48.

2. Beskrovny, *Russkaia armiia*, 1:260–64; Ordyn, *Pokorenie Finlandii*, 1:76–94.

3. Zavalishin, "O russkoi Shvedskoi voine 1741–1743gg," 71.

4. Ibid., 72.

5. "Repnin, V.," *RBS*, 16:85–89.

6. Frederick II's instruction of 1747 appears in Phillips, *Roots of Strategy*, 1:317.

7. *SIRIO*, 148: 458–62; on the Seven Years' War, see Maslovskii, *Russkaia armiia*.

8. Duffy, *Russia's Military Way*, 101; Pekarskii, "Pokhod russkikh v Prussiiu," 311–22. The "protocols" of the Conference for March 1756–March 1757 were published in *SIRIO*, vol. 136. Unfortunately their publication stopped with this volume. They allude to the "systematic plan" confirmed by the empress but did not include it. They made clear, however, that from the very beginning military operations aimed at Pomerania and Brandenburg (or Silesia) to bring about the "desired curtailment" of Prussia: 163, 309–26, 555. The Conference consisted of the chancellor (foreign minister), a former deputy chancellor, the procurator general, a field marshal, an admiral in charge of the navy department, the chief of the artillery, and the chief of the secret police.

9. Beskrovny, *Russkaia armiia*, 1:275–81; Duffy, *Russia's Military Way*, 81–91. Duffy gives somewhat smaller figures.

10. Beskrovny, *Russkaia armiia*, 1:275–81; Duffy, *Russia's Military Way*, 104–12.

11. Fleury de Saint-Charles, "Un attaché," 277–80.

12. Duffy, *Russia's Military Way*, 111.

13. Beskrovny, *Russkaia armiia*, 1:281–84; Duffy, *Russia's Military Way*, 112–16; Fleury de Saint-Charles, "Un attaché," 293–300; Menning, "Deep Strike," 13–14.

14. Beskrovny, *Russkaia armiia*, 1: 284–87; Duffy, *Russia's Military Way*, 116–18.

15. The standard work on this "first" Russo-Turkish war is Petrov, *Voina Rossii*. See also Rumiantsev, *Dokumenty*, vol. 2; Solov'ev, *Istoriia Rossii*; 14:357–69; and Kersnovskii, *Istoriia russkoi armii*, 1:125–37. For a discussion of the war's aims, see *Arkhiv Gosudarstvennogo Sovieta*, 1:1–18, 43, 142–43.

16. Solov'ev, *Istoriia Rossii*, 14:293.

17. Rumiantsev, *Dokumenty*, 2:174–75, 189–91.

18. Linda, "Pokhod russkikh voisk," 8–28.

19. Rumiantsev, *Dokumenty*, 2:117–18, 143–46, 150–53, 157–59, 172, 254–56, 316–19.

20. Beskrovny, *Russkaia armiia*, 1:488–93; Maslovskii, *Zapiski*, 2:241–59; "Reskripty . . . Seniavinu," 1368–82.

21. Solov'ev, *Istoriia Rossii*, 14:444–51; Rumiantsev, *Dokumenty*, 2:428–30, 443–44, 451–55, 473–76, 515–16, 541–43.

22. Beskrovny, *Russkaia armiia*, 1:495–507; Solov'ev, *Istoriia Rossii*, 10:10–21, 23–27; Maslovskii, *Zapiski*, 2:259–302; Petrov, *Voina Rossii*, 16–21; Rumiantsev, *Dokumenty*, 2:684–89, 697–700, 736–42, 762–63.

23. Kortua, *Russko-gruzinskie vzaimootnosheniia*, 160–69, 172–81, 191–82; Lang, *Last Years*, 207–8.

24. Beskrovny, *Russkaia armiia*, 1:521–22.

25. Petrov, *Vtoraia Turetskaia voina*; Maslovskii, *Zapiski*, 2:302–436; Beskrovny, *Russkaia armiia*, 1:520–70; Arkhiv Gosudarstvennogo Sovieta, 1:499–503.

26. Nordmann, *Grandeur et liberté de la Suède*, 374, 381–84.

27. Tolstoi, "Verel'skii mirnyi dogovor," 463; Beskrovny, *Russkaia armiia*, 1:579.

28. Beskrovny, *Russkaia armiia*, 1:524–82; Ordyn, *Pokorenie Finlandii*, 1:131–35, 439–49.

29. Roginskii, *Shvetsiia*, 41; Ordyn, *Pokorenie Finlandii*, 1:151–58; Brikner, "Konfederatsiia v An'iala v 1788 godu."

30. Ordyn, *Pokorenie Finlandii*, 1:76–77.

31. Ordyn, "Vyborgskaia pobeda," 84–113.

32. *SIRIO*, 51:9–11.

33. Magocsi, *Historical Atlas*, 70–72.

34. Lukowski, *Liberty's Folly*, 257–59; "Suvorov, A.," *RBS*, 20:49–56; Drake, "O srazhenii."

35. Sobieski, *Kampf um die Ostsee*, 202.

36. "Pis'mo grafa F. V. Rostopchina," 292–93.

37. "Suvorov, A.," *RBS*, 20:1–89, here 32.

38. "Iakobi. Nachertanie," 90–96, 99.

39. "Zubov, V.," in *RBS*, 7: 514–22, here 517–220; Dubrovin, "Pokhod."

40. LeDonne, *Russian Empire*, 145, 148.

41. "Iakobi. Nachertanie," 53–63, 80–84, 98; Lobanov-Rostovsky, *Russia and Asia*, 256.

## 5. Peripheral Deployment

1. The 1763 table is in *Stoletie voennogo ministerstva*, 4, annex, 35–41; see also Beskrovny, *Russkaia armiia*, 1:311, 317, 326. It is difficult to obtain accurate figures for the number of regiments at any given time, especially for the early 1760s; tables of organization are often incomplete. See also *PSZ*, vol. 44, part 1, 1763, no. 11735 and 1764, no. 12135.

2. *PSZ*, 16:1764, no. 12185.

3. *Entsiklopedicheskii slovar'*, 15:591.

4. *PSZ*, 13:1751, no. 9919 and 9921; Auerbach, *Besiedelung der Südukraine*, 14–16.

5. In 1762, Catherine was receptive to the advice of Münnich, who wanted another war with the Ottomans to expel them from Europe. See Hösch, "Das sogenannte," 181. On the influence of Grigorii Orlov and the Greek Grigorii Papaz-Ogli, see Sorel, *Question d'Orient*, 11–12.

6. *Entsiklopedicheskii slovar'*, 15:586–88; "Orenburgskoe kazach'e voisko," 100, gives a total of 5,887 Orenburg Cossacks for 1755, and Vitevskii, "Iaitskoe voisko," 425, refers to 6,124 Ural Cossacks for 1725.

7. Perdue, "Military Mobilization," 774–81; Barfield, *Perilous Frontier*, 292–94; Bergholz, *Parkition*, 382–404.

8. Karatanaev, "Istoricheskii ocherk," 55.

9. Beskrovny, *Russkaia armiia*, 1:311–15, 317–20; see also *PSZ*, 17:1764, no. 12494, vol. 19, no. 13649 and 1775, no. 14257.

10. Beskrovny, *Russkaia armiia*, 1:309.

11. *Ekaterina II i G. A. Potemkin*, 190–191.

12. RGVIA, f. Voenno-Uchenyi Arkhiv, d. 234, 1, 2–40b: deployment of 1781.

13. LeDonne, "Territorial Reform," 147–85.

14. RGVIA, f. 12, d. 48, 1, 6–14, here 10: deployment of June 1795.

15. Beskrovny, *Russkaia armiia*, 1:315–16, 321.

16. PSZ, vol. 43, part 1, 1796, no. 17606.

17. Bil'basov, "Prisoedinenie Kurliandii," 3, 9, 44–45.

18. Bardach, "Le Principe fédéraliste," 76.


6. *Economy, Culture, Client Societies*

1. Strumilin, *Ocherki ekonomicheskoi*, 323.

2. Beskrovny, *Russkaia armiia*, 1:86–87, 344–50.

3. Ibid., 103, 364–67.

4. Ibid., 375–80.

5. LeDonne, *Absolutism and Ruling Class*, 247–48, 280–81.

6. I borrow these terms from Ch'i, *Key Economic Areas*, 139, and Lattimore, *Studies in Frontier History*, 498.

7. Istomina, *Vodnye puti*, 58–62, 154–58, 160–62.

8. Ibid., 196–97, 208–209.

9. This section is based on Lodyzhenskii, *Istoriia russkogo tamozhennogo tarifa*, 86–97, 106, 113–18, 136–41, 152–58, and Semenov, *Izuchenie istoricheskikh*, 1:168–70, 2:22–33.

10. Chechulin, *Ocherki po istorii russkikh finansov*, 222.

11. Wortman, *Scenarios of Power*, 2:6.

12. See Lutwak's discussion of power and force in the appendix to *Grand Strategy of the Roman Empire*, 195–200.

13. Berelowitch and Medvedkova, *Histoire de Saint Petersburg*, 38–40.

14. Fuller, *Strategy and Power*, 84.

15. On Prokopovich, see J. Cracraft, "Feofan Prokopovich," in Garrard, *Eighteenth Century*, 75–105. See also Czartoryski, *Mémoires*, 1:335, 341.

16. Segel, *Literature of Eighteenth-Century Russia*, 1:166, 168, 174–77.

17. Johnston, *Cultural Realism*, 81.

18. Segel, *Literature of Eighteenth-Century Russia*, 182–92.

19. Czartoryski, *Mémoires*, 1:368–73.

20. Wortman, *Scenarios of Power*, 1:93.

21. Rogger, *National Consciousness*, 208–10; Black, *G.-F. Müller*, 115–20.

22. Brumfield, *History of Russian Architecture*, 232–49.

23. LeDonne, "Frontier Governors General," 173–74.

24. O. Medvedeva, "Bolgarskie zemli," in *Aleksandr I, Napoleon, i Balkany*, 107–16, here 113.

25. Zorin, "Krym v istorii russkogo samosoznaiia," 126, 134.

26. Cracraft, *Petrine Revolution*, 190.

27. Brumfield, *History of Russian Architecture*, 290.

28. Wortman, *Scenarios of Power*, 2:135, 170–171.

29. Lukowski, *Partitions of Poland*, 37–38.

30. Rogger, *National Consciousness*, 50, 53.

31. Solov'ev, *Istoriia Rossii*, 11:432.

32. Lukowski, *Partitions of Poland*, 187.

33. Solov'ev, *Istoriia Rossii*, 11:276–83; *Arkhiv kn. Vorontsova*, 2:71–93; "Mnenie russkikh," 140–63.

34. Stribrny, *Russlandpolitik*, 17–20, and Solov'ev, *Istoriia Rossii*, 14:168.

35. Trachevskii, *Soiuz kniazei*, 78.

36. Martens, *Recueil des traités et conventions*, 6: 134, 136.

37. Lukowski, *Partitions of Poland*, 143–45.

38. Bil'basov, "Prisoedinenie Kurliandii," 44–45.

39. Grot, "Sprengtporten'," 6–32, and Brikner, "Konfederatsiia v An'iala v 1788 godu," 750–68.

40. The process is traced in Kohut, *Russian Centralism and Ukrainian Autonomy*, 213, 216–22.

41. Lang, *Last Years*, 178–79, 181–83, 207–208; Kortua, *Russko-gruzinskie vzaimootnosheniia*, 136–40, 142–52, 172–81, 298–99; Kiniapina, *Kavkaz i Sredniaia Aziia*, 64–67, 75–77.

42. On the inner and outer periphery of the Heartland in the east, see LeDonne, *Russian Empire*, 3.

43. Vitevskii, "Iaitskoe voisko," 203–41, here 227.

44. Kasymbaev, *Gosudarstvennye deiateli*, 150–51, 179.

45. Khodarkovsky, *Where Two Worlds Met*, 231–35, and *Ocherki istorii Kalmytskoi ASSR*, 212–25.

46. Kasymbaev, *Gosudarstvennye deiateli*, 38, 46–48, 158–62, 181–90, and Olcott, *Kazakhs*, 34–44.

## 7. Strategic Penetration

1. Beskrovny, *Russkaia armiia*, 1:603–21.

2. Ibid., 1:621–31; Duffy, *Russia's Military Way*, 212–15, 217–22, 226–31.

3. Duffy, *Russia's Military Way*, 209–12; Piechowiak, "Anglo-Russian Expedition."

4. Menning, "Deep Strike," 16–17.

5. Beskrovny, *Russkaia armiia*, 2:24–37; *Vneshniaia politika Rossii* 2 (1961), 388–92; Chandler, *Campaigns of Napoleon*, 402–39; M. I. *Kutuzov—Sbornik dokumentov*, 2:1–354.

6. For this war, see Beskrovny, *Russkoe voennoe iskusstvo 19 veka*, 78–89; Ordyn, *Pokorenie Finlandii*, 1:375–402, 404–36; and Hubé, "Rossiia."

7. Apushkin, "Alandskaia ekspeditsiia," 24–26.

8. Josselson, *The Commander*, 55–58.

9. V-n, "Zimniaia ekspeditsiia," 23–26, 271–77.

10. Beskrovny, *Russkoe voennoe iskusstvo 19 veka*, 22.

11. Ibid., 55–57. The best source for this war is Lanzheron's account, "Voina s Turtsiei," rich in details on the operations and the jealousies among the imperial generals as well as information on the political situation in the Danubian principalities. For scholarly studies, see Dubrovin, "Kniaz' P. I. Bagration" and "Graf N. M. Kamenskii 2–1."

12. Josselson, *The Commander*, 92. For the War of 1812, see Tarle, *1812 god*, and Riehn, *1812*; see also Beskrovny, *Russkoe voennoe iskusstvo 19 veka*, 95–124; Josselson, *The Commander*, 90–157; Fuller, *Strategy and Power*, 177–218; and Chandler, *Campaigns of Napoleon*, 739–861. Last but not least, Clausewitz, *Campaign of 1812*. An immense number of documents pertaining to military preparations in 1810 and 1811 was published in *La Guerre nationale*. They tell us nothing about decision making, but a great deal about the views of some of the most important members of the high command. See, for example, Levin von Bennigsen's 1811 plan of offensive war against Napoleon (2:131–44); and Barclay's (1810?) plan of defensive war (vol. 1, part 1: 15–21), followed by his extensive position paper of 1811 calling for a defensive war and a strategic retreat accompanied by a scorched earth policy, which would defeat Napoleon's advantage of concentration and speed (4:17–107). Incidentally, Barclay dismissed Prussia vis-à-vis Russia—this "Oriental colossus of empire." Prussia as a state "had existed until now only in the spirit of Frederick the Great, its military reputation and its treasury," but its "insufficiently cemented parts" had just lost their reputation and treasure (4:33, 43).

One of the gems of the collection is a memorandum by a "retired captain" Krohne (otherwise unidentified), which came close to a definition of a grand strategy in the purely military sense: Russia by its geographical location constitutes a "base of strategic operations against the whole of Europe." As a result, it must be able to plan for war against England, the Turks, the Persians, the Swedes, Austria, and France. War against Sweden must aim at the heart of the kingdom; against the Turks, at reaching the Danube, the empire's "natural boundary," before striking at Constantinople; against France, at reaching the Rhine. A war against Prussia must aim at the capture of Berlin. See 2:299–325, here 300, 308, 310–11, 319, and 323.

Kutuzov's papers covering the operations of 1812 and early 1813 are in *M. I. Kutuzov. Sbornik dokumentov*, vol. 4–5.

13. For the 1813 campaign see Bogdanovich, *Istoriia voiny*; Chandler, *Campaigns*, 865–941 and Beskrovny, *Russkoe*, 127–44; Josselson, *The Commander*, 167–68 and Gallaher, "Political Considerations," 65–68.

14. Chandler, *Campaigns of Napoleon*, 945–1004, Beskrovny, *Russkoe voennoe iskusstvo 19 veka*, 148–57.

15. LeDonne, *Russian Empire*, 252–53.

16. Allen and Muratov, *Caucasian Battlefields*, 6–9.

17. Beskrovny, *Russkoe voennoe iskusstvo 19 veka*, 8–20; Bogdanovich, *Isoriia tsarstvovaniia*, 5:220–27, 237–39, 248–53.

18. Beskrovny, *Russkoe voennoe iskusstvo 19 veka*, 166–72; Shcherbatov, *General'-fel'd-marshal Kniaz' Paskievich*, 3:1–50. Curtiss, *Russian Army*, 21–45. Paulucci's memorandum is in *AKAK*, 5:983–91, here 987.

19. Jelavich, *Balkan Entanglements*, 245–48; Bogdanovich, *Istoriia tsarstvovaniia*, 6:20–36.

20. The text is in Bogdanovich, *Isoriia tsarstvovaniia*, 6:36–42.

21. Beskrovny, *Russkoe voennoe iskusstvo 19 veka*, 179–97. The classic history of the war is Moltke, *The Russians in Bulgaria and Rumelia*. See also Virtemberg, "Turetskii pokhod," and "Imperator Nikolai Pavlovich." For a very negative assessment, see Kagan, *Military Reforms*, 85–110.

22. Beskrovny, *Russkoe voennoe iskusstvo 19 veka*, 195–97.

23. Allen and Muratov, *Caucasian Battlefields*, 23–33, 43–45; Shcherbatov, *General'-fel'd-marshal Kniaz' Paskievich*, 3:100–232. See also Curtiss, *Russian Army*, 21–45.

24. Noradounghian, *Recueil d'actes internationaux*, 2:166–73, 232–35.

25. Curtiss, *Russian Army*, 75–95; "Dibich, I.," in *RBS*, 6:351–70, here 363–68; and Shcherbatov, *General'-fel'd-marshal Kniaz' Paskievich*, 4:1–208. For the memoirs of a participant, see Neelov, "Vospominaniia."

## 8. Dispersion of the Strategic Force

1. Beskrovny, *Russkaia armiia*, 2:17–21.

2. PSZ, 26:1801, no. 19951.

3. LeDonne, *Russian Empire*, 113–15.

4. Beskrovny, *Russkaia armiia*, 2:18, 21.

5. Wortman, *Scenarios of Power*, 1:208, 228.

6. PSZ, 29:1806, no. 22161 and 22174; 31:1810, no. 24389; Beskrovny, *Russkaia armiia*, 2:13–14.

7. PSZ, 31:1810, no. 24386.

8. Jones, *Art of War*, 342.

9 *PSZ*, 32:1812, no. 24975.

10. There are countless references to these troop movements in Nikolai Mikhailovich (Romanov), *Les Relations diplomatiques*, vols. 5–7.

11. Josselson, *The Commander*, 129–30, 133.

12. Ibid., 169; *PSZ*, 32:1813, no. 25357.

13. Bogdanovich, *Istoriia voiny*, 1:658–89.

14. *PSZ*, 32:1814, no. 25723; 5:1830, no. 3768; 10:1835, no. 8355.

15. *PSZ*, 33:1815, no. 26021 and 26022.

16. Beskrovny, *Russkaia armiia*, 2:19, 22; Curtiss, *Russian Army*, 107–108.

17. Lanzheron, "Russkaia armiia," 174.

18. Berelowitch and Medvedkova, *Histoire de Saint Petersburg*, 261–67.

19. *PSZ*, 31:1811, no. 24615 and 24704.

20. *PSZ*, 4:1829, no. 3199; E. Komarovskii, "Memuary," in *Derzhavnyi Sfinks*, 11–156, here 134.

21. *PSZ*, 34:1817, no. 26650 and 26784. On the Third Section, see Monas, *Third Section*; and Squire, *Third Department*.

22. *PSZ*, 33:1815, no. 25929; 1:1827, no. 1062; 11:1836, no. 9355.

23. Beskrovny, *Russkaia armiia*, 2: 36–38; Bogdanovich, *Istoriia tsarstvovaniia*, 5: 301–302, 343–67; and Pipes, "Russian Military Colonies."

24. Composition de l'armée russe, 1819. Ministère des Affaires étrangères, Archives diplomatiques, Paris. Vol. 27: Russie 1819–1827. Forces et colonies militaries, fol. 1–37.

25. Glinoetskii, "Russkii general'nyi shtab," 11:5–43, here 34–35.

26. *PSZ*, 34:1817, no. 27066.

27. *Kolachkovskii*, "Pol'sha," 409–38, here 409–10.

28. Beer, *Die Orientalische Politik*, 380.

29. Short biographies of the corps commanders (with portraits) are in *Rossiiskii Arkhiv* 7 (1996): 288–645.

30. Magocsi, *Historical Atlas*, 78–80.

31. Bogdanovich, *Istoriia tsarstvovaniia*, 5, annex, 41–42.

32. Veniukov, "Obshchii obzor," 211.

9. *Fortress Empire*

1. Beskrovny, *Russkaia armiia*, 2:284; Florinsky, *Russia*, 789. On Kankrin's pessimism, see Pintner, *Russian Economic Policy*, 19–26. See also Raeff, "Russia's Autocracy and Paradoxes of Modernization," in *Political Ideas*, 121.

2. Beskrovny, *Russkaia armiia*, 2:270. Thomas Owen gives lower figures: *The Corporation*, 2.

3. Gille, *Histoire économique et sociale de la Russie*, 145–46; Florinsky, *Russia*, 713; Parker, *Historical Geography*, 170.

4. Terras, *History of Russian Literature*, 147.

5. Beskrovny, *Russkaia armiia*, 2:277–84; Graf, "Oruzheinye zavody," 122–23.

6. Beskrovny, *Russkaia armiia*, 2:462–64.

7. Kabuzan, *Izmeneniia*, 107–15, 143–51.

8. LeDonne, *Absolutism and Ruling Class*, 279–83.

9. Beskrovny, *Russkaia armiia*, 2:482–83; Bogdanovich, *Istoriia tsarstvovaniia*, 5, annex, 16–17.

10. This section is based on Grochulska, "Conjoncture du Blocus continental," 127–28; Florinsky, *Russia*, 709–12, 789–91; Gille, *Histoire économique et sociale de la Russie*, 131–32,

154–57; Lodyzhenskii, *Istoriia russkogo tamozhennogo tarifa*, 159–64, 166–78, 185–96, 207; Bogdanovich, *Istoriia tsarstvovaniia*, 5:148–52, 6:200–203; and Parker, *Historical Geography*, 177–92.

11. LeDonne, *Russian Empire*, 61–70; Zlobin, "Diplomaticheskie otnosheniia," 73; Nikolai Mikhailovich, *Relations diplomatiques*, 4:93.

12. Martens, *Recueil des traités et conventions*, 6:362; Shil'der, "Rossiia," 45–46, 270.

13. Schulze Wessel, *Russlands Blick*, 103–4; Martens, *Recueil des traités et conventions*, 7:96–100; *SIRIO*, 119:530–31, 759–61. In 1811, the French ambassador to Petersburg had reported that "here, one considers Prussia to be a very weak state and one treats it as such": Nikolai Mikhailovich, *Relations diplomatiques*, 6:134; Czartoryski, *Mémoires*, 1:337.

14. *Vneshniaia politika Rossii*, 1:375–76; Martens, *Recueil des traités et conventions*, 3:19 and vol. 4, part 1, 149–50; Nikolai Mikhailovich, *Relations diplomatiques*, 6:265.

15. Bogdanovich, *Istoriia tsarstvovaniia*, 5:88–92, and Bogdanovich, "Smotr," 239.

16. The reader may detect a contradiction between this presentation and my description of the containment of Russia by the Germanic powers in *Russian Empire*, 147–54. The contradiction is more apparent than real: the Russians *expected* Prussia to behave like a client and Austria to remain friendly, while the two powers, despite their inferiority vis-à-vis the Russians and their mutual discord, were determined to resist Russian expansion.

17. See the account in "Persidskoe posol'stvo."

18. Nordmann, *Grandeur et liberté de la Suède*, 357–58; Ordyn, *Pokorenie Finlandii*, 2:295; Konttinen, "Central Bureaucracy," 208–9; Amburger, *Geschichte*, 514.

19. Amburger, *Geschichte*, 425–26; Goriainov, "K istorii," 178–80.

20. *Rossisskii Arkhiv* 7 (1996): 302–304, 351, 373, 392–93, 448, 463, 507–508, 603, 636–37.

21. This is discussed in Vernadsky, *Charte constitutionnelle*.

22. Kirby, *Baltic World*, 280.

23. Zhukovich, "Zapadnaia Rossiia," 212–13.

24. Khizniak, *Kievo-Mogilianskaia Akademiia*, 95–99.

25. Florinsky, *Russia*, 491.

26. Amburger, *Geschichte*, 465–67.

27. *PSZ*, vol. 27, no. 20598; 35:1818, no. 27542.

28. Wortman, *Scenarios of Power*, 1:173, 256.

29. On the formula, see Whittaker, *Origins of Modern Russian Education*, 4, 52, 94–96, 102.

30. Flynn, *University Reform*, 110–11, 115–19.

31. Wortman, *Scenarios of Power*, 1:261.

32. Ibid., 170, 181, 226, 308, 316–17.

33. Brumfield, *History of Russian Architecture*, 347.

34. Ibid., 348–51.

35. A. Pushkin, *Sobranie sochinenii*, 10 vols. (Moscow, 1974–78), here 10:31.

36. Martens, *Recueil des traités et conventions*, 11:265–66.

37. Petrovich, *Emergence of Russian Panslavism*, 45.

38. See, for example, Ivan Kireevskii, "On the Nature of European Culture," in Raeff, *Russian Intellectual History*, 174–207; Thaden, *Conservative Nationalism*, 32–35.

39. Wortman, *Scenarios of Power*, 1:309, 417.


*Conclusion*

1. For the distinction between inner and outer periphery, see LeDonne, *Russian Empire*, 3.

2. A poem by Adam Mickiewicz, "The Road to Russia," captures well this perception of mobility:

Who travels on these roads? Here swiftly ride
Snow-powdered troops of Russian cavalry,
And there are seen dark ranks of infantry,
With wagons, guns, kibitkas at their side.
By edict of the czar this regiment
Comes from the east to fight a northern foe;
That from the north to Caucasus is sent:
Whither they march, or why, they do not know—
And no one asks.
(Quoted in Lednicki, *Russia, Poland, and the West*, 51)

3. Czartoryski, *Mémoires*, 1: 75.
4. Heckscher, *Economic History of Sweden*, 15–16.
5. Ibid., 19.
6. Florinsky, *Russia*, 388–89.
7. Ibid., 488. On the 1839 currency reform see Pintner, *Russian Economic Policy*, 127–31, 190–214.
8. Florinsky, *History*, 787–90.
9. Curtiss, *Russian Army*, 314, 333, 342, 344, 352, 359. For the diplomatic background of the war, see Goldfrank, *Origins of the Crimean War*.
10. Fuller, *Strategy and Power*, 443.
11. Menning, *Bayonets Before Bullets*, 152–99.
12. Fuller, *Strategy and Power*, 462.
13. For a map of deployment, see Menning, *Bayonets Before Bullets*, 224–25.
14. Fuller, *Strategy and Power*, 462.
15. Gille, *Histoire économique et sociale de la Russie*, 165–68, 209–10; Menning, *Bayonets Before Bullets*, 217, 219.

# Bibliography

*AKAK* [*Akty sobrannye Kavkazskoiu Arkheograficheskoiu Kommissieiu*], 12 vol. Tiflis, 1866–1904.

*Aleksandr I, Napoleon, i Balkany*. Ed. V. Vinogradov. Moscow, 1997.

Allen, W., and R. Muratoff. *Caucasian Battlefields: A History of the Wars in the Turco-Caucasian Border, 1828–1921*. Cambridge, 1953.

Amburger, E. *Geschichte der Behördenorganisation Russlands von Peter dem Grossn bis 1917*. Leiden, 1966.

Ancel, J. *Géographie des frontières*. Paris, 1938.

Anisimov, E. *Podatnaia reforma Petra I*. Leningrad, 1982.

Apushkin, V. "Alandskaia ekspeditsiia 1808 goda." *Voennyi Sbornik*, 1908, 5:19–42, 6:27–52.

*Arkhiv Gosudarstvennogo Soveta*. Vol. 1 (1768–96gg.). Petersburg, 1869.

*Arkhiv Kniazia Vorontsova*, 40 vols. Moscow, 1870–95.

Auerbach, H. *Die Besiedelung der Südukraine in den Jahren 1774–1787*. Wiesbaden, 1965.

Bakhrushin, S. *Nauchnye trudy*. Vols. 3–4. Moscow, 1955–59.

Bardach, J. "Le Principe féderaliste et le principe unitaire de la législation de la Diète Polono-Lithuanienne de quatre ans (1788–1792)." *Acta Poloniae Historica* 70 (1994): 75–86.

Barfield, T. *The Perilous Frontier: Nomadic Empires and China*. Oxford, 1989.

Barrett, T. *At the Edge of Empire: The Terek Cossacks and the North Caucasus Frontier, 1700–1860*. Boulder, 1999.

Beauvois, D. *Histoire de la Pologne*. Paris, 1995.

Beer, A. *Die Orientalische Politik Oesterreichs seit 1774*. Leipzig, 1883.

Bellamy, C. "Heirs of Genghis Khan: The Influence of Tartar-Mongols on the Imperial Russian and Soviet Armies." *RUSI* 128 (1983): 52–60.

Berelowitch, W., and O. Medvedkova. *Histoire de Saint Petersburg*. Paris, 1996.

Berg, L. *Les régions naturelles de l'URSS*. Paris, 1941.

Bergholz, F. *The Partition of the Steppe*. New York, 1993.

Beskrovny, L. *Ocherk po istochnikovedeniiu voennoi istorii Rossii*. Moscow, 1957.

——. *Ruskaia armiia i flot v XVII veke*. Moscow, 1958. Cited as *Russkaia armiia*, 1.

——. *Russkaia armiia I flot v XIX veke*. Moscow, 1973. Cited as *Russkaia armiia*, 2.

——. *Russkoe voennoe iskusstvo 19 veka*. Moscow, 1974.

Bil'basov, A. "Prisoedinenie Kurliandii." *Russkaia Starina*, 1895, 1:3–55.

Black, J. *G.-F. Müller and the Imperial Russian Academy.* Montreal, 1987.

Blackwell, W. *The Beginnings of Russian Industrialization, 1800–1860.* Princeton, 1968.

Blanchard, I. *Russia's "Age of Silver."* London, 1989.

Bogdanovich, M. *Istoriia tsarstvovaniia imperatora Aleksandra I i Rossii v ego vremia.* 6 vols., Petersburg, 1869–71.

———. *Istoriia voiny 1813 goda za nezavisimost' Germanii.* 2 vols. Petersburg, 1863.

———. "Smotr pri Vertiu." *Voennyi Sbornik,* 1865, 8:231–44.

Bogoslovskii, M. *Oblastnaia reforma Petra Velikogo.* Moscow, 1902.

Boockmann, H. *Der Deutsche Orden.* 4th ed. Munich, 1994.

Brandenburg, N. "Kubanskii pokhod 1711 goda." *Voennyi Sbornik,* 1867, 3:29–42.

Braund, D. *Rome and the Friendly King: The Character of the Client Kingship.* New York, 1984.

Brikner, A. "Konfederatsiia v An'iala v 1788 godu. Materialy dlia istorii prisoedineniia Finliandii k Rossii." *Zhurnal Ministerstva Narodnogo Prosveshcheniia* (March 1868): 679–771.

Brumfield, W. *A History of Russian Architecture.* New York, 1993.

Brunhes, J., and C. Vallaux. *La Géographie de l'histoire.* Paris, 1921.

Cahen, G. *Historie des relations de la Russie avec la Chine sous Pierre le Grand.* Paris, 1912.

Camena d'Almeida, P. *Etats de la Baltique. Russie.* Paris, 1932.

Castex, R. *Strategic Theories,* ed. E. Kiesling. Annapolis, 1994.

Chandler, D. *The Campaigns of Napoleon.* New York, 1966.

Chechulin, N. *Ocherki po istorii russkikh finansov v tsarstvovanie Ekateriny II.* Petersburg, 1906.

Chen, V. *Sino-Russian Relations in the Seventeenth Century.* The Hague, 1966.

Ch'i, Ch'ao-ting. *Key Economic Areas in Chinese History.* London, 1906.

Christiansen, E. *The Northern Crusades. The Baltic and Catholic Frontier, 1100–1525.* London, 1980.

*Chteniia v imperatorskom obshchestve istorii I drevnostei Rossiiskikh pri Moskovskom Universitete.* 264 vols. Moscow, 1846–1918.

Clausewitz, C. *The Campaign of 1812 in Russia.* New York, 1995.

Collins, J. *Grand Strategy: Principles and Practices.* Annapolis, 1973.

Cracraft, J. *The Petrine Revolution in Russian Architecture.* Chicago, 1988.

Curtiss, J. *The Russian Army under Nicholas I, 1825–1855.* Durham, 1965.

Czartoryskii, A. *Mémoires du prince Adam Czartoryski.* 2 vols. Paris, 1887.

*Derzhavnyi Sfinks.* Moscow, 1999.

Donnelly, A. *The Russian Conquest of Bashkiria, 1552–1740.* New Haven, 1968.

Doyle, M. *Empires.* Ithaca, 1986.

Drake, L. "O srazhenii pri m. Matsiovitse 29 Sentiabria 1794 goda." *Voennyi Sbornik,* 1910, 10:1–40.

Dubrovin, N. "Graf N. M. Kamenskii 2–1. Turetskaia voina 1806–1812gg." *Voennyi Sbornik,* 1865, no. 5–8.

———. "Kniaz' P. I. Bagration. Turetskaia voina 1806–1812gg." *Voennyi Sbornik,* 1864, no. 11–12, 1865, no. 1–2.

———. "Pokhod grafa V.A. Zubova v Persiiu v 1796 godu." *Voennyi Sbornik,* 1874, 2:187–231; 3:5–32; 4:191–207; 5:5–33; 6:177–99.

Duffy, C. *Russia's Military Way to the West: Origins and Nature of Russian Military Power.* London, 1981.

Dyson, S. *The Creation of the Roman Frontier.* Princeton, 1985.

Eckhardt, J. "Der Livländische Landtag in seiner historischen Entwicklung." *Baltische Monatsschrift* 3 (1861): 38–78, 116–59.

*Ekaterina II i G.A. Potemkin. Lichnaia perepiska, 1769–1791.* Ed. V. Lopatin. Moscow, 1997.

Eliseeva, O. *Geopoliticheskie proekty G. A. Potemkina.* Moscow, 2000.

*Entsiklopedicheskii slovar'.* 82 vols. Petersburg, 1890–1904.

Erofeeva, I. *Khan Abulkhair: Polkovodets, pravitel' i politik.* Almaty, 1999.

Esper, T. "The Odnodvortsy and the Russian Nobility." *Slavonic and East European Review* 45 (1967): 124–34.

Fischer, A. *The Crimean Tatars.* Stanford, 1978.

Fleury de Saint-Charles. "Un attaché militaire francais à l'armée rusee (1759–60)." *Revue d'histoire diplomatique* 2 (1903): 261–301.

Florinsky, M. *Russia: A History and An Interpretation.* New York, 1953.

Flynn, J. *The University Reform of Tsar Alexander I, 1802–1835.* Washington, D.C., 1988.

Fox, E. *History in Geographic Perspective: The Other France.* New York, 1971.

Fuhrmann, J. *The Origins of Capitalism in Russia.* Chicago, 1972.

Fuller, W. *Strategy and Power in Russia, 1600–1914.* New York, 1992.

Gallaher, J. "Political Considerations and Strategy: The Dresden Phase of the Leipzig Campaign." *Military Affairs* 49 (1955): 65–68.

Garrard, J., ed. *The Eighteenth Century in Russia.* Oxford, 1973.

Gille, B. *Histoire économique et sociale de la Russie du moyen âge au vingtième siècle.* Paris, 1949.

Glinoetskii, N. "Russkii general'nyi shtab v tsarstvovanie imperatritsy Ekateriny II." *Voennyi Sbornik,* 1872, 1:5–64, 2:157–94; 1874, 10:187–250, 11:5–43, 12:189–272.

Goldfrank, D. *The Origins of the Crimean War.* New York, 1994.

Golosov, D. "Pokhod v Khivu v 1717 godu." *Voennyi Sbornik,* 1861, 10:303–64.

Got'e, I. *Time of Troubles: The Diary of Iurii Vladimirovich Got'e.* Ed. and trans. T. Emmons. Princeton, 1988.

Graf, F. "Oruzheinye zavody v Rossii." *Voennyi Sbornik* (1861): 9: 113-26, 10: 365–94.

Grochulska, B. "La Conjoncture du Blocus continental en Europe Centrale." *Acta Poloniae Historica* 21 (1970): 123–39.

Grot, I. "Sprengtporten', Shvedskii emigrant pri Ekaterine II." *Zhurnal Ministerstva Narodnogo Prosveshcheniia,* Jan.–Feb. 1885, 1–34; May–June 1885, 1–33.

*La Guerre nationale de 1812.* 6 vols. Paris, 1904–10.

Hatton, R. *Charles XII of Sweden.* London, 1968.

Haxlund, I. "When the Tsar Changed His Mind: A Momentous Incident in the Northern War." *Scando-Slavica* 49 (1997): 5–17.

Heckscher, E. *An Economic History of Sweden.* Cambridge, 1954.

Hekmat, M. *Essai sur l'histoire des relations politiques irano-ottomanes de 1722 à 1747.* Paris, 1937.

Hösch, E. "Das sogenannte 'griechische Project' Katharinas II." *Jahrbücher für Geschichte Osteuropas* 12 (1964): 168–206.

Hrushevsky, M. *A History of Ukraine.* New Haven, 1941.

Hubé, P. "Rossiia i Shvetsiia pered voinoi 1808–1809gg." *Voennyi sbornik,* 1908, no. 2–12; 1909, no. 1–12.

Hurewitz, J., ed. *The Middle East and North Africa in World Politics: A Documentary Record.* 2d ed. 2 vols. New Haven, 1975–79.

"Iakobi. Nachertanie k dvoistvennomu umnozheniiu polz s rasshireniem predelov ot storony Kitaia." *Chteniia,* 1858, 4:43–100.

"Imperator Nikolai Pavlovich i gr. Dibich-Zabalkanskii. Perepiska 1828–1830gg." *Russkaia Starina,* 1900, 1:95–110, 511–26, 765–80; 2:409–28; 3:891–934.

Istomina, E. *Vodnye puti Rossii vo vtoroi polivine XVIII–nachale XIX veka.* Moscow, 1982.

*Istoriia vneshnei politiki Rossii. Konets XV–XVIII vek.* Moscow, 1999.

Jelavich, B. *Balkan Entanglements, 1806–1914.* Cambridge, 1991.

——. *History of the Balkans.* 2 vols. Cambridge, 1983.

Johnston, A. *Cultural Realism, Strategic Culture, and Grand Strategy in Chinese History.* Princeton, 1995.

Jones, A. *The Art of War in the Western World.* Chicago, 1987.

Josselson, M. *The Commander: A Life of Barclay de Tolly.* New York, 1980.

Kabuzan, V. *Izmeneniia v razmeshchenii naseleniia Rossii v 18–pervoi polovine 19v.* Moscow, 1971.

Kagan, F. *The Military Reforms of Nicholas I.* London 1999.

Kaminski, A. *Republic vs Autocracy: Poland-Lithuania and Russia 1686–1697.* Cambridge, 1993.

Kappeler, A. *Russland Als Vielvölkerreich. Entstehung. Geschichte. Zerfall.* 2d ed. Munich, 1993.

Karatanaev, I. "Istoricheskii ocherk sluzhby Sibirskogo kazachego voiska." *Voennyi Sbornick,* 1903, 7:42–60; 8:46–60.

Kasymbaev, Z. *Gosudarstvennye deiateli kazakhskikh khanstv (XVIIIv.)* Almaty, 1999.

——. "Ekspeditsiia Bukhgol'tsa." *Istoricheskie nauki,* Alma Ata, 1 (1974), 33–39.

Keep, J. *Soldiers of the Tsar: Army and Society in Russia, 1462–1874.* Oxford, 1985.

Kennedy, P., ed. *Grand Strategies in War and Peace.* New Haven, 1991.

Kerner, R. *The Urge to the Sea.* Berkeley, 1942.

Kersnovskii, A. *Istoriia russkoi armii.* 4 vols. Moscow, 1992–94.

Khakhanov, A. "Iz istoriia snoshenii Gruzii s Rossiei v XVIIIv. Tsar Vakhtang VI i imperator Petr Velikii." *Zhurnal Ministerstva Narodnogo Prosveshcheniia,* May–June 1899, 102–12.

Khizniak, Z. *Kievo-Mogilianskaia Akademiia.* Kiev, 1988.

Khodarkovskii, M. *Where Two Worlds Met: The Russian State and the Kalmyk Nomads, 1600–1771.* Ithaca, 1992.

Kiniapina, N., et al. *Kavkaz i Sredniaia Aziia v vneshnei politike Rossii. Vtoraia polovina 18v–80-ie gody 19v.* Moscow, 1984.

Kinross, Lord. *The Ottoman Centuries.* New York, 1977.

Kirby, D. *The Baltic World, 1772–1793: Europe's Northern Periphery in an Age of Change.* London, 1995.

——. *Northern Europe in the Early Modern Period: The Baltic World, 1492–1772.* London, 1990.

*Kirgizskii krai. Rossiia. Polnoe geograficheskoe opisanie nashego otechestva,* vol. 18. Petersburg, 1913.

Kirilov, I. *Tvetushchee sostoianie vserossiiskogo gosudarstva.* Moscow, 1977.

Koch, H. *A History of Prussia.* New York, 1987.

Kohut, Z. *Russian Centralism and Ukrainian Autonomy, Imperial Absorption of the Hetmanate, 1760s–1830s.* Cambridge, 1988.

Kolachkovskii, K. "Pol'sha v 1814–31gg. (Iz vospominanii generala Klimentiia Kolachkovskogo)." *Russkaia Starina,* 1902, 1:623–40; 2:409–38, 553–74.

Komarovskii, E. "Zapiski," in *Derzhavnyi Sfinks,* 11–156.

Konstam, A. *Poltava, 1709: Russia Comes of Age.* London, 1994.

Konttinen, E. "Central Bureaucracy and the Restoration of Education in Early Nineteenth-Century Finland." *Scandinavian Journal of History* 21 (1996): 201–20.

Kortua, N. *Russko-gruzinskie vzaimootnosheniia vo vtoroi polovine XVIII veka.* Tbilisi, 1989.

Kostomarov, N. "Fel'dmarshal Minikn i ego znachenie v russkoi istorii." *Vestnik Evropy,* 1884, 4:510–64; 5:5–57.

Kotilaine, J. "In Defense of the Realm: Russian Arms Trade and Production in the Seventeenth and Early Eighteenth Century." Unpublished paper, Harvard University, 2000.

————. "Opening a Window on Europe: Foreign Trade and Military Conquest in Russia's Western Border in the Seventeenth Century." *Jahrbücher für Geschichte Osteuropas* 46 (1998): 494–530.

"Kratkaia khronologiia voennykh deistvii v Sibirii." *Voennyi Sbornik*, 1910, 9:203–18.

Lang, D. *The Last Years of the Georgian Monarchy, 1658–1832.* New York, 1957.

Lantzeff, G., and R. Pierce. *Eastward to Empire: Exploration and Conquest on the Russian Open Frontier to 1750.* Montreal, 1973.

Lanzheron, A. "Russkaia armiia v god smerti Ekateriny II." *Russkaia Starina*, 1895, 1:147–66 (March), 145–77 (April), 185–202 (May).

————. "Voina s Turtsiei 1806–1812gg." *Russkaia Starina*, 1907, no. 2–4; 1908, no. 1–4; 1909, no. 2–3; 1910, no. 3–4; 1911, no. 3.

Lattimore, O. *Studies in Frontier History.* Paris, 1962.

Lednicki, W. *Russia, Poland, and the West.* New York, 1954.

LeDonne, J. *Absolutism and Ruling Class: The Formation of the Russian Political Order, 1700–1825.* New York, 1991.

————. "Frontier Governors General, 1772–1825." *Jahrbücher für Geschichte Osteuropas* 47 (1999): 56–88; 48 (2000): 161–83, 321–40.

————. *The Russian Empire and the World, 1700–1917. The Geopolitics of Expansion and Containment.* New York, 1997.

————. The Territorial Reform of the Russian Empire, 1775–1796." *Cahiers du monde russe et soviétique* 23 (1982): 147–85, 24 (1983): 411–57.

————. "Ruling Families in the Russian Political Order, 1689–1825." *Cahiers du monde russe et soviétique* 28 (1987): 233–322.

Lerer, D. *La Politque française en Pologne sous Louis XV (1733–1772).* Toulouse, n.d.

Liddell Hart, B. *Strategy.* 2d ed. New York, 1991.

Linda, P. "Pokhod russkikh voisk v Gruziu v 1769–1771 godakh." *Voennyi Sbornik*, 1901, 9:8–28; 10:45–68; 12:60–77.

Lobanov-Rostovsky, A. *Russia and Asia.* Ann Arbor, 1951.

Lodyzhenskii, K. *Istoriia russkogo tamozhennogo tarifa.* Petersburg, 1886.

Longworth, P. *The Cossacks.* London, 1971.

Lord, R. *The Second Partition of Poland.* Cambridge, 1915.

Lukowski, J. *Liberty's Folly: The Polish-Lithuanian Commonwealth in the Eighteenth Century, 1697–1795.* London, 1991.

————. *The Partitions of Poland: 1772, 1793, 1795.* London, 1999.

Luttwak, E. *The Grand Strategy of the Roman Empire From the First Century* A.D. *to the Third.* Baltimore, 1976.

————. *The Grand Strategy of the Soviet Union.* New York, 1983.

Lystsov, V. *Persidskii pokhod Petra I, 1722–1723.* Moscow, 1951.

Mackinder, H. *Democratic Ideals and Reality.* New York, 1919.

Magocsi, P. *Historical Atlas of East Central Europe.* Seattle, 1993.

Manstein, C. *Contemporary Memoirs of Russia from the Year 1727 to 1744.* London, 1968.

Martens, F. *Recueil des traités et conventions conclus par la Russie avec les puissances étrangères.* 15 vols. Petersburg, 1874–1909.

Martonne, E. *Europe centrale.* 2 vols. Paris, 1930–31.

Maslovskii, D. *Russkaia armiia v Semiletniuiu voinu.* 3 vols. Moscow, 1886–91.

————. *Zapiski po istorii voennogo iskusstva v Rossii.* 2 vols. Petersburg, 1891 94.

Mediger, W. *Moskaus Weg nach Europa. Der Aufstieg Russlands zur europäischen Machtaat im Zeitalter Friedrches des Grossen.* Braunscheweig, 1952.

Menning, B. *Bayonets Before Bullets: The Imperial Russian Army, 1861–1914.* Bloomington, 1992.

——. "The Deep Strike in Russian and Soviet Military History." *Journal of Soviet Military Studies* 1 (1988): 9–28.

——. "Russian Military Innovation in the Second Half of the Eighteenth Century." *War and Society*, 2 (1984), 23–41.

Meurs, W., van. "Dmitrie Cantemir as Strategist." In *Biography and Romanian Studies*, ed. K. Treptow. Oxford, 1998.

*Mezhdunarodnye otnosheniia v Tsentral'noi Azii. XVII–XVIIIvv.* 2 vols. Moscow, 1989.

*M. I. Kutuzov—Sbornik dokumentov.* 5 vols. Moscow, 1950–1956.

Miliukov, P. *Gosudarstvennoe khoziaistvo Rossii v 1. Chetverti 18 stoletiia i reforma Petra Velikogo.* 2d ed. Petersburg, 1905.

"Mnenie russkikh gosudarstvennykh muzhei ob otnoshenii Rossii k Prussi pri imperatritse Elizavete." *Chteniia*, 1863, 1:115–64.

Moltke, H. von. *The Russians in Bulgaria and Rumelia in 1828 and 1829.* London, 1854.

Monas, S. *The Third Section: Police and Society in Russia Under Nicholas I.* Cambridge, 1961.

Myshlaevskii, A. "Rossiia i Turtsiia pered Prutskim pokhodom." *Voennyi Sbornik*, 1901, 1:1–35; 2:1–52.

Neelov, N. "Vospominaniia o Pol'skoi voine 1831 goda." *Voennyi Sbornik*, 1878, no. 2–11.

Nikolai Mikhailovich (Romanov), ed. *Les Relations diplomatiques de la Russie et de la France d'après les rapports des ambassadeurs d'Alexandre et de Napoléon 1808–1812.* 7 vols. Petersburg, 1905.

Noradounghian, G., ed. *Recueil d'actes internationaux de l'empire Ottoman.* 4 vols. Paris, 1897–1903.

Nordmann, C. *Grandeur et liberté de la Suède (1660–1792).* Paris, 1971.

*Ocherki istorii Kalmytskoi ASSR. Dooktiabr'skii period.* Moscow, 1967.

*Ocherki istorii SSSR. Period feodalizma, Rossiia vo vtoroi chetverti XVIIIv.* Moscow, 1957.

Odom, W. *The Collapse of the Soviet Military.* New Haven, 1998.

Olcott, M. *The Kazakhs.* Stanford, 1987.

Ordyn, K. *Pokorenie Finlandii.* 2 vols. Petersburg, 1889.

——. "Vyborgskaia pobeda i Rochensal'mskii pogrom." *Zhurnal Ministerstva Narodnogo Prosveshcheniia*, Jan.–Feb.1888, 84–113.

"Orenburgskoe kazach'e voisko." *Voennyi Sbornik* 3 (1874): 99–116.

Ostrowski, D. *Muscovy and the Mongols: Cross-Cultural Influences in the Steppe Frontier, 1304–1589.* Cambridge, 1998.

Owen, T. *The Corporation under Russian Law, 1800–1917.* New York, 1991.

Parker, G. *The Geopolitics of Domination.* London, 1988.

Parker, W. *An Historical Geography of Russia.* London, 1968.

Pekarskii, P. "Pokhod russkikh v Prussiiu pod nachalstvom fel'dmarshala Apraksina v 1757 godu." *Voennyi Sbornik*, 1858, 6:289–350.

Perdue, P. "Military Mobilization in Seventeenth and Eighteenth Century China, Russia, and Mongolia." *Modern Asian Studies* 30 (1996): 757–93.

"Persidskoe posol'stvo v Rossii 1828 goda." *Russkii Arkhiv*, 1889, 1:209–60.

Petrov, A. *Voina Rossii s Turtsiei i Pol'skimi konfederatami 1769–1774 god.* Petersburg, 1866.

——. *Vtoraia Turetskaia voina v tsarstvovanie imp. Ekateriny II, 1787–1791.* 2 vols. Petersburg, 1880.

Petrovich, M. *The Emergence of Russian Panslavism, 1856–1870.* New York, 1956.

Phillips, T., ed. *Roots of Strategy.* 3 vols. Harrisburg, 1985–91.

Piechowiak, A. "The Anglo-Russian Expedition to Holland in 1799." *Slavonic and East European Review* 41 (1962–63): 182–95.

Pintner, W. *Russian Economic Policy under Nicholas I.* Ithaca, 1967.

Pipes, R. *Russia under the Old Regime.* New York, 1974.

———. "The Russian Military Colonies, 1810–1831." *Journal of Modern History* 22 (1950): 205–19.

"Pis'mo grafa F.V. Rostopchina o sostoianii Rossii v kontse Ekaterininskogo tsarstvovaniia." *Russkii Arkhiv*, 1878, 1:292–98.

Plokhii, S. *The Cossacks and Religion in Early Modern Ukraine.* New York, 2001.

Pokrovsky, M. *Chinese-Russian Relations.* New York, 1949.

*Polnoe Sobranie Zakonov Rossiiskoi Imperii, 1649–1913 (PSZ).* 234 vols. 1830–1916.

Portal, R. *L'Oural au XVIII siècle.* Paris, 1950.

Raeff, M. *Political Ideas and Institutions in Imperial Russia.* Boulder, 1994.

———. *Russian Intellectual History: An Anthology.* New York, 1966.

Ragsdale, H., ed. *Imperial Russian Foreign Policy.* Cambridge, 1993.

"Report gosudaryne imperatritse grafa Minikha o chisle voisk v nachale 1732 goda." *Chteniia*, 1867, 3:97–98.

"Reskripty i ukazy imp. Ekateriny II-i k A.N. Seniavinu." *Russkii Arkhiv*, 1871, 1351–1408.

Riasanovsky, N. *The Image of Peter the Great in Russian History and Thought.* New York, 1985.

Riehn, R. *1812: Napoleon's Russian Campaign.* New York, 1991.

Roberts, M. *The Swedish Imperial Experience, 1560–1718.* Cambridge, 1979.

Rogger, H. *National Consciousness in Eighteenth-Century Russia.* Cambridge, 1960.

Roginskii, V. *Shvetsiia i Rossiia. Soiuz 1812 goda.* Moscow, 1978.

Rossiiskii Gosudarstvennyi Voenno-Istoricheskii Arkhiv (RGVIA). Moscow.

Rousset, J. *Recueil historique d'actes, négociations, mémoires et traitéz.* 21 vols. The Hague, 1728–1755.

Rumiantsev, P. *Dokumenty.* Ed. P. Fortunatov. 2 vols. Moscow, 1953.

*Russkii biograficheskkii slovar' (RBS).* 25 vols. Petersburg, 1896–1918.

*Sbornik Imperatorskogo Russkogo Istoricheskogo Obshchestva (SIRIO).* 148 vols. Petersburg, 1867–1916.

Schulze Wessel, M. *Russlands Blick auf Preussen.* Stuttgart, 1995.

Scott, F. *Sweden: The Nation's History.* Minneapolis, 1977.

Segel, H. *The Literature of Eighteenth-Century Russia: An Anthology.* 2 vols. New York, 1967.

Semenov, A. *Izuchenie istoricheskikh svedenii o Rossisskoi vneshnei torgovle i promyshlennosti s poloviny XVII—go stoletiia po 1858 goda.* Petersburg, 1859.

Shatina, N. "Altyn-khany Zapadnoi Mongolii v XVIIv." *Sovetskoe vostokovedenie* 6 (1949): 383–95.

Shaw, D. "Southern Frontiers of Muscovy, 1550–1700." In *Studies in Russian Historical Geography*, ed. J. Bater and R. French. 2 vols. 1: 117–42. London, 1990.

Shcherbatov, A. *General'-fel'd-marshal Kniaz' Paskievich. Ego zhizn' i deiatel'nost'.* 7 vols. Petersburg, 1888–1904.

Shil'der, N. "Rossiia v eia otnosheniiakh k Evrope 1806–1815gg." *Russkaia Starina*, 1888, 1: 269–379; 1809, 1: 1–52.

Sobieski, W. *Der Kampf um die Ostsee von den ältesten Zeiten bis zur Gegenwart.* Leipzig, 1933.

Solov'ev, S. *Istoriia Rossii s drevneishikh vremen.* 15 vols. Moscow, 1959–66.

Sorel, A. *La Question d'Orient au XVIII siècle. Le partage de la Pologne et le Traité de Kainardj.* 3d ed. Paris, 1902.

Squire, P. *The Third Department, the Establishment and Practices of the Political Police in the Russia of Nicholas I.* Cambridge, 1968.

Stevens, C. *Soldiers on the Steppe.* DeKalb, 1995.

*Stoletie voennogo ministerstva.* Ed. D. Skalon. 13 vols. Petersburg, 1902–14.

Stribrny, W. *Die Russlandpolitik Friedrichs des Grossen, 1764–1786.* Würzburg, 1966.

Strumilin, S. *Ocherki ekonomicheskoi istorii Rossii SSSR.* Moscow, 1966.

Subtelny, O. *Ukraine: A History.* Toronto, 1994.

*SVIM. Sbornik voenno-istoricheskikh materialov.* 14 vols. Petersburg, 1892–1904.

Tarle, E. *1812 god.* Moscow, 1961.

———. *Ekspeditsiia russkogo flota v Arkhipelag v 1769–1774gg.* Moscow, 1945.

———. *Severnaia voina I Shvedskoe nashestvie na Rossiiu.* Moscow, 1958.

———. *Borodino.* Moscow, 1962.

Terras, V. *A History of Russian Literature.* New Haven, 1991.

Thaden, E. *Conservative Nationalism in Nineteenth-Century Russia.* Seattle, 1964.

Tolstoi, D. "Verel'skii mirnyi dogovor s Shvetsieiu 3-go Avgusta 1790 goda (po dokumentam iz arkhiva grafa Igel'stroma)." *Russkii Arkhiv,* 1887, 3:427–520.

Trachevskii, A. *Soiuz kniazei i nemetskaia politika Ekateriny II, Fridrikha II, Iosifa II, 1780–1790gg.* Petersburg, 1877.

"Turetskaia voina pri imperatritse Anne." *Russkii Arkhiv,* 1878, 1:255–74.

*Ural' i Priural'e. Rossiia. Polnoe geograficheskve opisanie nashego otechestva.* Vol. 5. Petersburg, 1914.

VanCreveld, M. *Supplying War: Logistics from Wallenstein to Patton.* Cambridge, 1977.

Veniukov, M. "Obshchii obzor postepennogo rasshireniia russkikh predelov v Azii i sposobov oborony ikh." *Voennyi Sbornik,* 1872, 1:195–228.

Vernadsky, G. *La Charte constitutionnelle de l'Empire russe de l'an 1820.* Paris, 1933.

———. *A History of Russia: The Tsardom of Muscovy, 1547–1682.* 2 vols. New Haven, 1969.

Virtemberg (Württemberg). "Turetskii pokhod 1828 goda. Zapiski Printsa Virtenberga." *Russkaia Starina,* 1880, 1:79–94, 527–44, 781–800; 2:429–48; 3:43–56.

Vitevskii, V. "Iaitskoe voisko do priiavleniia Pugacheva." *Russkii Arkhiv,* 1879, 1:273–304, 401–93; 2:377–428; 3:203–41, 377–402, 435–58.

Vneshniaia politika Rossii XIX I nachala XX veka. Dokumenty Rossiiskogo Ministerstva inostrannykh del. *Ed. A. Narochnitskii. Moscow, 1960.*

V-n, F. "Zimniaia ekspeditsiia 1809 goda cherez Kvarken." *Voennyi Sbornik,* 1900, 7:1–26; 8:271–89.

Wakeman, F. *The Fall of Imperial China.* New York, 1975.

Wallerstein, I. *The Modern World System 1.* New York, 1974.

Whittaker, C. *The Origins of Modern Russian Education: An Intellectual Biography of Count Sergei Uvarov, 1786–1855.* DeKalb, 1984.

Wójcik, Z. "The Separatist Tendencies in the Grand Duchy of Lithuania in the Seventeenth Century." *Acta Poloniae Historica* 69 (1994): 55–62.

Wortman, R. *Scenarios of Power, Myth, and Ceremony in Russian Monarchy.* 2 vols. Princeton, 1995–2000.

Zagorovskii, V. *Belgorodskaia cherta.* Voronezh, 1969.

*Zapiski o slobodskikh polkakh s nachala ikh poseleniia do 1766 goda.* Kharkov, 1812.

Zasedateleva, I. *Terskie kazaki.* Moscow, 1971.

Zavalishin, I. I. "O russkoi Shvedskoi voine 1741–1743gg." *Rossiiskii Arkhiv,* 6(1995), 56–75.

Zhukovich, P. "Zapadnaia Rossiia v tsarstvovanie imperatora Pavla." *Zhurnal Ministerstva Narodnogo Prosveshcheniia,* Sept.–Oct. 1916, 186–275.

"Zhurnal o voennykh operatsiiakh s 1733 po 1737g." *Sbornik voenno-istoricheskikh materialov* 3 (1893): 58–301.

Zlobin, K. "Diplomaticheskie otnosheniia mezhdu Rossieiu i Shvetsieiu v pervye gody tsarstvovaniia imp. Aleksandra I do prisoedineniia Finliandii k Rossii." *SIRIO,* 2:1–95.

Zolotarev, V., ed. *Istoriia voennoi strategii Rossii.* Moscow, 2000.

Zorin, A. "Krym v istorii russkogo samosoznaiia," *Novoe literaturnoe obozrenie* 31: (1998): 123–43.

"Zur livländischen Landtagsgeschichte des 18. Jahrhunderts." *Baltische Monatsschrift* 18 (1869): 247–88, 428–74; 19 (1870): 84–99, 146–54.

# Index

Alexander I, 8, 125, 161, 165, 184, 203, 205, 206, 207, 211, 222
Alexei Mikhailovich, 12, 20, 37
Andrusovo, Treaty of, 21
Anna Ivanovna, 7, 67, 86, 127, 141
Augustus II, 22, 38, 39, 63, 64, 66
Austria, 61, 65–66, 67, 87, 89–92, 97, 104, 166, 167, 207–208
"awesomeness," 7, 48, 57, 65, 81, 139, 140, 141, 144, 208, 209, 218, 230, 236

Bagration, Petr, 159, 162, 163, 184, 185, 211, 217
Baltic Germans, 68–70, 112, 140, 147, 210, 226
Barclay de Tolly, Michael, 159, 163, 164, 165, 166, 167, 175, 184, 185, 186, 188, 217
Bashkirs, 74, 77, 86
Biron, Ernst, 69, 127, 147
Bothnia, Gulf of, 40, 92, 159
Bukhgolts, Ivan, 42–43
Buxhöwden, Friedrich von, 156, 157, 158

canals, 57, 134–36, 199
Cantemir, family, 74
Catherine II, 8, 94, 98, 105, 106, 134, 139, 142, 144, 205, 214, 222
Caucasus. See Georgia
Charles XII, 4, 22, 38, 39, 40, 65, 100
Cherkasskii, Alexander, 43–44, 73, 76

Chernyshev, Zakhar, 92, 95, 103, 104, 108, 119, 126
client states and societies, 5, 25, 37, 61–81, 112, 144, 145–62, 205–12, 218, 225–27
Continental System, 162, 198, 203–204
Cossacks
  Azov, 72
  Black Sea, 122
  Don, 71–72, 86, 87, 121, 156, 211
  Greben, 72, 121
  Orenburg, 76, 115, 122, 150
  Siberian, 75, 115
  Terek, 72, 121
  Ukrainian, 20, 25–27, 70–71, 111–12, 114, 117, 121, 122, 143, 148–49, 210, 226
  Ural, 33, 76, 115, 117, 122, 150
Crimean Khanate, 11, 27, 28, 29, 37, 94, 96, 98, 121, 148
Czartoryski, Adam, 7, 140, 141, 207, 210, 226

deep strategic penetration, 38, 40, 41, 44, 45, 61, 139, 156, 167, 176, 221, 232
deployment, 44, 48, 50, 51, 52, 61, 130, 182, 183, 191, 223, 224
  of 1725, 45–48
  of 1743, 50–52
  of 1763, 108–16
  of 1781, 119–120
  of 1796, 120–33, 125–31
  of 1801, 178–82
  of 1819, 188–90, 191–97

Diebitsch, Hans von, 172–73, 175, 186, 194, 196
Dolgorukov, Grigorii, 64
Dolgorukov, Vasilii, 96, 110

economic policy, 52–57, 132–34, 136, 137, 198–203, 227–28
Elizabeth (empress), 8, 86, 137, 141, 143
empires. *See also* Austria; Prussia
    Chinese, 34–35, 115, 140, 150, 151, 220
    Ottoman, 10, 11, 25, 139, 149, 160, 171
    Persian, 99, 208, 220
    Polish, 3, 4, 10, 20, 26, 63–64, 100, 103, 104, 115, 119, 126, 147, 157, 165, 193, 194, 210, 214, 226, 237
    Swedish, 19, 20, 22, 64–65, 205
Ermolov, Alexei, 171, 196, 209

Finland, 17, 65, 102, 147, 158, 184, 192, 194, 205, 209–10,
force structure, 45, 116, 123, 177–78, 182–83, 186–87, 224
fortification lines, 27, 36, 48–50, 114, 120–121, 122, 123, 130
Fortress Empire, 128–129, 138, 145, 152, 168, 186, 187, 194, 197, 198, 199, 202, 204, 209, 212, 214, 215, 216, 218, 224, 230
Fortress Russia, 47, 59, 128–129, 134, 144, 145, 205, 223
Frederick II, 66, 87–92, 100, 108, 142, 145–146, 206
"friendly kingdom." *See* Austria

gendarmes, 167, 187–88, 191
Georgia, 72, 99, 105, 149, 169–70, 172, 196, 211
Golitsyn, Alexander, 94, 95, 108
Golitsyn, Boris, 76
Golitsyn, Vasilii, 7, 27–28
Golovin, Fedor, 35
Golovin, Nikolai, 86
Got'e, Iurii, 9
governors general, 210, 211–12
grand strategy, 5, 6–9, 52–53, 58, 61, 85, 94, 145, 160, 219, 230, 233
Greigh, Samuel, 101
Gustav III, 100–102, 147, 210

Heartland, 3, 6, 23, 29, 32, 40, 57, 58, 61, 139, 142, 155, 162, 166, 168, 170, 230, 236, 237

hostages, 62, 140
Hoven, Otto von der, 127, 147

Iakobi, Ivan, 105, 106
Internal Guard, 187, 192, 197
Ivan IV, 4, 11, 19, 26, 38

Johnston, Alastair, 4

Kalmyks, 33, 72, 77–79, 86, 92, 117, 150–151, 226
Kankrin, Egor, 198, 204, 205
Kazakhs, 33, 34, 36, 79–80, 130, 151, 226
Kazan Tatars, 150
Kirilov, Ivan, 75
Kutuzov, Mikhail, 157, 161, 163, 164, 165, 183, 184, 185, 217
Kvarken, 39, 159

Lacy, Peter, 86
land militia. *See* fortification lines
Leszczynski, Stanislas, 38, 40, 64, 71
Likharev, Ivan, 43
Lomonosov, Mikhail, 140, 141, 142
Luttwak, Edwards, 5, 235–36

Manchu dynasty. *See* empires, Chinese
Mazepa, Ivan 70, 140
military expenditures, 133, 201–202
military–industrial complex, 6, 54, 135, 137, 228
military settlements, 188, 195, 216
moats, 24, 25, 40, 41, 92, 97, 158, 159, 161, 171, 174, 205, 208, 220
Moldavia and Wallachia, 23, 73–74, 94, 95, 97, 157, 161, 172, 207, 211, 212
Mongols, 6, 9, 156, 221, 236
Müller, Gerhard, 142
Münnich, Burchard von, 94, 96, 113, 140

Nadir Shah, 42, 52, 73
Napoleon, 38, 157, 160, 164, 165, 166, 167, 206
Nepliuev, Ivan, 80
New Serbia, 114, 195
Nicholas I, 198, 206, 209, 211, 212, 215, 216, 222, 230, 231
Northern War. *See* wars, Russo–Swedish
Nystadt, Treaty of, 39, 64

Ochakov steppe, 98, 99, 100, 107, 122, 130
Odessa, 136
Ordin–Nashchokin, Afanasii, 37
Orenburg, 30
Orthodoxy, 10, 141, 142, 143, 145, 212, 214, 217
Ottoman empire. *See* empires, Ottoman

Panin, Petr, 95, 96, 110, 116
paper money, 133–34, 201–202
paradomania, 144, 216, 227
Paskievich, Ivan, 171, 174, 194, 209, 215, 231
Patkul, family, 22, 68, 70
Paul I, 123, 127, 136, 138, 144, 214
Paulucci, Filippo, 8, 171, 193
Persian empire. *See* empires, Persian
Polish empire. *See* empires, Polish
Poltava, battle of, 39
Poniatowski, Stanislas, 103, 146
Potemkin, Grigorii, 98, 99, 100, 117, 118–119, 121, 126, 215
Prokopovich, Feofan, 140
Prussia, 66–67, 87, 89–92, 104, 120, 145–46, 157, 165, 167, 206–207
Pushkin, Alexander, 144, 217

Razumovskii, Kirill, 143
Repnin, Nikolai, 103, 144, 210, 212
Repnin, Vasilii, 87
Rumiantsev, Nikolai, 203, 207
Rumiantsev, Petr, 90, 92, 94–98, 99, 117–18, 122, 126, 146
Russia and Europe, 9

Saltykov, Petr, 91, 96, 108
Schwartzenberg, Karl von, 165, 166, 167, 185
serfdom, 140, 143, 199, 200, 215, 228
Seven Years' War, 89–92, 226, 227, 229
Siberia. *See* theaters, eastern

Slavianoserbia, 114, 195
Slavophiles, 217
Spiridov, Grigorii, 95
Strandmann, Gustav, 126, 131
strategic force, 45, 47–48, 50, 52, 111–14, 116, 117, 122, 123, 177, 179, 197, 223–25
Suvorov, Alexander 98, 100, 105, 122, 155–56
Swedish Empire. *See* empires, Swedish

tariff, 58–60, 137–138, 203–205, 229
Teutonic Knights, 10, 11, 19, 68, 119, 128
theaters
    eastern, 11, 29–36, 67, 74, 122–23, 130–31, 182, 197, 220–21
    southern, 11, 23–29, 67, 128–30, 180–182, 194–96, 210
    western, 11, 15–22, 61, 126–28, 178–80, 191–94
Thirteen Years' War, 3, 22
Tilsit agreement, 157, 203
Totleben, Gottlieb von, 95–96
Trediakovskii, Vasilii, 140

universities, 212–14

Volynskii, Artemii, 79

wars
    Russo–Chinese, 106–107
    Russo–Crimean, 7, 27, 42, 50, 221
    Russo–French, 40, 155–57, 162–68
    Russo–Persian, 41–42, 105–106, 168–71
    Russo–Polish, 3, 19–21, 50, 104, 174–75
    Russo–Swedish, 3, 18–21, 38–39, 40, 85–87, 100–103, 157–59, 222

Zubov, Valerian, 105
Zunghars, 31, 33, 35–36, 74, 79, 155